Practical Project EVM: The Application of Earned Value Management to Project Monitoring and Controlling

M. Jeffery Tyler, PMP

Printed in the United States of America

First Printing, 2011

ISBN-13: 978-1-467928-05-2
ISBN-10: 1467928054

CreateSpace
7290 B. Investment Drive
Charleston, SC 29418
USA

https://www.createspace.com/Contact.jsp

Preface

Some might ask why another EVM book and I would agree if this book were of the same philosophy and format as most EVM books on the market and in the classrooms. The biggest rejection of earned value tools, techniques and process comes from the very people who need them the most, the project and program managers. For decades the PM profession has monitored and controlled the schedule and costs of projects much the same way a person given their first checkbook might conduct their personal fiduciary responsibilities in not keeping up with their check register and thinking, I've still got checks, I must still have money.

I've sat in many a project and program review listening as PMs glossed over their fiduciary responsibilities not even addressing their deviations from their schedule and cost baselines. These project and program managers assume more resources will be provided to cover the resources they've squandered for lack of understanding the simple earned value tools, techniques and process associated with successful monitoring and controlling. In any time whether it is one of austerity or one of bountiful plenty, we cannot afford to waste our resources. I asked myself why this trend exists with highly trained, educated and intelligent PMs. As I commenced to writing numerous on ground and online PM courses for different universities, colleges, corporations, and government entities, I found a common theme the books I sought to use for the courseware I was developing for my customers-they were all Greek. Every book I sought to use as a source for my courses endeavored to make earned value management the most comprehensive conceptual, compilation of confusing criteria known to management. In short, they were not simplistic approaches to earned value that could be used on the real-life everyday job.

Having spent fifteen years in the government in major space and aviation systems acquisition, and twenty years in civilian industries as a project, program and executive manager, I found that the tools, techniques and process I repeatedly came to use coincided with the basic EVM tools, techniques and process promoted by the Project Management Institute (PMI) in the preparation for the Project Management Professional (PMP) certification. In writing this book, I sought to provide the basics in the most simplified manner possible. I wrote a story, drawn from real-life, no-kidding, actual events as the basis of my scenario to provide the reader background material to develop their earned value management skills against. The Ansari X-Prize competition really happened but, not in the way I present it. Burt Rutan was and is a space and aviation icon and his Scaled-Composites company, along with Herb Iverson really exists but I've fictionalized their roles in the scenario I've placed the reader into. Why do I use the Estes model rocket as the basis for my real rocket project you might ask? At one time as the director of the Department of Defense space training courses, part of our training involved field trips to space related locations. One of these was to the then McDonald-Douglas assembly plant for the NAVSTAR GPS satellite's Delta II medium lift launch vehicle. Each rocket was an individual project and not an operation in that each satellite was built differently and required the launch vehicle to be assembled with modifications, much like a diesel-electric locomotive is individually built and not an assembly line product. While in discussions with the plant PM, I was told that there is little difference in assembling a scaled model rocket and the Delta II rocket. There were just more parts, and they were bigger. Later, as I was trying to get my graduate students to get their minds around just how to build a good detailed (decomposed) Work Breakdown Structure, I remembered this association. My students, with their fictitious projects were trying to build the Boulder dam, the Space Shuttle or they were trying to build a bird house. To level the playing field and since, at the time, my students were mostly from the space arena, I struck on the thought of using model rocket instructions as a basis for my students to use in developing their project work breakdown structures. This was something they could relate to but not in such detail that the material distracted from learning the methodology. Having been in major systems acquisition, I was familiar with the use of making proof-of-concept and demonstration-validation vehicles. Additionally, having done some work with Burt Rutan and Herb Iverson on some classified military projects, and knowing about Burt's work with scaled-down versions of real test vehicles for extracting flight data prior to going FSD (Full Scale Development) I pulled all of this together to provide my students with a hypothetical learning environment that they could work within to apply the proven tools, techniques and processes and top give them a real-life feel in their academic projects. In doing this I went to the Estes Model Rocketry plant, which happened to be nearby at the time and secured their permission to use their rocket instructions as a learning tool for my students to use in developing their work breakdown structures that became the foundations for their scope, schedule, costing, staffing, risk analysis, quality and procurement actions in applying their learned project management tools, techniques and processes to their projects. In writing this book I once again took the diverse yet complementary entities to form a hypothetical scenario as the background for this book. I use and show what is being used by successful PMs on the job to monitor and control their project variances from the approved project baseline and no more. As the PM who reads, uses, and follows the tools, techniques and processes in this book becomes more and more proficient in his or her profession, I would recommend delving into the deeper and more conceptual uses of EVM formulae as part of one's professional development. Use this book to get started. It's written somewhat like a novel. Enjoy the read. Enjoy EVM. It can be rewarding to you as a professional project or program manager.

TABLE OF CONTENTS

Earned Value Management (EVM) is the standard monitoring and controlling methodology for the vast majority of multimillion dollar projects. But, what about small and medium sized projects? The purpose of this book is to provide a simple basic understanding of the use of EVM for the average PM that allows for the monitoring and control of a project's schedule and costs without deterring his or her focus from the daily management and leadership that is essential for project success. There are two thoughts on the management of projects. And, these philosophies paint the poles of the spectrum of project management. The first is management through attention to detail. "The devil is in the details." If you manage the detail, the rest will follow." "Pay attention to details. " These quotes are often ballyhooed around industry as a prescription for project success as if the more detail paid to the accounting of the numbers the greater the chance of success. Any PM worth their salt knows this usually substitutes for the lack of good management and leadership. On the other hand, getting out there and leading your project without paying attention to the project controls is like flying, or for that matter driving, without watching your gauges. You're moving in the right direction but overlooking the health-checks of your project will cause catastrophic failure in getting to your successful completion. What is needed is the ability for the PM to guide the project to completion with a useable "cross-check" of the project's health while still allowing for the focus to be on "flying" the project. As a young pilot I was continually reminded, "Fly the plane first, then cross-check your gauges. Fly the plane, and then communicate. Fly the plane, and then fly the mission." In many instances, where I've been asked to assess the reasons behind unsuccessful projects, I've found that the PM, the project leader, lost his or her focus on guiding the project towards successful completion because they took their eyes off the goal to attend to either too much numbers control while losing sight of what was causing the numbers to say what they were saying or, to attend to too much "hands-on" direction and not understand what the warnings the instruments (numbers) were saying. If you can't tell by now, I'm telling you that "flying" your project is like flying a plane. Fly the plane but, keep a good cross-check of your instruments and what they are telling you so you can correctly understand deviations from the norm and make adjustments before the situation gets out of hand and you crash your project into the ground. As I've cautioned new PMs in an earlier book, "Plan your plan to the finest detail. Only show the highest level of your planning. Manage the difference." (Tyler M. , 1998) Decide just what does all of this mean to my project and to me as a PM?

- Is my project on budget?
    - By exactly how much $$$?
    - This month and cumulatively?
- Is my project on schedule?
    - By exactly how much $$$, time, and deliverables?
    - This month and cumulatively?
- If there is variance....what is causing it to occur?
    - What is the root cause of Schedule or Cost variance?
- What is the forecast for upcoming budget and schedule performance?
    - Can I complete this project as planned, or must I make changes?

These are the basic questions any PM needs to focus on. The rest is statistical analysis reserved for strategic synthesis and evaluation. These four basic questions are the basis of EVM and what the PM needs to know. Well, If the Program Manager is not using Earned Value.......then what magic is being used to monitor and assess performance and progress with respect to $$$ and time? Good question, I'm glad you asked it. The Sarbanes-Oxley law set into effect a due diligence requirement for all Program and Project Managers to exercise management and report performance. If the PM is not using EVM to support management and reporting......then what is being used to stay out of jail?

Chapter 1: Overview / Introduction

So, how am I going to help you fly your project while maintain a good cross-check of your project's health? Great question! I'm glad you asked that. In this chapter and the following chapters, I will guide you through the management of a fictitious project, drawing from a real-life scenario, while showing you how to read your Earned Value gauges without bogging you down in the numbers. This way you can manage your project without taking your eyes off successfully completing it. We will be using the Ansari X-Prize competition as our launch point (no pun intended) for this hands-on experience. The Ansari X-Prize competition takes many forms. You may remember that the manned space-flight competition was recently won by Burt Rutan with his Spaceship-One. The Ansari X-Prize also covers other completions but we will draw from the space competition for our purposes. In our scenario, we will fictitiously be in the Ansari X-Prize completion that is the follow-on to the manned space flight competition. In our scenario, the competition builds on the manned competition to show the feasibility of commercial cargo launch vehicles that can take cargo into space, to the space station, and return to be used again within weeks of the primary launch. In our scenario, Burt Rutan and his real-life company, Scaled Composites (http://www.scaled.com/), is a testing facility for competitors that want to test fly a seven-eight's scale demonstration test vehicles to work out the bugs before committing to a full size version. This is a normal part of a system development in both aviation and space systems development. Test vehicles are full of wiring and boxes that are built in for the testing and cannot be removed after the testing therefore these test vehicles are considered experimental only and can no longer be of any use after the testing. As you might think, this could be expensive to build a one-time test vehicle just for testing. What usually happens is that a scaled-down version is assembled and tested. The object is to scale down the cost of the test vehicle without scaling the size down to the point that the test data is irrelevant. Ergo, the seven-eighth scale test models.

Chapter 1: The Scenario

In our scenario, Burt Rutan is not a competitor in the X-Prize reusable cargo launch vehicle competition. However, his company, Scaled-Composites is globally known for the testing of scaled-down demonstration-validation (DEMVAL) test models. You may remember the flight of The Rutan Model 76 Voyager back in the mid-80's. This was the first aircraft to fly around the world without stopping or refueling. It was piloted by Dick Rutan (Burt's brother) and Jeana Yeager. Some other scaled DEMVALs include:

- MODEL 97: Microlight
- MODEL 115: Starship
- MODEL 133: ATTT
- MODEL 143: Triumph
- MODEL H1, H2: Stars & Stripes
- MODEL 151: ARES
- General Motors Ultralite Show Car
- MODEL 226: Raptor
- MODEL 247: VisionAire Vantage
- MODEL 271: V-Jet II
- MODEL 281: Proteus
- MODEL 309: Adam M-309
- MODEL 311: Virgin Atlantic GlobalFlyer
- MODEL 316: SpaceShipOne
- MODEL 318: White Knight
- MODEL 326: Northrop Grumman X-47A
- MODEL 339: SpaceShipTwo
- MODEL 348: WhiteKnightTwo (Scaled Composites , 2010)

As you can see, Scaled-Composites is the go-to company for the Ansari X-Prize competitors to use for testing of their DEMVAL rockets before going into what is called Full-Scale Development (FSD). The only problem is, Scaled-Composites isn't capable of launch vehicle assembly. So, Burt Rutan has decided to outsource the assembly only, of the DEMVAL launch vehicles. As you might guess, our company, Space Systems Technologies Corporation (Yeah, I thought it was such an original name too) won the RFP (Request For Proposal) and, we are tasked to assembly only, the different competition DEMVAL test vehicles before the competitors go into FSD. Please be aware of the sensitivity of this contract. We will be assembling the different competitors DEMVAL test vehicles as separate projects in an overall assembly program for this contract. As such, we must ensure absolute confidentiality between competitors. If you are using this book in the classroom you must remember not to share your knowledge of the project you are working on with classmates working on other similar rocket assembly projects. This is called compartmentalization and must be maintain for security reasons. You will be the PM taking over the Gauchito rocket assembly project. You will be provided with the background information regarding the Gauchito DEMVAL to help you place yourself into the scenario. You are into the execution phase of the project with the Gauchito project plan to draw your information from. Additionally, you built a Gauchito Project Workbook, in MS Excel®. This is an abridged selection of the information you will need to manage your project. You might consider using this workbook instead of wading through the mass of information in the Gauchito project plan. You will be expected to build your Earned Value Management (EVM) tools, techniques and processes (TT&P) into a viable EVM managed project without losing sight of the successful completion of the project. I wish we had the time and opportunity to actually assemble this rocket as we move the EVM processes to avail you a true hands-on experience. But, time and materials do not allow for this. We will be using a modified version of the actual Gauchito Ansari X-Prize rocket engineering specifications (SPECS). In order to tailor the real-life scenario down to something a student can use without being overwhelmed with project activities, I've applied for and received the permission from the Estes Model Rocket Company to use their model rocket assembly instruction sheet in lieu of the actual Gauchito engineering specs. This way you can concentrate on the EVM TT&P without being overwhelmed with the myriad aspects of a full-scaled assembly project. Now, let's jump into the scenario and apply the EVM TT&P you will learn as we go through this experience. I hope you will have as much fun learning as you will playing this scenario. By the time you finish reading, and studying, this book I hope for you to be able to construct a project scope control system based on a decomposed WBS, calculate the different types of project budget estimates, conduct Earned Value Management (EVM), analyze potential resource conflicts, and evaluate strategies to ensure effective resource allocation. This is a fancy way of saying you will be able to take a project's work breakdown structure or the outline of your project's scope, and break it down into its smallest activities called work packages. Then you will be able to take this fully decomposed WBS and expand it into an estimate of work in hours by the different workers by their skills, total up each worker's effort in hours, multiply that by the pay rate for that skill or, use an average (blended) rate to come up with the total cost by worker and the total labor cost for the project. In addition to this you will do the same for the other two categories of cost and schedule control, that is, the material and the equipment being used on the project. Remember there is a difference between the three categories of labor, material and equipment. We'll cover this later in the book. Next you will learn, understand and apply the different pertinent formulae that will aid you in maintaining control of your project's schedule and its costs. We'll even play around with different potential issues that cause issues to a project's costs and schedule management. Last but not least, we will look at different strategies to help you effectively utilize your assigned resources for the maximum return. In doing this you will use tools, software and techniques to establish a project baseline and control cost and schedule. Topics in this book include preparing PERT/CPM networks, estimating time and resources, creating the project baseline, controlling the baseline, crashing the network, optimization and heuristics techniques for resource allocation, earned value management, and statistical control tools. Now let's jump into the case scenario. Imagine yourself working for a company called Space Systems Technologies Corporation and you've just finished planning a project with the assigned Project Manager (PM) but, something's up. The Gauchito project (the one you expect to work on as one of the team leads for the PM) has had its project plan approved by the Senior Vice President for Engineering. This guy is your project sponsor and will provide all the necessary resources for the team to complete the project. However, his administrative assistant just called and you've been summoned to his office regarding the Gauchito project. On the way to the office you go over everything that might have caused you to be called to the SVP's office instead of the project PM. The project's been approved and we're ready to g execution so, what's at issue? Nothing good comes to mind as you walk into the SVP's office...

Chapter 1: Become Acquainted with Earned Value Management-The Situation

Congratulations! A project where you were part of the team planning just won approval and your VP sponsor only made minor adjustments to your proposed schedule and cost estimates. Of course, you really know she wouldn't buy off on those fifty new computers being added to the project for higher quality and efficiency. Except now the person designated the project manager in the project charter has major family issues and is off the project. You've been designated as the new project manager since you have a good working knowledge of the project's planning. Now, don't you wish you had paid more attention in the planning meetings with the team? Well, now you have to execute on the schedule and the costs you and the team agreed to meet. Should be simple right? Not! Staying on schedule and on costs is an anomaly and works only in sterile environments that aren't affected by weather, people, shipping, price increases and a host of other unforeseen events that will play havoc with you keeping your project on schedule and at cost to its completion. You're in luck. There are quite a few techniques for monitoring and controlling project schedules and costs. They cover the spectrum from top-of-the-head management of time and costs to highly granular computer tracking systems. Depending on the project each end of the spectrum has been used. However, the most common technique used for both schedule and cost management is earned value management (EVM). This is a project management technique used since the 1960's for measuring project progress in an objective manner combining measurements of project scope performance, schedule performance, and cost performance into a single integrated and understandable methodology. Now don't get me wrong here. EVM can be made more difficult that it needs to be for the most common projects. The great thing about earned value is that it can be scaled to fit projects from small simple ones to extremely large and complicated ones. The sad thing is, many project and program managers don't understand the basics of EVM. In that your VP sponsor of your project just happened to mention that she would be evaluating your performance as a PM on your ability to monitor and control your schedule and cost through EVM techniques, you might just take some time and get to know this proven and widely used methodology of project schedule and cost control. Earned value methodology is becoming the global standard in both the private and public sector. The U.S. Office of

Management and Budget (OMB) establishes the criteria for government use of EVM. Many projects must do EVM but not all. EVM typically applies only to projects that exceed $20 million of value; are some flavor of Cost-Incentive based; or involve IT development/procurement. (BUDGET, 2005) And the OMB Circular a-11 dated 2007 has the complete definition of the requirements for practicing EVM. (BUDGET, 2010) In the public sector, earned value management is mandated for high cost government projects in the United States and many other countries are following the suit. Many commercial organizations are now adopting EVM as a basic tool to manage projects. What I want to do here is provide you an simple analysis of the principles, tools, and techniques for controlling project cost and schedule. You will learn the use of easy-to-use tools, software and techniques to establish a project baseline and control cost and schedule. You do know what a project baseline is don't you? It's that spend plan you provided to your sponsor in your project plan presentation that stated what resources you would be using at what time. All of these expenditures added up to a total expenditure of your organization's resources. Faced with this knowledge you know that:

- You will have to examine the general problems inherently faced in similar projects from the perspective of project scope, time and cost.
- You will have to compare different project scheduling and cost tools as solutions to be implemented for this project.
- You'll have to use the approved Work Breakdown Structure (WBS) to setup a resource based schedule and,
- You'll have to examine the purpose of EVM on this project.

A little background first. Your project is one of a number of "assembly only" projects for different DEMVAL (Demonstration-Validation) scaled models of the full rockets that will compete in the Ansari X Prize competition. The Ansari X Prize (formerly the X Prize) was a US$10,000,000 prize, offered by the X-PRIZE Foundation, for the first non-government organization to launch a reusable manned spacecraft into space twice within two weeks. It was modeled after early 20th-century aviation prizes and aimed to spur development of low-cost spaceflight. The prize was won on October 4, 2004, 47th anniversary of the Sputnik 1 launch, by the Tier One project using the experimental space plane SpaceShipOne. The Ansari Foundation now wants to commercially place a cargo launch vehicle into space on a recurring basis. To do this Scaled Composites, the company that placed the SpaceShipOne into space has asked our corporation (Space Systems Technical Corporation or SSTC) to assembly for them to test 7/8th scale demonstration-validation rockets to identify any future manufacturing issues and to extrapolate the necessary data for a full sized rocket to be provided to the different competitors. By using a single organization, knowledgeable in rocket assembly, Scale Composites feels the quality standards will remain consistent.

Figure 1 - SpaceShipOne

Our specific project team has been sub-contracted by Burt Rutan's Scaled Composites through our parent SSTC, with assembling the Gauchito rocket to meet Scaled Composites requirements based on the Gauchito Rocket plans. A project plan was built against the Estes Gauchito Rocket plans provided by Pablo de Leon and Associates who have contracted with Scaled Composites to build a 7/8ths scale model of the follow-on rocket for competition.

Figure 2 - Gauchito Cargo Rocket

Pablo de Leon and Associates (Pablo de Leon y Asociados) is an Argentine-based team formed to design, build and operate a suborbital space transportation system. The team was created to compete for the Ansari X Prize and was accepted by the X Prize Foundation on February 10, 1997. The team is formed by Argentine specialists in several fields, including propulsion, mechanical design, aerodynamics, thermal systems, cryogenics, computer science, etc. The team now intends to compete in the second Ansari X Prize for reusable cargo rockets to resupply the International Space Station (ISS). Pablo de Leon, Team Leader, is an Argentine aerospace engineer with wide experience in space systems design, project management and development of space vehicles and components. More than 42 scientists, engineers, technicians and volunteers have worked on this program for years in order to one day achieve the first orbital manned flight in Latin America. The team, conscientious of the past, believes it is necessary to learn from those who preceded us and reach a level of technological development comparable with the times. If Argentina wants to be once more an industrialized nation, it feels it must invest heavily in science and technology. That is why Pablo de Leon and Associates are working in this project, because they believe it is valuable, and it will help to inspire a new generation of young Argentines and Latin Americans. Pablo de Leon and Associates do not have the facilities to build a 7/8th model of their full-up rocket, and they need specific extrapolated data from test flights. This is why Scaled Composites was chosen for the task. However, Scaled Composites has outsourced the assembly of the scaled rocket to Kaplan Technical Corporation because we specialize in the assembly of spacecraft on a project basis.

The VESA "Gauchito" is a conventional style rocket launch vehicle, using 4 hybrid rocket engines in cluster configuration. The length of the full scaled "Gauchito" is 12 meters without the escape tower, with a diameter of 2.20 meters in the main body, and 6.60 meters including the aerodynamic fins. The weight of the full scaled rocket is 8,000 kilograms while the empty weight is 2,400 kilograms. The capsule can accommodate 1 crewmember with a maximum weight of 300 kilograms of cargo. The capsule maintains a controlled atmosphere of oxygen and nitrogen, and the crew will use full pressure suits with 100% oxygen. The propulsion system of the "Gauchito" was designed by Prof. Jorge Lassig. It combines safety, economy, and reusability. The propellant grain, shaped as a cylinder and using several channels with geometrical shapes is placed in the combustion chamber. The "Gauchito" uses 4 hybrid rocket engines, which burns Polyester Resin as propellant and liquid oxygen (LOX) as oxidizer for 60 seconds. The throttle can be regulated, and the engines are re-startable. The propulsion system has redundant safety devices and can be stopped in case of malfunction. The total thrust is 250,000 newtons (52,910 lb). Each engine uses 380 kilograms of polyester resin and 1,080 kilograms of LOX. This requires a volume of 4 m3 for the 4 rocket engines. The LOX is feed by high pressure nitrogen coming from an additional tank located at the top of the rocket body. The total length of the rocket body is almost 8 meters, with a 2 meters diameter. The pressurized nitrogen tank is ½ meter diameter and the spherical LOX tank is 2 meters diameter. The longitude of each motor tube is 3,3 meters with a diameter of .60 meter. Our Engineering Design Team has planned out the assembly project for the Gauchito 7/8th scale rocket. (Tyler, 1995-2010)

The most common technique used for both schedule and cost management is earned value management (EVM), a project management technique used for measuring project progress in an objective manner that combines measurements of project scope performance, schedule performance, and cost performance within a single integrated methodology. Earned value methodology is becoming the global standard in both the private and public sector. In the public sector, earned value management is mandated for all the government projects in the United States and many other countries are following the suit. Many commercial organizations are now adopting EVM as a basic tool to manage projects. This book provides an analysis of the principles, tools, and techniques for controlling project cost and schedule. You will learn the use of tools, software and techniques to establish a project baseline and control cost and schedule. Topics include estimating time and resources, creating the project baseline, controlling the baseline, crashing the network, optimization and heuristics techniques for resource allocation, earned value management, and statistical control tools.

Chapter 1: Setting the project scope.

Recent industry studies have shown that the single factor that has the greatest impact on project schedule is "requirements volatility," or the number, significance, and timing of changes to the project scope after work has begun. Proper scope planning can reduce, if not eliminate these changes to your project scope. In planning the scope of a project, you are setting parameters, like building the box to hold the project plan. The plan is the detail of how the project will be accomplished. The project scope tells you what is inside and what is outside the box. It sets limits on the project. Good project scope planning is a defense against "scope creep" that gradual (or not-so-gradual) expansion of the project as it unfolds. When planning the scope of a project, it is also important to establish the difference between the necessary components and deliverables and components that are desirable but not absolutely necessary. Once you have planned the scope of the project, you can plan to deliver the required solution. This solution comes in parts known as **deliverables**. (M. Jeffery Tyler, 2009) Deliverables, according to Max Wideman, are measurable, tangible, verifiable items that must be produced to complete the project. Often used more narrowly in reference to an external deliverable, which is a deliverable that is subject to approval by the project sponsor or customer. (Wideman, 2005) As such, deliverables become deliverables when any tangible and verifiable. You will need to take the customer's Contract Data Requirements List or CDRL-normally a Department of Defense term but being used in industry more and more-and convert the deliverables into your project tasks. Notice that the Gauchito project plan has done this in the planning process as the tasks in the Gauchito project Work Breakdown Structure (WBS). You will need to validate the WBS against the engineering specs (Estes instruction sheet) before proceeding with applying your Earned Value Management (EVM) Tools, Techniques & Processes (TT&P) as part of your first assignment. The WBS serves as the basis for the project schedule and a number of other essential project elements. The difference levels of the WBS are usually broken into:

- 1 Program
  - 1.1. Project
    - 1.1.1. Task

1.1.1.1. Subtask

1.1.1.1.1. Work Package

1.1.1.1.1.1. Level of Effort

1.1.2. Task

1.1.2.1. Subtask

1.1.2.1.1. Work Package

1.1.2.1.1.1. Level of Effort ((Kerzner, 2003)

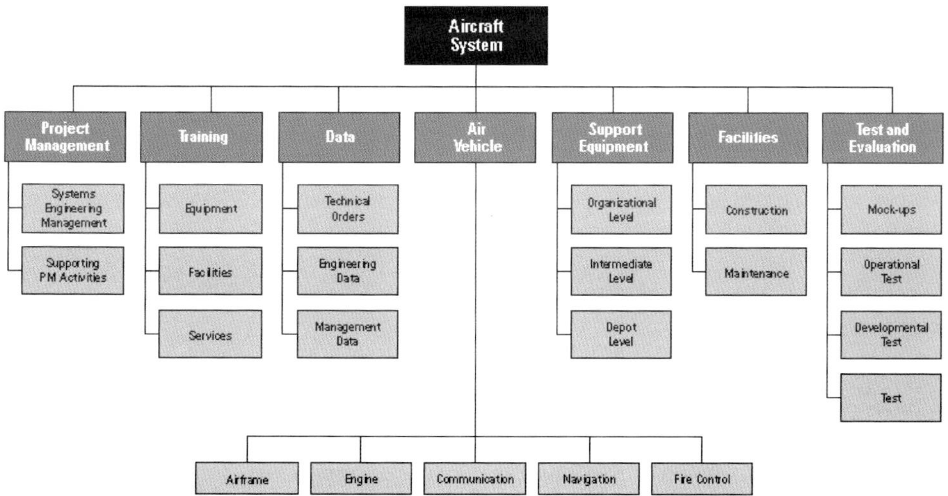

(Project Managment Institute, 1998)

The work breakdown structure displays the project scope in an organized fashion by grouping all project deliverables into hierarchical levels according to detail. Each descending level represents an increasingly detailed description of the project elements. (Defense, 2005) Although each project is unique, the underlying structures of many projects will resemble each other to some extent. Using WBS templates from similar projects can greatly expedite the scope definition process. Creating a work breakdown structure requires the project manager and the project team to Meet with key personnel in all areas associated with the project, review the project scope statement for all high-level deliverables, brainstorm all major areas and phases, and breakdown each phase into smaller groups by considering how much to accomplish the phase. Once the phase is defined, begin developing lower level elements, tasks and work packages, identify any additional high-level deliverables that will be necessary to complete the project scope, organize the highest-level deliverables, Level 1, into a "tree" or outline structure, and then organize any lower-level deliverables that have been identified, Level 2 or below, under their related Level 1 deliverables.

Decomposition is a technique for further defining the scope of work involved in a project by breaking down each high-level deliverable into its components just like outlining the thoughts of a narrative document. It involves subdividing each high-level deliverable into smaller, more manageable components, until each is defined in sufficient detail to facilitate estimating, monitoring, and control. Each level of decomposition is drawn or indented to show its relation to the next higher and lower levels and should be arranged to reflect how the work of the project will actually be accomplished. Once all deliverables have been defined, each is given a code or identifier to indicate its level in the WBS. The resulting decomposition for training would look like the following. Proper definition requires that each item be individually scheduled, budgeted and assigned to a specific owner who will accept responsibility for its satisfactory completion. Decomposition should reduce each item to a level where accurate cost and duration estimates can be made by the project team. Items that are too large or complex to be accurately estimated should be broken down even further. Detailed decomposition of deliverables that occur later in the project schedule may have to be deferred until the project progresses and more is known.

Decomposing project deliverables requires the project manager and the project team to analyze each Level 1 deliverable to determine its next lower-level elements, Level 2, analyze each Level 2 deliverable to determine its next lower-level elements, Level 3, and then continue to decompose the deliverables into lower-level deliverables (Level 4, etc.) until each is in sufficient detail to enable effective estimating, monitoring, and control. BIG HINT HERE: Just remember that those completed end items called deliverable will become your tasks to work towards completing in your project. You need to break those deliverables-now tasks down into smaller activities for better controlling. As you've just read tasks are broken down into two or more subtasks or, if this is the lowest level of the work to be accomplished, work packages. Yes, you can go from a task to two or more work packages. OR, you can break a task into two or more subtasks which then can be further broken down into more subtasks and continuing until the lowest level which becomes the work package. To simplify, the highest level of your project scope outline is the task derived from the associated deliverable. The lowest level of your scope outline will be the work package to which you apply effort, or work. This application of work to a work package is usually time but can also be a resource for a fixed resource such as material or equipment. We'll talk about scheduling material and equipment later. Let's concentrate on setting your scope with a fully decomposed Work Breakdown Structure. Just remember:

- Program
  - Project
    - Task
      - Subtask
        - Work Package
          - Level of Effort or,

- Task (activity that when complete becomes deliverable)
  - Subtask (any level of activities between the task and the work package)
    - Work Package (lowest level of activity in the WBS)
      - Level of Effort (work in time/duration applied to work package)

You might, at this time, take a look at the Gauchito Project plan, located in Appendix-A of this book. In there you will find the Work Breakdown Structure you and the team developed in your project planning. Since this is the scope of the project that has been approved by your sponsor you need to go with this (unless you want to go back into the planning process again) to build out your MS Project schedule and apply your resources for monitoring and controlling. Remember that MS Project is basically a MS Excel workbook on steroids with User Interfaces (UI's). When you open MS Project you will be in the Gantt view. All the Gantt view is, is an Excel spreadsheet with a Bar Chart to the right. As you populate the cells in the spreadsheet the bar chart will depict the information you are inserting. All the bars will line up with the current date. This is called a Start-Start relationship in precedence diagramming which we will cover later.

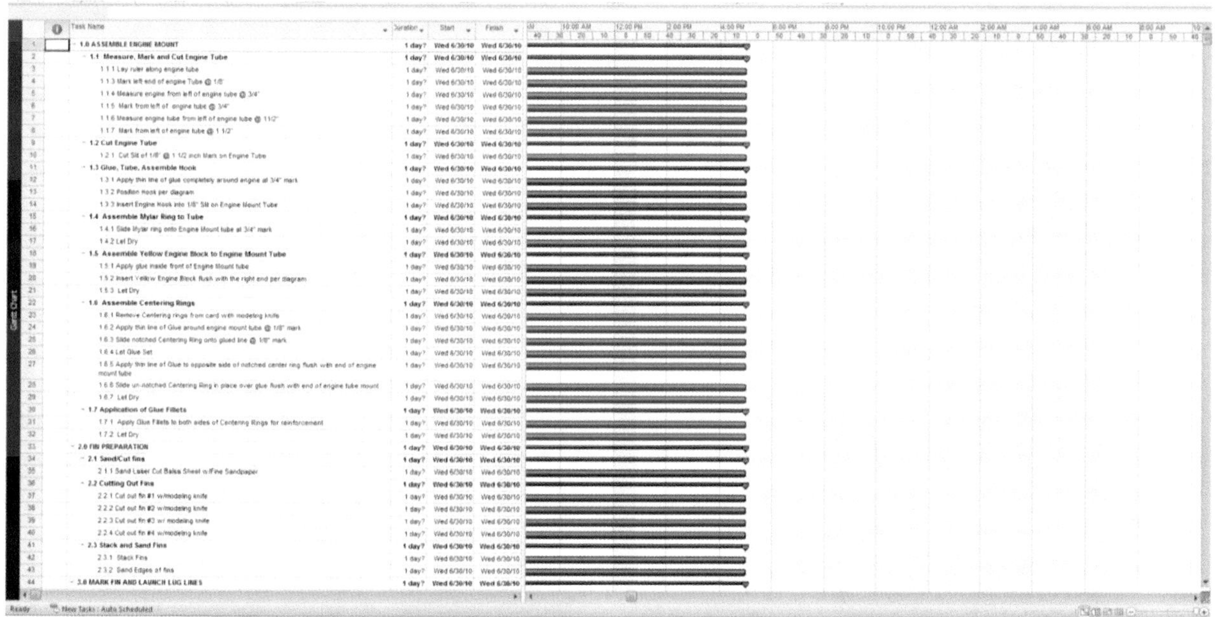

	Task Name	Duration	Start	Finish
1	1.0 ASSEMBLE ENGINE MOUNT	1 day?	Wed 6/30/10	Wed 6/30/10
2	1.1 Measure, Mark and Cut Engine Tube	1 day?	Wed 6/30/10	Wed 6/30/10
3	1.1.1 Lay ruler along engine tube	1 day?	Wed 6/30/10	Wed 6/30/10
4	1.1.3 Mark left end of engine Tube @ 1/8"	1 day?	Wed 6/30/10	Wed 6/30/10
5	1.1.4 Measure engine from left of engine tube @ 3/4"	1 day?	Wed 6/30/10	Wed 6/30/10
6	1.1.5 Mark from left of engine tube @ 3/4"	1 day?	Wed 6/30/10	Wed 6/30/10
7	1.1.6 Measure engine tube from left of engine tube @ 11/2"	1 day?	Wed 6/30/10	Wed 6/30/10
8	1.1.7 Mark from left of engine tube @ 1 1/2"	1 day?	Wed 6/30/10	Wed 6/30/10
9	1.2 Cut Engine Tube	1 day?	Wed 6/30/10	Wed 6/30/10
10	1.2.1 Cut Slit of 1/8" @ 1 1/2 inch Mark on Engine Tube	1 day?	Wed 6/30/10	Wed 6/30/10
11	1.3 Glue, Tube, Assemble Hook	1 day?	Wed 6/30/10	Wed 6/30/10
12	1.3.1 Apply thin line of glue completely around engine at 3/4" mark	1 day?	Wed 6/30/10	Wed 6/30/10
13	1.3.2 Position hook per diagram	1 day?	Wed 6/30/10	Wed 6/30/10
14	1.3.3 Insert Engine Hook into 1/8" Slit on Engine Mount Tube	1 day?	Wed 6/30/10	Wed 6/30/10
15	1.4 Assemble Mylar Ring to Tube	1 day?	Wed 6/30/10	Wed 6/30/10
16	1.4.1 Slide Mylar ring onto Engine Mount tube at 3/4" mark	1 day?	Wed 6/30/10	Wed 6/30/10
17	1.4.2 Let Dry	1 day?	Wed 6/30/10	Wed 6/30/10
18	1.5 Assemble Yellow Engine Block to Engine Mount Tube	1 day?	Wed 6/30/10	Wed 6/30/10
19	1.5.1 Apply glue inside front of Engine Mount tube	1 day?	Wed 6/30/10	Wed 6/30/10
20	1.5.2 Insert Yellow Engine Block flush with the right end per diagram	1 day?	Wed 6/30/10	Wed 6/30/10
21	1.5.3 Let Dry	1 day?	Wed 6/30/10	Wed 6/30/10
22	1.6 Assemble Centering Rings	1 day?	Wed 6/30/10	Wed 6/30/10
23	1.6.1 Remove Centering rings from card with modeling knife	1 day?	Wed 6/30/10	Wed 6/30/10
24	1.6.2 Apply thin line of Glue around engine mount tube @ 1/8" mark	1 day?	Wed 6/30/10	Wed 6/30/10
25	1.6.3 Slide notched Centering Ring onto glued line @ 1/8" mark	1 day?	Wed 6/30/10	Wed 6/30/10
26	1.6.4 Let Glue Set	1 day?	Wed 6/30/10	Wed 6/30/10
27	1.6.5 Apply thin line of Glue to opposite side of notched center ring flush with end of engine mount tube	1 day?	Wed 6/30/10	Wed 6/30/10
28	1.6.6 Slide un-notched Centering Ring in place over glue flush with end of engine tube mount	1 day?	Wed 6/30/10	Wed 6/30/10
29	1.6.7 Let Dry	1 day?	Wed 6/30/10	Wed 6/30/10
30	1.7 Application of Glue Fillets	1 day?	Wed 6/30/10	Wed 6/30/10
31	1.7.1 Apply Glue Fillets to both sides of Centering Rings for reinforcement	1 day?	Wed 6/30/10	Wed 6/30/10
32	1.7.2 Let Dry	1 day?	Wed 6/30/10	Wed 6/30/10
33	2.0 FIN PREPARATION	1 day?	Wed 6/30/10	Wed 6/30/10
34	2.1 Sand/Cut fins	1 day?	Wed 6/30/10	Wed 6/30/10
35	2.1.1 Sand Laser Cut Balsa Sheet w/Fine Sandpaper	1 day?	Wed 6/30/10	Wed 6/30/10
36	2.2 Cutting Out Fins	1 day?	Wed 6/30/10	Wed 6/30/10
37	2.2.1 Cut out fin #1 w/modeling knife	1 day?	Wed 6/30/10	Wed 6/30/10
38	2.2.2 Cut out fin #2 w/modeling knife	1 day?	Wed 6/30/10	Wed 6/30/10
39	2.2.3 Cut out fin #3 w/ modeling knife	1 day?	Wed 6/30/10	Wed 6/30/10
40	2.2.4 Cut out fin #4 w/modeling knife	1 day?	Wed 6/30/10	Wed 6/30/10
41	2.3 Stack and Sand Fins	1 day?	Wed 6/30/10	Wed 6/30/10
42	2.3.1 Stack Fins	1 day?	Wed 6/30/10	Wed 6/30/10
43	2.3.2 Sand Edges of fins	1 day?	Wed 6/30/10	Wed 6/30/10
44	3.0 MARK FIN AND LAUNCH LUG LINES	1 day?	Wed 6/30/10	Wed 6/30/10

Be sure that your WBS is correctly entered into MS Project exactly as it is identified in the Gauchito Project Plan WBS in appendix WT: WBS at tracked level on page 20. BE sure to indent each level of activity accordingly as we discussed above. Activity 1.0, or 1. should be the first task in this case. Some organizations will have you set the project as your 1.0 or 1. In order to track multiple projects with one MS Project file where your Gauchito project would be 1.0 and the Canadian Arrow project might be 2.0 and the Alpha Rocket project might be 3.0 and so on. However, in our case our company, Space Systems Technologies, Inc. maintains the MS Project file separately due to confidentiality of proprietary information between rocket designers and our customer Scaled Composites specifically requires compartmentalization of our files. So, we will name our file for the project and the first task will be labeled 1.0 or in MS project 1. The second task will be 2.0 or 2, the third 3.0 or 3. and so on. The Gauchito project plan WBS would look like this:

1.0 ASSEMBLE ENGINE MOUNT

1.1 Measure, Mark and Cut Engine Tube

1.1.1 Lay ruler along engine tube

1.1.3 Mark left end of engine Tube @ 1/8'

1.1.4 Measure engine from left of engine tube @ 3/4"

1.1.5 Mark from left of engine tube @ 3/4"

1.1.6 Measure engine tube from left of engine tube @ 11/2"

1.1.7 Mark from left of engine tube @ 1 1/2"

1.2 Cut Engine Tube

1.2.1 Cut Slit of 1/8" @ 1 1/2 inch Mark on Engine Tube

1.3 Glue, Tube, Assemble Hook

1.3.1 Apply thin line of glue completely around engine at 3/4" mark

1.3.2 Position Hook per diagram

1.3.3 Insert Engine Hook into 1/8" Slit on Engine Mount Tube

1.4 Assemble Mylar Ring to Tube

1.4.1 Slide Mylar ring onto Engine Mount tube at 3/4" mark

1.4.2 Let Dry

1.5 Assemble Yellow Engine Block to Engine Mount Tube

1.5.1 Apply glue inside front of Engine Mount tube

1.5.2 Insert Yellow Engine Block flush with the right end per diagram

1.5.3 Let Dry

1.6 Assemble Centering Rings

1.6.1 Remove Centering rings from card with modeling knife

1.6.2 Apply thin line of Glue around engine mount tube @ 1/8" mark

1.6.3 Slide notched Centering Ring onto glued line @ 1/8" mark

1.6.4 Let Glue Set

1.6.5 Apply thin line of Glue to opposite side of notched center ring flush with end of engine mount tube

1.6.6 Slide un-notched Centering Ring in place over glue flush with end of engine tube mount

1.6.7 Let Dry

1.7 Application of Glue Fillets

1.7.1 Apply Glue Fillets to both sides of Centering Rings for reinforcement

1.7.2 Let Dry

2.0 FIN PREPARATION

2.1 Sand/Cut fins

2.1.1 Sand Laser Cut Balsa Sheet w/Fine Sandpaper

2.2 Cutting Out Fins

2.2.1 Cut out fin #1 w/modeling knife

2.2.2 Cut out fin #2 w/modeling knife

2.2.3 Cut out fin #3 w/ modeling knife

2.2.4 Cut out fin #4 w/modeling knife

2.3 Stack and Sand Fins

2.3.1 Stack Fins

2.3.2 Sand Edges of fins

3.0 MARK FIN AND LAUNCH LUG LINES

3.1 Cut - Tape

3.1.2 Cut out tube marking guide

3.1.2 Tape tube marking guide around body tube

3.1.3 Mark body tube at arrows

3.1.4 Mark Launch Lug Line as LL on Body tube

3.2 Remove guide, connect fins and lug lines, extend LL line

3.2.1 Remove Tube Marking guide from body tube

3.2.2 Connect Fins using door frame

3.2.3 Connect launch lug lines using door frame

3.3 Extend Launch Lug Line

3.3.1 Extend launch lug line 3 3/4" from end of tube

4.0 INSERTING ENGINE MOUNT

4.1 Mark inside of tube @ 5/8" where LL is

4.1.1 Measure inside tube to 5/8" position on tube

4.1.2 Mark inside tube at 5/8"

4.2 Glue Tube

4.2.1 Measure inside rear of body tube to 1 3/4' position on tube

4.2.2 Use finger to smear glue 1 3/4" inside rear of body tube along LL.

4.3 Assemble Engine Hook

4.3.1 Align engine hook with LL line

4.3.2 Insert engine mount into body tube until centering ring is even w/the 5/8" glue mark

4.3.3 Let Dry

4.4 Gluing Center Body Ring

4.4.1 Locate scrap piece of balsa to apply glue

4.4.2 Apply glue to centering/body tube joint

4.4.3 Let Dry

5.0 ATTACH FINS

5.1 Attach Fin #1

5.1.1 Apply thin layer of glue to edge of fin

5.1.2 Allow to dry (1 minute for model)

5.1.3 Apply second layer of glue to edge of fin

5.1.4 Attach Fin to body tube along one of fin lines flush w/end

5.2 Attach Fin #2

5.2.1 Apply thin layer of glue to edge of fin#2

5.2.2 Allow to dry (1 minute for model)

5.2.3 Apply second layer of glue to edge of fin #2

5.2.4 Attach Fin #2 to body tube along one of fin lines flush w/end

5.3 Attach Fin #3

5.3.1 Apply thin layer of glue to edge of fin #3

5.3.2 Allow to dry (1 minute for model)

5.3.3 Apply second layer of glue to edge of fin #3

5.3.4 Attach Fin #3 to body tube along one of fin lines flush w/end

5.4 Attach Fin #4

5.4.1 Apply thin layer of glue to edge of fin #4

5.4.2 Allow to dry (1 minute for model)

5.4.3 Apply second layer of glue to edge of fin #4

5.4.4 Attach Fin #4 to body tube along one of fin lines flush w/end

5.5 Check Fin Alignment

5.5.1 Check Fin #1 Alignment as shown in diagram

5.5.2 Check Fin #2 Alignment as shown in diagram

5.5.3 Check Fin #3 Alignment as shown in diagram

5.5.4 Check Fin #4 Alignment as shown in diagram

5.6 Allow glue to dry

5.6.1 Let Glue Set

5.6.2 Stand Rocket on end

5.6.3 let glue dries completely

6.0 ATTACH SHOCK CORD

6.1 Cut out shock cord mount

6.1.1 Cut out shock cord from front page

6.2 First Glue Application

6.2.1 Attach shock cord to shock cord mount

6.2.2 Apply glue to shock cord mount

6.2.3 Fold edge of shock cord mount forward over glued shock cord

6.3 Second Glue Application

6.3.1 Apply glue to shock cord mount

6.3.2 Fold forward again-see diagram for clarification

6.4 Squeeze and Hold

6.4.1 Squeeze shock cord/shock cord mount tightly

6.4.2 Hold for 1 minute

6.5 Attaching Shock Cord Mount

6.5.1 Glue mount 1" inside body tube

6.5.2 Hold until glue sets

6.5.3 Let Dry Completely

7.0 ASSEMBLE NOSE CONE

7.1 Glue nose cone

7.1.1 Apply plastic cement to inside rim of nose cone

7.1.2 Press Nose Cone Insert into place over plastic cement inside of nose cone rim

7.1.3 Let Dry Completely

8.0 ATTACH PARACHUTE/SHOCK CORD

8.1 Attach Lines

8.1.1 Pass shroud line on parachute through eyelet

8.2 Attach Parachute

8.2.1 Pass parachute through loop in shroud-look to diagram for clarification

8.3 Tie Lines

8.3.1 Tie shock cord to nose cone using a double knot

9.0 ATTACH LAUNCH LUG

9.1 Glue launch lines

9.1.1 Glue LL centered onto LL Line on rocket body

9.2 Application of Glue Fillets

9.2.1 Apply glue fillets along launch lug

9.2.2 Apply glue fillets along fin/body tube joints

9.2.3 Smooth each fillet with finger

9.2.4 Let glue dry completely

10.0 PAINTING THE ROCKET

10.1 Apply first coat

10.1.1 Spray rocket with white primer

10.1.2 Let Dry

10.2 Sand

10.2.1 Sand entire rocket

10.3 Apply final coat

10.3.1 Spray completed rocket with white second coat of primer

10.3.2 Let Dry

10.3.3 Spray Nose Cone with Copper paint

10.3.4 Let Dry

11.0 APPLICATION OF DECALS

11.1 Apply first decal

11.1.1 Remove First decal from back sheet

11.1.2 Place on Rocket where indicated

11.1.3 Rub decal to remove bubbles

11.2 Apply second decal

11.2.1 Remove second decal from backing sheet

11.2.2 Place on Rocket where indicated

11.2.3 Rub decal to remove bubbles

11.3 Apply third decal

11.3.1 Remove third decal from backing sheet

11.3.2 Place on Rocket where indicated

11.3.3 Rub decal to remove bubbles

11.4 Apply fourth decal

11.4.1 Remove fourth decal from backing sheet

11.4.2 Place on Rocket where indicated

11.4.3 Rub decal to remove bubbles

11.5 Apply fifth decal

11.5.1 Remove fifth decal from backing sheet

11.5.2 Place on Rocket where indicated

11.5.3 Rub decal to remove bubbles

11.6 Apply sixth Decal

11.6.1 Remove sixth decal from backing sheet

11.6.2 Place on Rocket where indicated

11.6.3 Rub decal to remove bubbles

11.7 Apply seventh Decal

11.7.1 Remove seventh decal from backing sheet

11.7.2 Place on Rocket where indicated

11.7.3 Rub decal to remove bubbles

12.0 APPLYING CLEAR COAT

12.1 Apply clear coat to entire rocket

12.1.1 Apply clear coat to entire rocket

12.1.2 Dry Completely

13.0 DISPLAY NOZZLE ASSEMBLY

13.1 Spray Nozzle Base White

13.1.1 Paint Nozzle #1 w/Silver Paint Pen

13.1.2 Paint Nozzle #2 w/ Silver Paint Pen

13.1.3 Paint Nozzle #3 w/ Silver Paint Pen

13.1.4 Paint Nozzle #4 w/ Silver Paint Pen

13.1.5 Allow to dry

13.2 Apply Glue

13.2.1 Apply glue to tab on nozzle #1

13.2.2 Place Nozzle #1 into hole on base

13.2.3 Apply glue to tab on nozzle #2

13.2.4 Place Nozzle #2 into hole on base

13.2.5 Apply glue to tab on nozzle #3

13.2.6 Place Nozzle #3 into hole on base

13.2.7 Apply glue to tab on nozzle #4

13.2.8 Place Nozzle #4 into hole on base

14.0 ROCKET PREFLIGHT

14.1 Prepare Rocket

14.1.1 Remove Nose Cone from Rocket

14.1.2 Locate recovery wadding

14.1.3 Insert 4-5 loosely crumpled squares of recovery wadding

14.2 Spike

14.2.1 Pull parachute into a spike-see diagram for clarification

14.3 Fold

14.3.1 Fold parachute according to diagram

14.4 Roll

14.4.1 Roll parachute according to diagram

14.5 Re-insert

14.5.1 Wrap lines loosely around rolled parachute-see diagram for clarification

14.5.2 Insert parachute into body tube of rocket

14.5.3 Insert shock cord into body tube of rocket

14.5.4 Insert nose cone into body tube of rocket

15.0 PREPARE FOR TEST LAUNCH

15.1 Insert Engine

15.1.1 Remove engine

15.1.2 Insert tip to touch propellant

15.1.3 Insert engine into rocket

Notice the indents will cause any higher level activities within a specific task to be bolded in MS Project. What this is telling you is that every bolded activity will total the levels of effort (work) from the next indented activities below it. If an activity is NOT bolded, then you know it is a work package and it is at that level you will input effort or work (usually in time or duration). By now you may have noticed that there places where only one work package is identified below a subtask. You are correct. There should be two or more subordinate activities below a higher activity. But hey, you were part of that team that planned this out so work with it. Just remember that when breaking an activity down it should be broken down into two or more subordinate activities. Now you know.

If you copy and paste the above WBS into MS Project, the WBS numbering will also follow. You don't want to do this. Every scheduling tool like MS Project provides you with a capability of numbering your activities according to the incremental indentations. Try this out on MS Project. (Instructions for setting up MS Project are at the end of this chapter.

Never, never reveal your WBS to your customer past the third level of subordinate tasks. Else, they will micro-manage you into ruin. (Tyler M. J., 1998)

Chapter 1: Estimating time and resources.

Now that we have our scope defined, we need to provide our time and resources. Time is not considered a resource but must be accounted for. An example of this concept can be seen in activity 1.6.7 Let Dry. You must allow the glue to dry but, you won't assign a person to glue drying. Look at your cost estimate in your Gauchito Project Workbook. Looking across the skill sets in ROW 2 for activity 1.6.7 you will see that there is no Level of Effort (hours) assigned to any of the resources but there is to the DUMMY resource. This is a technique used in an old network diagramming method called Activity on the Arrow (AOA) Diagramming Method or ADM. In this method time was accounted for with what was called Dummy Activities. In the Project Evaluation Review Technique (PERT) that we are using in MS Project (see MS Project Network Diagram), even though the activity is accounted for with "Nodes" we account for the use of time with a 'Dummy" resource to account for the use of time. In our example here the 8 hours of drying time is assigned to a dummy resource. No pay scale is applied but time is still accounted for in your schedule development. Schedule development means determining start and finish dates for project activities. If the start and finish dates are not realistic, the project is unlikely to be finished as scheduled. The schedule development process must often be iterated (along with the processes that provide inputs, especially duration estimating and cost estimating) prior to determination of the project schedule. The project schedule includes planned start and expected finish dates for the project elements that costs will be allocated to. This information is needed in order to assign costs to the time period when the cost will be incurred. Activity definition involves identifying and documenting the specific activities that must be performed in order to produce the deliverables/tasks, sub-tasks and work packages identified in the work breakdown structure. Implicit in this process is the need to define the activities such that the project objectives will be met. Activity sequencing involves identifying and documenting interactivity dependencies. Activities must be sequenced accurately in order to support later development of a realistic and achievable schedule. Sequencing can be performed with the aid of a computer (e.g., by using project management software) or with manual techniques. Manual techniques are often more effective on smaller projects and in the early phases of larger ones when little detail is available. Manual and automated techniques may also be used in combination. Cost budgeting involves allocating the overall cost estimates to individual work items in order to establish a cost baseline for measuring project performance. This involves the integration of project scope, work, durations, sequencing and labor/equipment/material resources into a comprehensive plan for iterative expenditure of all project resources in a cumulative process. (Dr Dan Patterson, 2010)

The key to the success of most projects is obtaining the right people in the right quantities to do the work. People can include a host of project-related personnel such as project team members, support staff, contractors, and customer resources. This requires understanding the nature of the work to be performed and identifying the knowledge and skills that will be needed. The project manager, in conjunction with the project sponsor and other key stakeholders, must review the WBS, activities list, and network diagram to determine the nature and extent of the work. From this understanding, they can identify the types of knowledge and skills that will be needed, along with an estimate of the actual number of people needed. Doing this well requires the experience to understand and anticipate people's productivity and how to best divide up the work. In addition, the project manager should project when during the life of the project certain people will be needed so that they can be effectively phased in. (Tyler M. J., 2009) In addition to people, resource planning involves determining what equipment and materials will be needed for the project, and in what quantities. Materials will normally include anything that is consumed in the course of creating the project deliverables. Equipment can include any tools, machinery, and computing equipment that will be required. Since identifying and estimating all required resources can be a difficult task, it is best to focus separately on each deliverable and the related activities. The "owners" of each deliverable shown in the WBS must make an estimate of the type and number of resources they expect will be necessary to complete their work. (Kerzner, 2003) Knowledge of the resources that can be made available to the project is needed before resource requirements can be finalized. Although the equipment and material resource pool can be important, the more important factor in resource planning is knowledge of the pool of qualified and potentially available people. This information will generally be provided to the project manager by the managers of the functional organizations who will ultimately release the people. This resource pool description helps project managers understand whether or not their requirements can be satisfied or must be adjusted. Comparing the resource estimates to projected availability will indicate which requirements can be satisfied and which cannot. When faced with shortages, the project manager must either develop alternative approaches to satisfying the project scope statement or document why project objectives cannot be met within the current constraints. When estimating the cost of the project, project managers normally review cost data from past projects to serve as a model for the current estimation. This is called analogous estimating. Team members analyze historical cost figures to determine the funding requirements for their own assignments. In doing so, close attention is made to project specific conditions that affect cost estimates. Cost estimates can be adjusted to account for differences in current and past project conditions (e.g. inflation, operating conditions). (Tyler M. J., 2009) Data from previous project experiences, if available, can be analyzed to provide a baseline of comparison for improving cost estimates. This information can be obtained from project files, commercial cost estimating databases, and/or people with appropriate experience and responsibility. To the extent that the current project parallels the circumstances of another project, past cost estimates and actuals can be used as a model for estimating. Past cost estimates and actuals should be adjusted to the extent that present project circumstances differ from previous projects. The first step is to simply apply the appropriate rates to the various resources or resource categories for the cumulative amount of those resources to be applied to the project. Most projects only require the use of average, rather than specific, rates. The average salary rate of each labor type, for instance, usually provides sufficient accuracy. The costs associated with each category of project resources should be calculated separately and then totaled for the overall project. Costs can also be subtotaled for each phase of a project, such as for design, development, testing, and delivery. Estimating and tracking project costs provide valuable historical data for future projects. There are normally three iterations of project estimates. These are the Order of Magnitude Estimate, the Budget Estimate, and the Definitive Estimate. The Order of Magnitude Estimate is an approximate estimate made without detailed data. It is produced from cost capacity curves normally used during the formative stages of an expenditure program and is used for initial evaluations of project. Other terms for an Order of Magnitude Estimate are:

- "Guesstimates"
- SWAG
- Conceptual estimate
- Preliminary estimate

The range of this estimation is -25% to +75% of expenditure at project completion. Budget Estimates are prepared from equipment details, flow sheets, equipment layouts, initial specifications and staffing assessments. These estimates are used for obtaining the funds required for the project and receiving approval of the project. Other terms for the Budget Estimate are:

- Appropriation estimate
- WAG
- Control estimate
- Design estimate

The range of the Budget estimation is -10% to +25% of expenditure at project completion. Definitive Estimates are prepared from well-defined information, engineering specifications and other reliable information. This type of estimate is used for proposals, bid evaluations, contract changes, and any additional work. Other terms for the Definitive Estimate are:

- Check estimate
- Final estimate
- Lump sum estimate
- Tender estimate
- Post contract change estimate

The range of estimation for the Definitive Estimate is -5% to +10% of expenditure at project completion. Standard project estimating, according to Harold Kerzner follows three techniques-Parametric, Analogous, and Engineering (bottom-up or Grass roots). (Kerzner, 2003) According to the Project Management Institute, there are nine estimating techniques utilized in project management. (PMI, 2008) The Department of Defense specifies four techniques that also entail the first four from the PMI and we'll consider these four. (Department of Defense, 1992) First, there is the parametric estimation also know as statistical estimation. Parametric estimation is a statistical method of estimating using database of similar elements or a model that generates an estimate based on system performance and/or design characteristics of chosen model. This technique is very reliable if projects compared are similar, and the historical information used is accurate. A good point to this estimating is that the model used can be scalable between small and large projects. Second, there is the use of historical data. Historical results estimating uses data from past project files, commercial or cost estimating databases and uses team knowledge with Subject Matter Expert (SME) contributions. The third cost estimating technique is the analogous estimation. This type of estimation is also called "top down" estimating. Analogous estimating applies to actual costs of a similar project and requires the estimator to make a subjective judgment relative to the similarities between the two projects. Insurance and Mortgage Adjusters use this method of estimation. A version of this technique is called the extrapolation estimation method. Extrapolation estimation uses actual test data to extrapolate for a proposed project. Prototyping is an example of extrapolation estimating. Extrapolation estimating is used in many modern products such as aircraft, cars, software programs, and real estate products. The purpose of the Gauchito demonstration-validation rocket is for the extrapolation of test flight data to validate the final design and project cost factors for the final rocket assembly. The fourth and most reliable estimating technique for project management, as well as the most versatile type of estimating, is the bottom-up estimation. Your Gauchito project plan utilizes this type estimation. The bottom-up estimate is also called the "engineering" method or the grass-roots estimating method. It is the most detailed method of estimating. This estimating starts at lowest level of work (work package) in the WBS. The lower the WBS is decomposed, the easier it is to use this method. Hours are applied to the work packages and then "roll-up" to sub-total for subordinate tasks or activities and then to tasks or activities to provide a bottom-up developed estimate. Use of this estimate allows for costing by task or activity. Should a task or activity be eliminated, the entire project costing does not have to be recalculated since each task is modularized. Computerized tools are used in many of the previously mention estimating techniques. Computerized tools are software tools used to allow "what if" scenarios to be modeled. An example of computerized tools is using a spreadsheet for the bottom up estimating technique. (Tyler M. J., 2009) Take a look at the Gauchito Project Workbook.xls file for an example of how this is used in the Gauchito project.

Chapter 1: Thought Question

Draw from your personal and professional experiences to address the topic below for the Threaded Discussion. Remember that this is a discussion, so keep your responses succinct and to the point. Respond to at least three of your classmates.

After a historic presidential election in the United States, officials and citizens are focused on the transition program and the initial priorities of the new administration. In the context of a worldwide economic crisis, the pressing questions on people's mind are: What new programs and projects will be initiated? What will be cut? How will the administration prioritize the campaign promises made to different stakeholders?

It will be imperative to cultivate and promote a portfolio mindset and apply the principles of portfolio management at every level to address these crucial questions. Whether in government, your organization or department, or at a personal level, a portfolio mindset can provide strategic focus. It can ensure that you are working on the right projects with the right priorities, and are not being bogged-down, or stuck, on low-value initiatives.

According to the Standard for Portfolio Management, a portfolio is a collection of projects or programs and other work that are grouped together to facilitate the effective management of that work to meet strategic business objectives. Portfolio management focuses on the processes to identify, select, prioritize, govern, measure and report on the projects and programs to achieve specific business objectives.

In your estimation, a portfolio mindset requires that, at any point in time, managers:

a) Inventory all of the projects and programs in the portfolio, and be familiar with them

b) Focus on the big picture with clarity of purpose and based on strategic objectives

c) Continuously assess and balance priorities based on the four R's – reward (benefit), risk, resources and relationship (the impact of doing a project on other projects that are existing or planned). (Duggal, 2008)

Choose the position that you feel is most relevant to the preceding comments regarding having a portfolio mindset and substantiate your premise with referenced citation. Be sure to write your initial post according to APA format using citations/examples to substantiate your position and give credit to your references at the bottom of your post. Be sure to synthesize your analysis of the reading as a conclusion and then evaluate your synthesis.

Chapter 1: Chapter Synthesis and Evaluation

Project Scope Management involves ensuring that the project does enough work, and only enough work, to deliver the business purpose of the project successfully. It is primarily concerned with the project's boundaries - inclusion as well as exclusion, and includes the following processes: Project Initiation - committing the organization to the project; Scope Planning - developing the work breakdown structure; Scope Change Control - controlling changes to project scope; Scope Verification - assuring that the project has been done correctly. Reference: PMI® Guide to The Project Management Body of Knowledge

The biggest problem that can face a project is not meeting the agreed deadline: It has been widely said that delivering on time is the most important issue, and that users will sacrifice functionality in order to meet their deadlines. Imagine the project manager's ideal: a beautifully designed project plan, which will deliver, early and under budget, all the functionality the user has requested. Why does it seem never to happen that way? When customers initiate a project, they do so with a certain concept of the end result. If the project manager does his job well, that idea will be translated into a scope document of some kind. However, once things get started the customer starts to learn more, and realizes that what he originally asked for is not what he needs, so he initiates a scope change or a change request. Additionally, the business needs usually change over the course of the project so that what was originally contracted for, requires major changes. And, in many cases, the marketplace changes and what was originally contracted for must be delivered early in order to be first to market even if the product has bugs or deficiencies.

What can a good project manage do in these diverse and dynamic conditions? First, collaborate with your customer. Studies show the more the customer is involved in the process; the less likely it is that there will be surprises. Understand the customer's expectations. Requirements definition is the basis of scope definition. However, customers do not define requirements. They define expectations; what they expect to see as a result of your project. Filter all impacts to your scope. Scope change is the death of many a project. Cross-walk all impacts to your scope against the organization's strategic and operational goals and objectives. If the scope change doesn't provide a strong business case, push back. Be flexible but, be realistic also. M. Mitchell Waldrop, in his book, *Complexity: The Emerging Science at the Edge of Order and Chaos*, states that a project manager must have ... a willingness to let go of control and walk on the "edge of chaos." (Waldrop, 1992) But don't let chaos take control of your project. Remember, you are the first and the final decision-maker for your project and, you customer. Once you control the scope, then you can control the schedule and costs of your project.

Chapter 1: Test Your Knowledge

Take the following practice quiz. Identify those where you are weak and then reinforce yourself.

1. Scope Management
   a) Is concerned with naming all activities performed, the end products which result, and the resources of the project manager
   b) Entails managing the project's work content
   c) Is a subset of configuration management and as such is performed by CM specialists
   d) Is not a concern of the project manager
   e) None

2. The scope statement provides
   a) A basis for future decisions about the project
   b) A baseline to accomplish verification measures
   c) A baseline to evaluate potential scope changes
   d) All
   e) b and c only

3. The project life-cycle can be describes as:
   a) Project concept, project planning, project execution, and project close-out
   b) Project planning, work authorization, and project reporting
   c) Project planning, project control, project definition, WBS development and project termination
   d) Project concept, project execution, and project reporting
   e) All

4. Customer influence in the project process is:

a) Essential in accurately documenting the goals and objectives of the project
b) Meddlesome and will slow down the process
c) A minor consideration because the customer has difficulty in stating what he wants
d) Best handled by the sales department
e) None

5. A project is defined as:
   a) A coordinated undertaking of interrelated activities directed toward a specific goal that has a finite period of performance
   b) A large, complex undertaking with many objectives, multiple sources of funding and no discernible end point
   c) An undertaking of interrelated activities directed toward a specific goal that can be accomplished in less than one year
   d) A group of activities headed by a project manager who has cradle-to-grave life cycle responsibility for the end product
   e) All

6. Creation of project objectives
   a) Allows for data collection and analysis and progress reporting against which standards of performance can be measured
   b) Is accomplished by selection of measurable variables against which performance can be judged
   c) Is required before funding of the project by the project sponsor
   d) All
   e) a and b only

7. The Project Charter
   a) Expresses upper management commitment to the project
   b) Provides the authority by which the project may proceed

c) Establishes the organizational structure within which the project will operate

d) Specifies the overall objectives and timeframes of this project

e) All

8. A program is characterized as

   a) A grouping of similar projects having no definite end that supports the product(s) from cradle to grave

   b) A grouping of related tasks lasting one year or less

   c) A unique undertaking having a definite time period

   d) A project with a cost over $1 million

   e) None

9. The Project Charter is developed by

   a) Senior management

   b) The customer

   c) The project manager

   d) Both a and c

   e) None

10. A clear definition of the users' needs serves as the direct basis for the . . .

    a) Functional requirement

    b) Work Breakdown Structure

    c) Project cost estimate

    d) Selection of personnel

    e) Termination decision

11. A technical requirement has which of these characteristics?

    a) Typically describe physical dimensions and performance requirements

    b) Easy to understand

c) A communication tool between the user and the design team

d) Written in non-technical language

e) Developed in cooperation with the user

12. Selection criteria for project selection include . . ..

a) Cost vs. benefits

b) Risk

c) Contribution towards organizational goals

d) Rate of return

e) All

13. Scope management is:

a) a project control function

b) employs change control

c) a work authorization process

d) considers Cost, Quality and Schedule

e) all

14. The sequential steps that define the process for successfully completing a project is:

a) Implementation Plan

b) Development Plan

c) critical path

d) Management Plan

e) a life cycle

Chapter 1: Application Exercise

Since you are the new PM for the Gauchito project, and the company schedule monitoring and controlling software tool is Microsoft Project® you will need to familiarize yourself with the tool immediately. Your sponsor wants your fully decomposed Work Breakdown Structure (WBS) set up in MS Project, also referred to as MPP for its file extension, and in his Drop Box within the week. Here's what you will need to do:

Set up and familiarize yourself with MS Project (MPP) tool following the Gauchito Rocket Assembly Project. If you are unfamiliar with MS Project or, need some refreshing, go the Appendix A learning modules and become very familiar with this tool. Failure to do so will adversely affect your ability to properly conduct the qualitative and quantitative analysis required for successful completion an industry standard EVM application. Following the engineering specifications for the rocket assembly of the Gauchito 7/8 scale demonstration-validation rocket from your Engineering Specs (Gauchito Rocket.ppt and Gauchito Rocket Product Description in Doc Sharing) build a fully decomposed **Work Breakdown Structure (WBS) in MS Project** and become familiar with the different screens and input User Interfaces (UI's) associated with the tool. If you need further instructions, go to the MS Project web page and click on the associated tutorial provided and then conduct your initial setup of the project and according to the Gauchito Project Plan.doc. WARNING: Do not copy the WBS directly from the project plan without auditing it carefully with the Engineering Specifications (Estes Instructions). It has omissions and mistakes that will degrade your performance if blindly copied. Be sure that all information is correctly transferred to your MS Project file such as project start dates, durations, predecessors, and resources.

Chapter 2: Chapter Overview / Introduction

Well, you now have your approved Gauchito schedule updated into a scheduling tool. Not bad for someone that wasn't paying too much attention when the project planning was taking place. Now how are we going to execute on this schedule to keep the project on track time wise and cost wise? You're good with the questions now. Let's look at what we have and what we need to now do to develop out our planning tool further. First we need to have a common understanding of just what earned value is. Once we have a common understanding, we can apply the basic elements of earned value to calculate just how well the Gauchito project is performing. It's kind of like a health report. Then we need to formulate how we can get back on track if we've drifted of track. Let's take a look at the purpose of using earned value management in monitoring and controlling this project.

Earned Value Management (EVM) is a technique used to track the progress and status of a project and to forecast the likely future performance of the project. EVM techniques integrate the scope, schedule, and cost of the project into a single comprehensive analytical picture of project health.

Good planning coupled with effective use of EVM techniques will reduce a large amount of issues arising out of schedule and cost overruns. EVM techniques address a lot of stakeholder's questions in a project, related to the performance of the project. EVM techniques can be used to show past performance of the project, current performance of the project, and predict the future performance of the project by use of statistical techniques. To do this we need to establish what is called a starting point or baseline to move forward. Remember in the project presentation, the PM you are replacing presented your project sponsor, the VP for Engineering, with her project budget or Spend Plan. Most projects calculate their expenditures over time in what is called a spend plan. Now the Online Business Dictionary defines a spending plan as an

Aggregate budget comprising of departmental or individual budgets for an accounting period, program, or project. (n.a., 2010) Notice the term aggregate. This means that you have to keep a running total of your expenditures over time; a cumulative set of totals that reflect what has been spent incrementally over the past period since the beginning of the project. Now you have to graph this running total. Because projects tend to start of slow as the beginning, gain momentum in the middle, and then get slower as the work is completing the effort can be incrementally graphed like a bell-curve:

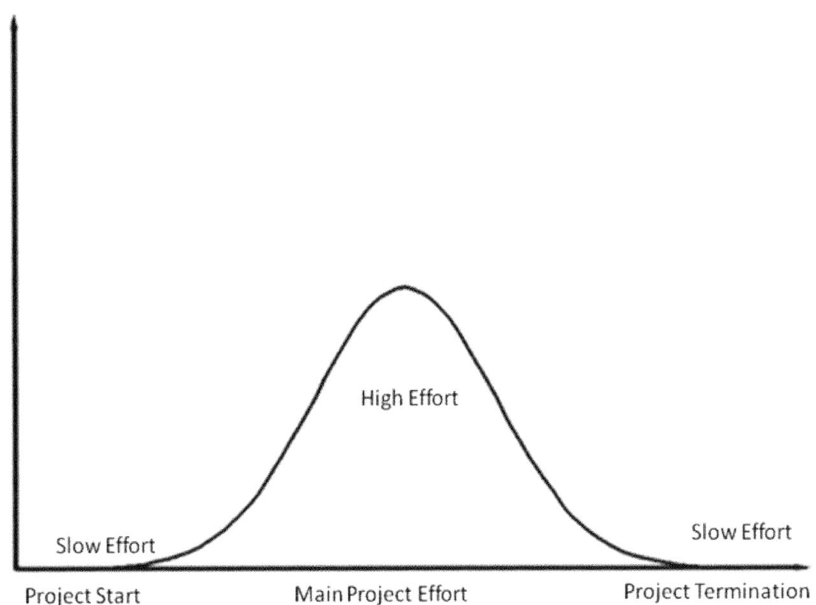

Figure 02.01-Incremental Expenditures Over Time

But, what if we want to graph the cumulative expenditure totals over time and not the incremental expenditures over time. It's like plotting each month's expected expenditures added to the previous monthly expenditures over time. So, month one would be added to month two and then months one and two would be added to month three and so on. Graphing this would not product the bell-curve we looked at previously. Cumulative totals will result in a diagonal line graph that looks like this:

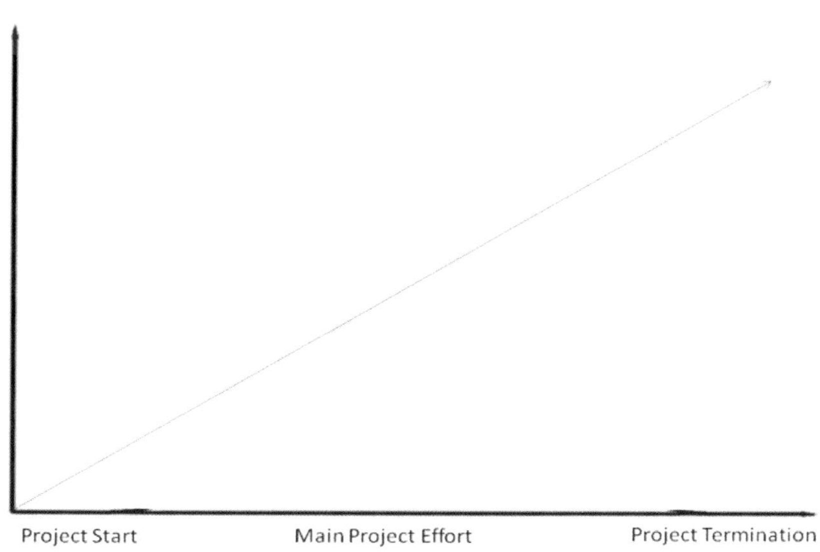

Figure 02.02-Cumulative Equal Expenditures over Time

This graph reflect that your project spent the same exact amount of expenditures in each incremental period (day, week, month, etc.) over the life of the project. Many projects, especially government projects are managed this way. However, a project is normally slow to start, picks up speed and then slows down as it winds down at the end. If we were to graph the real cumulative effort of a project over its lifecycle it might look like this:

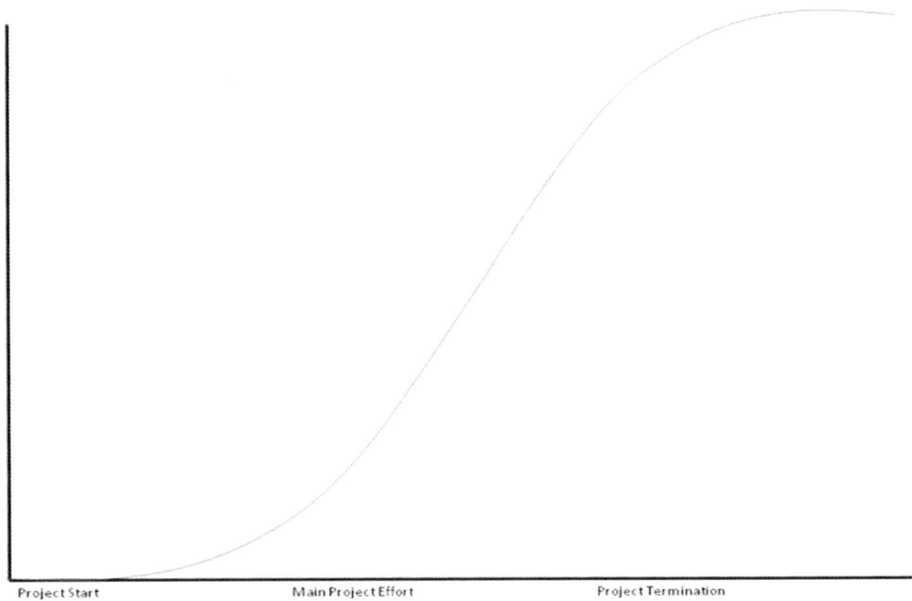

Figure 02.03 Project Lifecycle as a Cumulative S-Curve

Chapter 2: Creating the project baseline.

Estimated costs must be totaled by period to create a time-phased cost baseline for effective project cost tracking. Variances to the cost baseline may or may not actually impact the overall cost budget for the project or require corrective action. Projects frequently under spend in the early phases and then overspend in later phases to make up for the slow start. In other cases, however, cost overruns early in the project foretell the probability of even larger problems as the project progresses. The cost baseline is the tool for tracking costs and identifying possible cost problems. Creating a time-phased cost baseline requires summarization of project cost estimates by time period (typically hourly, monthly or quarterly). (Tyler M. J., 2009) Projects often require the use of items with long lead-times that must be ordered well in advance of their actual use on the project. The spending plan is created to reflect these differences and authorize purchases out of synch with the cost budget. Creating a spending plan requires you to identify items, such as custom parts or complex equipment, that must be ordered in advance of their actual use or application on the project, determine when these items must be ordered or purchased and itemize any differences with the cost budget, identify personnel usage by time period labor expenditure on the project, and then determine when these personnel are to be utilized and itemize any differences with the cost budget. How do I do this you might ask? Again, a good question. Take a look at the Gauchito Project Workbook on your Appendix-B. Look at the Spend-Plan Baseline.

CATEGORY	Week 1	Week 2	Week 3	Week 4	Week 5	Week 6	Week 7	Week 8
Labor	7 350.00	7 350.00	7 350.00	11 550.00	4 200.00	4 200.00	12 600.00	15 400.00
Material	10 900.00	0.00	0.00	100.00	5 800.00	0.00	365.00	4 320.00
Equipment / parts	175.00	0.00	0.00	625.00	0.00	0.00	225.00	0.00
TOTAL	18 425.00	7 350.00	7 350.00	12 275.00	10 000.00	4 200.00	13 190.00	19 720.00
CUMULATIVE	**18,425.00**	**25,775.00**	**33,125.00**	**45,400.00**	**55,400.00**	**59,600.00**	**72,790.00**	**92,510.00**

CATEGORY	Week 9	Week 10	Week 11	Week 12	Week 13	Week 14	Week 15	Week 16	
Labor	2 880.00	5 600.00	5 600.00	5 600.00	1 400.00	2 800.00	2 800.00	1400	98 000.00
Material	2 875.00	645.00	0.00	2 400.00	0.00	300.00	0.00	50000	77 705.00
Equipment / parts	0.00	0.00	0.00	0.00	0.00	0.00	0.00	0	1 025.00
TOTAL	5 675.00	6 245.00	5 600.00	8 000.00	1 400.00	3 100.00	2 800.00	51 400.00	**176,730.00**
CUMULATIVE	**98,185.00**	**104,430.00**	**110,030.00**	**118,030.00**	**119,430.00**	**122,530.00**	**125,330.00**	**176,730.00**	

Figure 02.04

Notice how the Gauchito project team planned out the expenditures of the project over its life in weekly increments just like we've been discussing. All three categories of expenditure are accounted for-labor, material and equipment/parts. The planned incremental (weekly in this case)expenditure of these categories can be drawn from the Material & Equipment (M&E) Forecast for material and equipments and, from comparing the derived percentage of work form the Cost Estimate with the planned schedule from the Gantt chart. Okay, this sounds confusing but, in reality it is quite simple. The M&E Forecast is straight forward. Here it is from the Gauchito Project Workbook:

Code	Item	Cost	Week 1	Week 2	Week 3	Week 4	Week 5	Week 6	Week 7	Week 8	Week 9	Week 10	Week 11	Week 12	Week 13	Week 14	Week 15	Week 16
	Equipment	**$1,025**	**$175**	**$0**	**$0**	**$625**	**$0**	**$0**	**$225**	**$0**	**$0**	**$0**	**$0**	**$0**	**$0**	**$0**	**$0**	**$0**
	Scissors x 10	$100							$100									
	Pencil x10	$25	$25															
	Ruler x10	$50	$50															
	Modeling Knife x 5	$100	$100															
	Guide, Tube Marking	$500				$500												
	Tool, Framing x 1	$125				$125												
	Tool, Fin Alignment x 1	$125							$125									
	Material	**$77,705**	**$10,900**	**$0**	**$0**	**$100**	**$5,800**	**$0**	**$365**	**$4,320**	**$2,875**	**$645**	**$0**	**$2,400**	**$0**	**$300**	**$0**	**$50,000**
	Guide, Shock Cord Mount	$250							$250									
	Sand Paper (Course)	$75	$75															
	Sand Paper (Fine)	$75	$75															
	Glue	$150	$150															
	Cement	$120								$120								
	Tape, Masking	$100				$100												
	Primer, Spray	$110										$110						
	Paint, Spray (White)	$160										$160						
	Paint, Spray (Clear)	$125										$125						
	Pen, Paint (Silver)	$250										$250						
	Tube, Body BT-58	$5,800					$5,800											
	Block, Engine EB-5B	$5,000	$5,000															
	Cord, Shock, Rubber	$115							$115									
	Hook, Mini Engine EH-3	$300	$300															
	Tube, Engine Mount BT-5	$500	$500															
	Ring, Retainer (Mylar)	$250	$250															
	Sheet, Decal #60859	$650												$650				
	Card, Centering Ring RA5-58	$550	$550															
	Lug Launch LL-2A	$375									$375							
	Fins, Laser Cut x4	$4,000	$4,000															
	Parachute Assembly 12' x 1	$2,500									$2,500							
	Base, Nozzle, Display x 1	$750												$750				
	Nozzles x 4	$1,000												$1,000				
	Cone, Nose x 1	$3,000								$3,000								
	Insert, Nose Cone x 1	$1,200								$1,200								
	Wadding, Recovery x 1pk	$300														$300		
	Engine Assembly, A10-3T x 1	$50,000																$50,000
		TOTAL	**$22,150**	**$0**	**$0**	**$1,450**	**$11,600**	**$0**	**$1,180**	**$8,640**	**$5,750**	**$1,290**	**$0**	**$4,800**	**$0**	**$600**	**$0**	**$100,000**

Activity List | Decomposed WBS | Cost Estimate | Spend Plan-Baseline | GANTT Schedule | Network Diagram | M& E Forecast

Figure 02.05

The full cost of each piece of material and equipment is considered spent the first time it is needed. This is a principle used in industry for a couple of reasons. The first is that the procurement or contracting office can consolidate specific material or equipment needs in order to seek a more conducive contracting agreement with vendors. Let's say that you will need, according to the Gauchito M&E Forecast, $645 worth of paint products over a two week period. By consolidating the entire purchase into one buy your procurement office can contract a volume price. Now, let's just expand that out to the entire assembly program for our company. Let's say we have 10 rocket assembly projects using similar resources across the company. We can then do a one-time buy of the paint products through one vendor, with one bid and reap the savings of a volume buy. Now, what if this were a full up rocket assembly with say, $6450 worth of paint products being expended over a two month increment. Contracting for one buy at one time reaps the volume savings. Okay, you say, but where do we put all the paint products if we don't have the storage space or, don't want to incur the cost of storage? Again, a good question. I'm glad you asked that. Your procurement folks will set up a delivery schedule there by allowing for delivery from the vendor as you need it while committing the funds up front helping the vendor to provide a set cost delivery of goods from that end. In this way your company and the vendor have a win-win situation. The second reason is more for you and your project. By committing the funds up front you're fenced or, locked-in the entire use of those funds for your project and for fiduciary responsibility, your company must ensure those funds are committed for the use they were contracted towards. This ensures your project's funding isn't realigned without fiduciary liability from executive management and, if your funding is realigned, you can legally reset your scope with the customer through management reserve from the company and not contingency reserve from your project. But how do you figure the cost of labor for your spend plan? The Gantt chart is matched to the spend plan with the same increments, in this case, by the week. However, the definitive cost estimate utilizes tasks against the labor skills on the project (see across the top of the Cost Estimate in the Gauchito Project Workbook).

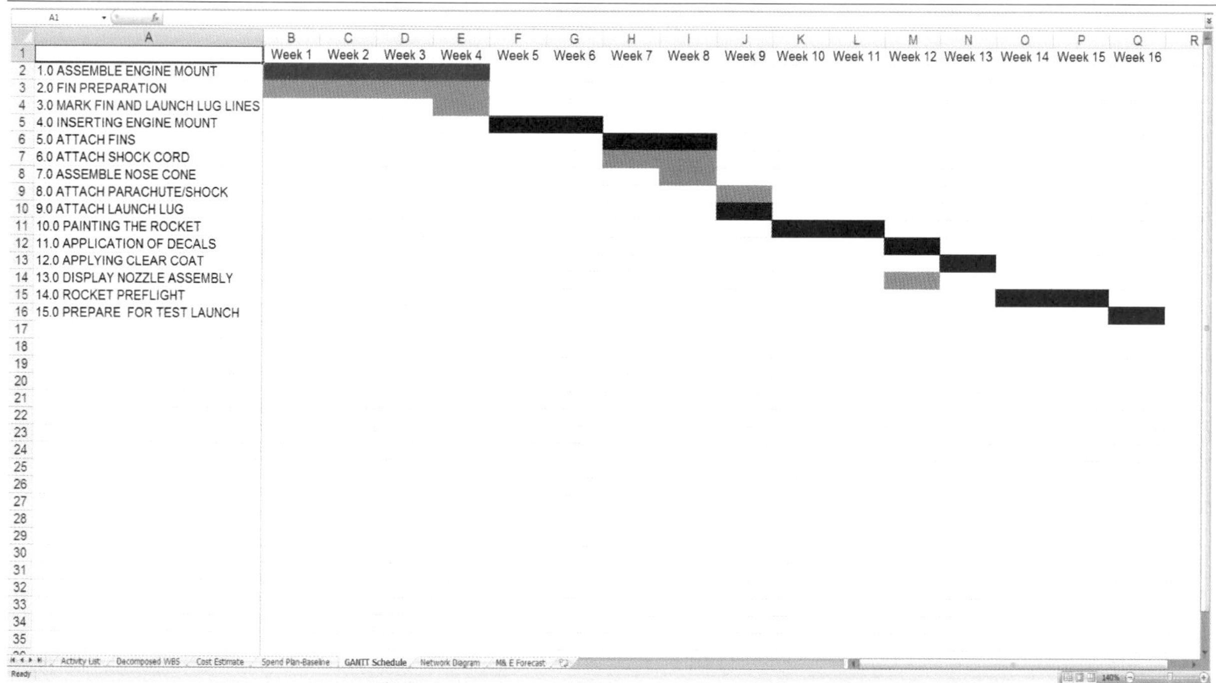

Figure 02.06

How do you calculate say, total work for the Fitter, the Draftsman, the Gluer, and the Cutter for the Engine Mount Assembly over the four weeks the Gantt chart indicate this activity will run. Remember you are estimating the expenditure of your project funds over incremental periods, in this case, over the 16 weeks the project plan has the assembly scheduled. Therefore, you can estimate the expenditure of labor funds for the engine mount assembly task (or, activity) by using a common denominator. The best common denominator to use is percentage of funds expended. That's a fancy term for figuring how much each skill set will cost you for their work each week. Many organizations will make this easier for calculation by smoothing the rate structure or, averaging the rates for the skills being used. This is called a "blended" rate. How does this work you ask? You sure do come up with great questions. Notice in the Gauchito Project Workbook, under the Cost Estimate tab, on line 226, you have each individual skill set hourly rate. Look to the right of these differing rates to cell L226. The formula in that cell is the average of all the different resource hourly rates. This is the project's blended rate for all the skills being utilized on the project. Now, there's a caveat here. If you use outsourced labor through a contract (i.e. contract employees) you must, for legal reasons, keep the blended rates separate, one blended rate for company employees and one blended rate for contract employees. Just adjust your calculations to comply with this legal requirement. Okay, now we know we are going to use blended rates and percentage of hours expended to figure out how much project labor funding is going to be expended weekly by task activity. Looking only at the task level for the Engine

Mount Assembly we can develop the following formula to use:

$$\frac{\text{Work x Rate}}{\text{Time}} = \text{Expenditure}$$

In our example we have 55 hours of work (remember you don't pay for Dummy work since it only constitutes time) multiplied by the Blended rate of $36/hour divided by 4 weeks of work on this activity. So, you the have:

$$\frac{(55 \times 36)}{4} = \$495\text{/week spent for the Engine Mount Assembly task.}$$

But, notice that you also have another task being executed in the first week, the Fin Preparation task. Calculating the expenditure for that activity results in the following:

$$\frac{(30 \times 36)}{4} = \$270\text{/week spent for the Fin Preparation task.}$$

Combining the expenditure of these two tasks shows labor at $765 per week for each of the four weeks. However, a cursory look at the workbook shows that the company instilled additional organizational funding that was indicated in appendix H of the Gauchito Project Plan. This being the case, we choose to follow the approved project plan's figures. Remember, the definitive cost estimate is just that, estimation. What is presented to the sponsor and is approved, reflects what the project is to receive going into execution. So, let's use appendix H of the Gauchito Project Plan as our source for our workbook as depicted. By applying the percentage of labor in each week we get $7,350 for the first three weeks to accomplish tasks 1.0 and 2.0. The addition task 3.0 in week 4 ups the labor costs to $11.550 and so on. Now the planned value of your labor expenditures can be laid out for the project:

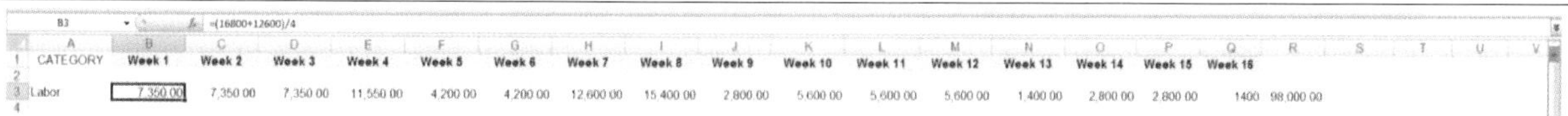

CATEGORY	Week 1	Week 2	Week 3	Week 4	Week 5	Week 6	Week 7	Week 8	Week 9	Week 10	Week 11	Week 12	Week 13	Week 14	Week 15	Week 16	
Labor	7,350.00	7,350.00	7,350.00	11,550.00	4,200.00	4,200.00	12,600.00	15,400.00	2,800.00	5,600.00	5,600.00	5,600.00	1,400.00	2,800.00	2,800.00	1400	98,000.00

Figure 02.07

Going to the M&E Forecast tab we find the planned value of our material expenditures are estimated to be thus:

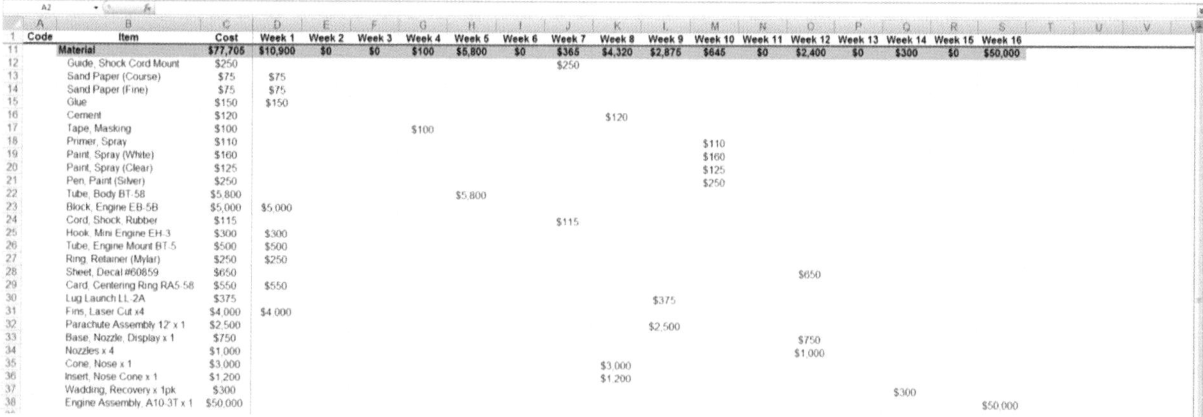

Code	Item	Cost	Week 1	Week 2	Week 3	Week 4	Week 5	Week 6	Week 7	Week 8	Week 9	Week 10	Week 11	Week 12	Week 13	Week 14	Week 15	Week 16
	Material	**$77,705**	**$10,900**	**$0**	**$0**	**$100**	**$5,800**	**$0**	**$365**	**$4,320**	**$2,875**	**$645**	**$0**	**$2,400**	**$0**	**$300**	**$0**	**$50,000**
	Guide, Shock Cord Mount	$250							$250									
	Sand Paper (Course)	$75	$75															
	Sand Paper (Fine)	$75	$75															
	Glue	$150	$150															
	Cement	$120								$120								
	Tape, Masking	$100				$100												
	Primer, Spray	$110										$110						
	Paint, Spray (White)	$160										$160						
	Paint, Spray (Clear)	$125										$125						
	Pen, Paint (Silver)	$250										$250						
	Tube, Body BT-58	$5,800					$5,800											
	Block, Engine EB-5B	$5,000	$5,000															
	Cord, Shock, Rubber	$115							$115									
	Hook, Mini Engine EH-3	$300	$300															
	Tube, Engine Mount BT-5	$500	$500															
	Ring, Retainer (Mylar)	$250	$250															
	Sheet, Decal #60859	$650												$650				
	Card, Centering Ring RA5-58	$550	$550															
	Lug Launch LL-2A	$375									$375							
	Fins, Laser Cut x4	$4,000	$4,000															
	Parachute Assembly 12' x 1	$2,500									$2,500							
	Base, Nozzle, Display x 1	$750												$750				
	Nozzles x 4	$1,000												$1,000				
	Cone, Nose x 1	$3,000								$3,000								
	Insert, Nose Cone x 1	$1,200								$1,200								
	Wadding, Recovery x 1pk	$300														$300		
	Engine Assembly, A10-3T x 1	$50,000																$50,000

Figure 02.08

Finally, we use the same M&E Forecast to show that the planned value of our equipment expenditures to be:

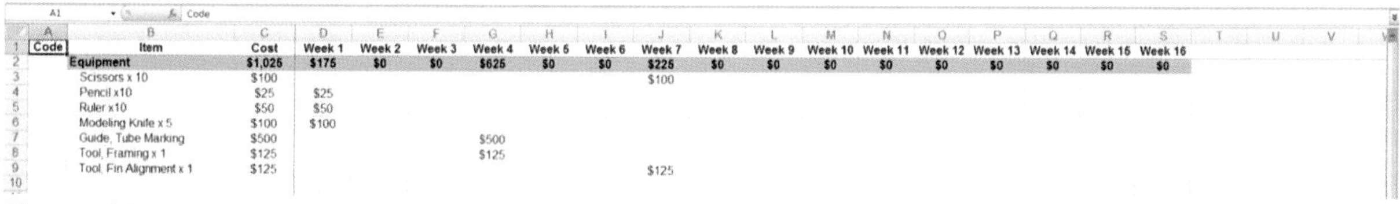

Code	Item	Cost	Week 1	Week 2	Week 3	Week 4	Week 5	Week 6	Week 7	Week 8	Week 9	Week 10	Week 11	Week 12	Week 13	Week 14	Week 15	Week 16
	Equipment	**$1,025**	**$175**	**$0**	**$0**	**$625**	**$0**	**$0**	**$225**	**$0**	**$0**	**$0**	**$0**	**$0**	**$0**	**$0**	**$0**	**$0**
	Scissors x 10	$100							$100									
	Pencil x10	$25	$25															
	Ruler x10	$50	$50															
	Modeling Knife x 5	$100	$100															
	Guide, Tube Marking	$500				$500												
	Tool, Framing x 1	$125				$125												
	Tool, Fin Alignment x 1	$125							$125									

Figure 02.09

It's now just a matter of plugging these planned expenditures into a schedule for their anticipated need. Remember we commit equipment and material expenditures at the first time they are planned to be used and then schedule for their delivery as required. Doing this we can build the Project Spend Plan or Budget:

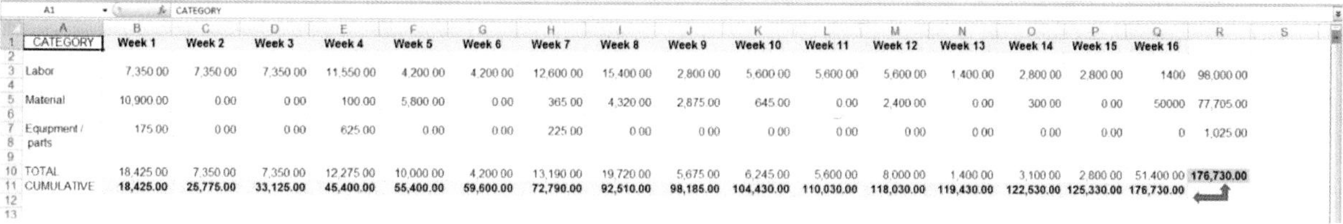

CATEGORY	Week 1	Week 2	Week 3	Week 4	Week 5	Week 6	Week 7	Week 8	Week 9	Week 10	Week 11	Week 12	Week 13	Week 14	Week 15	Week 16	
Labor	7,350.00	7,350.00	7,350.00	11,550.00	4,200.00	4,200.00	12,600.00	15,400.00	2,800.00	5,600.00	5,600.00	5,600.00	1,400.00	2,800.00	2,800.00	1400	98,000.00
Material	10,900.00	0.00	0.00	100.00	5,800.00	0.00	365.00	4,320.00	2,875.00	645.00	0.00	2,400.00	0.00	300.00	0.00	50000	77,705.00
Equipment / parts	175.00	0.00	0.00	625.00	0.00	0.00	225.00	0.00	0.00	0.00	0.00	0.00	0.00	0.00	0.00	0	1,025.00
TOTAL	18,425.00	7,350.00	7,350.00	12,275.00	10,000.00	4,200.00	13,190.00	19,720.00	5,675.00	6,245.00	5,600.00	8,000.00	1,400.00	3,100.00	2,800.00	51,400.00	**176,730.00**
CUMULATIVE	**18,425.00**	**25,775.00**	**33,125.00**	**45,400.00**	**55,400.00**	**59,600.00**	**72,790.00**	**92,510.00**	**98,185.00**	**104,430.00**	**110,030.00**	**118,030.00**	**119,430.00**	**122,530.00**	**125,330.00**	**176,730.00**	

Figure 02.10

If we use the graphing capabilities of Excel we can take this information (data) and chart it out into what is referred to as the project baseline or Planned Value (PV):

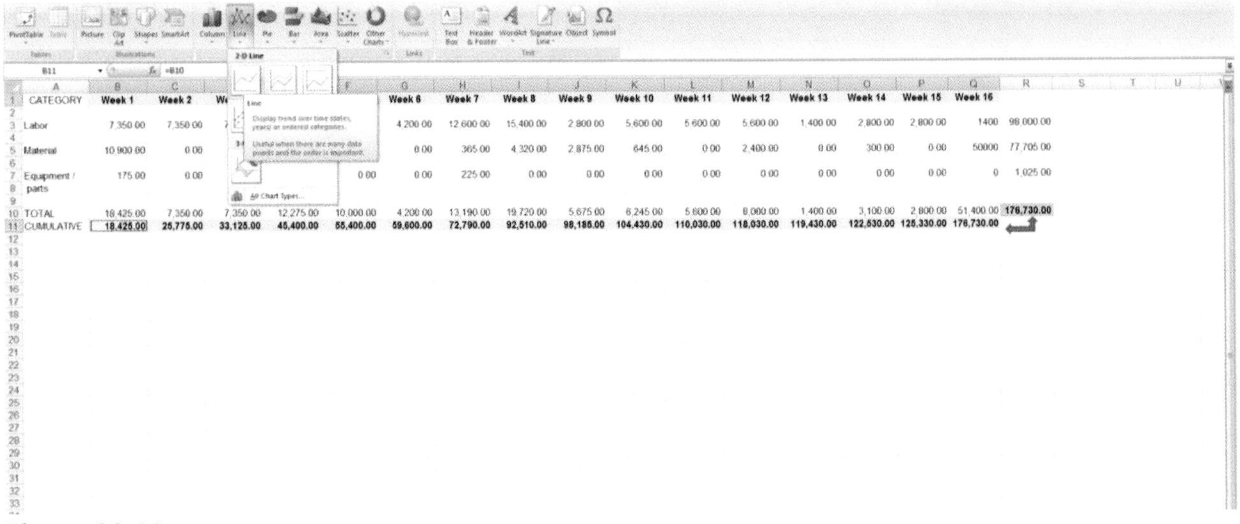

CATEGORY	Week 1	Week 2	We			Week 6	Week 7	Week 8	Week 9	Week 10	Week 11	Week 12	Week 13	Week 14	Week 15	Week 16	
Labor	7,350.00	7,350.00				4,200.00	12,600.00	15,400.00	2,800.00	5,600.00	5,600.00	5,600.00	1,400.00	2,800.00	2,800.00	1400	98,000.00
Material	10,900.00	0.00				0.00	365.00	4,320.00	2,875.00	645.00	0.00	2,400.00	0.00	300.00	0.00	50000	77,705.00
Equipment / parts	175.00	0.00			0.00	0.00	225.00	0.00	0.00	0.00	0.00	0.00	0.00	0.00	0.00	0	1,025.00
TOTAL	18,425.00	7,350.00	7,350.00	12,275.00	10,000.00	4,200.00	13,190.00	19,720.00	5,675.00	6,245.00	5,600.00	8,000.00	1,400.00	3,100.00	2,800.00	51,400.00	176,730.00
CUMULATIVE	18,425.00	25,775.00	33,125.00	45,400.00	55,400.00	59,600.00	72,790.00	92,510.00	98,185.00	104,430.00	110,030.00	118,030.00	119,430.00	122,530.00	125,330.00	176,730.00	

Figure 02.11

Just highlight the time increments and the cumulative totals (identified for you in yellow) with your cursor. Now click on the Insert tab and then on the Line Chart selector and Line command. As the information window states, "Line charts are used to display trends over time." This is exactly what you are doing with the earned value cumulative totals lined out. Click on the line chart and you will get something like this:

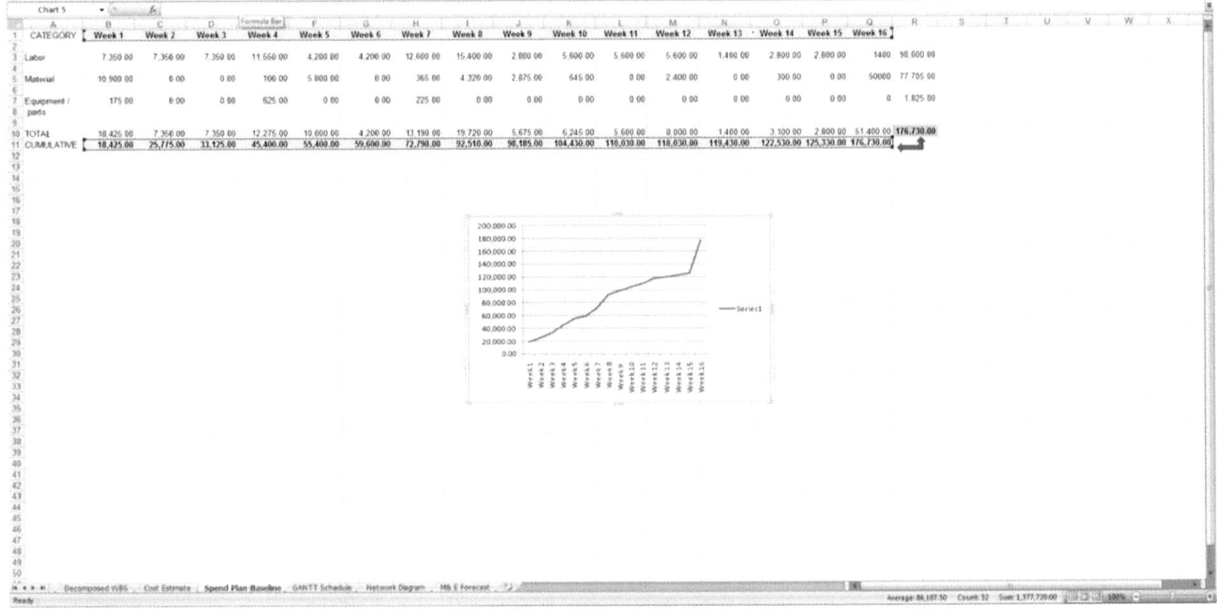

CATEGORY	Week 1	Week 2	Week 3	Week 4	Week 5	Week 6	Week 7	Week 8	Week 9	Week 10	Week 11	Week 12	Week 13	Week 14	Week 15	Week 16	
Labor	7,350.00	7,350.00	7,350.00	11,550.00	4,200.00	4,200.00	12,600.00	15,400.00	2,800.00	5,600.00	5,600.00	5,600.00	1,400.00	2,800.00	2,800.00	1400	98,000.00
Material	10,900.00	0.00	0.00	100.00	5,800.00	0.00	365.00	4,320.00	2,875.00	645.00	0.00	2,400.00	0.00	300.00	0.00	50000	77,705.00
Equipment / parts	175.00	0.00	0.00	625.00	0.00	0.00	225.00	0.00	0.00	0.00	0.00	0.00	0.00	0.00	0.00	0	1,025.00
TOTAL	18,425.00	7,350.00	7,350.00	12,275.00	10,000.00	4,200.00	13,190.00	19,720.00	5,675.00	6,245.00	5,600.00	8,000.00	1,400.00	3,100.00	2,800.00	51,400.00	176,730.00
CUMULATIVE	18,425.00	25,775.00	33,125.00	45,400.00	55,400.00	59,600.00	72,790.00	92,510.00	98,185.00	104,430.00	110,030.00	118,030.00	119,430.00	122,530.00	125,330.00	176,730.00	

Figure 02.12

Now just play around with the graph chart until you have it the way you want. I like mine like this:

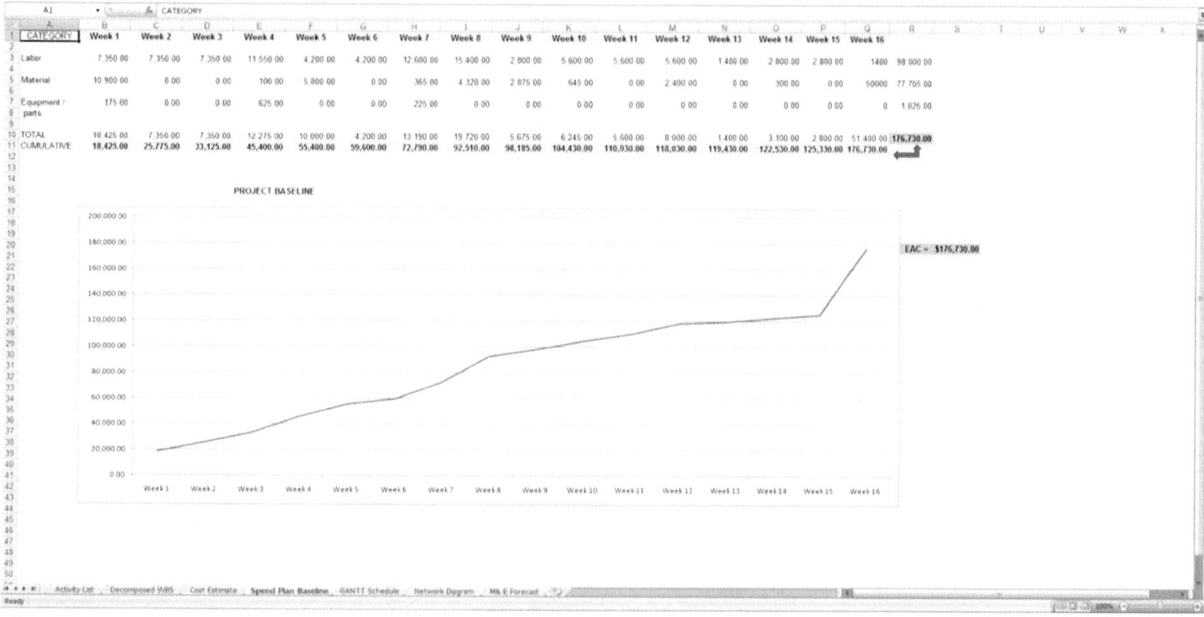

CATEGORY	Week 1	Week 2	Week 3	Week 4	Week 5	Week 6	Week 7	Week 8
Labor	7,350.00	7,350.00	7,350.00	11,550.00	4,200.00	4,200.00	12,600.00	15,400.00
Material	10,900.00	0.00	0.00	100.00	5,800.00	0.00	365.00	4,320.00
Equipment / parts	175.00	0.00	0.00	625.00	0.00	0.00	225.00	0.00
TOTAL	18,425.00	7,350.00	7,350.00	12,275.00	10,000.00	4,200.00	13,190.00	19,720.00
CUMULATIVE	18,425.00	25,775.00	33,125.00	45,400.00	55,400.00	59,600.00	72,790.00	92,510.00

CATEGORY	Week 9	Week 10	Week 11	Week 12	Week 13	Week 14	Week 15	Week 16	
Labor	2,800.00	5,600.00	5,600.00	5,600.00	1,400.00	2,800.00	2,800.00	1400	98,000.00
Material	2,875.00	645.00	0.00	2,400.00	0.00	300.00	0.00	50000	77,705.00
Equipment / parts	0.00	0.00	0.00	0.00	0.00	0.00	0.00	0	1,025.00
TOTAL	5,675.00	6,245.00	5,600.00	8,000.00	1,400.00	3,100.00	2,800.00	51,400.00	176,730.00
CUMULATIVE	98,185.00	104,430.00	110,030.00	118,030.00	119,430.00	122,530.00	125,330.00	176,730.00	

Figure 02.13

Be sure to show your Estimation At Completion (EAC) for readers to understand what they are looking for at the end of the project. You will need to type this in since Excel doesn't do it for you. I would also title the chart as the Project Baseline so there's no mistaking it by the accounting folks or executive management. Notice that this project baseline reflects the trend value of cumulative expenditures planned for over the life of the project from start to completion. This baseline is also called the Planned Value or PV. It is also call the Budgeted Cost of Work Scheduled or BCWS. Both terms are used in industry and it would behoove you to know both so you don't get yourself mixed up in front of executive management. Execs like to trade the terms in discussing projects with PM to see how quick they are on their feet.

Now that we have the project baseline established and we have the tool to measure any deviation from the expected expenditures, we can start to apply some forms of measurement against this baseline.

Chapter 2: Earned value management.

The terminology used in Earned Value Analysis (EVA), now referred to as Earned Value Management (EVM) is undergoing a change within industry. A short comparison is as follows:

- Earned Value Analysis (EVA) = Earned Value Management (EVM)
- Budgeted Cost of Work Scheduled (BCWS) = Planed Value (PV)
- Budgeted Cost of Work Performed (BCWP) = Earned Value (EV)
- Actual Cost of Work Performed (ACWP) = Actual Costs (AC)

The usage of terminology for EV in the PMBOK, section 7.3.2 is somewhat nebulous. (Stackpole, Cynthia et al, 2008) Care should be given in ensuring you understand both the old (BCWS, BCWP, ACWP) and the new terms PV, EV, AC) and don't get them mixed up. For the purposes of this book, both the old terms and new terms were utilized for the convenience of the reader. Both terms are used in industry and in Project Management Professional (PMP) examinations. The new terms are currently found in the Guide to the PMBOK, 2000 and subsequent editions. The 1996 edition used only the old terms. The Earned Value approach allows the project to compare cost and schedule variances concurrently, thus allowing the project manager to take a comprehensive view of the project's progress. When used properly earned value becomes a highly effective management tool for cost and schedule control as well as a performance reporting mechanism to upper management. Earned Value consists of three functions:

- Budget Cost of Work Scheduled (BCWS) which is the same as planned value (PV) budget or the baseline
- Actual Cost of Work Performed (ACWP) which is the amount of actual costs (AC) costs to perform task
- Budgeted Cost of Work Performed (BCWP) which is the earned value (EV) or what the project is really worth at a given point in time

Chapter 2: Spreadsheet control tools.

Spreadsheets are the choice of project management EVM tools. Even cost and control tools such as Microsoft's Project Professional, Oracle's Primavera and Planview's Planview are based on spreadsheets. Many third party EVM tools are also based on spreadsheets. In fact this book uses a simple version of a spreadsheet-based EVM control tool found in Appendix-G called the Gauchito Blank Template.xls. Please take the time to play around with this template but be careful to use a clean template to work the assignments in this book. Another example of a developed EVM control tool can be also found in Appendix-F called EVM Project Example.xls. This tool is a derivative of a major telecom project EVM control tool. Adding multiple project EVM control tools together can provide a program EVM control tool. An example of this is also in Appendix-E called A Program EVM Example.xls. As you become more proficient in your own EVM TT&P, you will start to develop your own personal tools whether they are personally developed, product applications, or third part spreadsheets. Just be sure you are comfortable and proficient with the use of the EVM control tool you use for your project. As for the assignments in the Gauchito project, you will be expected to utilize the provided Gauchito Blank Template for courseware standardization.

Before we get into setting the scope and the requirements of the project, let's take a quick look at what makes up earned value management.

Chapter 2: What is Earned Value Management?

Earned Value Management (EVM) is a technique used to track the progress and status of a project and to forecast the likely future performance of the project. EVM techniques integrate the scope, schedule and cost of the project into a single comprehensive analytical picture of project health. Good planning coupled with effective use of EVM techniques will reduce a large amount of issues arising out of schedule and cost overruns. EVM techniques address a lot of stakeholder's questions in a project, related to the performance of the project. EVM techniques can be used to show past performance of the project, current performance of the project and predict the future performance of the project by use of statistical techniques.
The Earned Value approach allows the project to compare cost and schedule variances concurrently, thus allowing the project manager to take a comprehensive view of the project's progress. When used properly earned value becomes a highly effective management tool for cost and schedule control as well as a performance reporting mechanism to upper management. Earned Value consists of three functions:

- Budget Cost of Work Scheduled/Planned Value (BCWS/PV) which is the same as **planned** budget or the baseline
- Actual Cost of Work Performed/Actual Costs (ACWP/AC) which is the amount of **actual** costs to perform task
- Budgeted Cost of Work Performed/Earned Value (BCWP/EV) which is the **earned value** or what the project is really worth at a given point in time

These three functions plotted on a graph provide the Cumulative Cost Curve (S Curve) as depicted below.

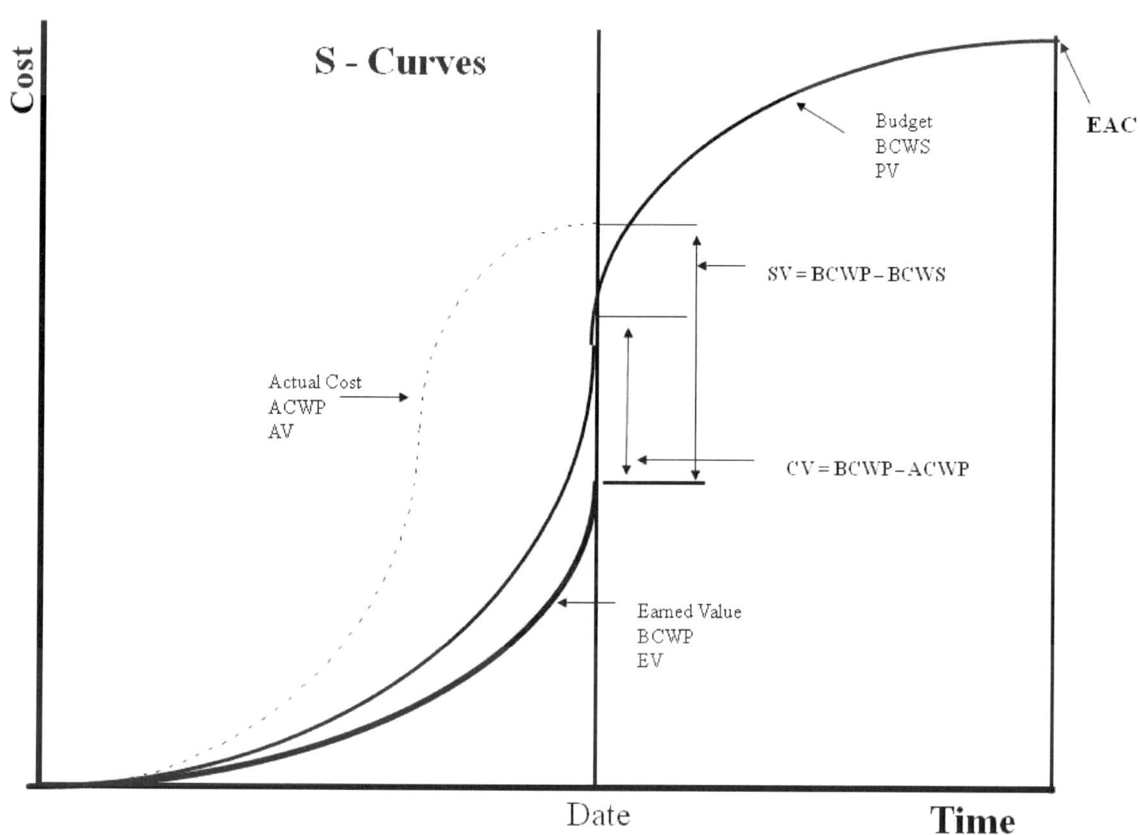

Figure 02.14
(Tyler M. J., Lecture Notes, 1993-2010)

Chapter 2: The Purpose of Earned Value Management.

EVM as it was practiced from the 1950s-1995 did require substantial investment in people and systems. The practice required a small army of schedulers and budget analysts. Processes were manual. And large mainframe computers were needed to crunch the numbers (which required lab-coated computer wizards to operate). All in all, the practice of EVM could only be done by large companies that could afford the overhead. Typically this meant defense contractors that were having the costs underwritten by the government. What changed this picture was the introduction of client-server, mid-range platforms that replaced the cumbersome main frames. In the last 5 years in particular, it has become common to see applications that can run EVM on a laptop....by a single analyst. A few years ago this function took dozens of people plodding through laborious manual processes. EVM can be done quickly and efficiently, without the outlay of capital resources that was previously required. Some EV applications cost under $500. And you don't need highly expert wizards to operate the system. The EVM functions can even be out-sourced. A great problem is that many older managers and executives simply do not understand that the world has changed in the past 10 years. They are stuck in the time warp of their past experience. They remember EVM as incredibly labor intensive and difficult to do. (Chadick, 2011)

Also, Project Managers, especially the older ones, get glassy-eyed when they see the numbers, accounting, budget, calculations, etc., that comprise EVM. Their typical response is to relegate to Finance & Accounting as a budget function....not a function worthy of their managerial attention. Of course, we know that this attitude is totally misguided. EV is about PERFORMANCE; It is explicitly not a bean-counter function. The PMs who fail to embrace their EVM are abrogating responsibility for their management. And they are not practicing rigorous, due diligence in the management of their program.

Earned value (EV) is one of the most sophisticated and accurate methods for measuring and controlling project schedules and budgets. Earned value has been used extensively in large projects, especially in government projects. PMI is a strong supporter of the earned value approach because of its ability to accurately monitor the schedule and cost variances for complex projects. (Haughey, 2010) The term "Earned Value" is gaining in popularity around project management circles as if it is some wonderful new concept to be embraced. Yet, it has been in use since the 1960s when the Department of Defense adopted it as a standard method of measuring project performance. Today, it is both embraced and shunned, often in response to prior experience or stories told "in the hallway." The opponents will generally cite the cost and effort to make it work, and the limited benefit derived from its implementation. The proponents will cite the cost savings to the project overall, the improved analysis, communication and control derived from its implementation. No doubt, the two camps have vastly different experiences to formulate their perceptions. (Wilkens, 1999)

Chapter 2: Setting Up the EVM Tool

Now that you understand the basics of setting up an EVM tool, let's make one of our own. Starting with a blank Excel spreadsheet let's set the spend plan to address the project activities at the task level and the time increments as weekly. Your initial spend plan should look this:

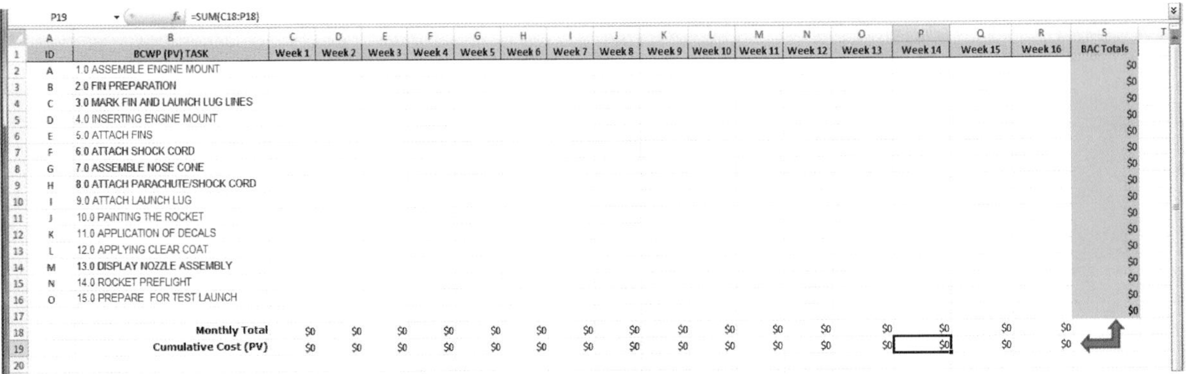

P19 =SUM(C18:P18)

ID	BCWP (PV) TASK	Week 1	Week 2	Week 3	Week 4	Week 5	Week 6	Week 7	Week 8	Week 9	Week 10	Week 11	Week 12	Week 13	Week 14	Week 15	Week 16	BAC Totals
A	1.0 ASSEMBLE ENGINE MOUNT																	$0
B	2.0 FIN PREPARATION																	$0
C	3.0 MARK FIN AND LAUNCH LUG LINES																	$0
D	4.0 INSERTING ENGINE MOUNT																	$0
E	5.0 ATTACH FINS																	$0
F	6.0 ATTACH SHOCK CORD																	$0
G	7.0 ASSEMBLE NOSE CONE																	$0
H	8.0 ATTACH PARACHUTE/SHOCK CORD																	$0
I	9.0 ATTACH LAUNCH LUG																	$0
J	10.0 PAINTING THE ROCKET																	$0
K	11.0 APPLICATION OF DECALS																	$0
L	12.0 APPLYING CLEAR COAT																	$0
M	13.0 DISPLAY NOZZLE ASSEMBLY																	$0
N	14.0 ROCKET PREFLIGHT																	$0
O	15.0 PREPARE FOR TEST LAUNCH																	$0
																		$0
	Monthly Total	$0	$0	$0	$0	$0	$0	$0	$0	$0	$0	$0	$0	$0	$0	$0	$0	
	Cumulative Cost (PV)	$0	$0	$0	$0	$0	$0	$0	$0	$0	$0	$0	$0	$0	$0	$0	$0	

Figure 02.15

Notice that the expected totals for each task budgeted at completion are summed at the right (highlighted in green). Additionally, the weekly expenditures are totaled at the bottom. This allows us to then add each weekly total cumulatively so we can see the entire amount of expenditures anticipated at each weekly increment. The formula is simple for this, week 1 = week 1, week 2 = week 1 + week 2, week 3 = week 1 + w 2 + week 3, and so on. According to the Gauchito project plan the duration of the project is expected to take 16 weeks. The cumulative total of the weeks in week 16 should also equal the total of all the Tasks BAC totals. Notice that the blue highlighted double arrow identifies that the two sets of totals should be the same amount. If this isn't true, there is a miscalculation in your spend plan.

But, you say, numerous tasks extend beyond the weekly increments. So, how do we indentify the weekly amount of a task executed over multiple weeks? Great question! This shows you're getting into this. For labor only, you just need to identify the percentage of each task expended in each of the weeks it is executed. But, is this the latest information we have? This was just for the initial planning and does not necessarily represent the Planned Value or PV for the project. Let's look back at our MS Project schedule that we built out using the latest information:

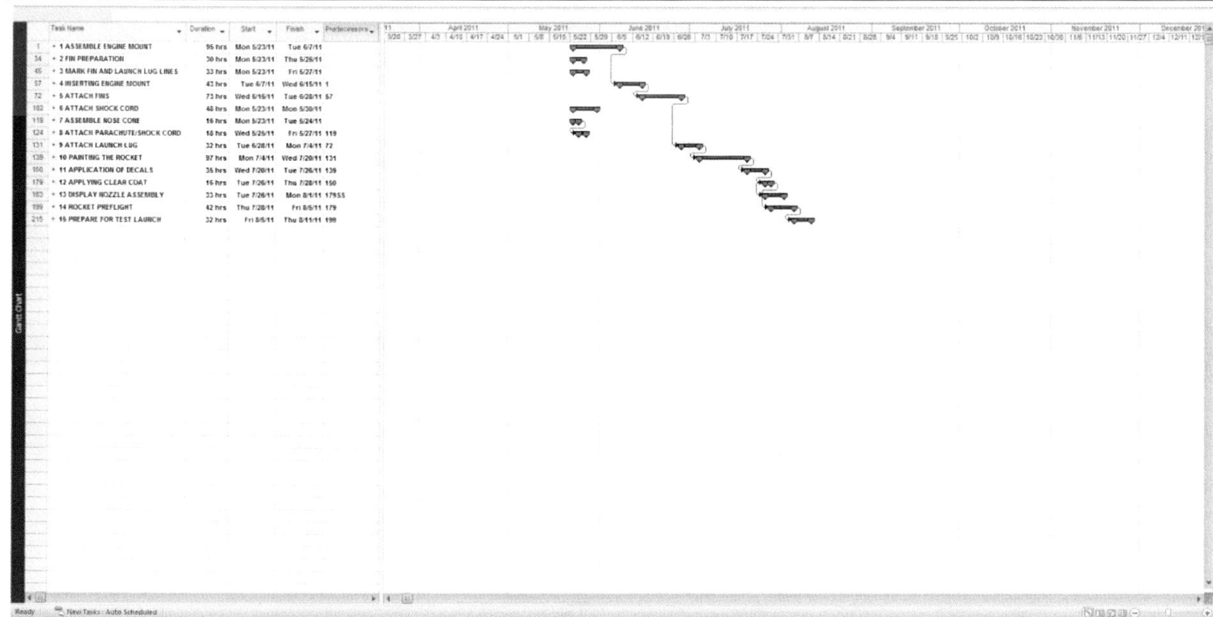

	Task Name	Duration	Start	Finish	Predecessors
1	1 ASSEMBLE ENGINE MOUNT	95 hrs	Mon 5/23/11	Tue 6/7/11	
34	2 FIN PREPARATION	30 hrs	Mon 5/23/11	Thu 5/26/11	
45	3 MARK FIN AND LAUNCH LUG LINES	33 hrs	Mon 5/23/11	Fri 5/27/11	
57	4 INSERTING ENGINE MOUNT	43 hrs	Tue 6/7/11	Wed 6/15/11	1
72	5 ATTACH FINS	73 hrs	Wed 6/15/11	Tue 6/28/11	57
102	6 ATTACH SHOCK CORD	48 hrs	Mon 5/23/11	Mon 5/30/11	
119	7 ASSEMBLE NOSE CONE	16 hrs	Mon 5/23/11	Tue 5/24/11	
124	8 ATTACH PARACHUTE/SHOCK CORD	18 hrs	Wed 5/25/11	Fri 5/27/11	119
131	9 ATTACH LAUNCH LUG	32 hrs	Tue 6/28/11	Mon 7/4/11	72
139	10 PAINTING THE ROCKET	97 hrs	Mon 7/4/11	Wed 7/20/11	131
150	11 APPLICATION OF DECALS	35 hrs	Wed 7/20/11	Tue 7/26/11	139
179	12 APPLYING CLEAR COAT	16 hrs	Tue 7/26/11	Thu 7/28/11	150
183	13 DISPLAY NOZZLE ASSEMBLY	33 hrs	Tue 7/26/11	Mon 8/1/11	179SS
199	14 ROCKET PREFLIGHT	42 hrs	Thu 7/28/11	Fri 8/5/11	179
215	15 PREPARE FOR TEST LAUNCH	32 hrs	Fri 8/5/11	Thu 8/11/11	199

Figure 02.16

From the Gauchito project workbook you will notice that the Gantt chart does not reflect the Network Diagram. This is because a Gantt chart on a spreadsheet is a gross representation of the reality of the project. As you might imagine, using just a bar chart to manage day-to-day activities can result in deviations from the project baseline. Using a tool like MS Project allows for the granularity necessary for managing the project at the work package level while using a spreadsheet based Gantt provides the high-level representation of the project's performance for general decision making. Providing a work package level granularity at your project review will inundate executive management with minutiae and distract from your purpose of providing information on major issues that need to be resolved. Attention to detail is necessary in the day-to-day aspects of project management. But, the project management must be able to zoom out and look at the task level performance of that project as well. You need to use the micro-level tools daily to stay abreast of the project and identify deviations from the baseline to immediately bring the project back on line. However, when presenting the project as a whole, performance needs to be viewed at the task level. Remember that tasks, once completed become the deliverables of the project. It is at this level that the sponsor and the customer/user, and major stakeholders like the functional managers and back office managers, will be keeping track of your project as well as a host of other projects. *Plan your plan to the finest detail. Only show the highest level of your planning. Then, manage the difference.* (Tyler M. J., 1998)

You may have notice by now that MS Project does not allow for Finish-Finish relationships at the Summary Task level. In order for its algorithms to work, tasks that have shorter durations, when fast-tracked with tasks that have longer durations need to has Start-Start precedence relationships. Just remember is the task is not on the critical path, it can float as you need it but it must commence the same time as the other tasks it is being fast-tracked with.

Now that we know the subtleties between a tool like MS Project and a tool like the EVM tool, we can now build out a calculation sheet for our EVM tool focusing on activity at the task level, setting the precedence of the task level activities, the duration, and the blended rate of $35.00/hour but at a weekly rate (remember our increments are weekly not hourly) to arrive at a budgeted at completion cost for each task.

ID	Job Description	Immediate Predecessors	Planned Duration (Weeks)	Staff (Number)	Rate/Person/Week	Task Cost (BAC)	1Mos Effort to Date (Wks)	% Complete	Outstanding Durtation (Wks)	Staff Level	ACWP (AC)
A	1.0 ASSEMBLE ENGINE MOUNT	Start	2	4	$1,440	$11,520		0%			$0
B	2.0 FIN PREPARATION	Start	1	3	$1,440	$4,320		0%			$0
C	3.0 MARK FIN AND LAUNCH LUG LINES	Start	1	3	$1,440	$4,320		0%			$0
D	4.0 INSERTING ENGINE MOUNT	A	2	3	$1,440	$8,640		0%			$0
E	5.0 ATTACH FINS	D	1	3	$1,440	$4,320		0%			$0
F	6.0 ATTACH SHOCK CORD	Start	2	3	$1,440	$8,640		0%			$0
G	7.0 ASSEMBLE NOSE CONE	Start	1	2	$1,440	$2,880		0%			$0
H	8.0 ATTACH PARACHUTE/SHOCK CORD	G	1	1	$1,440	$1,440		0%			$0
I	9.0 ATTACH LAUNCH LUG	E	1	1	$1,440	$1,440		0%			$0
J	10.0 PAINTING THE ROCKET	I	1	4	$1,440	$5,760		0%			$0
K	11.0 APPLICATION OF DECALS	J	1	1	$1,440	$1,440		0%			$0
L	12.0 APPLYING CLEAR COAT	K	1	1	$1,440	$1,440		0%			$0
M	13.0 DISPLAY NOZZLE ASSEMBLY	K	1	3	$1,440	$4,320		0%			$0
N	14.0 ROCKET PREFLIGHT	L	1	2	$1,440	$2,880		0%			$0
O	15.0 PREPARE FOR TEST LAUNCH	N	1	1	$1,440	$1,440		0%			$0
			24 weeks Level of Effort								
	Blended Rate=	$1,440	11 weeks duration								

Figure 02.17

Using the Gauchito Project Workbook and the Network Diagram tab, we can identify the critical path task activities in red for reference and set the Immediate Predecessors. Our durations will be rounded up or down for the use of resource expenditures. Otherwise, you will project expenditure of all your planned resources well before the project is completed. Now we can use this data to build out the Gauchito EVM tool. Let's just look at the first task. The Assemble Engine Mount will start on the first week of the project, take 2.4 weeks (95 hours) rounded down to two weeks utilizing 4 team members at a blended rate of $1,440/week ($36/hr. x 40 hrs./week = $1,440/week) for a total Budget At Completion labor cost of $11,520. Before we can place the labor data into the Gantt Tab we need to include any anticipated expenditures in equipment and material. So let's go to the Gauchito Project Workbook and look at the M&E Forecast. The Material and Equipment Forecast is just that, a prediction of when you expect to use the material and equipment and the cost of that expenditure. Let's take a look at what an M&E Forecast looks like.

Code	Item	Cost	Week 1	Week 2	Week 3	Week 4	Week 5	Week 6	Week 7	Week 8	Week 9	Week 10	Week 11	Week 12	Week 13	Week 14	Week 15	Week 16
	Equipment	**$1,025**	**$1,025**	**$0**	**$0**	**$0**	**$0**	**$0**	**$0**	**$0**	**$0**	**$0**	**$0**	**$0**	**$0**	**$0**	**$0**	**$0**
	Scissors x 10	$100	$100															
	Pencil x10	$25	$25															
	Ruler x10	$50	$50															
	Modeling Knife x 5	$100	$100															
	Guide, Tube Marking	$500	$500															
	Tool, Framing x 1	$125	$125															
	Tool, Fin Alignment x 1	$125	$125															
	Material	**$77,705**	**$15,685**	**$2,500**	**$5,800**	**$0**	**$0**	**$375**	**$270**	**$650**	**$1,875**	**$550**	**$50,000**	**$0**	**$0**	**$0**	**$0**	**$0**
	Guide, Shock Cord Mount	$250	$250															
	Sand Paper (Course)	$75	$75															
	Sand Paper (Fine)	$75	$75															
	Glue	$150	$150															
	Cement	$120	$120															
	Tape, Masking	$100	$100															
	Primer, Spray	$110							$110									
	Paint, Spray (White)	$160							$160									
	Paint, Spray (Clear)	$125									$125							
	Pen, Paint (Silver)	$250										$250						
	Tube, Body BT-58	$5,800			$5,800													
	Block, Engine EB-5B	$5,000	$5,000															
	Cord, Shock, Rubber	$115	$115															
	Hook, Mini Engine EH-3	$300	$300															
	Tube, Engine Mount BT-5	$500	$500															
	Ring, Retainer (Mylar)	$250	$250															
	Sheet, Decal #60859	$650								$650								
	Card, Centering Ring RA5-58	$550	$550															
	Lug Launch LL-2A	$375						$375										
	Fins, Laser Cut x4	$4,000	$4,000															
	Parachute Assembly 12' x 1	$2,500		$2,500														
	Base, Nozzle, Display x 1	$750									$750							
	Nozzles x 4	$1,000									$1,000							
	Cone, Nose x 1	$3,000	$3,000															
	Insert, Nose Cone x 1	$1,200	$1,200															
	Wadding, Recovery x 1pk	$300										$300						
	Engine Assembly, A10-3T x 1	$50,000											$50,000					
		TOTAL	**$16,710**	**$2,500**	**$5,800**	**$0**	**$0**	**$375**	**$270**	**$650**	**$1,875**	**$550**	**$50,000**	**$0**	**$0**	**$0**	**$0**	**$0**

Cost Estimate | Spend Plan-Baseline | GANTT Schedule | Network Diagram | M& E Forecast

Figure 02.18

It looks like you will be expending most of your material and equipment the first week, don't let that fool you. Yes, you will be spending the money the first week but many of those items will also be used throughout the project. A good technique that has been proven over the decades with project management is to frontload your equipment and material. What does this mean? Good question. It means that you commit your total funds for any piece of equipment or material the first time it is to be used on the project. If you have say, $50 worth of glue to be used in week 1 and then another $50 worth of glue to be used in week 2 and the final $50 worth of glue to be used in week 4, commit the total amount of $150 the first week when you need only the first third. You do this for a couple of reasons. First, your procurement department can get a cheaper rate if all the glue is bought in volume at one time. But you don't have anywhere to store the rest of the glue you say? Not to worry. Let the procurement department take the savings by buying in volume and then set up a delivery schedule with the glue vendor to deliver one-third the first week, one-third the second week, and the last third the fourth week. Now, you've saved the organization money by buying volume (savings remains in your project account as contingency reserve) and you've let the vendor store the remainder for you until you need it. Remember there's another reason for committing the funds up front? As a project moves through its lifecycle, there are times that monies need to be moved from project to project by executive management to keep all projects healthy. Just because you are fiduciarily responsible doesn't mean that you won't have funds moved out of your project to help someone who wasn't or couldn't be so. The commitment of funds locks those funds or "fences" the funds for contracted requirements and cannot be pulled from your project. Just remember to set up a delivery schedule with all of your vendors when you do this.

So, let's add $1,025 worth of equipment and $15,685 worth of material to the $5,760 worth of labor in our first week's column in our EVM tool for the Planned Value (PV) chart in the EVM tool, BCWS Gantt tab.

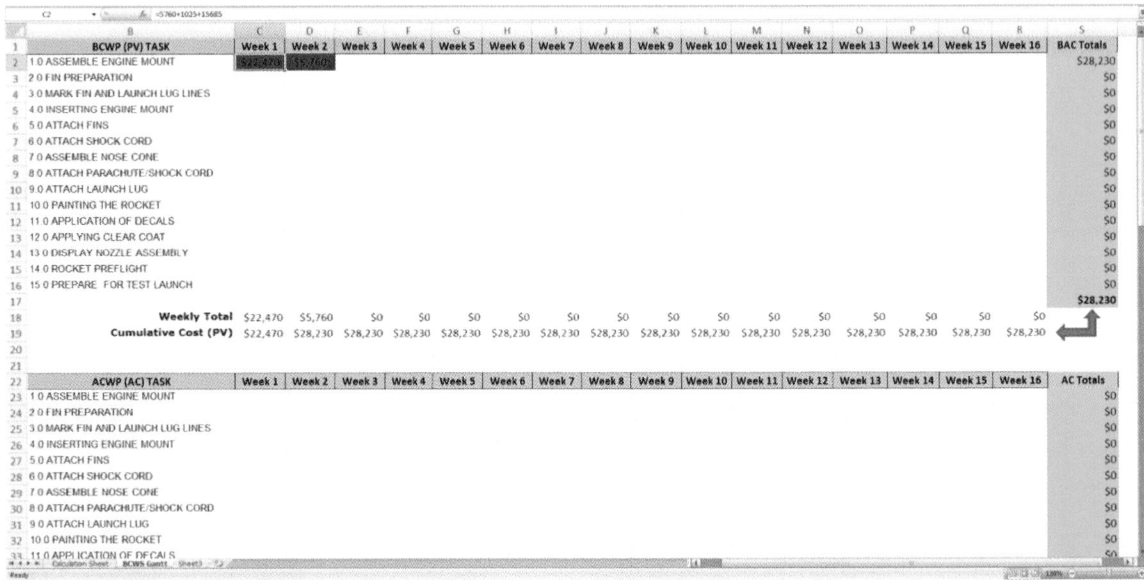

C2 =5760+1025+15685

BCWP (PV) TASK	Week 1	Week 2	Week 3	Week 4	Week 5	Week 6	Week 7	Week 8	Week 9	Week 10	Week 11	Week 12	Week 13	Week 14	Week 15	Week 16	BAC Totals
1.0 ASSEMBLE ENGINE MOUNT	$22,470	$5,760															$28,230
2.0 FIN PREPARATION																	$0
3.0 MARK FIN AND LAUNCH LUG LINES																	$0
4.0 INSERTING ENGINE MOUNT																	$0
5.0 ATTACH FINS																	$0
6.0 ATTACH SHOCK CORD																	$0
7.0 ASSEMBLE NOSE CONE																	$0
8.0 ATTACH PARACHUTE/SHOCK CORD																	$0
9.0 ATTACH LAUNCH LUG																	$0
10.0 PAINTING THE ROCKET																	$0
11.0 APPLICATION OF DECALS																	$0
12.0 APPLYING CLEAR COAT																	$0
13.0 DISPLAY NOZZLE ASSEMBLY																	$0
14.0 ROCKET PREFLIGHT																	$0
15.0 PREPARE FOR TEST LAUNCH																	$0
																	$28,230
Weekly Total	$22,470	$5,760	$0	$0	$0	$0	$0	$0	$0	$0	$0	$0	$0	$0	$0	$0	
Cumulative Cost (PV)	$22,470	$28,230	$28,230	$28,230	$28,230	$28,230	$28,230	$28,230	$28,230	$28,230	$28,230	$28,230	$28,230	$28,230	$28,230	$28,230	

ACWP (AC) TASK	Week 1	Week 2	Week 3	Week 4	Week 5	Week 6	Week 7	Week 8	Week 9	Week 10	Week 11	Week 12	Week 13	Week 14	Week 15	Week 16	AC Totals
1.0 ASSEMBLE ENGINE MOUNT																	$0
2.0 FIN PREPARATION																	$0
3.0 MARK FIN AND LAUNCH LUG LINES																	$0
4.0 INSERTING ENGINE MOUNT																	$0
5.0 ATTACH FINS																	$0
6.0 ATTACH SHOCK CORD																	$0
7.0 ASSEMBLE NOSE CONE																	$0
8.0 ATTACH PARACHUTE/SHOCK CORD																	$0
9.0 ATTACH LAUNCH LUG																	$0
10.0 PAINTING THE ROCKET																	$0
11.0 APPLICATION OF DECALS																	$0

Figure 02.19

Notice in the formula bar that task 1.0 labor for the first week ($11,520/2 for each week of activity) of $5,760 has the equipment and material expenditures added to it and the second week for task 1.0 only hast the labor inserted. You can validate this calculation by checking the BAC Totals for task 1.0 and see that the total of $28,230 = $11,520 (2 weeks labor) + $1,025 (equipment) + $15,685 (material). The same cumulative total is also shown in cell D18 for the expenditure through week 2. Now you have the start of your EVM tool that shows you a high-level Gantt (at the task level) and your planned value (PV) of that activity. Color in each task's activity in the week that the work is to be done and insert the expenditures for labor, equipment and material to fill out your project's planned value for the life of the project. Use the color red to identify activities on the critical path and another color to identify activities not on the critical path. To give you an idea of this, let's do one more activity not on the critical path, task 2.0 Fin Preparation. Going back to the Gantt on your MS Project tool you will see that task 2.0 will take and, because of MS Project, has a Start-Start relationship with task 1.0. On your Calculation Sheet tab in your EVM tool we see that task 2.0 starts at the beginning of the project, has a duration of 1 week, utilizes 3 team members at a rate of $1,440 per week for a total of $4,320 BAC. Putting this into the PV chart of your EVM tool results in the following:

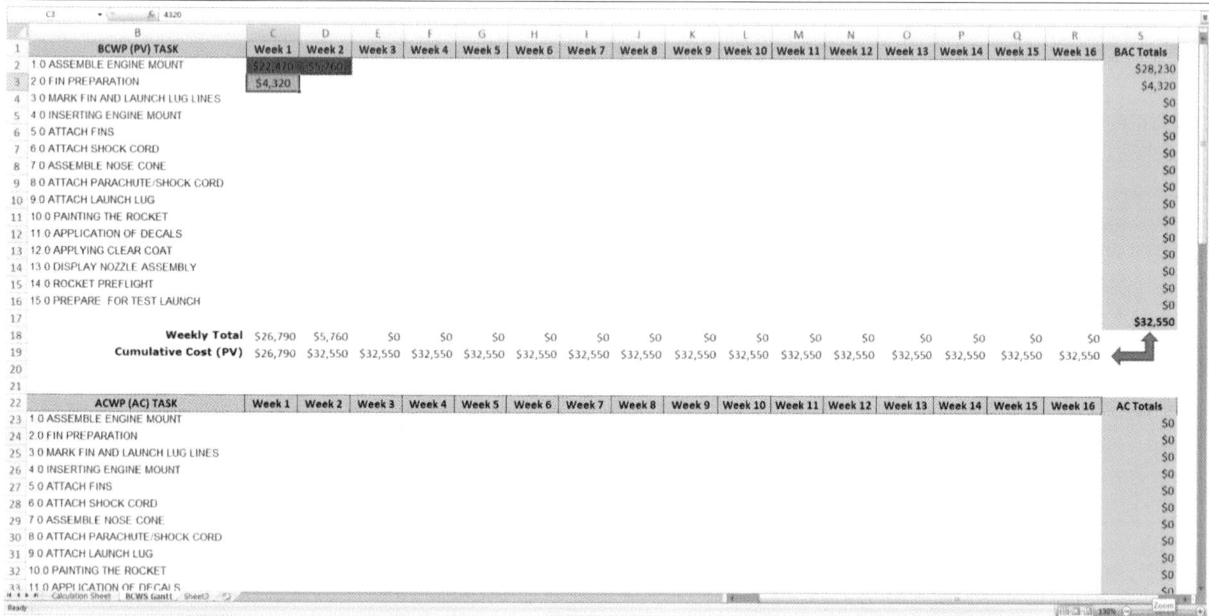

BCWP (PV) TASK	Week 1	Week 2	Week 3	Week 4	Week 5	Week 6	Week 7	Week 8	Week 9	Week 10	Week 11	Week 12	Week 13	Week 14	Week 15	Week 16	BAC Totals
1.0 ASSEMBLE ENGINE MOUNT	$22,470	$5,760															$28,230
2.0 FIN PREPARATION	$4,320																$4,320
3.0 MARK FIN AND LAUNCH LUG LINES																	$0
4.0 INSERTING ENGINE MOUNT																	$0
5.0 ATTACH FINS																	$0
6.0 ATTACH SHOCK CORD																	$0
7.0 ASSEMBLE NOSE CONE																	$0
8.0 ATTACH PARACHUTE/SHOCK CORD																	$0
9.0 ATTACH LAUNCH LUG																	$0
10.0 PAINTING THE ROCKET																	$0
11.0 APPLICATION OF DECALS																	$0
12.0 APPLYING CLEAR COAT																	$0
13.0 DISPLAY NOZZLE ASSEMBLY																	$0
14.0 ROCKET PREFLIGHT																	$0
15.0 PREPARE FOR TEST LAUNCH																	$0
																	$32,550
Weekly Total	$26,790	$5,760	$0	$0	$0	$0	$0	$0	$0	$0	$0	$0	$0	$0	$0	$0	
Cumulative Cost (PV)	$26,790	$32,550	$32,550	$32,550	$32,550	$32,550	$32,550	$32,550	$32,550	$32,550	$32,550	$32,550	$32,550	$32,550	$32,550	$32,550	

ACWP (AC) TASK	Week 1	Week 2	Week 3	Week 4	Week 5	Week 6	Week 7	Week 8	Week 9	Week 10	Week 11	Week 12	Week 13	Week 14	Week 15	Week 16	AC Totals
1.0 ASSEMBLE ENGINE MOUNT																	$0
2.0 FIN PREPARATION																	$0
3.0 MARK FIN AND LAUNCH LUG LINES																	$0
4.0 INSERTING ENGINE MOUNT																	$0
5.0 ATTACH FINS																	$0
6.0 ATTACH SHOCK CORD																	$0
7.0 ASSEMBLE NOSE CONE																	$0
8.0 ATTACH PARACHUTE/SHOCK CORD																	$0
9.0 ATTACH LAUNCH LUG																	$0
10.0 PAINTING THE ROCKET																	$0
11.0 APPLICATION OF DECALS																	$0

Figure 02.20

Notice that the Gantt shows the activity in gray (not on critical path) for a total labor of $4,320 and no equipment or material expenditures because we accounted for all equipment and material expenditures with the task 1.0 activity. You can break down your equipment and material by activity by week but you will find it time consuming to do so. Another way to account for the equipment and material is to add additional rows under the tasks, one for equipment expenditures and one for material expenditures. Excel is versatile enough to let you do this. Continue to do this for all activities for labor, material and equipment for your project to flesh out your planned value. As you do so you will notice that other parts of the EVM tool start to populate as well.

Chapter 2: Navigating the EVM Tool

Down towards the bottom left portion of the BCWS Gantt tab worksheet you will notice that the Cumulative Cost Curve or the project S-Curve is starting to take shape.

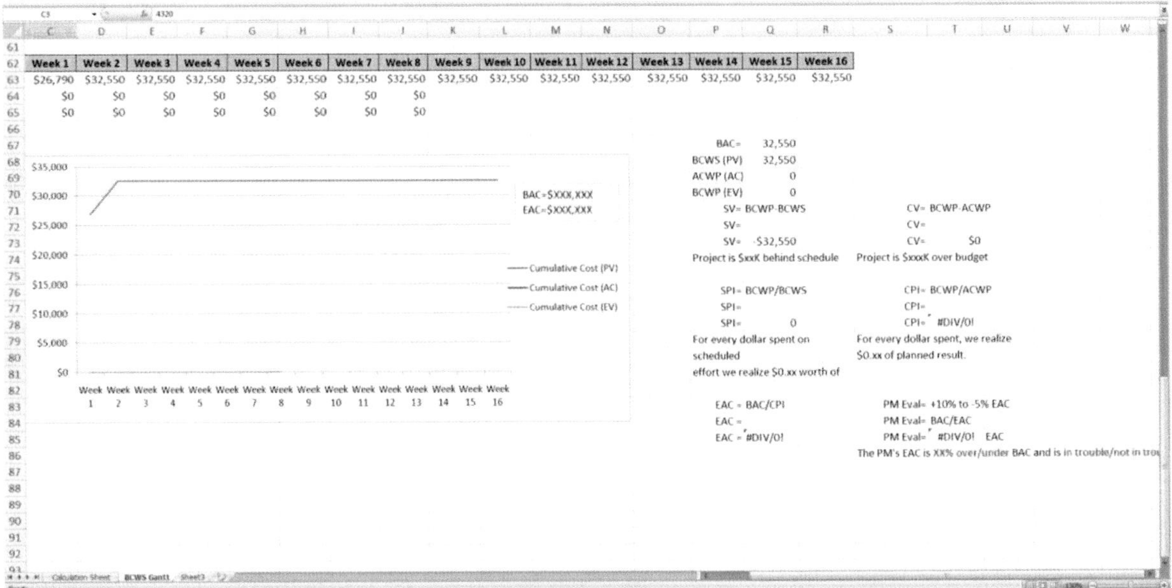

Figure 02.21

As you populate the rest of the Gauchito task activities you will see this continues to provide graphic resolution to the planned value of your project. You will also notice that to the right of the Cumulative Cost Curve graph there are sets of formulae whose totals are being populated as you fill in your PV chart. At cell P67 we have the project's BAC being populated for us. This is just a copy of the total BAC fro, cell S17 but provides you a specific location for this figure. Just below it is the same figure reflecting cell J19 which is the cumulative value of the project in the eighth week. We've set this as a marker because we know we have to present an update for the project in week eight. We can change the cell location to reflect which week we want to look at depending on which week we want to focus our attention for the PV. The same goes for ACWP (AC) below it and for the BCWP (EV) just below that. We know that schedule Variance is BCWP-BCWS or EV-PV so, let's set that formula just below using cell Q70 minus cell Q68. Now we have a running total for any given time for our SV. As we change our markers to reflect which we are in with the project lifecycle, each of our EVM formulae will reflect the results. For the CPI we should have an error since we are dividing BCWP (EV) by ACWP (AC) which are both zero at this time. As we populate our actuals, ACWP or AC and our earned value, BCWP or EV, we will see these cell populated as well. Let's go ahead and input some bogus numbers into the PV chart to flesh out the planned value so we can populate the AC chart. NOTE: the figures from this point on do not reflect the actual figures from the Gauchito project plan. Any use of these figures as submissions for the exercises at the end of the chapters will result in incorrect tabulations. It will also show that you got lazy and just copied and pasted numbers without understanding what you are doing.

Chapter 2: Thought Question

As a PM you would like to use earned value analysis to track progress on internal projects, but your organization established your project in a weak matrix environment where salaries are confidential. What should you do?

A. Figure salary costs only for workers who are willing to disclose their salary to you.

B. Get confidential organizational salary data after a promise to do your reports only at home.

C. Estimate salaries for workers on your projects and use the estimates in your earned value analysis.

D. Salary amounts that are not 100 percent accurate are worthless, so do not bother.

From the four choices, choose and substantiate your position with cited reference. Be sure to write your initial post according to APA format using citations/examples to substantiate your position and give credit to your references at the bottom of your post. Be sure to synthesize your analysis of the reading as a conclusion and then evaluate your synthesis. (Institute, Quick Quiz, 2008)

Chapter 2: Chapter Synthesis and Evaluation

In this Chapter, we examined the purpose of earned value management (EVM) as we applied the basic elements of EVM and calculate the EV Performance Measures to formulate EV Completion Measures just as you will in the business environment. Be sure to maintain proficiency with this as it will come in handy as we proceed with the monitoring and controlling of the Gauchito project's schedule and costs.

Chapter 2: Test Your Knowledge

Take the following practice quiz. Identify those areas of Organizational Planning where you are weak and then reinforce yourself.

1. Using the time reference problem, which task is completed?

TASK	BCWS	ACWP	BCWP
Survey	500	2000	400
Remove Debris	2000	3500	2000
Dig hole	3000	2000	2800
Emplace forms	1200	1000	1100
Pour Concrete	5000	3000	2500

a. Pour concrete

b. Survey

c. Dig hole

d. Remove debris

2. On November 1, $1,000 worth of work on a task was supposed to have been done (BCWS); however, the BCWP was $850. Calculate the schedule variance.

a.-$100

b.$100

c.$150

d.-$150

3. If the project committed $1,000 worth of work resources but only completed $850 worth of work, what is the Cost Variance?

a. Cannot calculate from the information provided

b.$1,500

c.-$150

d.$150

4. The Cost Performance Index (CPI) measures:

a. cost of work performed vs. planned costs.

b. work performed vs. planned work.

c. work performed vs. cost of work performed.

d. direct costs vs. indirect costs.

5. The computation for Cost Performance Index is:

a. BCWP-BCWS

b. BCWP-ACWP

c. BCWP/ACWP

d. ACWP/BCWP

6. The Cost Performance Index is computed as:

a. budget cost of work performed divided by actual cost of work performed

b. budget cost of work performed minus actual cost of work performed

c. budget cost of work performed minus budget cost of work scheduled

d. budget cost of work scheduled divided by budget cost of work performed

Chapter 2: Application Exercise

Now that the project sponsor has agreed with your WBS from last week's submission, you understand the WBS is the foundation of the project. Based on the information from the Gauchito project plan, your company finance department provided you with the following:

Table 02.01: Original Task List and Budgeted Effort

ID	Job Description	Immediate Predecessors	Planned Duration (Weeks)	Staff (Number)	Rate/Person/Week	Task Cost (BAC)
A	1.0 ASSEMBLE ENGINE MOUNT	Start	2	4	$1,440	$11,520
B	2.0 FIN PREPARATION	Start	1	3	$1,440	$4,320
C	3.0 MARK FIN AND LAUNCH LUG LINES	Start	1	3	$1,440	$4,320
D	4.0 INSERTING ENGINE MOUNT	A	2	3	$1,440	$8,640
E	5.0 ATTACH FINS	D	1	3	$1,440	$4,320
F	6.0 ATTACH SHOCK CORD	Start	2	3	$1,440	$8,640
G	7.0 ASSEMBLE NOSE CONE	Start	1	2	$1,440	$2,880
H	8.0 ATTACH PARACHUTE/SHOCK CORD	G	1	1	$1,440	$1,440
I	9.0 ATTACH LAUNCH LUG	E	1	1	$1,440	$1,440
J	10.0 PAINTING THE ROCKET	I	1	4	$1,440	$5,760

K	11.0 APPLICATION OF DECALS	J	1	1	$1,440	$1,440
L	12.0 APPLYING CLEAR COAT	K	1	1	$1,440	$1,440
M	13.0 DISPLAY NOZZLE ASSEMBLY	K	1	3	$1,440	$4,320
N	14.0 ROCKET PREFLIGHT	L	1	2	$1,440	$2,880
O	15.0 PREPARE FOR TEST LAUNCH	N	1	1	$1,440	$1,440

You notice that the accounting guys are running with a blended rate for all skill sets to include the outsourced contracted fitters. Since this is the latest information you include it in your Project Workbook to supersede what was provided in the Gauchito project plan.

- Using your MPP solution for chapter one and the information drawn from the scenario and charts in the Gauchito project plan and the Gauchito Project Workbook you and your team put together for working reference, input the necessary data for Cost, Work, Duration, Start, Finish and Predecessors as provided for the Gauchito project into the Gauchito EVM Tool Template.
- Cut your **baseline** in MPP since this is now the approved BAC.
- Using the information in the Gauchito Project Plan, your Gauchito Project Workbook your team put together as working references, and your company provided EVM Tool Template, construct in the EVM tool template a Gantt bar graph for the project BCWS (PV).

CONSIDERATIONS:

- All work packages within a subtask are executed in serial (F-S) fashion.

- All subtasks within a task are executed in a serial (F-S) fashion.
- All tasks (deliverables) are executed according to the Gauchito project plan appendix WG: Gantt.

Compare the resultant Gantt charts in MS Project and in your EVM Tool.

- What differences can be noticed?
- Which tool is better for schedule control? Why?
- Which tool is better for cost control? Why?

Chapter 3: Chapter Overview / Introduction

In this chapter, you will look how quality standards are necessary for the success of projects and how the identification of risk events, the qualification of these events and the quantification of their outcomes can minimize failure. You will see how some risks can be mitigated through the prudent use of vendor selection and proper contracting. This unit will comprise about eleven hours of effort depending on the level of your study habits.

Schedule development means determining start and finish dates for project activities. If the start and finish dates are not realistic, the project is unlikely to be finished as scheduled. The schedule development process must often be iterated (along with the processes that provide inputs, especially duration estimating and cost estimating) prior to determination of the project schedule. The project schedule includes planned start and expected finish dates for the project elements that costs will be allocated to. This information is needed in order to assign costs to the time period when the cost will be incurred. Activity definition involves identifying and documenting the specific activities that must be performed in order to produce the deliverables/tasks, sub-tasks and work packages identified in the work breakdown structure. Implicit in this process is the need to define the activities such that the project objectives will be met. Activity sequencing involves identifying and documenting interactivity dependencies. Activities must be sequenced accurately in order to support later development of a realistic and achievable schedule. Sequencing can be performed with the aid of a computer (e.g., by using project management software) or with manual techniques. Manual techniques are often more effective on smaller projects and in the early phases of larger ones when little detail is available. Manual and automated techniques may also be used in combination.

Cost budgeting involves allocating the overall cost estimates to individual work items in order to establish a cost baseline for measuring project performance.

This involves the integration of project scope, work, durations, sequencing, and labor/equipment/material resources into a comprehensive plan for iterative expenditure of all project resources in a cumulative process. As we go through this chapter describe the elements of a schedule, see if you can set up a complete project schedule using MS Project, assign your estimates using MS Project, create, schedule, assign, and level your project resources using MS Project, sequence project work package using MS Project, assign task priorities in MS Project, and baseline your project in MS Project and in MS Excel.

Chapter 3: Schedule Development

Schedule development and control for a project requires determining start and finish dates for all of the activities. If these dates are not realistic, the project will be in jeopardy of completion. The project manager is concerned not only with establishing realistic activity start and finish date but also with influencing the factors which create schedule changes to ensure that changes are beneficial. If he or she determines that the schedule has changed, the project manager is responsible for managing the actual changes as they occur. Schedule development and control must be thoroughly integrated with the other project processes to ensure a coordinated sequence of events with resources being applied at the proper time. Project team members normally input the tasks, durations, and dependencies for their assignments manually to the project manager or into a project software program. The software automatically calculates each member's schedules and displays those activities along the critical path. If done manually, the project manager accomplishes this task. With the advent of project scheduling software, computers usually accomplish this action. All the schedules can then be linked together into a project activity network for analysis.

Chapter 3: Calculating Your Preliminary Project Schedule

The most frequently used approach for calculating the time driven project schedule is the Critical Path Method (CPM). CPM essentially identifies the longest time path through the schedule (The longest cumulative duration). More than one critical path through a schedule is possible when the durations are equal. The addition of durations on the "critical path" not only determines when the project will likely finish, but also the earliest and latest possible dates for all the other activities to start and finish. The difference between the earliest and latest possible finish dates is called "float," since the completion of the activity can occur anywhere between the two dates without affecting the overall project completion date. Another way to define the critical path is that it is the path (or paths) through the schedule with "zero float." Any activities that are completed after their "late finish" dates automatically become part of the critical path and threaten to delay the overall project completion. Calculating the preliminary project schedule requires the following tasks:

- Input all activities, dependencies, and durations into a common use project management software program
- If all activities are tied with predecessor and successor relationships to the project start and finish milestones, then the program will automatically calculate the critical path along with the scheduled project start and finish dates
- If such a program is not available, then follow each path through the schedule and manually determine the early and late finish dates for all activities
- Identify those activities on the critical path (those with zero float where the early and late finish dates are the same)
- The critical path will determine the date for the finish milestone and, thereby, the earliest possible completion date for the overall project

Chapter 3: Calculating Your Resource Leveled Project Schedule

The network diagram and the resulting preliminary schedule were based upon activity duration estimates and the logical relationships among those activities, without regard to resource loading issues. The schedule must now be analyzed to determine the reasonableness of the inherent resource loading assumptions. For example, although technically, there may be no obstacles to performing two tasks in parallel, they may have to be completed by the same resource. This can result in impossible situations where the same piece of equipment is scheduled to be used on two different places at the same time or a key individual is scheduled to work full time on two activities simultaneously. In these cases, the timing of activities must be shifted if the resource constraints cannot be overcome. Leveling project resources requires:

- Ensuring all activities have assigned owners
- Creating a resource profile showing the cumulative workload for all activities by time period proposed in the preliminary schedule
- Identifying times when people have unrealistic workloads (consistently over 8 hours/day or 40 hours/week)
- Should all of the alternatives fail to level the project over-allocations effectively, determining what additional resources will be necessary to make the schedule realistic

Caution: Remember, *"A woman can produce a baby in nine months. However, nine women cannot produce a baby in one month." (Tyler, 1998)*

Many computer based software programs can automatically level your over-allocations of resources. They do this by spreading the resource over time and, in many cases, extend the project well past the planned completion date. Address resource leveling with prudence. Take a look at Appendix-A, How to use MS Project. In there you will see the techniques for setting up a schedule in a computer based software program. MS Project is excellent for building schedules in a Gantt format based on a PERT methodology. You can also have an excellent network diagram built at the same time saving you immense pain and loss of time.

Chapter 3: Document Your Schedule Assumptions

Since all schedules are built upon currently available knowledge, projections, and assumptions, it is important to document those key assumptions for validation and later reference. Assumptions typically include: the availability of key resources, timely performance of outside contractors, stability of product requirements, availability of enabling technology, etc. If these assumptions are later found to be invalid, negative impact to the project schedule is likely to occur. These assumptions will also be used as inputs to the following related processes:

- Risk Identification
- Risk Quantification
- Response Development

Documenting schedule assumptions requires the following three tasks be performed:

- Review activities on the critical path and identify assumptions that, if later invalidated, would negatively impact the schedule
- Identify any other key schedule assumptions

Document those assumptions and their potential negative impact on the project schedule

Chapter 3: Update Your Resource Requirements

Your initial estimates of resource levels required to fulfill the project scope statement will invariably change as a result of the knowledge gained through the detailed scheduling processes. These changes, which can be of any type or quantity, need to be reflected in the resource requirements as defined in Resource Planning in *A Guide to the PMBOK*. Updating resource requirements requires:

- Identifying changes from earlier resource estimates
- Reflecting those changes in the resource requirements defined in Resource Planning

Chapter 3: Setting up the Actuals in the EVM Tool

After we flesh out the planned value for a project we now have an idea as to when resources will be committed and how much will be committed. If we had actually used the correct figures from the Gauchito project plan we would have realized a Cumulative Cost Curve that reflected the one in the Gauchito project plan. As we move into execution we can input the actual expenditure when they happen. So first we copy the figures for the PV chart and past them into the AC chart like this:

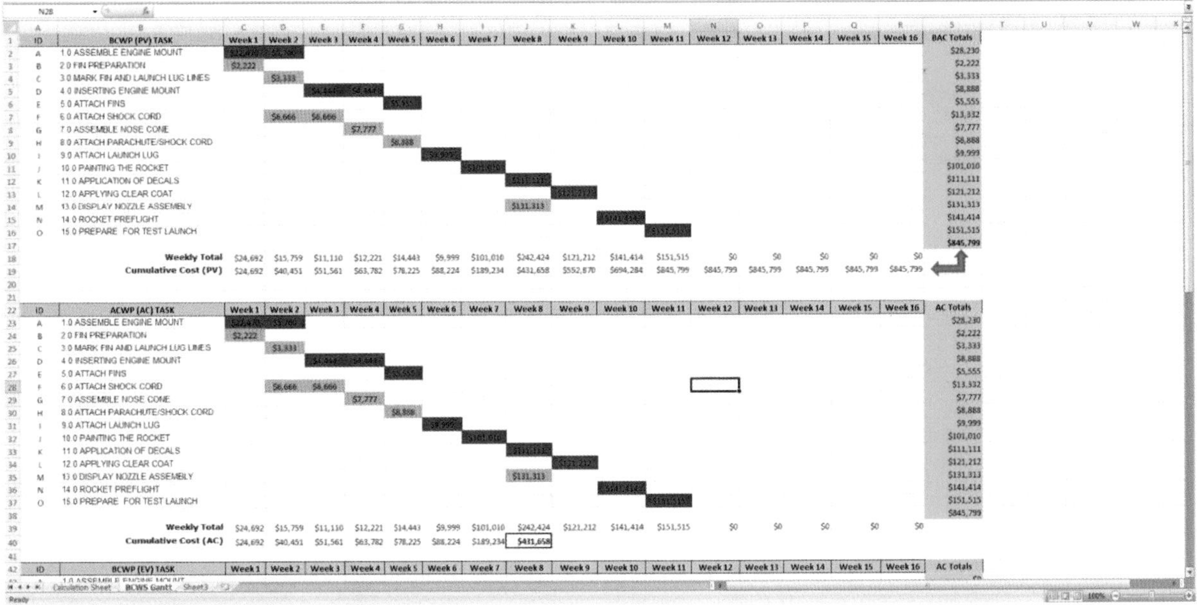

ID	BCWP (PV) TASK	Week 1	Week 2	Week 3	Week 4	Week 5	Week 6	Week 7	Week 8	Week 9	Week 10	Week 11	Week 12	Week 13	Week 14	Week 15	Week 16	BAC Totals
A	1.0 ASSEMBLE ENGINE MOUNT	[illegible]	[illegible]															$28,230
B	2.0 FIN PREPARATION	$2,222																$2,222
C	3.0 MARK FIN AND LAUNCH LUG LINES		$3,333															$3,333
D	4.0 INSERTING ENGINE MOUNT			[illegible]	[illegible]													$8,888
E	5.0 ATTACH FINS					[illegible]												$5,555
F	6.0 ATTACH SHOCK CORD		$6,666	$6,666														$13,332
G	7.0 ASSEMBLE NOSE CONE				$7,777													$7,777
H	8.0 ATTACH PARACHUTE/SHOCK CORD					$8,888												$8,888
I	9.0 ATTACH LAUNCH LUG						[illegible]											$9,999
J	10.0 PAINTING THE ROCKET							[illegible]										$101,010
K	11.0 APPLICATION OF DECALS								[illegible]									$111,111
L	12.0 APPLYING CLEAR COAT									[illegible]								$121,212
M	13.0 DISPLAY NOZZLE ASSEMBLY								$131,313									$131,313
N	14.0 ROCKET PREFLIGHT										[illegible]							$141,414
O	15.0 PREPARE FOR TEST LAUNCH											[illegible]						$151,515
																		$845,799
	Weekly Total	$24,692	$15,759	$11,110	$12,221	$14,443	$9,999	$101,010	$242,424	$121,212	$141,414	$151,515	$0	$0	$0	$0	$0	
	Cumulative Cost (PV)	$24,692	$40,451	$51,561	$63,782	$78,225	$88,224	$189,234	$431,658	$552,870	$694,284	$845,799	$845,799	$845,799	$845,799	$845,799	$845,799	

ID	ACWP (AC) TASK	Week 1	Week 2	Week 3	Week 4	Week 5	Week 6	Week 7	Week 8	Week 9	Week 10	Week 11	Week 12	Week 13	Week 14	Week 15	Week 16	AC Totals
A	1.0 ASSEMBLE ENGINE MOUNT	[illegible]	[illegible]															$28,230
B	2.0 FIN PREPARATION	$2,222																$2,222
C	3.0 MARK FIN AND LAUNCH LUG LINES		$3,333															$3,333
D	4.0 INSERTING ENGINE MOUNT			[illegible]	[illegible]													$8,888
E	5.0 ATTACH FINS					[illegible]												$5,555
F	6.0 ATTACH SHOCK CORD		$6,666	$6,666														$13,332
G	7.0 ASSEMBLE NOSE CONE				$7,777													$7,777
H	8.0 ATTACH PARACHUTE/SHOCK CORD					$8,888												$8,888
I	9.0 ATTACH LAUNCH LUG						[illegible]											$9,999
J	10.0 PAINTING THE ROCKET							[illegible]										$101,010
K	11.0 APPLICATION OF DECALS								[illegible]									$111,111
L	12.0 APPLYING CLEAR COAT									[illegible]								$121,212
M	13.0 DISPLAY NOZZLE ASSEMBLY								$131,313									$131,313
N	14.0 ROCKET PREFLIGHT										[illegible]							$141,414
O	15.0 PREPARE FOR TEST LAUNCH											[illegible]						$151,515
																		$845,799
	Weekly Total	$24,692	$15,759	$11,110	$12,221	$14,443	$9,999	$101,010	$242,424	$121,212	$141,414	$151,515	$0	$0	$0	$0	$0	
	Cumulative Cost (AC)	$24,692	$40,451	$51,561	$63,782	$78,225	$88,224	$189,234	$431,658									

ID	BCWP (EV) TASK	Week 1	Week 2	Week 3	Week 4	Week 5	Week 6	Week 7	Week 8	Week 9	Week 10	Week 11	Week 12	Week 13	Week 14	Week 15	Week 16	AC Totals

Figure 03.01

We do this because we need a replica of the PV to work from as we go into execution and made adjustments to this replica without disturbing our approved PV that we need to continue to work from. Let's jump ahead to week 4 for our monthly Project Review. For instructional purposes let's say everything is going fine and we are exactly on target as we planned. The AC chart will look like this:

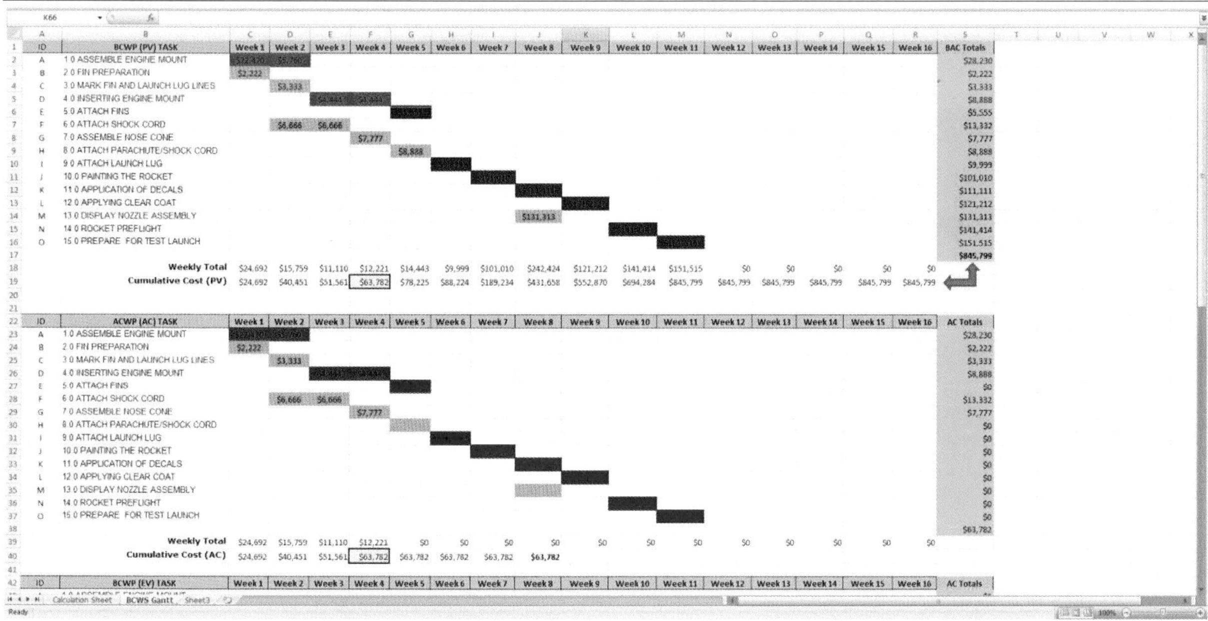

ID	BCWP (PV) TASK	Week 1	Week 2	Week 3	Week 4	Week 5	Week 6	Week 7	Week 8	Week 9	Week 10	Week 11	Week 12	Week 13	Week 14	Week 15	Week 16	BAC Totals
A	1.0 ASSEMBLE ENGINE MOUNT	$22,470	$5,760															$28,230
B	2.0 FIN PREPARATION	$2,222																$2,222
C	3.0 MARK FIN AND LAUNCH LUG LINES		$3,333															$3,333
D	4.0 INSERTING ENGINE MOUNT			[illegible]	[illegible]													$8,888
E	5.0 ATTACH FINS					[illegible]												$5,555
F	6.0 ATTACH SHOCK CORD		$6,666	$6,666														$13,332
G	7.0 ASSEMBLE NOSE CONE				$7,777													$7,777
H	8.0 ATTACH PARACHUTE/SHOCK CORD					$8,888												$8,888
I	9.0 ATTACH LAUNCH LUG						[illegible]											$9,999
J	10.0 PAINTING THE ROCKET							[illegible]										$101,010
K	11.0 APPLICATION OF DECALS								[illegible]									$111,111
L	12.0 APPLYING CLEAR COAT									[illegible]								$121,212
M	13.0 DISPLAY NOZZLE ASSEMBLY								$131,313									$131,313
N	14.0 ROCKET PREFLIGHT										[illegible]							$141,414
O	15.0 PREPARE FOR TEST LAUNCH											[illegible]						$151,515
																		$845,799
	Weekly Total	$24,692	$15,759	$11,110	$12,221	$14,443	$9,999	$101,010	$242,424	$121,212	$141,414	$151,515	$0	$0	$0	$0	$0	
	Cumulative Cost (PV)	$24,692	$40,451	$51,561	$63,782	$78,225	$88,224	$189,234	$431,658	$552,870	$694,284	$845,799	$845,799	$845,799	$845,799	$845,799	$845,799	

ID	ACWP (AC) TASK	Week 1	Week 2	Week 3	Week 4	Week 5	Week 6	Week 7	Week 8	Week 9	Week 10	Week 11	Week 12	Week 13	Week 14	Week 15	Week 16	AC Totals
A	1.0 ASSEMBLE ENGINE MOUNT	[illegible]	[illegible]															$28,230
B	2.0 FIN PREPARATION	$2,222																$2,222
C	3.0 MARK FIN AND LAUNCH LUG LINES		$3,333															$3,333
D	4.0 INSERTING ENGINE MOUNT			[illegible]	[illegible]													$8,888
E	5.0 ATTACH FINS																	$0
F	6.0 ATTACH SHOCK CORD		$6,666	$6,666														$13,332
G	7.0 ASSEMBLE NOSE CONE				$7,777													$7,777
H	8.0 ATTACH PARACHUTE/SHOCK CORD																	$0
I	9.0 ATTACH LAUNCH LUG																	$0
J	10.0 PAINTING THE ROCKET																	$0
K	11.0 APPLICATION OF DECALS																	$0
L	12.0 APPLYING CLEAR COAT																	$0
M	13.0 DISPLAY NOZZLE ASSEMBLY																	$0
N	14.0 ROCKET PREFLIGHT																	$0
O	15.0 PREPARE FOR TEST LAUNCH																	$0
																		$63,782
	Weekly Total	$24,692	$15,759	$11,110	$12,221	$0	$0	$0	$0	$0	$0	$0	$0	$0	$0	$0	$0	
	Cumulative Cost (AC)	$24,692	$40,451	$51,561	$63,782	$63,782	$63,782	$63,782	$63,782									

ID	BCWP (EV) TASK	Week 1	Week 2	Week 3	Week 4	Week 5	Week 6	Week 7	Week 8	Week 9	Week 10	Week 11	Week 12	Week 13	Week 14	Week 15	Week 16	AC Totals

Figure 03.02

You will notice that we moved our markers from the J column to the F column to reflect week 4. So, where BCWS (PV) equaled J19 originally, it now reflects F19 to show the PV for week 4. Additionally, the ACWP=F40 and the BCWP (EV)= F60 all to reflect the week 4 performance figures. You may have noticed that the AC chart, while it reflects the Gantt bars in red and gray does not hold any values after week 4. This is because the AC chart only displays the actual costs that have been spent and not any projected costs as the PV chart displays. You can't display what you haven't spent to date, only what has been spent. Good so far? Great! Now let's set up the earned value through week 4. Again, earned value is what the project is worth at the present time and we are concerned with the project up to week 4.

Since the project is exactly on the baseline, we can surmise that the EV will be exactly like the AC and you will be correct. It should look like this:

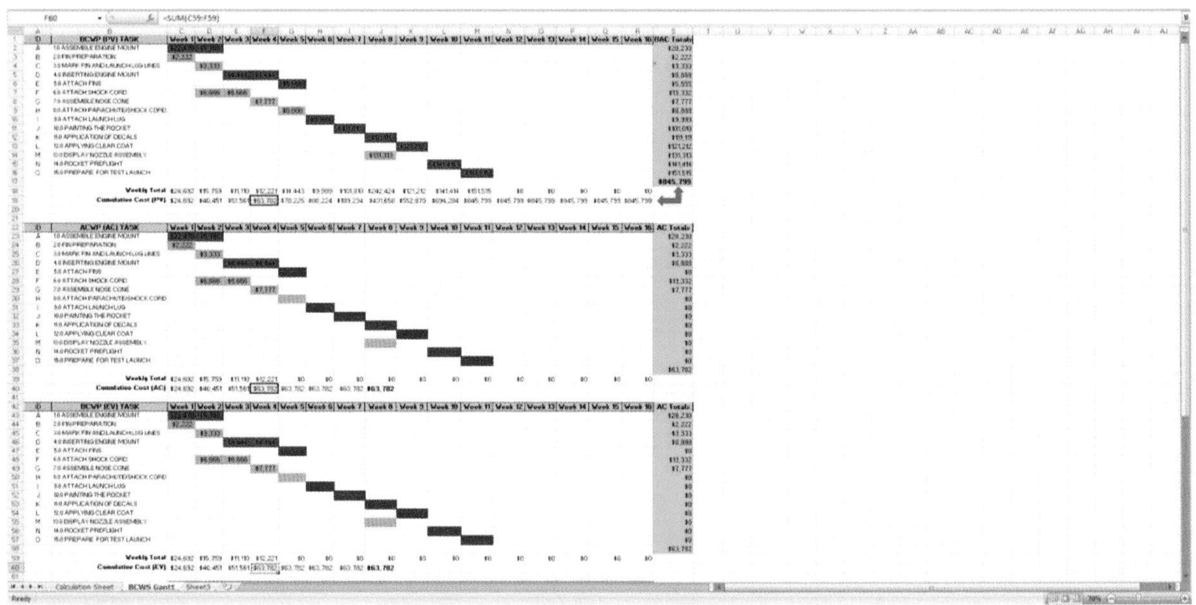

Figure 03.03

If we take a look at the Cumulative Cost Curve, we will notice that both the AC and the EV lines are right on with the PV showing that the project is on track without any variance. Good for us! Now let's see what happens when we get off the baseline and our project has variance.

Chapter 3: Setting Up the EVM Tool with Variance Shown

Let's assume that as we move into our week 8 Project Review we had a week's slippage in our task 5.0 Attaching the Fins. This meant we spent another week's worth of labor but not any equipment or material expenditures we indicated in our planned value chart. Why is this? This is because your payroll will continue but equipment and material can sit without incurring additional expenditures unless they have to be warehoused and you will then account for that in your actuals chart. Let's now populate the AC chart to reflect the project through the eighth week showing one week of slippage for task 5.0.

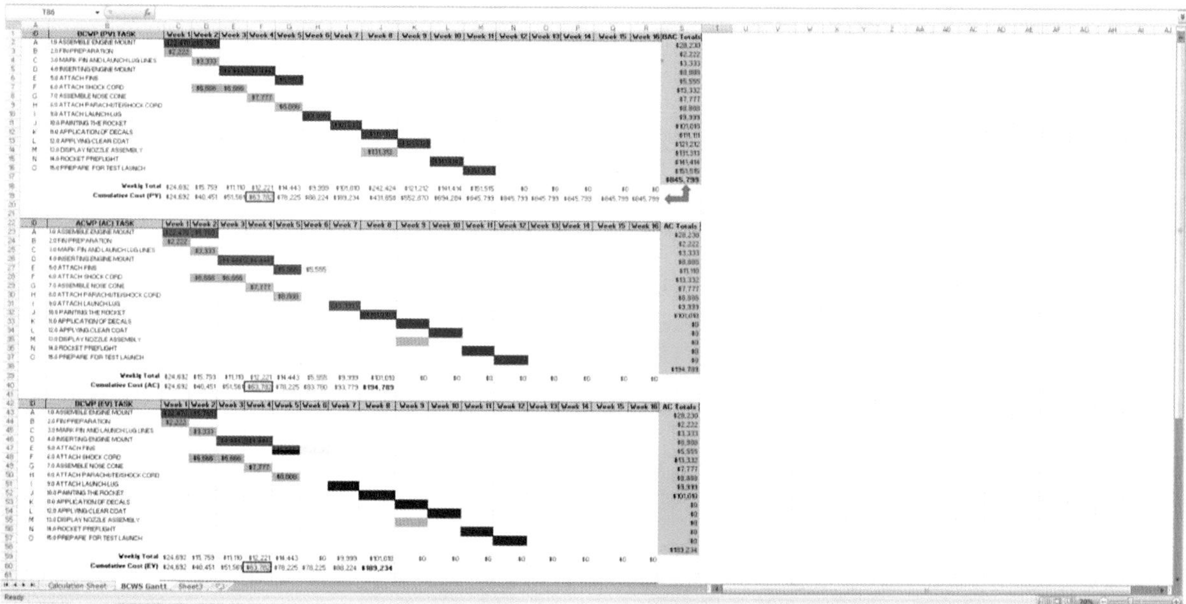

Figure 03.04

You will notice that the slippage for task 5.0 is accounted for in the AC chart with both the Gantt and the cost values (yellow cell). However the additional costs for the extra week is not indicated in the EV chart although the Gantt still reflects the slippage (yellow cell). And, all other costs and value are carried only to the eighth week. Now we have three charts that show what we planned on expending for the entire project (PV chart), what has been spent to date (AC chart), and what the project is worth to date (EV chart).

Navigating over to the Formulae Area, we can analyze the following:

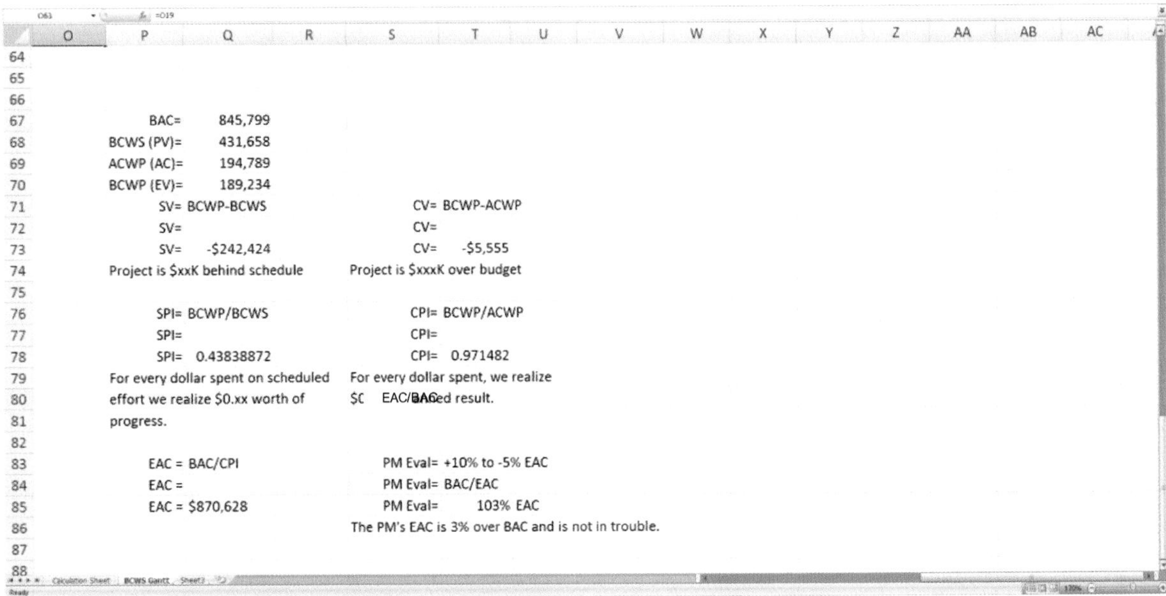

Figure 03.05

Our variances are as follows:

- Schedule Variance (SV)= -$242,424
    - The project is $242K behind schedule
- Cost Variance (CV)= -$5,555
    - The project is $6K over budget
- Schedule Performance Index (SPI)= 0.44
    - For every dollar spent on scheduled effort we realize $0.44 worth of progress
- Cost Performance Index (CPI)= 0.97
    - For every dollar spent, we realize $0.97 of planned result
- What was budget to us from the organization (BAC) remains $845,799
- What we expect to spend (at this rate) at the end of the project (EAC) is now $870,628

We can then synthesize the following conclusion:

Since a project manager is expected to bring a project in within +10% to -5% of the BAC and the project is projected to come in at 103% of the BAC, this is a +3% VAC and the project and the project manager are within performance expectations and will live to see another day.

This is how we use the EVM tool to show us project performance and by extension, the project manager's performance. The project manager will use this performance monitoring tool to help show executive management hoe he or she intends to bring the project back on track using his or her magical PM powers.

Chapter 3: Discussion Question

You know the obvious things to do to control costs on your project like selecting less experienced team members and watching the cost of materials. But are there hidden costs you might be overlooking?

A. The only way to control costs is to use internal staff and buy materials at a discount.

B. Hidden costs result only when team members overestimate their activity time.

C. If you have a hardware project, the price of electricity is always a hidden cost.

D. There may be hidden costs in the way the schedule is arranged and executed.

From the four choices, choose and substantiate your position with cited references. Be sure to write your initial post according to APA format using citations/examples to substantiate your position and give credit to your references at the bottom of your post. Be sure to synthesize your analysis of the reading as a conclusion and then evaluate your synthesis.

Chapter 3: Thought Question

You know the obvious things to do to control costs on your project like selecting less experienced team members and watching the cost of materials. But are there hidden costs you might be overlooking?

A. The only way to control costs is to use internal staff and buy materials at a discount.

B. Hidden costs result only when team members overestimate their activity time.

C. If you have a hardware project, the price of electricity is always a hidden cost.

D. There may be hidden costs in the way the schedule is arranged and executed.

From the four choices, choose and substantiate your position with cited reference. Be sure to write your initial post according to APA format using citations/examples to substantiate your position and give credit to your references at the bottom of your post. Be sure to synthesize your analysis of the reading as a conclusion and then evaluate your synthesis. Remember that this is a discussion, so keep your responses succinct and to the point. Respond to at least three of your colleagues. (Institute, 2008)

Chapter 3: Chapter Synthesis and Evaluation

Nothing gets built on schedule or within budget.

((Tyler M. J., 1998)

The purpose of a Schedule Management Plan is to establish standard guidelines and procedures for managing changes to the project schedule. The schedule management plan may be part of, or an extension to, organization policy. Those who develop it should be responsible for establishing and implementing the management approach and the controls for the project. A schedule management plan is an output of the schedule development process, as referenced in the Guide to the PMBOK. Work to reduce the duration of your activities. "You are evaluated on bringing the project in on time, under budget, and meeting the requirements. You keep your customer by showing him your added value.

(Tyler M. J., 1998) Try adding more resources to some of your activities. If you assign more people or equipment, you might be able to reduce the time required. However, be careful. Remember Tyler's law on Over-Allocation. Allow more time in the workday. Allow for overtime or add another shift. Run a cost-benefit analysis to see if doing so is cost effective. Allow more workdays in your schedule. Use a weekend but, again, you must realize a cost benefit to your project. Project management software tools were originally conceived for use on large single projects. Over the last decade it has become apparent that the vast majority of users of project management tools are actually involved in a number of small, inter-related projects. This is known to many as program management. Many industries have been forced to provide additional products and functions aimed at bending the single project tool to make it more appropriate to the multi-project environment. These tools all assume a fundamental model of the multi-project planning process and this model carries with it considerable problems. So what is the right tool for the project manager to use in scheduling the project? Many companies will tell that to use their tool will make you a great project manager. Remember this. A software-scheduling tool is just a tool. If you don't know how to use the tool or what it's function is, you'll never achieve control over your project. A hammer is a tool. Use of a hammer does not make you a carpenter. Mastery of the hammer moves you in the direction of being a good carpenter. Master the tool then understand how it is to be used in the overall scheme of things.

Chapter 3: Test Your Knowledge

Take the following practice quiz. Identify those areas of Organizational Planning where you are weak and then reinforce yourself.

1. Free float is the amount of time that an activity may be delayed without affecting the:
   a) Early start of the succeeding activities.
   b) Late start of the succeeding activities.
   c) Project finish.
   d) Cost of the project.
   e) Late finish of any parallel activities.

2. The critical path is calculated by
   a) determining which tasks have the least amount of total slack.
   b) subtracting the end date of task one from the start date of task two.
   c) totaling the time for all activities.
   d) determining the shortest path through the network.
   e) determining the determining which tasks have the most slack

3. Which of the following is indicative of negative float?
   a) The late start date is earlier than the early start date.
   b) The critical path supports the imposed end date.
   c) The early finish date is equal to the late finish date.
   d) When leads are employed in the schedule.
   e) The project is sinking.

4. The critical path in a schedule network is the path that:
   a) Takes the longest time to complete
   b) Must be done before any other tasks
   c) Allows some flexibility in scheduling a start time

d) Is not affected by schedule slippage

e) All of the above

5. The first step in building a PERT/CPM network is to:
   a) Create a work-breakdown structure
   b) Create a flow chart
   c) Determine the critical path
   d) Show task relationships
   e) *None

6. The purpose of a dummy activity in an activity-on-arrow diagram is to
   a) Show a dependency
   b) Identify a task that could be replaced by another
   c) Take the slack time into account
   d) Show a task that is not necessarily needed
   e) Denote a milestone

7. As a project is carried out and slack time is consumed on individual tasks, the slack left over for the remaining tasks is:
   a) Reduced
   b) Insignificant
   c) Unchanged
   d) Increased
   e) Doubled

8. As a control tool, the bar chart (Gantt) method is most beneficial for:
   a) Rearranging conflicting tasks
   b) Depicting actual versus planned tasks
   c) Showing the outer dependencies of tasks
   d) a and c

e) a and b

9. Fast tracking means to:
   a) Speed up a project through parallel tasks
   b) Swap one task for another
   c) Reduce the number of tasks if possible
   d) b and c
   e) *None

10. The key purpose of project control is to:
    a) Keep the project on track
    b) Plan ahead for uncertainties
    c) Generate status reports
    d) Develop the project road map
    e) *All
11. The actual configuration of a PERT/CPM network ________________________ the amount of resources that can be devoted to the project.
    a) Is heavily dependent upon
    b) Increases
    c) Is not affected by
    d) Does not require
    e) Is the only means for determining
12. In crashing a task, you would focus on:
    a) As many tasks as possible
    b) Non-critical tasks
    c) Accelerating performance of tasks on critical path
    d) Accelerate performance by minimizing cost
    e) a and d

Chapter 3: Application Exercise

Your first month's Project Review (weeks 1-4) is coming up with your sponsor and customer. Herb Everson, the chief engineer from Scaled Composites will be in attendance representing his company. Your financial specialist from the accounting department provides you with the following information:

Table 03.01: Progress at the End of Month Eight

ID	TASK	EFFORT to DATE (Person Weeks)	Outstanding Duration (Weeks)	Staff
A	1.0 ASSEMBLE ENGINE MOUNT	12	0	0
B	2.0 FIN PREPARATION	3	0	0
C	3.0 MARK FIN AND LAUNCH LUG LINES	3	0	0
D	4.0 INSERTING ENGINE MOUNT	3	1	3
E	5.0 ATTACH FINS	0	1	2
F	6.0 ATTACH SHOCK CORD	6	0	0
G	7.0 ASSEMBLE NOSE CONE	2	0	0
H	8.0 ATTACH PARACHUTE/SHOCK CORD	1	0	0
I	9.0 ATTACH LAUNCH LUG	0	1	1
J	10.0 PAINTING THE ROCKET	0	1	4
K	11.0 APPLICATION OF	0	1	1

	DECALS			
L	12.0 APPLYING CLEAR COAT	0	1	1
M	13.0 DISPLAY NOZZLE ASSEMBLY	0	1	3
N	14.0 ROCKET PREFLIGHT	0	1	2
O	15.0 PREPARE FOR TEST LAUNCH	0	1	1

- Using this latest information, update your MS Project tool and your EVM tool.
- Ensure you have metrics for the following:
    - Schedule Variance (SV)
    - Schedule Performance Index (SPI)
    - Cost Variance (CV)
    - Cost Performance Index (CPI)
    - Estimate at Completion (EAC)
    - Variance at Completion (VAC)
    - Estimate to Complete (ETC)
- Submit your completed tools (MPP and XLS) to your instructor.

Chapter 4: Chapter Overview / Introduction

There are a variety of earned value tools to use in the monitoring and control of a project's schedule and costs. Numerous hardware and software application promise to make project monitoring/controlling an easy and effective process. In reality, the successful monitoring and control of projects falls back on the project manager's ability to understand the schedule and cost issues, what are the pertinent causes and what is the best way to manage these issues towards resolution. Think back to your primary school teacher explaining why you need to know the multiplication table. In your mind you only needed a calculator and a minimal amount of understanding regarding its use. So, you "borrowed" your father's TI 400xti or whatever was the classic handheld computation device of the day. This thing could plot graphs, display scientific notation, convert hexadecimal to binary and provide you trigonometry functions. But, you got lost in all the bells and whistles when the teach ask you simple multiplication problems. The same thing happened later in secondary school or later in college in your trig classes when all you wanted to do was plug and chug the numbers and get the answer (the correct one hopefully) to the problem.

This is the same situation with using earned value tools whether they are embedded into applications like MS Project, Planview and Oracle's Primavera or they are add-ins for Excel or your favorite spreadsheet. If you don't understand and comprehend the need, purpose and mechanics behind software application or hardware devices, how do you know you have the correct answer? Standing in front of your sponsor and other executives of the organization is not the time to decide you need you know how to use EVM tools. That's why you're reading this chapter, to better understand the principles behind the tools. Besides, Burt Rutan, our customer, has told our company that his company wants an accounting of time and cost expenditures against what we proposed to win the bid. Bottom line, you're being graded on the performance of the Gauchito rocket assembly project. If that doesn't wake you up and take notice you have to be catatonic.

So, what's the purpose and how do you use these tools to keep your project on time and cost? Again, I'm glad you asked. Let's take a look...

Chapter 4: Purpose for the EVM Tool

Remember that multiplication table in primary school we just talked about? What was its purpose? Your teacher probable told you that it was a tool to aid you in arriving at the correct answer and that if you memorized it life would be a lot easier. Similarly, an EVM tool is used to aid the project manager, and others in arriving at consensus as to the health of a project based on the value it was planned to achieve compared with the value it has earned to date compared with the actual costs expended to date. This should tell you that an EVM tool should consist of three trend lines: a trend line that reflects the life of the project as planned, a shorter trend line that reflects what the project is worth from the project start date to the current date, and a trend line that reflects what the accounting folks say the project has cost the organization from the project start date to the current date. The tool should be capable of comparing these three trend lines an algorithmic manner to result in some form of performance reporting. This should immediately bring to mind that a spreadsheet should be the basis for any good EVM tool and, for the most part spreadsheet are the foundations for EVM tools. Earned value has been monitored by project and program managers using spreadsheets for decades. I'm giving my age away when I tell you that project health and performance was followed accounting sheet before there were electronic spreadsheets. Technology has made monitoring the performance of project much easier today with electronic spreadsheets. Project managers used the electronic versions like VisiCalc, Lotus 1-2-3, and other electronic spreadsheets to build out self developed EVM tools (it was called Earned Value Analysis or EVA back then) to aid in monitoring and controlling schedule and cost for projects. Today they use Excel as the industry EVM tool and most EVM tools are based on Excel to include MS Project. Here is an example of a spreadsheet based EVM tool form the 1990's. The names and values have been altered to protect the guilty:

Budget Description: 1998 Y2K Update		App Mgr Name	Larry App
Application Name: Network Application		Project Coord Name	Jeff Coord
Phase: Conversion Analysis		VP Name	Patrice Vice
Work Request #	120742	Director Name	Bob Ector
Work Request Name		Authorized Dep'ts	2895
Project #		Date	6/6/1998
Company #			
SHL Project Code #			

		Jan	Feb	Mar	Apr	May	Jun	Jul (1998)	Aug	Sep	Oct	Nov	Dec	Total
Internal (MCI Staff)	**Hours**	38	41.5	44	29.5	413	413	413	40	40	40	40	0	1,552
	Rate	38	38	38	38	38	38	38	38	38	38	38	38	
	$	1,444	1,577.00	1,672.00	1,121.00	15,694.00	15,694.00	15,694.00	1,520.00	1,520.00	1,520.00	1,520.00	-	58,976
External (Contractors)														
Grade	**Hours**					40	48	38	40	48	40	40	50	344
	Rate	56	56	56	56	56	56	56	56	56	56	56	56	
	$	-	-	-	-	2,240.95	2,689.14	2,128.90	2,240.95	2,689.14	2,240.95	2,240.95	2,801.19	19,272
Grade	**Hours**													-
	Rate		-	-	-	-	-	-	-	-	-	-	-	
	$	-	-	-	-	-	-	-	-	-	-	-	-	-
Grade	**Hours**													-
	Rate		-	-	-	-	-	-	-	-	-	-	-	
	$	-	-	-	-	-	-	-	-	-	-	-	-	-
Total Contractor	**Hours**	-	-	-	-	40	48	38	40	48	40	40	50	344
	$	-	-	-	-	2,241	2,689	2,129	2,241	2,689	2,241	2,241	2,801	19,272
Capital (Detail Items)														
Hardware	**$**							15000						15,000
Software	**$**													-
Other Costs (Detail Items)														
Team/Factory Costs	**$**					27,457.32								27,457
Travel	**$**							1500						1,500
	$													-
Total 1998	**$**	1,444	1,577	1,672	1,121	45,392	18,383	34,323	3,761	4,209	3,761	3,761	2,801	122,206

Ass/Req Analysis Coding Test FVO Roll-Out

90.00% 81.00% 88.00% 77.00% 56.00% 17.00%

Figure 04.01

We start with the organization's standard project spend plan or budget spreadsheet and fill in the planned expenditures for the life of the project. These resources are derived from the locked scope in the fully decomposed work breakdown structure to which is added the labor resources, to which is added the levels of effort at the work package level and totaled up to the next levels up to the tasks. This is then totaled by skill with either blended/banded/averaged rate or individual rates calculated and allocated by increments, in this case months.

For the basic tool we can then set up a matrix of cost expenditures to provide the Actual Cost of Work Performed (ACWP) which is the amount of actual costs (AC) costs to perform task to look something like this:

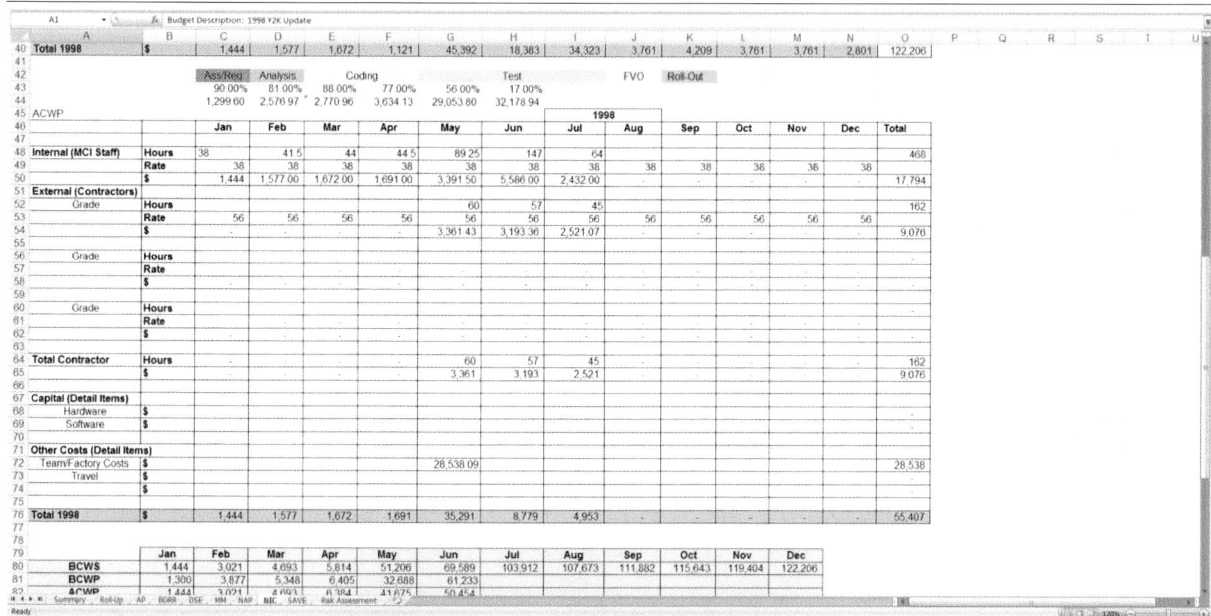

A1 — Budget Description: 1998 Y2K Update

	A	B	C	D	E	F	G	H	I	J	K	L	M	N	O
40	Total 1998	$	1,444	1,577	1,672	1,121	45,392	18,383	34,323	3,761	4,209	3,761	3,761	2,801	122,206
41															
42			Ass/Req	Analysis	Coding			Test		FVO	Roll-Out				
43			90.00%	81.00%	88.00%	77.00%	56.00%	17.00%							
44			1,299.60	2,576.97	2,770.96	3,634.13	29,053.80	32,178.94							
45	ACWP								1998						
46			Jan	Feb	Mar	Apr	May	Jun	Jul	Aug	Sep	Oct	Nov	Dec	Total
47															
48	Internal (MCI Staff)	Hours	38	41.5	44	44.5	89.25	147	64						468
49		Rate	38	38	38	38	38	38	38	38	38	38	38	38	
50		$	1,444	1,577.00	1,672.00	1,691.00	3,391.50	5,586.00	2,432.00	-	-	-	-	-	17,794
51	External (Contractors)														
52	Grade	Hours					60	57	45						162
53		Rate	56	56	56	56	56	56	56	56	56	56	56	56	
54		$	-	-	-	-	3,361.43	3,193.36	2,521.07	-	-	-	-	-	9,076
55															
56	Grade	Hours													-
57		Rate		-	-	-	-	-	-	-	-	-	-	-	
58		$	-	-	-	-	-	-	-	-	-	-	-	-	-
59															
60	Grade	Hours													-
61		Rate		-	-	-	-	-	-	-	-	-	-	-	-
62		$	-	-	-	-	-	-	-	-	-	-	-	-	-
63															
64	Total Contractor	Hours	-	-	-	-	60	57	45	-	-	-	-	-	162
65		$	-	-	-	-	3,361	3,193	2,521	-	-	-	-	-	9,076
66															
67	Capital (Detail Items)														
68	Hardware	$													-
69	Software	$													-
70															
71	Other Costs (Detail Items)														
72	Team/Factory Costs	$					28,538.09								28,538
73	Travel	$													-
74		$													-
75															
76	Total 1998	$	1,444	1,577	1,672	1,691	35,291	8,779	4,953	-	-	-	-	-	55,407
77															
78															
79		Jan	Feb	Mar	Apr	May	Jun	Jul	Aug	Sep	Oct	Nov	Dec		
80	BCWS	1,444	3,021	4,693	5,814	51,206	69,589	103,912	107,673	111,882	115,643	119,404	122,206		
81	BCWP	1,300	3,877	5,348	6,405	32,688	61,233								
82	ACWP	1,444	3,021	4,693	6,384	41,675	50,454								

Summary / Roll-Up / AP / BORR / DSE / MM / NAP / NIC / SAVE / Risk Assessment

Figure 04.02

The projects worth can then be derived by removing any additional cost that were not planned for but resulted in slippage:

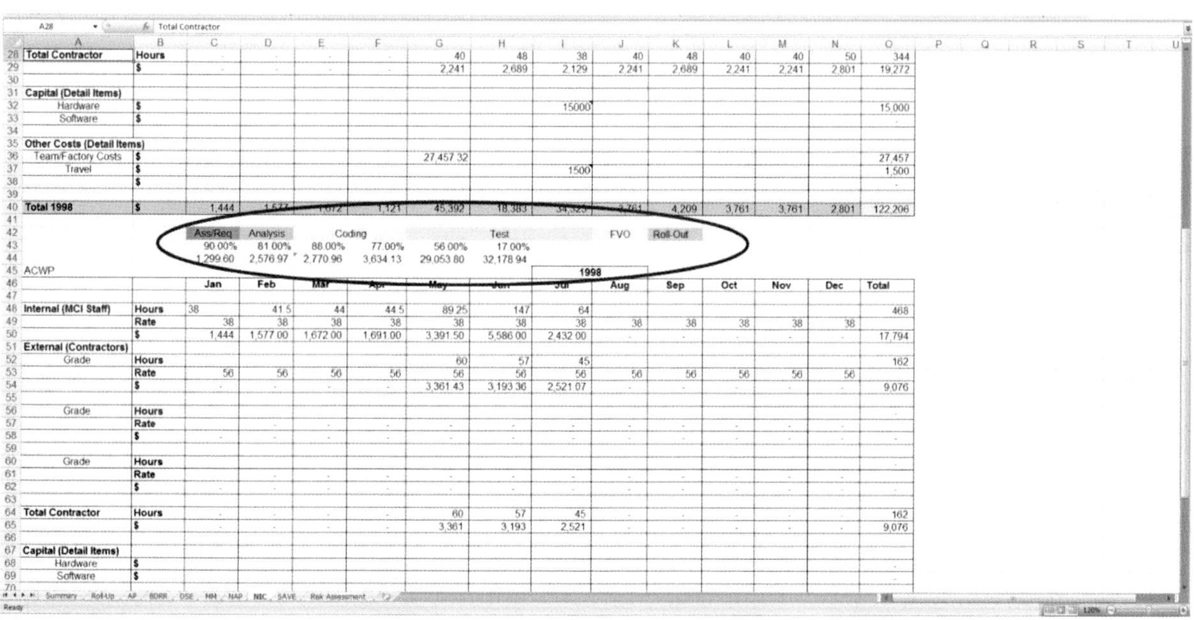

A28 — Total Contractor

	A	B	C	D	E	F	G	H	I	J	K	L	M	N	O
28	Total Contractor	Hours	-	-	-	-	40	48	38	40	48	40	40	50	344
29		$	-	-	-	-	2,241	2,689	2,129	2,241	2,689	2,241	2,241	2,801	19,272
30															
31	Capital (Detail Items)														
32	Hardware	$							15000						15,000
33	Software	$													-
34															
35	Other Costs (Detail Items)														
36	Team/Factory Costs	$					27,457.32								27,457
37	Travel	$							1500						1,500
38		$													-
39															
40	Total 1998	$	1,444	1,577	1,672	1,121	45,392	18,383	34,323	3,761	4,209	3,761	3,761	2,801	122,206
41															
42			Ass/Req	Analysis	Coding			Test		FVO	Roll-Out				
43			90.00%	81.00%	88.00%	77.00%	56.00%	17.00%							
44			1,299.60	2,576.97	2,770.96	3,634.13	29,053.80	32,178.94							
45	ACWP								1998						
46			Jan	Feb	Mar	Apr	May	Jun	Jul	Aug	Sep	Oct	Nov	Dec	Total
47															
48	Internal (MCI Staff)	Hours	38	41.5	44	44.5	89.25	147	64						468
49		Rate	38	38	38	38	38	38	38	38	38	38	38	38	
50		$	1,444	1,577.00	1,672.00	1,691.00	3,391.50	5,586.00	2,432.00	-	-	-	-	-	17,794
51	External (Contractors)														
52	Grade	Hours					60	57	45						162
53		Rate	56	56	56	56	56	56	56	56	56	56	56	56	
54		$	-	-	-	-	3,361.43	3,193.36	2,521.07	-	-	-	-	-	9,076
55															
56	Grade	Hours													-
57		Rate		-	-	-	-	-	-	-	-	-	-	-	
58		$	-	-	-	-	-	-	-	-	-	-	-	-	-
59															
60	Grade	Hours													-
61		Rate		-	-	-	-	-	-	-	-	-	-	-	-
62		$	-	-	-	-	-	-	-	-	-	-	-	-	-
63															
64	Total Contractor	Hours	-	-	-	-	60	57	45	-	-	-	-	-	162
65		$	-	-	-	-	3,361	3,193	2,521	-	-	-	-	-	9,076
66															
67	Capital (Detail Items)														
68	Hardware	$													-
69	Software	$													-

Summary / Roll-Up / AP / BORR / DSE / MM / NAP / NIC / SAVE / Risk Assessment

Figure 04.03

(Tyler M. J., NIS Y2K EVM Workbook, 1998)

Chapter 4: Pieces and Parts of the EVM Tool

The best approach to building your own EVM tool is first to take what your organization uses as its format for budgets or spend plans. I see that Space Systems Technology Corporation, your organization, uses something similar to the example project spend plan located in Appendix H, so let's use that to start with.

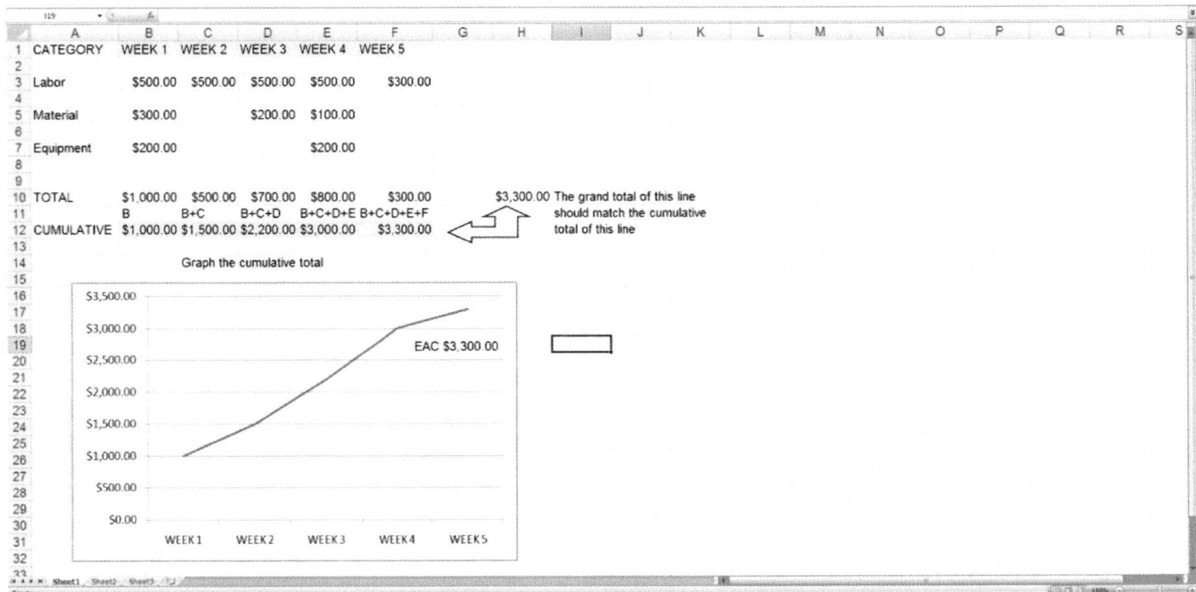

CATEGORY	WEEK 1	WEEK 2	WEEK 3	WEEK 4	WEEK 5	
Labor	$500.00	$500.00	$500.00	$500.00	$300.00	
Material	$300.00		$200.00	$100.00		
Equipment	$200.00			$200.00		
TOTAL	$1,000.00	$500.00	$700.00	$800.00	$300.00	$3,300.00
	B	B+C	B+C+D	B+C+D+E	B+C+D+E+F	
CUMULATIVE	$1,000.00	$1,500.00	$2,200.00	$3,000.00	$3,300.00	

Figure 04.04

Notice that a spend plan or budget is merely an incremental accounting for what is expected to be spent over the life of the project encompassing the three major resource that will be expended over time, that is; Labor resources, equipment resources, and material resources. Labor addresses the cost expenditures for all the human resources to be expended to accomplish the work directly related to the scope of the project. In other words, only the work that can be mapped directly back to the work breakdown structure set at the work package level. Any labor expense that cannot be found as a work package in the WBS is not reflected in the project's spend plan or budget. This means any and all back office work, and in many cases, the project manager's work and any Program Management Office work for the project. Let's keep this clean okay? Your spend plan or project budget must only reflect the resources directly attributed to effecting the accomplishment of the tasks of the project. This keeps the accounting clean and easier to audit. Your organization has standard charges that it will add to the cost of the project to account for supporting labor on the project. This includes labor like the procurement specialist or contracting specialist that will help you procure your labor, equipment and material needed for the project. Any contract labor will be included as part of the work packages in the WBS and will be included in your spend plan. This goes for any procurement costs for equipment and materials.

So, now you have your categories of labor, material and equipment listed down the left column and you have your increments (in this case, weeks) across the top row. Now, all you have to do is figure out what your expenditures are planned to be for each category over time. For most projects, if you are new to this, it's best to keep the expenditures at the task level and follow these expenditures accordingly.

Chapter 4: Thought Question

By now you have been exposed to different abbreviations such as BAC, ETC and EAC in Earned Value Management. Are the Budget at Completion (BAC) and the Estimate at Completion (EAC) the same thing?

A. At the project start, Budget at Completion equals Estimate at Completion—but that can change.

B. Estimate at Completion and Estimate to Complete are the same thing.

C. Each organization designs its own terms to describe what a project will cost.

D. All projects vary, so after you budget costs estimate your accuracy with ETC.

From the four choices, choose and substantiate your position with cited reference. Be sure to write your initial post according to APA format using citations/examples to substantiate your position and give credit to your references at the bottom of your post. Be sure to synthesize your analysis of the reading as a conclusion and then evaluate your synthesis. Remember that this is a discussion, so keep your responses succinct and to the point.

Chapter 4: Chapter Synthesis and Evaluation

Consider the use of a Cost management plan, the purpose of which is to establish standard guidelines and procedures for controlling changes to the project budget. The procedures should include a definition of the severity levels of potential impacts to costs, who needs to be involved, a description of how cost variances will be managed and how the resulting decisions will be incorporated and communicated. A great deal of confusion can also result in projects when terminology and records are undefined. A definitions and records section is provided for that purpose.

When it comes to planning your budget, plan for the worst events to happen. Expect the best events to happen. You will never be surprised or disappointed. (Tyler M. J., 1998)

Chapter 4: Test Your Knowledge

Take the following practice quiz. Identify those areas of Organizational Planning where you are weak and then reinforce yourself.

1. The Cost Performance Index (CPI) measures:
   a) floating costs vs. sunk costs
   b) work performed vs. cost of work performed.
   c) cost of work performed vs. planned costs.
   d) work performed vs. planned work.
   e) direct costs vs. indirect costs.

2. When comparing the cost of competing projects, which of the following is typically NOT considered?
   a) Opportunity costs.
   b) Direct costs.
   c) Sunk costs.
   d) Indirect costs.
   e) Burden rates.

3. The computation for Cost Performance Index is:
   a) BCWP/ACWP
   b) BCWP-ACWP
   c) BCWP-BCWS
   d) ACWP/BCWP
   e) ACWP-BCWS

4. The following types of cost are relevant to making a financial decision except:
   a) unavoidable costs

b) opportunity costs

c) direct costs

d) sunk costs

e) none

5. The Cost Performance Index is computed as:

   a) budget cost of work performed divided by actual cost of work performed

   b) budget cost of work performed minus actual cost of work performed

   c) budget cost of work performed minus budget cost of work scheduled

   d) budget cost of work scheduled divided by budget cost of work performed

   e) actual cost of work scheduled divided by budget cost of work performed

6. Life Cycle Costing:

   a) is the concept of all costs within the total life of a project

   b) is an activity devoted to optimizing cost/performance

   c) is an activity of appraising the cost and technical performance of a completed project

   d) is a process of predicting the life of a project

   e) all

7. Managerial Reserves are:

   a) allowances to account for price changes that can occur over the life of the project due to inflation

   b) accounts to allocate and maintain funds for contingency purposes

   c) Incentive fees paid to managers for good performance

   d) funds used to offset poor cost or schedule estimates

   e) all

8. Sunk costs are

a) Future costs held in reserve
b) Costs invested in commodities
c) Overhead costs
d) Tax credits
e) Expended costs over which we have no more control

9. Cost variance (CV) is which of the following equations?
   a) CV = BCWP = BCWS
   b) CV = BCWP - ACWP
   c) CV = SV / BCWS
   d) 1 and 3

10. Which of the following can best describe cost budgeting?
    a) The process of establishing budgets, standards, and a monitoring system by which the investment cost of the project can be measured and managed.
    b) The process of developing the future trends along with the assessment of probabilities, uncertainties, and inflation that could occur during the project.
    c) The process of assembling and predicting costs of a project over its life cycle.
    d) The process of gathering, accumulating, analyzing, monitoring, reporting, and managing the costs on an on-going basis.
11. Which of the following is a direct project cost?
    a) Lighting and heating for the corporate office
    b) Employee health care
    c) Piping for an irrigation project
    d) a and b

12. Which of the following can best describe cost controls?
    a) The process of gathering, accumulating, analyzing, monitoring, reporting, and managing the costs on an on-going basis.

b) The process of developing the future trends along with the assessment of probabilities, uncertainties, and inflation that could occur during the project.
c) The process of assembling and predicting costs of a project over its life cycle.
d) The process of establishing budgets, standards, and a monitoring system by which the investment cost of the project can be measured and managed.

13. If the project was supposed to have $1,000 worth of work accomplished but only completed $850 worth of work, what is the Scheduled Variance?
    a) -$150
    b) $150
    c) $1,500
    d) Cannot calculate from the information provided
    e) None

14. If $850 worth of work is completed, but it actually cost $900 to perform the work, what is the Cost Variance?
    a) Cannot calculate from the provided information
    b) $50
    c) -$50
    d) None

15. Sunk costs are:
    a) dollars that have not been invested but are in the management reserve.
    b) cost that vary in total depending upon the activity of the project as compared to fixed costs.
    c) another name for labor cost since these costs are already budgeted.
    d) dollars already invested in the project and regardless of what is done will not affect the project's outcome.
    e) a and c

16. Reserve funds are set aside to be used when:
    a) anticipated problems have been identified but not completely expected
    b) an up-scope of the project requires additional funds to compensate the initial budget
    c) they are needed for the sporadic fluctuation in potential labor rates when a union contract is under negotiation.
    d) none

17. Cost control is concerned with:
    a) influencing the factors which create a change to the cost baseline
    b) managing the actual changes when and as they occur
    c) insuring that the customer knows that the project budget is under or over budget
    d) a and b
    e) b and c

18. Which is the most conservative of the work completion rules:
    a) 0/100 Rule
    b) 50/50 Rule
    c) 20/80 Rule
    d) 100/100 Rule
    e) None

19. Which is considered the earned value?
    a) Budgeted Cost of Work Scheduled
    b) Budgeted Cost of Work Performed
    c) Actual Cost of Work Performed
    d) Budgeted at Completion
    e) b and d

20. What does a positive Cost Variance indicate?

a) A cost under run
b) The project is over budget
c) There were not enough dollars allocated in the budget for the budget item
d) The project is behind
e) None

21. What does a negative Schedule Variance indicate?

a) The project is behind in the schedule
b) Up-scope is causing cost overruns
c) The project is ahead of schedule
d) The project is on schedule
e) None

22. The BCWS is $10,000 and the BCWP was determined to have a $7,000 worth, and the ACWP is $5,000. What is the Cost Variance?

a) $2,000
b) -$2,000
c) $3,000
d) -$3,000
e) Cannot calculate the answer since not enough data is available

23. The BCWS is $10,000 and the BCWP was determined to have a $7,000 worth, and the ACWP is $5,000. What is the Cost Variance percent?

a) 29%
b) -48%
c) 50%
d) 60%

e) Cannot calculate the answer since not enough data is available

24. If a CV was positive and the SV was positive, what does this indicate?
    a) The project is under budget and ahead of schedule
    b) The project is over budget but on schedule
    c) The project is under budget but behind schedule
    d) Cannot tell from the information given
    e) The project is on budget and on schedule
25. If the variable cost of producing a unit is $100 per unit and all fixed costs equals $2,500, what will be the cost of producing ten extra units?
    a) $1,000
    b) $3,500
    c) $25,000
    d) $1,500
    e) None

26. What is the purpose of the contingency money in a cost estimate?
    a) Provides money to cover uncertainties in the estimate within the defined scope and schedule
    b) Money to cover changes in scope
    c) Money to cover unforeseen natural disasters
    d) a and b
    e) a and c

Chapter 4: Application Exercise

Using the information from your updated MPP and XLS file prepare for your upcoming project review. The only event you think may be an issue at the project review is the delay, by one week of getting the outsourced fitters on site. This delayed the project until the second week but payroll continued. Plot your Gantt schedule on your Gauchito EVM Tool provided by your company for PV (BCWS), EV (BCWP) and AC (ACWP). Ensure all items on the EVM are documented. Identify the following as a bullet paper to refer to in your project review:

- What the (approved) BAC is
- What the (projected) EAC is
- What the current SV is
- What the current CV is
- What is the current SPI?
- What is the current CPI?
- What is the VAC and are you in trouble? Why or why not?

Explain what you can do to bring the variance back on baseline in terms of project objectives (time, cost, quality).

- Submit your MPP, XLS and DOC files to your instructor.

Chapter 5: Chapter Overview / Introduction

You're doing great. The team has come together and worked through the early dynamics that is part of team building. Your Gauchito project, while getting off to a wobbly start is humming along here in the eighth week and you are looking forward to meeting with Herb Everson the customer representative (CR) from Scaled Composites. You have some things to go over with him and you want to ensure you have his best understanding of the progress of the rocket assembly project before you address some possible issues that might be coming up. You've heard rumor to the effect that Scaled Composites may be conducting the test launch preparation at its own site out in California for all the rocket assembly projects and you want to discuss what this might mean to the project.

Timely and specific feedback on the situational condition of a project is critical to the success of the project, and enables the project manager to identify and isolate problems early in the project lifecycle and then make the necessary corrections that keep the project on target and on budget. Earned Value Management (EVM) has, over time, proven to be the single most effective performance measurement tool and feedback mechanism for managing projects and programs. In this chapter will look at the basic methodologies needed integrate the management of scope, schedule, and cost through the project baseline. Remember that the cost baseline is a time-phased budget that will be used to measure and monitor cost performance on the project. It is developed by summing estimated costs by period and is usually displayed in the form of an S-curve. When there are changes to the scope of the project there are corresponding changes to the schedule, the cost, the quality of the project as well. Studies have shown the principle cause of project failure is the inability to manage the scope of the project. Good management entails defining the scope of the project and holding as close to that scope as possible, verifying with the customer the product or service is within the scope, and controlling any the inevitable changes to the project scope. The Project Management Institute defines scope definition as subdividing the major project deliverables (as identified in the scope statement) into smaller, more manageable components. Scope verification is the process of formalizing acceptance of the project scope by the stakeholders. And, scope change control is focused on influencing the factors which create scope changes to ensure that changes are beneficial, determining that a scope change has occurred, and managing the actual changes when and if they occur.

Chapter 5: Scope Change Control

Even the slightest changes to the scope of the project can have significant implications for other areas of the project plan, including schedule, costs, quality and risks, as well as customer satisfaction. That is why it is so important to manage requests for scope changes in a disciplined manner, as described in the scope management plan and the overall change control system. Complying with the scope management plan and overall change control system requires the project manager to perform the following tasks:

- Review the scope change guidelines and procedures with the project team, as defined in the scope management plan and overall change management system.
- Require that all requests for scope changes be formally managed.
- Review team progress and work products to ensure that no unauthorized scope changes take place.

It is important to understand the underlying causes of requests for changes to the scope prior to making any decisions. The most frequent causes of scope change requests include:

- Errors or Omissions. Since it is often difficult for customers to accurately describe their requirements during project planning, they discover more about what they really want in the final product as the project progresses. They then have a tendency to want to change their requirements after specification and development has begun, resulting in schedule delays and cost increases.

- Value-Adding Opportunities. Unforeseen opportunities to add value to the project often present themselves after the project begins, such as the advent of new technology. Engineering and development personnel, who would like to have their newly discovered ideas, included in the current project, normally request changes of this type. The best solution is usually to maintain the scope of the current project if newly discovered opportunities do not have sufficient value to offset the risks involved.

- Competitive Pressures. Competition does not stand still during a project, and competitors may come out with new products with new features or functionality while the project is underway. This can force a project team to reevaluate its plans and make changes to the product design in order to remain competitive.

- Schedule Slippage. Schedule slippage, forces project teams to consider reducing the scope of their projects. If it appears that the original schedule cannot be realistically achieved, but the customer cannot accept a later completion date, then either the project scope must be reduced or more resources applied to bring it in on time. The importance of considering the full implications of changing the scope of the project cannot be overstated. Increasing the scope, through the addition of new features or functionality, will always add unanticipated complexity to the project and will normally result in slipping the original schedule. On the other hand, reducing the scope in an attempt to bring a slipping schedule in on time will usually result in customer disappointment and dissatisfaction.

There is a technique to control scope changes called configuration management. Configuration management can provide appropriate levels of review and approval for changes. This provides focal points for those seeking to make changes. Configuration management provides, through the project manager, a single point of input to contracting representatives

For any change to the project scope it is imperative to know:

- What is the cost of the change and is it justifiable?
- What is the impact on quality and the cost of additional quality checks?
- Is the change really required?
- What is the impact on the schedule?

Chapter 5: Analyzing Changes to Project Scope

Analyzing requests for project scope changes requires the project manager to first identify the root cause of the change. This must be done quickly and efficiently working with the SMEs (Subject Matter Experts) on the team, with the project sponsor, and with the user or the customer. In your case, Herb Everson is the CR and you, working with your team leads and project sponsor need to estimate the benefits and costs of making any changes to the Gauchito project by identifying the implications of the scope change to the other elements of the project plan, including the schedule, the cost, and the quality level of the assembly.

Once you have done this, you need to assess the risks involved with making the change or changes, then assess the direct impact on your customer, Scaled Composites and be ready to discuss with Herb Everson the CR, your sponsor, and the functional managers that are supporting the project the ramifications of making the proposed changes.

Chapter 5: Authorizing Changes to Project Scope

Once the affected stakeholders have thoroughly evaluated the potential impacts of a scope change request, the action must be properly authorized and its results monitored. Resources must be prepared to make the change in a timely manner, and further action may be required if the change does not take place as planned. Authorizing and monitoring scope changes requires the project manager to ensure the proposed action is properly authorized as defined in the scope management plan and change control system. Normally this is accomplished by using a change control form (CCF, usually a company form) that specifies the change and the purpose for the change. Additionally, the CCF will specify the impact of the change on the projects management objectives in time, cost and quality. The CCF must be reviewed, discussed and accepted or rejected by a change control board (CCB) usually made up of stakeholders directly affected by the scope changes. This usually, but may not include the customer or user, each of the functional mangers that are providing resources to the project and in some cases the sponsor. The project manager, by nature of his or her position must be part of the CCB since any changes will directly affect the future progress of the project. The project manager then ensures the responsible people are prepared to make the change in a timely manner. This will mean a re-planning of the project by going back and configuring the WBS to reflect the scope change, reconstruction of the resource allocation matrix for additional resources or the removal of resources, the restructuring of the duration estimate to roll-up the new levels of effort to address the changes in the scope of the project, the re-calculation if the project costs and the re-cutting of the project baseline or planned value (PV). Once this is completed, the project manger must run the actuals of the project to date to being the project up to date with the new scope changed but showing the resources already spent.

Having established the planned value (PV) with new baseline and EAC, and with the actuals (AC) recalculated to date, the earned value of the project must now be calculated to show the new project worth and any variances as a result. All of this will require feedback or formal status reporting on the change to the affected stakeholders. In this case, once you have your changes and their implications calculated you need to set up a project review with the affected stakeholders to evaluate the actual versus planned progress of the change for validation, rejection and then initiate further action as needed.

Chapter 5: Updating Changes to Project Scope

All changes to the product scope which in turn, change the project scope must be formally reflected in the affected project documents, including requirements, specifications, designs, the scope statement and work breakdown structure. Not keeping scope-related documents current can cause confusion later in the project, such as during test plan development and final customer acceptance. The documents should be updated continually to reflect the most recent scope-related decisions. This provides a current source of information for all involved and creates a project history that will be needed for future reference and learning. In updating scope-related project documents the project manager is responsible for updating affected documents, utilizing a consistent version control numbering system to identify each document update and effective date, reviewing the updated documents for completeness and distribute as needed to affected project stakeholders, and documenting the causes of scope variances, rationale for decisions, along with other lessons learned from the change to become part of the project history file as a reference for current and future projects.

Chapter 5: Updating Affected Project Documents

Once it is decided that there will need to be a change in the scope and the proper forms are submitted to you, the project manager, you will need to run the changes through your project tools to recalculate the impact to the project's earned value. Before this can be done, however, you will need to lock the old project for archiving and future reference. In MPP and in your EVM tool you save your files with annotation in the file name to show they are now archive files. It can be as simple as taking the existing file name and adding the work ARCHIVED to the front of the back of the file name. Then go into the file properties in your File Explorer and set the file for archiving as shown below:

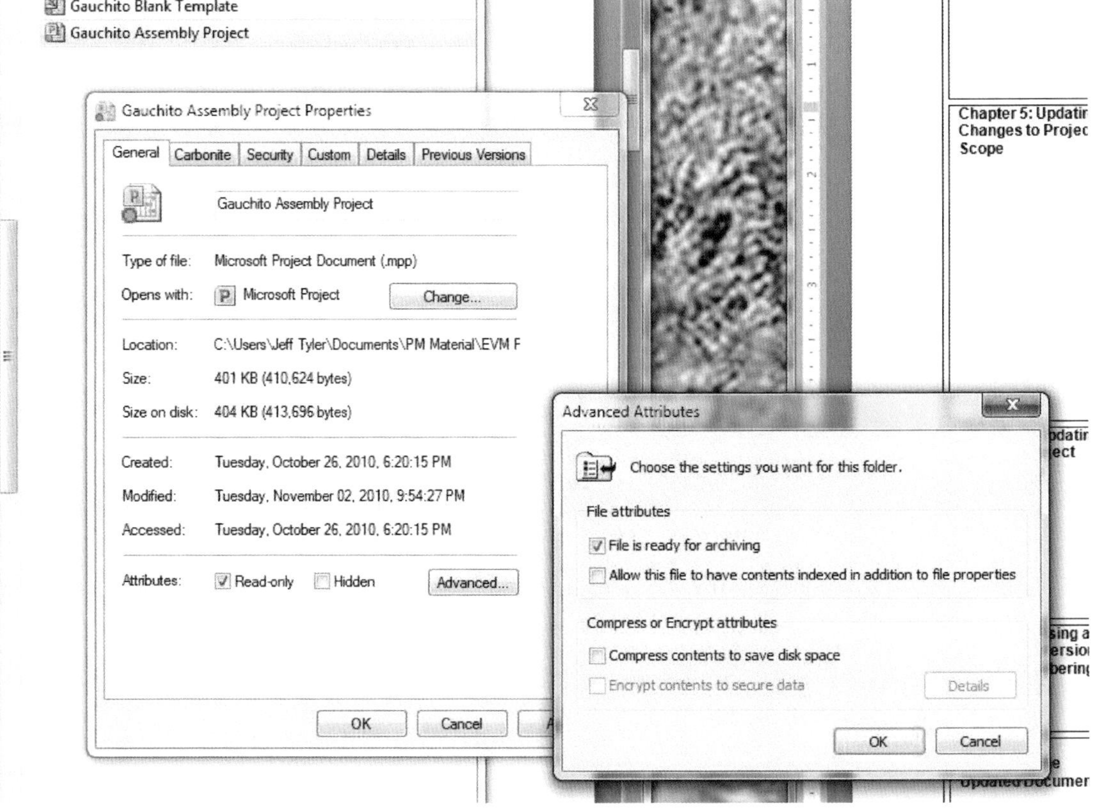

Figure 05.01

Once this is accomplished, save the archive file in the appointed place and proceed to make your updated changes the MPP file and the Excell EVM tool. Be sure to save both files with new file names in accordance with the organization's file convention protocols and version controls.

Chapter 5: Using a Consistent Version Control Numbering System

A formal change control management system provides set procedures for updating the status of changes to project deliverables as a result of changes to the project scope. This means that all changes must be capable of being mapped back to the original scope of the project as derived from the original project deliverables. As such each subsequent change to the preceding changes must be tracked. One of the easiest methods is to use the year-month-day-version number techniques. This can be marked as yymmdd-version#. For example the first approved and implemented change on December 15, 2011 would read 111215-001 allowing for up to 999 changes in one day, an unlikely occurrence. This allows for tracking by year, the month, then day, then version on a given day. Be aware there is no set version control standard and many different techniques are used. As the project manager, it is incumbent on you to know the organizational version control system or VCS. Some organizations use an automated system like the Microsoft SharePoint sites that will allow for revisions and will keep track of them for you. Just be sure you use the proscribed methodology, but use a common version control numbering system that is understood by all project stakeholders.

Chapter 5: Reviewing the Updated Documents

Normally, multi-month projects are reviewed by the project sponsor, customer/user and specific stakeholders on a monthly basis. It is in these project reviews that any variances in schedule and costs are discussed and decisions made. The project manager must be prepared to address the reasons for these variances from the original baseline and what is being done to rectify these variances. In reviewing the updated project documents, project performance is determined based on variance in relation to previous EVM documents. Again, the project's performance and, as an extension, the project manager's performance is evaluated base on the projected EAC from the current variance to the end of the project. A trend analysis is conducted based on the current variance out to the end of the project to provide a new EAC. This trended EAC is then compared to the BAC and any difference is the Variance At Completion (VAC). The formula for this is VAC=BAC-EAC. A healthy project (and a healthy PM) has a VAC within a window of +10% to -5%. In other words a $1M project can only have a projected (trended) VAC within $1.1M to $950K. Outside of this projected window, the project and the project manager are considered unhealthy and require executive management intercession. In some cases the project manager is removed for cause. If it's not obvious to you by now, you need to understand that the project manager must continually remain knowledgeable of the health of the project based on a continuous review of the current EVM documentation compared to earlier versions.

Chapter 5: Documenting the Scope Variances

It is only with documenting the causes of the scope changes that an objective monitoring of the variances to the baseline can be conducted and proper mitigation of deviations from the baseline be acted on. By documenting the scope variances, the project manager has a basis for immediate actions to address the variances and if necessary, inform the sponsor and customer/user as to the situation with options to correct the deviations and receive concurrence for actions to rectify the variance. In doing so, the sponsor and the customer/user become co-actionaries in the process. "Visionaries have ideas. Actionaries see them through. Dictionaries just talk about them." (Charland, 2010) You can't take action without a point to start from and you can't move in a direction until you know where you are and where you want to go from there. This is the reason for weekly project status reports and for periodic project reviews with the major project stakeholders. IT is up to you, the project manager to compile all the information on project baseline variances from your status reports into a project review. MS Project can help you with this.

After you've entered the basic information about your project, you may want to print it and review the plan. To make it easy to identify your project, you can add headers, footers, and page numbers. If you want to review certain areas of the plan, you can change to another view, customize the view to show only the information you need, and print it. You can add project information to the header, footer, or legend of a view. The project information can be data you entered (such as your company's name or manager's name) or data provided by Microsoft Project (such as the page number or project finish date). You can choose the project information that adds the most impact to your printed view. Be sure to note that to format project information, you will need to select the ampersand (&) that precedes it, or select the entire line, and then click Format Text Font . Select the font, font style, size, and color you want; select the Underline check box if you want; and then click OK. To add a title, page number, or other project information, On the File menu, click Page Setup, then click the Header, Footer, or Legend tab.

Click the Left, Center, or Right tab. In the text box, place the insertion point where you want to add the project information. In the General and Project fields boxes, click each type of information you want, and then click Add. Microsoft Project will use the information you typed into the Project Information and Properties dialog boxes to fill in each type of information. To see what a project view will look like when printed, click Print Preview.

Before printing a view, it is useful to see what the information will actually look like when printed. You can adjust the page orientation and size, edit headers, footers, and legends, and set print options. To print a view from the screen using the default settings, just click Print. Most often, a printed view includes only the information that's displayed on your screen when you use the Print command. When you want to print what you see on your screen, print a view. You can print sheet views, graph views, and most chart views, that is, any view except form views and the Relationship Diagram view. Again, please note that to change the default print settings, click Print on the File menu, and then specify the printer and printer properties, the print range, the number of copies, and the date range. To see the results of your changes immediately, click Preview in the Print dialog box. To print a standard report On the View menu, click Reports.

Then click the report type you want, and then click Select. Click the specific report you want to print, and then click Select. Click Print. Your report will be a predefined set of detailed information about a specific part of your plan. Microsoft Project provides more than 20 predefined reports; for example, the Who Does What report automatically includes each resource's task assignments, as well as the work, delay, and start and finish dates for each assignment. Should you need to distribute project information online Microsoft Project puts the communication potential of the Internet at your fingertips with a variety of Internet and Intranet features.

With Microsoft Project, you can communicate project plans and collect project information from team members. You can copy information as a static picture and save the picture in a Web-compatible file format and, you can distribute documents on the Internet or Intranet as they related to your project. You can include information from a Microsoft Project schedule in an HTML document for the World Wide Web. Microsoft Project uses import/export maps to determine which fields are exported to HTML format and may use a template to determine how and where the information is displayed in the HTML file. You can create or edit both the HTML import/export maps and the HTML templates. To publish information in Web format On the File menu, click Save As Web Page. If necessary, type a name for the exported file in the File name box, and then click Save. In the Import/export map list, click the name of the map you want to use for exporting your data, such as Export to HTML using standard template. Note, you can define a new map or edit an existing map by clicking New Map. Click Save. You can even edit the sample templates that Microsoft Project provides for creating formatted HTML files from exported data or you can create your own templates.

You can copy information as a static picture from the active Microsoft Project. View and paste it into any program capable of displaying graphical information as images. You can also save the picture in a Web-compatible file format for use on the Web. In many views, you can copy a picture of the entire view or select and copy a portion of the view. Select the rows in your project you want to copy or display the area you want to copy on your screen. On the Edit menu, click Copy Picture. Under Render image, specify how you want the image rendered:

To copy the information for display on a screen, such as for a Microsoft PowerPoint slide, click For screen. To copy the information as it would be printed, click For printer. To copy the information as a GIF image file, for use in a Web page or in other programs, click To GIF image file, and then specify the path and file name you want to copy the image to. Under Copy, click Rows on screen to copy all visible portions of your plan, or click Selected rows to copy only the row you have selected. To copy information for a range of dates other than those currently displayed in the timescale, under Timescale, enter a starting and ending date in the From and To boxes. Click OK. Switch to the program where you want to paste the Microsoft Project information, and then paste the picture using the program's Paste command.

Chapter 5: So, What Does This All Mean?

Projects are dynamic and they change for a variety of reasons. While these the cause of changes may vary, the effect is essentially that the scope will be changed in some way. Changes in time (slippage or early completion) affect costs and or quality which in turn require a reassessment of scope. Changes in cost affect time and or quality which in turn affect the scope. Changes in quality affect costs and time which, in turn, affect the scope. This is because the scope is the definition of the project. Variance monitored with EVM is controlled by adjusting cost, time, quality which in turn change the scope and the completion of the tasks that become the project deliverables. Should there be a change in the expected deliverables, there is will be a change in the scope of the project which, in turn will affect cost, time (the schedule) and/or the quality of the project.

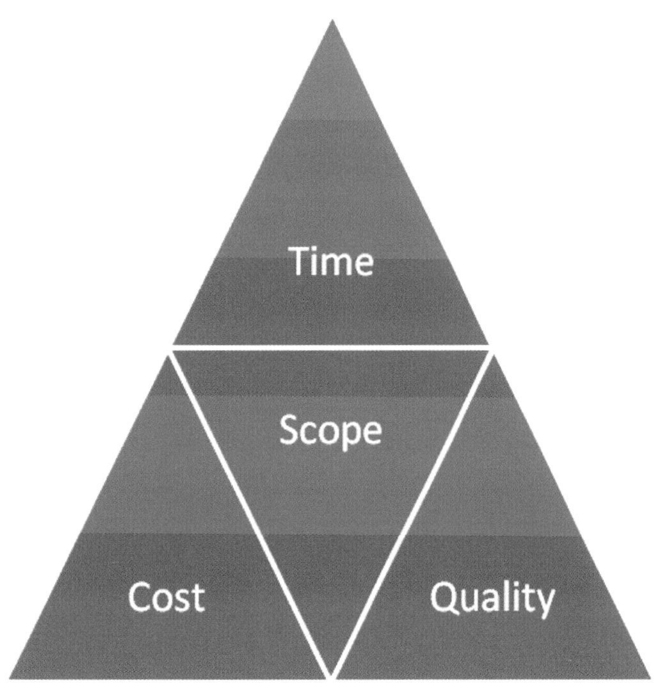

Figure 05.02 Project Core Interrelationships

It is incumbent upon the project manager to ensure that adjustments are assessed and enacted on each of these four core areas of the project when even one is adjusted. If the customer/user changes the scope, you must adjust the schedule, costs (resources) and quality accordingly. If the sponsor changes the costs (resources) you must adjust the scope, schedule and quality accordingly. If the schedule changes, you will need to adjust the scope, costs and quality accordingly. If the quality of the project has been affected, you will need to adjust the scope, schedule and cost accordingly. Each of these four project areas are interdependent on each other and require the experienced project manager to balance their adjustments as they relate to each other.

Chapter 5: Thought Question

Recently your project exceeded its estimate and the customer insisted that you and your organization absorb the extra costs. Is this fair?

A. No, but since you don't want the customer to sue your organization you should pay the costs.

B. It depends on the way your contract was written, but probably the customer is correct.

C. Usually the performing organization and the customer split overruns 70/30.

D. Ask the customer if they will pay the full amount this time for a 10% discount next time.

(Institute P. M., 2008)

Chapter 5: Chapter Synthesis and Evaluation

In this chapter we examined the use of performance reporting as part of a project review. Both activities- performance reporting and project reviews- while essential to good project management are rarely, if ever utilized, as they should be. Variances will always exist, unless there is perfect execution of the Project Plan. Variances are not always a bad omen, or cause of concern, or an indicator of poor management. Significant variances are those variances that break predetermined thresholds, require management attention, and corrective action. A significant variance may mean the original plan was inappropriate, or the earned value technique was not appropriate, or the actuals were incorrect. Significant variances inform management that something needs to be examined, analyzed and proper corrective action instituted. The proper use of performance reporting during the execution and controlling phases of the project can ensure a smooth administrative closure. Just remember that you can't tell which way the train left the station by only looking at the track. (Tyler M. J., 1998)

In chapter 5 we will be presenting updates from the project in PowerPoint as part of your project review presentation. By unit 6 you will have seen how to use software tools in MS Project and Excel to aid you in monitoring and controlling your project. But, in unit 6 you will be hand calculating your project earned value. Be sure you look over the formulae in Cost References (see the flyleaf) before you have to hand calculate in chapter 6.

Chapter 5: Test Your Knowledge

Take the following practice quiz. Identify those where you are weak and then reinforce yourself.

1. The Cost Performance Index (CPI) measures:
   a) floating costs vs. sunk costs
   b) work performed vs. cost of work performed.
   c) cost of work performed vs. planned costs.
   d) work performed vs. planned work.
   e) direct costs vs. indirect costs.

2. The computation for Cost Performance Index is:
   a) BCWP/ACWP
   b) BCWP-ACWP
   c) BCWP-BCWS
   d) ACWP/BCWP
   e) ACWP-BCWS

3. The Cost Performance Index is computed as:
   a) budget cost of work performed divided by actual cost of work performed
   b) budget cost of work performed minus actual cost of work performed
   c) budget cost of work performed minus budget cost of work scheduled
   d) budget cost of work scheduled divided by budget cost of work performed
   e) actual cost of work scheduled divided by budget cost of work performed

4. Cost variance (CV) is which of the following equations?
   a) CV = BCWP - BCWS
   b) CV = BCWP - ACWP

c) CV = SV / BCWS
d) 1 and 3

5. Cost controls can be best described by which of the following?
   a) The process of gathering, accumulating, analyzing, monitoring, reporting, and managing the costs on an on-going basis.
   b) The process of developing the future trends along with the assessment of probabilities, uncertainties, and inflation that could occur during the project.
   c) The process of assembling and predicting costs of a project over its life cycle.
   d) The process of establishing budgets, standards, and a monitoring system by which the investment cost of the project can be measured and managed.

6. If the project was supposed to have $1,000 worth of work accomplished but only completed $850 worth of work, what is the Scheduled Variance?
   a) -$150
   b) $150
   c) $1,500
   d) Cannot calculate from the information provided
   e) None

Chapter 5: Application Exercise

It's now week eight into the project. Everything is going well except that Scaled Composites (the customer) has, for financial reasons, dropped the Test Launch Preparation deliverable effectively removing task 15 from the scope of the project You've been asked to re-plan your project with these changes taken into consideration and present your new revamped baseline to your sponsor and Herb Everson for acceptance. Be sure to take into account any management reserve needed as a result of this change in scope.

- Build a new MS Project (without baseline set) file with the current information and the proposed scope changes.
- Transfer the necessary data over to a new Gauchito EVM template showing only the planned value and proposed baseline. Be sure that you include any changes during the course of the project lifecycle.
- Write your presentation into a bulleted talking paper to refer to during your presentation.
- Build your talking points into a PowerPoint presentation that includes:
    - Background situation
    - Proposed Gantt schedule
    - Proposed revised spend plan/budget
    - Proposed baseline

Chapter 6: Chapter Overview / Introduction

The project manager is fiduciarily responsible for tracking all expenditures in time and costs (resources) throughout execution to maintain cost and schedule control. The project manager must continually remind the team that one of the objectives of the project to complete the project without incurring any additional costs in resources or time and to avoid changes to the initial project baseline. As actual on-going changes in costs and schedule are incurred, team members need to report actual hours expended for each resource, one-time costs, and the percentage completion of each activity. This provides the basis for Earned Value Analysis (EVA). Major cost variances or requests for additional resources are to be reported as impacts to the budget or spend plan. All changes that affect the client must be reported and authorized by upper management before final billing arrangements are made. Earned Value Management is concerned with influencing factors that create change to the project baseline, determining that the project baseline has changed, and managing actual changes when and as they occur. This chapter is a review of the basics to be the platform to launch into the more advanced aspects of EVM and will cover:

- Work completion methods
- Earned value (EV) concept and terms
- Cross-checking of all control procedures to ensure compliance
- Analyzing requests for changes to the cost baseline
- Authorizing and monitoring changes to the cost baseline
- Updating the cost baseline and related documents

Chapter 6: Work Completion Methods

Some of the most important data point of control information is the data that shows how much work has been completed. Several methods are used in project management to determine the amount of task completion.

The **0/100 Rule** is used to determine what percent of the task is complete. The assumption is that the value of the project is none until all work is finished. At completion, all of the Budgeted Cost of Work Scheduled (BSCS or baseline) for the task is applied to its appropriate amount. This is considered to be a very conservative approach.

The **20/80 Rule** is based on the concept of Pareto's Rule. Once the task is started, the project manager assumes a 20% completion and applies 20% of the BCWS against the account. When the task is finished, the remaining 80% is charged to budget and compared with The Actual Cost of Work Performed (ACWP). The task assumes only a small amount of value until it completed. This method is cautious, but is less conservative than the 0/100 rule.

The **50/50 Rule** may be the most popular method of showing a task's progress. This assumes that once the task is begun, 50% of its BCWS is charged to the project account. When the task is completed, the remaining amount is charged to the project account and compared to the ACWP.

Chapter 6: Earned Value (EV) Concepts and Terms

The terminology used in Earned Value Analysis (EVA), now referred to as Earned Value Management (EVM) is undergoing a change within industry. A short comparison is as follows:

- Earned Value Analysis (EVA) = Earned Value Management (EVM)
- Budgeted Cost of Work Scheduled (BCWS) = Planed Value (PV)
- Budgeted Cost of Work Performed (BCWP) = Earned Value (EV)
- Actual Cost of Work Performed (ACWP) = Actual Costs (AC)

The explanation of EV in the PMBOK, section 7.3.2 is somewhat nebulous. (Stackpole, Cynthia et al, 2008) Care should be given in ensuring you understand both the old and the new terms and don't get them mixed up. For the purposes of this book, both the old terms and new terms were utilized for the convenience of the reader. Both terms are used in industry and in Project Management Professional (PMP) examinations. The new terms are currently found in the Guide to the PMBOK, 2000 and subsequent editions. The 1996 edition used only the old terms.

The Earned Value Management approach allows the project manager to compare cost and schedule variances concurrently, thus allowing the project manager to take a comprehensive view of the project's progress. When used properly earned value becomes a highly effective management tool for cost and schedule control as well as a performance reporting mechanism to upper management. Earned Value consists of three functions:

- Budget Cost of Work Scheduled (BCWS) which is the same as **planned value (PV)** budget or the baseline
- Actual Cost of Work Performed (ACWP) which is the amount of **actual costs (AC)** costs to perform task
- Budgeted Cost of Work Performed (BCWP) which is the **earned value (EV)** or what the project is really worth at a given point in time

These three functions plotted on a graph provide the Cumulative Cost Curve (S Curve) as depicted below.

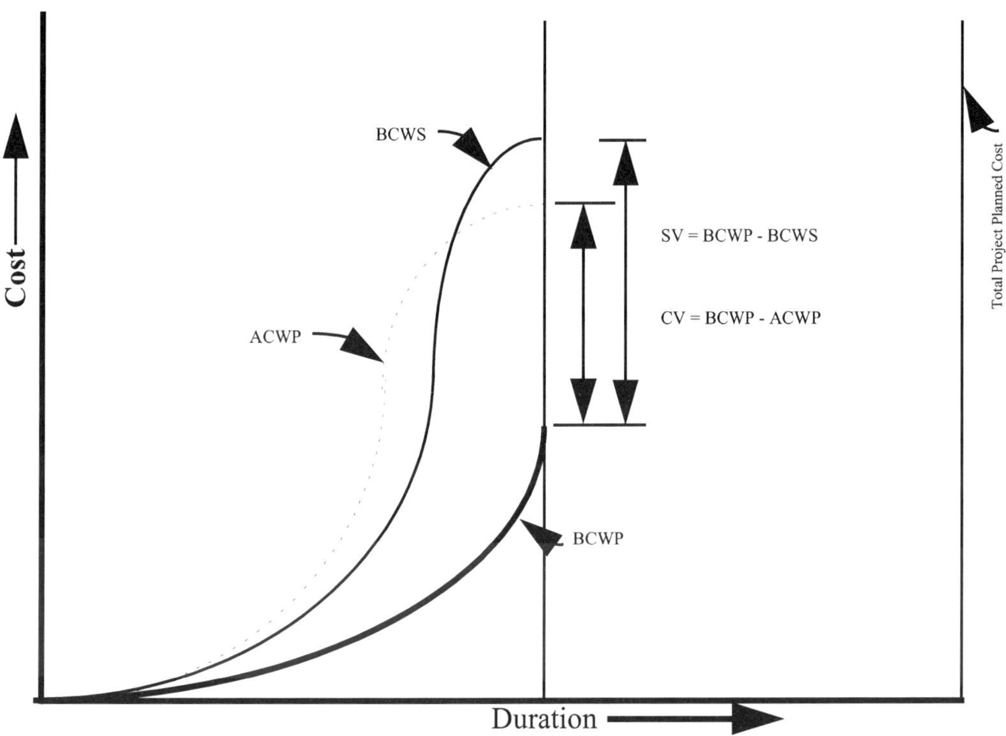

Figure 06.01 Baseline or PV S-Curve with EV and AC Values for Variance

The combination of BCWS and ACWP or budgeted amount of cost for completed work shows the Cost Variance (CV) of the project.

CV = BCWP – ACWP or EV-AC

If the amount is positive the project has a cost under run.

If the amount is negative, the project has a cost overrun.

You must take into account the schedule of the completion of the project if, at this time, it is behind or ahead of schedule.

The combination of BCWP and BCWS or planned work to what was actually accomplished shows the Schedule Variance (SV) of the project.

SV = BCWP – BCWS or EV-PV

If the amount is positive the project ahead of schedule.

If the amount is negative, the project is behind schedule.

The combination of the Cost Variance (CV) to the Schedule Variance results in some heuristic factors that say volumes about a project:

If CV is positive & SV is negative then task not started or not enough resources applied.

If CV is negative and SV is negative, then costs are overrun.

If CV is negative and SV is positive, money was spent to crash schedule.

If CV is positive and SC is positive, then project is under budget and ahead of schedule.

The Schedule Variance percent and the Cost Variance percent will provide an idea of how much the project is deviating from the project plan.

SV% = (SV/BCWS) X 100

CV% = (CV/BCWP) X 100

The Cost/Schedule Performance Index can explain how efficiently the project work is being accomplished.

$$CPI = \frac{BCWP}{ACWP}$$

If CPI > 1.0, then there is exceptional performance

If CPI < 1.0, then performance is poor

Budgeted At Completion (BAC) is the sum of all budgets (BCWS) allocated to the project or the project baseline. This is what the total effort of the project should cost.

Estimated At Completion (EAC) is defined as either the hour or dollar amount that provides a realistic appraisal of the project work performed. The formula for EAC is:

EAC = [(ACWP/BCWP) X BAC]

EAC is the sum of all direct and indirect costs to date plus the estimate of all authorized work remaining.

Variance at Completion (VAC) provides the best estimate of the total cost at the completion of the project.

Chapter 6: Cross-Check All Control Procedures to Ensure Compliance

Changes to the cost baseline can have significant implications for others areas of the project plan, including scope, time, quality, risk, procurement, and staffing. That is why it is so important to manage requests for changes to the cost baseline in a disciplined manner, as described in the cost management plan and the overall change control system. Complying with the cost management plan and overall change control system requires:

- Reviewing the guidelines and procedures for making changes to the cost baseline with the project team, as defined in the cost management plan and overall change management system
- Requiring that all requests for cost baseline changes be formally managed
- Reviewing the rate of project expenditures to ensure that no unauthorized changes to the cost baseline take place

Chapter 6: Analyzing Requests for Changes to the Cost Baseline

It is important to understand the underlying causes of requests for changes to the cost baseline prior to making any decisions. The most frequent causes of such change requests are errors or omissions made during cost estimating. Since it is often difficult for team members to accurately estimate project resource requirements during the planning process, they discover more about what is required to achieve project objectives as the work progresses. Team members have a tendency to want to revise their cost estimates when they are surprised by unanticipated and costly activities and problems, resulting in pressures to reduce the project scope, add resources, or shortcut quality control measures. Other sources of requests to change the cost baseline include: changes in customer's plans that may require additional resources to achieve earlier completion; internal, competitive, and customer-driven pressures to broaden the project scope; general organizational pressures to reduce expenses, and the occurrence of significant, unplanned events. Analyzing requests for changes to the cost baseline requires:

- Identifying the root cause of the change request
- Comparing the benefits of making the change to the proposed increase in costs
- Identifying the implications of the cost change on the other elements of the project plan, including scope, time, and quality
- Assessing the risks involved with making the change
- Assessing the direct impact on the customer, if any
- Discussing the implications of making the change with key project stakeholders, especially the project sponsor and upper management

Chapter 6: Authorize and Monitor Changes to the Cost Baseline

Once the team has thoroughly evaluated the potential impacts of a change request, the action must be properly authorized and its results monitored. Every effort should be made to maintain the current cost baseline by looking for alternative approaches to getting the work completed. Authorizing and monitoring changes to the cost baseline requires:

- Attempting to contain costs in other areas before authorizing increasing the baseline
- Ensuring the proposed action is properly authorized as defined in the cost management plan and change control system
- Requiring feedback or formal status reporting on the change
- Evaluating the actual versus planned costs after authorizing the change
- Initiating further action as needed

Chapter 6: Update the Cost Baseline and Related Documents

All cost-related changes must be formally reflected in the cost baseline and spending plan. Not keeping cost-related documents current can cause confusion, such as when attempting to compare actual costs with the cost baseline. These documents should be updated continually to reflect the most recent cost-related decisions. This provides a current source of information for all involved and creates a project history that will be needed for future reference and learning. Updating cost-related project documents requires:

- Making changes to the cost baseline and spending plan
- Using a consistent version control numbering system to identify each document update and effective date
- Reviewing the updated documents for completeness and distribute as needed to affected project stakeholders
- Documenting the causes of cost variances, rationale for decisions, along with other lessons learned from the change to become part of the project history file as reference for current and future projects

Chapter 6: Thought Question

How do you manage expectations on a project where the original sponsors change midway through the work? Do you change the scope in these cases?

A. Stop work on the project until you are asked by the new sponsor to continue. If the project continues, start fresh with a new baseline.

B. Meet with the new sponsor to explain the business value of the project, but keep the original baseline so that your metrics are not disturbed.

C. Check with the new sponsor to see if his or her business objectives for the project are the same as the original sponsor. Alter the scope if it makes practical sense to do so.

D. Continue with the project as though there had been no change in sponsorship until you hear differently. Although the individual sponsor changed, the technical requirements did not.

In organizations with robust project management practices, getting a different sponsor is a major change for the project and the project team. How you as the project manager react depends on the type of organization involved and the reason for the switch.

Organizational Situations: If your organization funds all projects out of a common fund, the sponsor may be a management cheerleader but not paying for the costs of the work out of his or her own departmental pocket. In this situation, you are more likely to be expected to continue the project as planned. In other work places, the sponsor's budget is the source of your project funding. This sponsor may be more likely to adjust project goals and constraints.

Change Reasons: You may have a new sponsor because your current sponsor was promoted (or demoted). The entire unit or company may restructure, moving personnel to new positions. Your management team may have experienced a corporate takeover or purchased a subsidiary.

Expansion may have necessitated a new hire come into this position. Regardless, you need to be poised to brief the latest manager on your project.

Sponsor Briefing

Your first act should be to introduce yourself as the project manager and set up a meeting to discuss how the sponsor intends for you to move forward with the project. If this person is new to the company, he or she will need a week or so to adjust before he or she is prepared to make effective business decisions. Continue the work of the project until you can have a discussion about the project's future.

There are five useful discussion points you should try to cover when you talk to the new sponsor and take back to your team.

- Come prepared to present the original goals of the project and the business value it is expected to provide to the organization. Bring the original metrics of time, budget and quality, and show the percentage that has currently been completed and the amount of time it will take to finish it as planned.
- Ask the sponsor, especially the one that will be funding it directly, if his or her vision includes continuing the project with these same parameters, or what a new direction should be.
- Find out if the sponsor wants you to temporarily continue the work of the project as originally planned, stop immediately until he or she has time to assess how to proceed, or finish it as planned.
- If the new manager knows that there need to be new goals/budget or other changes, set up a second meeting to get those details.
- This first meeting is also a good time to ask what kinds of reports he or she would like to see. Not every sponsor wants or needs the same kind of information about a project. Bring samples of choices.

Scope Adjustment: If the changes to scope prove to be small, you can use traditional ways to show and document their effect on your original baseline. For big shifts, you can re-baseline in Microsoft Project or other automated software so that the project is now working toward the adjusted goals. A new sponsor will want the project statistics to show success in meeting objectives.

Protect the corporate budget and your team's morale with an organized plan for updating and accommodating a changing sponsor. Your reputation as a project manager will start out on a solid foundation with this new manager. (B. Davis, 2010)

Chapter 6: Chapter Synthesis and Evaluation

Many assumptions are made during project planning regarding resource availability. Once you move into the execution phase of your project these assumptions must now be made to happen. All too often, funding, team members, or key pieces of equipment/hardware will still be still committed to work from previous projects or engaged in functional commitments at project execution time. It is your responsibility, as the project manager, with the support of the project sponsor, to free up these resources from other commitments in order to perform the activities as scheduled. The timely transition to action has a direct impact on the project's ability to meet the demands of the schedule timelines. You are also responsible for ensuring that project has the needed resources to accomplish the work. The use of earned value management allows you, as the project manager to quickly assess variances from the project baseline, identify the causes and move to rectify the causes behind the variances to bring the project back online. Remember, the best decisions, utilizing the best information, too late, are, by definition, the wrong decisions. (Tyler M. J., 1998)

Chapter 6: Lesson Synthesis and Evaluation

If you're not keeping score, how do you know how far you have come? Project control is about ensuring that the project is on target and the correct results are being achieved. The critical success factor in a control process is good planning. Many cultures do not reward good plans; they reward controlling against the plan. It is important to develop good plans and adjust as more information is gathered through the control process. The Project Manager must be able to define what each team member is expected to accomplish and to determine that it is accomplished. When it comes to planning your budget, plan for the worst events to happen. Expect the best events to happen. You will never be surprised or disappointed. (Tyler M. J., 1998)

Chapter 6: Application Exercise

Now that you have a solid understanding of how Earned Value Management is conducted and how to use the EVM Tool, understand that many organizations do not use such tools but rely on the basic principles you have learned in this course. As such, you now have the opportunity to display your understanding of EVM principles using just the basic formulae. You may use any tools we have utilized in this course (Excel, MPP, EVM Tool) or you may calculate the assignment longhand. *If you choose to calculate longhand, ALL calculations must be shown or you will be deducted points.*

Project Background:

Note: The following problem is taken from a standardized, globally-used EVM assessment and reflects the basics of EVM.

To maintain their competitive position in the robotics market, the RAMBOTICS Corporation needs to develop a new generation robot.

They have initiated a project to achieve this goal. The project will commence 1 January 2010.

The project is comprised of the tasks in Table 1 (next page). Predecessors, task duration, and the number of personnel required to achieve the task in that duration are also provided.

Part 1: Requirements

Construct a Gantt Bar Chart for the project and determine Budget At Completion (BAC) for the project. Assume that RAMBOTICS Corporation has access to unlimited resources; that personnel cost are blended costs at $10,000 per month per person, and that there are no project costs other than personnel costs. A task cannot commence until all its predecessors have been completed.

Table 06.01: Original Task List and Budgeted Effort

ID	Job Description	Immediate Predecessors	Planned Duration (Months)	Staff (Number)
A	Electrical Design	Start	4	6
B	Assemble Boards	A	4	3
C	Test Boards	B	2	2
D	Software Design	Start	4	1
E	Programming	D	2	2
F	Software Testing	E	2	2
G	Robot Body Design	A	4	2
H	Robot Construction	G	2	2
I	Final Assembly	C,F,H	2	2

Part 2: Earned Value Calculations

After eight months project progress is determined as detailed in Table 2. Predecessors remain the same.

Table 06.02: Progress at the End of Month Eight

ID	Job Description	Effort to Date (Person Months)	Outstanding Duration (Months)	Staff Number
A	Electrical Design	30	0	0
B	Assemble Boards	9	1	3
C	Test Boards	0	2	2
D	Software Design	4	0	0
E	Programming	8	1	2
F	Software Testing	0	4	2
G	Robot Body Design	6	1	2
H	Robot Construction	0	2	2
I	Final Assembly	0	2	2

Part 2: Earned Value Calculations

Using the information in Table 2 (prior page), and the original details, update your Gantt Chart showing the remaining work, and estimate the PV (BCWS), AC (ACWP) and EV (BCWP) for each task at the end of month eight.

For the project:

- What is the Cost Variance (CV)?
- What is the Schedule Variance (SV)?
- What is the Cost Performance Index (CPI)?
- What is the Schedule Performance Index (SPI)?
- What is the Estimate at Completion (EAC)?

Grading: Final Project

You'll need to respond to these questions as part of Unit 6's tracking progress assignment.

6.1 Gantt Chart

6.1.1 Correctly depicts task level Gantt?

6.1.2 Correctly depicts task precedence relationships?

6.1.3 Correctly depicts task durations?

6.1.4 Correctly depicts resource levels?

6.2 Gantt Chart Updated (8 month progress tracking)

6.2.1 Correctly depicts Effort to Date?

6.2.2 Correctly depicts Outstanding Duration?

6.2.3 Correctly depicts Staffing Changes?

6.3 EVM Performance Measures (8 month progress)

6.3.1 Cost Variance (CV) correctly calculated?

6.3.2 Schedule Variance (SV) correctly calculated?

6.3.3 Cost Performance Index (CPI) correctly calculated?

6.3.4 Schedule Performance Index (SPI) correctly calculated?

Appendices

Appendices: Contents

These appendices offer the reader tool templates, examples to follow, and information for help in completing the assigned chapter exercises:

Appendix-A: The Gauchito Rocket Assembly Project Plan©

Ansari X Prize Gauchito Rocket

Mohave, California

Table of Contents

Executive Summary:

Space Systems Technologies Corporation "SSTC" is a World Wide Leader in providing business solutions. Space Systems Technologies Corporation will engineer and build a 7/8 scale model of the Ansari X Gauchito Rocket. The projects start date is May 22, 2011 the end date is July 26, 2011. The order of magnitude estimate for the project budget will be **$63,000.00**.

With the requirements in this project, the Project Scope, Project Proposal, Budget Utilization, Cost, Constraints, Requirements, Project Plan, Responsibilities and the Risk Factors, have all been discussed and worked on.

Space Systems Technologies Corporation the engineering firm has contracted for the following reasons:

- The personnel are highly skilled and experienced in the field.
- Over 30 years experience in successful engineering.

In conclusion, Space Systems Technologies Corporation is a firm specializing in the production of built to scale fully functioning models.

Key Stakeholders:

Pablo de Leon & Associates along with the members of Space Systems Technologies Corporation are the key stakeholders for the Ansari X Gauchito Rocket project. Burt Rutan and the Scaled Composites Corporation is the direct customer for whom this assembly project is invoiced.

Business needs:

Pablo de Leon & Associates requires Space Systems Technologies Corporation to build a functioning scaled rocket based on their design for entry into the Ansari X Prize Cup. This scaled rocket prototype will allow Pablo de Leon to test their design for reduced cost and prove the feasibility of building a full sized rocket.

Proposal 7/8 Scale Ansari X Gauchito Rocket:

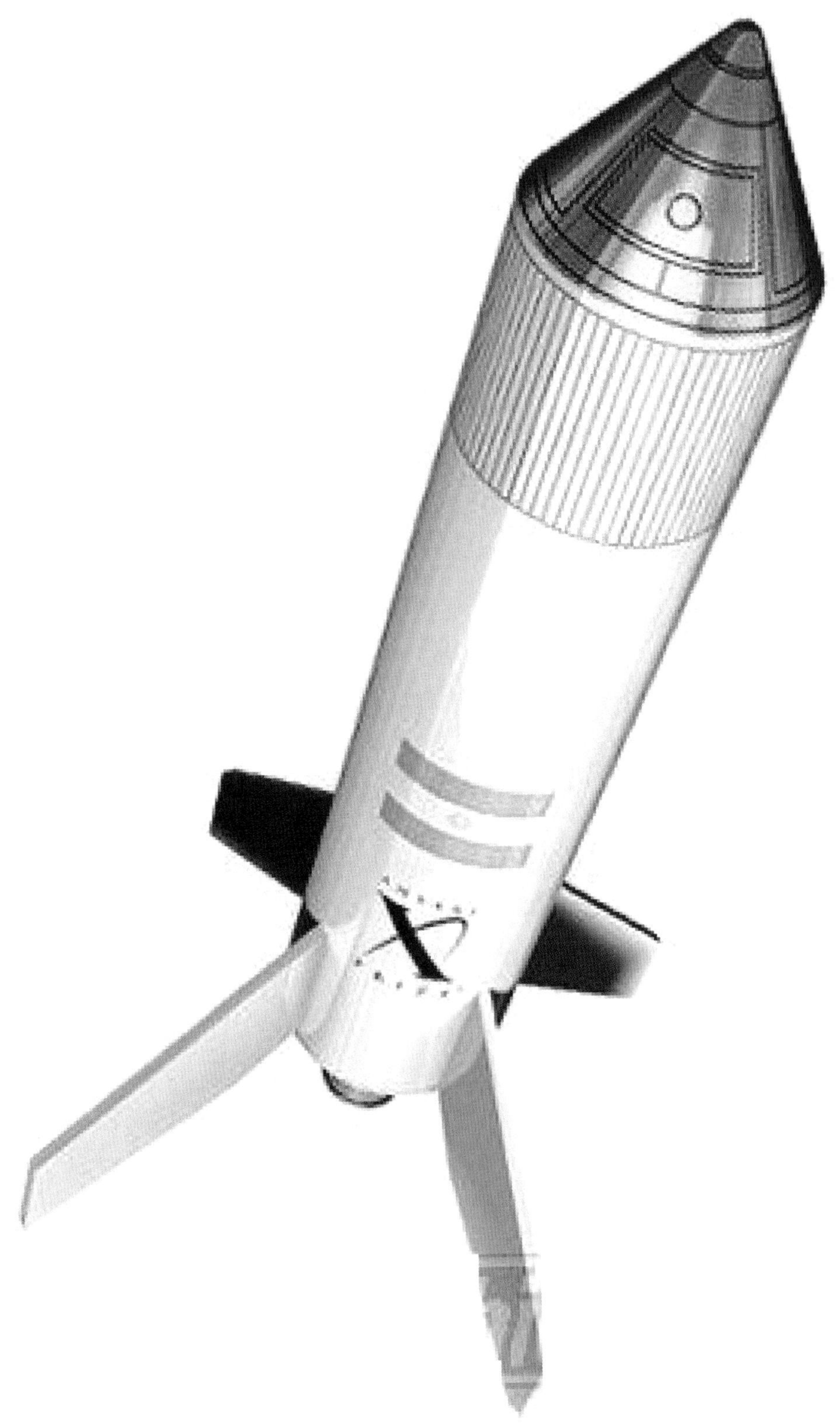

1.0 Scope Management Plan:

1.1 Scope Definition

The project scope for the Gauchito rocket will be defined by the project charter and preliminary scope statement as well as the scope management plan and all approved change requests. The work breakdown structure presents the project deliverables in a hierarchical manner and the definition will include the completed work breakdown structure down to the work package level. The work breakdown structure will be based upon the construction plan, which will be strictly adhered to. In order to ensure proper definition of scope the Project Manager will meet with all of the key personnel regarding every facet of this project. All phases of the project will be broken down according to amount of effort required into smaller work packages.

1.2 Scope Documentation

The project scope will be documented through an engineering specs descriptive document that is provided by the customer and has been inputted into the project charter. If there are any discrepancies between the product description and the product requirements, as the product description states the rocket must be 37 feet long, the project charter requires a 7/8 scale which is a 43 foot long rocket, then the project manager and the team will discuss this with the customer and define the actual length. There will be an internal central database set up for this project specifically to allow all project team members access to the same information regarding the exact scope for this project. All documentation specific to this project shall be archived and tracked within this database.

1.3 Scope Verification

The project scope shall be verified through the project scope statement, the project scope management plan, a constant communication with the project sponsor to ensure the deliverables are being met and understood. An inspection of each deliverable shall be performed and shall be compared to the construction plan and the work breakdown structure. The scope deliverables are understood to be as follows:

1.0 ASSEMBLE ENGINE MOUNT

2.0 FIN PREPARATION

3.0 MARK FIN AND LAUNCH LUG LINES

4.0 INSERTING ENGINE MOUNT

5.0 ATTACH FINS

6.0 ATTACH SHOCK CORD

7.0 ASSEMBLE NOSE CONE

8.0 ATTACH PARACHUTE/SHOCK CORD

9.0 ATTACH LAUNCH LUG

10.0 PAINTING THE ROCKET

11.0 APPLICATION OF DECALS

12.0 APPLYING CLEAR COAT

13.0 DISPLAY NOZZLE ASSEMBLY

14.0 ROCKET PREFLIGHT

15.0 PREPARE FOR TEST LAUNCH

1.4 Scope Management

The project scope will be managed through the utilization of change requests to the project and shall be reviewed by the subject matter expert it affects, the project manager, and the sponsor. Identification of any risk to the project regarding the change as well as the effect on the schedule of the project and cost will be considered. No changes will be approved until the project manager and team meet with the sponsor to validate the scope. The project manager and customer need to meet to get the customers feedback on any requested changes after they have been validated through the scope to ensure that all of the deliverables are still being met if the change is approved. The project manager and the sponsor must both sign off and approve any changes requested. Any and all corrective actions that are suggested will be considered in the same manner as the requested changes. Corrective actions that need to be taken will be signed off on by the project manager and the sponsor and will be implemented by the project manager. The following change order form will be utilized during the duration of this project.

Project Scope Change Order

Project Name: Ansari X Prize Cup-Gauchito Rocket

Project Manager: Julie Davis

Project Tracking Number: PMGT 605-001 Date:

Summary of Change:

Rationale for Change:

Brief overview of the impact of this change on . . .

- Project schedule:

- Quality of deliverables:

- Costs:

- Stakeholders and/or core team members:

- Other deliverables, including amount and quality:

Change approved by (signatures):

Sponsor Jeff Tyler: ______________________________________ Date: __________

Project Manager Julie Davis: _________________________________ Date: ________

The project scope will also be managed through the project scope statement, the work breakdown structure, the project scope management plan, performance reports, as well as any approved change requests, and all work performance information. The implemented change control procedures will be followed with no exceptions, Variance analysis shall be utilized when needed.

1.5 Scope Control

The project scope will be controlled by utilizing the project scope statement, work breakdown structure, work breakdown structure dictionary, project scope management plan, all project performance reports, all approved change requests, and work performance information, which are the scope inputs of the project. The tools used will be the change management plan, variance analysis, any replanning needed to stay within the scope of the project and on task to complete the deliverables, as well as the utilization of the configuration management system. The outputs for the scope control will include any project scope updates, all work breakdown structure updates, all scope baseline updates, any requested changes, any recommended corrective actions, any organizational process asset updates, and any updates to the project management plan. All changes, including a preliminary high-level evaluation of schedule, cost, and labor etc..., will be presented to the Configuration Control Board "CCB" immediately as time is of the essence in the short-term project to determine if any changes should be approved.

1.5.1 Causation of Scope Changes

Please note the most frequent causes of scope change requests include:

- Errors in Omissions-Change in requirements which would result in schedule delays and cost increases which are not allowed in this project at all, due to the short time frame and the race to win the Ansari X Prize.
- Value-Adding Opportunities-The unforeseen advent of new technology that could add value to the project. Maintain the scope of the project if the new opportunity does not have sufficient return on investment value to offset any risk that could be involved utilizing the new product. We are contracted to utilize only those tool sets which were previously agreed upon. No changes will be acceptable unless signed off on by the CCB, The PM, and the Sponsor.
- Competitive Pressures-Other competitors getting closer to being the first do develop the rocket that will win the contest may cause our team to have to up the schedule and work holidays and weekends.
- Schedule Slippage- Can sometimes force the team to reduce the scope of the project. This is not an option with this project as it is so detailed and short term. Do not forget this team wants to be first to have a fully functioning rocket to enable Pablo de Leon & Associates to win the Ansari X Prize Cup.

1.6 Scope Development & Breakdown

Process for developing the WBS from the detailed scope statement will be completed through the use of subject matter experts "SME's". A project team review will be conducted after the project manager breaks down each deliverable into the level of the work package, where it can be assigned to one person, and a cost control account created for that work package, which must be less than 80 hours. For example, cutting and sanding the fins is decomposed into cutting fins as one task and sanding fins as one task. . The tasks may then each be further decomposed further into Cutting fin #1, Sanding fin #1, with a work package for each fin for cutting, and one for sanding.

1.7 Formal Scope Verification

Formal verification of the deliverable will be done through the utilization of the WBS, the Project Charter, the Scope Management Plan as well as any signed, approved change requests and updates. This will be done through reviewing the deliverables and their requirements at each milestone by the PM and Sponsor.

1.8 Formal Acceptance

Formal acceptance of deliverable will be obtained through the above stated verification process so that when the Rocket is complete, the customer can review all of the formal verification requirements and test procedures that the sponsor previously signed off on with the PM. Formal acceptance is considered complete when the customer comes to pick up the rocket no later than 3 days after completion of contract deliverables.

2.0 Schedule Management Plan:

Objectives

The purpose of this document is to define and document how changes to the schedule will be managed for this project.

Overview

The project shall be managed by means of an established Work Breakdown Structure (WBS). This WBS shall be the basis for establishing project schedule and for definition of project tasks and deliverables. The Project Manager (PM) shall collect actual completion and resource utilization data from the team members in order to calculate actual performance against predicted cost and schedule. This data shall be presented to the program manager in the form of a weekly project status report.

Task status and resource utilization statistics shall be reported to the PM utilizing the elements of the WBS. The project shall be controlled using Microsoft Project to establish project tasks, dependencies and schedule. WBS activity decomposition shall be such that tasks can be completed in a maximum one week time frame. Credit for task progress shall only be awarded upon task completion. Team members shall provide weekly statistics on resource expenditures by task as well as information concerning task completion. This information shall then be compiled to provide schedule status to the Sponsor.

2.1 Assumptions

- The materials and equipment will arrive one week prior to project start date
- All necessary personnel will be available at the time of the project start
- The contracts will be followed as written without any delays or difficulties

2.2 Schedule Variance Response Process

Once the project schedule is base-lined, the PM is responsible to ensure that actual effort, start and end dates are entered for each activity. This data is essential to establish whether schedule variances exist. When variance is required the PM is the primary decision maker, for Major Problems the Sponsor will be the ultimate decision maker.

2.3 Major Problems

- On a regular basis, but not less than once per week the PM will create an earned value report. Using this report, the PM will identify and isolate both positive and negative schedule variances.
- When a variance exceeds +/- 5% the PM must determine what is causing the variance and decide if the variance requires corrective action.
- If corrective action is required, it is up to the discretion of the Sponsor as to whether a schedule change request is necessary, or if the variance can be absorbed within the existing project schedule. If a schedule change request is necessary, it is submitted through the standard schedule change control procedures as outlined below.
- Notification will be sent to the Sponsor and all Functional Managers via email, when required a copy of the signed change request form will be attached.

2.4 Minor Problems

- Minor variances will be absorbed into project through schedule changes or shifting of project resources.

2.5 Schedule Change Control Processes

1.1. All schedule modifications must go though the following Change Control process:

1) Identify and assess the schedule change.
2) Fill out a "*Change Request Form*" and submit the "*Change Request Form*" along with required supporting documentation to the PM.
3) The PM will review the change request and may possibly request additional documentation prior to review by the CCB.
4) The CCB will evaluate the change. Using the "*Change Request Form*", the CCB will mark the change as:

   1.1.4.1. Approved, in which case the PM will incorporate the change and adjust other project planning factors as necessary.

1.1.4.2. Approved pending additional supporting documentation, in which case the PM will specify and coordinate gathering of the required documentation, incorporate the change and adjust other project planning factors as necessary.

1.1.4.3. Denied, in which case the PM will notify the requestor of the status and reason for denial.

5) The PM will document the Change Request outcome and as necessary update WBS and schedule documentation if impacted.

2.6 Schedule References

A WBS for the level the project will be tracked is in Appendix WT.

Resource Leveled Project Plan is available in Appendix WR.

Time based Network Diagram is available in Appendix ND.

Milestone Chat is available in Appendix MM

Change Request form is in Appendix CR

Appendix MM: Milestones

Name	Finish Date
1.0 ASSEMBLE ENGINE MOUNT	6/5/2011
2.0 FIN PREPARATION	5/25/2011
3.0 MARK FIN AND LAUNCH LUG LINES	5/30/2011
4.0 INSERTING ENGINE MOUNT	6/9/2011
5.0 ATTACH FINS	6/16/2011
6.0 ATTACH SHOCK CORD	5/26/2011
7.0 ASSEMBLE NOSE CONE	5/23/2011
8.0 ATTACH PARACHUTE/SHOCK CORD	6/2/2011
9.0 ATTACH LAUNCH LUG	6/22/2011
10.0 PAINTING THE ROCKET	6/29/2011
11.0 APPLICATION OF DECALS	7/6/2011
12.0 APPLYING CLEAR COAT	7/7/2011
13.0 DISPLAY NOZZLE ASSEMBLY	7/13/2011
14.0 ROCKET PREFLIGHT	7/20/2011
15.0 PREPARE FOR TEST LAUNCH	7/26/2011

Appendix CR: Change Request Form

Project Name:

Date Request Submitted:

Title of Change Request

Change Order Number:

Submitted by: (name and contact information)

Change Category:

☐**Scope** ☐**Schedule** ☐**Cost** ☐**Technology** ☐**Other**

Description of change requested:

Events that made this change necessary or desirable:

Justification for the change/why it is needed/desired to continue/complete the project:

Impact of the proposed change on:

Scope:

Schedule:

Cost:

Staffing:

Risk:

Other:

Suggested implementation if the change request is approved:

Required approvals:

Name/Title	Date	Approve/Reject

Reference:

Schwable, Kathy, Information Technology Project Management, Fourth Edition, Thomson Course Technology, 2011.

Found at www.course.com/mis/schwable4e.

Appendix WT: WBS at tracked level

Name	Duration	Start Date	Finish Date
1.0 ASSEMBLE ENGINE MOUNT	**95**	**5/22/2011**	**6/5/2011**
1.1 Measure, Mark and Cut Engine Tube	*35*	*5/22/2011*	*5/26/2011*
-1.2 Cut Engine Tube	*2*	*5/26/2011*	*5/26/2011*
-1.3 Glue, Tube, Assemble Hook	*7*	*5/26/2011*	*5/30/2011*
-1.4 Assemble Mylar Ring to Tube	*9*	*5/30/2011*	*5/30/2011*
-1.5 Assemble Yellow Engine Block to Engine Mount Tube	*10*	*5/31/2011*	*5/31/2011*
-1.6 Assemble Centering Rings	*22*	*6/1/2011*	*6/2/2011*
-1.7 Application of Glue Fillets	*10*	*6/5/2011*	*6/5/2011*
2.0 FIN PREPARATION	**30**	**5/22/2011**	**5/25/2011**
-2.1 Sand/Cut fins	*8*	*5/22/2011*	*5/22/2011*
-2.2 Cutting Out Fins	*12*	*5/23/2011*	*5/24/2011*
-2.3 Stack and Sand Fins	*10*	*5/24/2011*	*5/25/2011*
3.0 MARK FIN AND LAUNCH LUG LINES	**33**	**5/22/2011**	**5/30/2011**
-3.1 Cut - Tape	*13*	*5/22/2011*	*5/25/2011*
-3.2 Remove guide, connect fins and lug lines, extend LL line	*16*	*5/25/2011*	*5/30/2011*
-3.3 Extend Launch Lug Line	*4*	*5/30/2011*	*5/30/2011*
4.0 INSERTING ENGINE MOUNT	**43**	**6/6/2011**	**6/9/2011**
-4.1 Mark inside of tube @ 5/8" where LL is	*7*	*6/6/2011*	*6/6/2011*
-4.2 Glue Tube	*5*	*6/6/2011*	*6/7/2011*
-4.3 Assemble Engine Hook	*18*	*6/7/2011*	*6/8/2011*
-4.4 Gluing Center Body Ring	*13*	*6/9/2011*	*6/9/2011*
5.0 ATTACH FINS	**73**	**6/12/2011**	**6/16/2011**
-5.1 Attach Fin #1	*10*	*6/12/2011*	*6/13/2011*
-5.2 Attach Fin #2	*10*	*6/12/2011*	*6/13/2011*
-5.3 Attach Fin #3	*10*	*6/12/2011*	*6/13/2011*
-5.4 Attach Fin #4	*10*	*6/12/2011*	*6/13/2011*
-5.5 Check Fin Alignment	*16*	*6/13/2011*	*6/15/2011*
-5.6 Allow glue to dry	*17*	*6/15/2011*	*6/16/2011*
6.0 ATTACH SHOCK CORD	**44**	**5/22/2011**	**5/26/2011**
-6.1 Cut out shock cord mount	*5*	*5/22/2011*	*5/22/2011*
-6.2 First Glue Application	*12*	*5/22/2011*	*5/24/2011*
-6.3 Second Glue Application	*8*	*5/24/2011*	*5/25/2011*
-6.4 Squeeze and Hold	*6*	*5/25/2011*	*5/25/2011*
-6.5 Attaching Shock Cord Mount	*13*	*5/25/2011*	*5/26/2011*

7.0 ASSEMBLE NOSE CONE	**16**	**5/22/2011**	**5/23/2011**
-7.1 Glue nose cone	*16*	*5/22/2011*	*5/23/2011*
8.0 ATTACH PARACHUTE/SHOCK CORD	**18**	**5/30/2011**	**6/2/2011**
-8.1 Attach Lines	*7*	*5/30/2011*	*5/31/2011*
-8.2 Attach Parachute	*5*	*5/31/2011*	*6/1/2011*
-8.3 Tie Lines	*6*	*6/1/2011*	*6/2/2011*
9.0 ATTACH LAUNCH LUG	**32**	**6/19/2011**	**6/22/2011**
-9.1 Glue launch lines	*4*	*6/19/2011*	*6/19/2011*
-9.2 Application of Glue Fillets	*28*	*6/19/2011*	*6/22/2011*
10.0 PAINTING THE ROCKET	**64**	**6/22/2011**	**6/29/2011**
-10.1 Apply first coat	*16*	*6/22/2011*	*6/23/2011*
-10.2 Sand	*8*	*6/23/2011*	*6/23/2011*
-10.3 Apply final coat	*40*	*6/26/2011*	*6/29/2011*
11.0 APPLICATION OF DECALS	**35**	**6/29/2011**	**7/6/2011**
-11.1 Apply first decal	*5*	*6/29/2011*	*6/29/2011*
-11.2 Apply second decal	*5*	*6/29/2011*	*6/30/2011*
-11.3 Apply third decal	*5*	*6/30/2011*	*6/30/2011*
-11.4 Apply fourth decal	*5*	*6/30/2011*	*7/3/2011*
-11.5 Apply fifth decal	*5*	*7/3/2011*	*7/5/2011*
-11.6 Apply sixth Decal	*5*	*7/5/2011*	*7/5/2011*
-11.7 Apply seventh Decal	*5*	*7/5/2011*	*7/6/2011*
12.0 APPLYING CLEAR COAT	**16**	**7/6/2011**	**7/7/2011**
-12.1 Apply clear coat to entire rocket	*16*	*7/6/2011*	*7/7/2011*
13.0 DISPLAY NOZZLE ASSEMBLY	**32**	**7/10/2011**	**7/13/2011**
-13.1 Spray Nozzle Base White	*18*	*7/10/2011*	*7/11/2011*
-13.2 Apply Glue	*14*	*7/12/2011*	*7/13/2011*
14.0 ROCKET PREFLIGHT	**42**	**7/13/2011**	**7/20/2011**
14.1 prepare	*13*	*7/13/2011*	*7/17/2011*
14.2 Spike	*4*	*7/17/2011*	*7/17/2011*
14.3 Fold	*4*	*7/17/2011*	*7/18/2011*
14.4 Roll	*4*	*7/18/2011*	*7/18/2011*
14.5 Re-insert	*17*	*7/18/2011*	*7/20/2011*
15.0 PREPARE FOR TEST LAUNCH	**32**	**7/21/2011**	**7/26/2011**
-15.1 Insert Engine	*32*	*7/21/2011*	*7/26/2011*

Appendix WG: Gantt

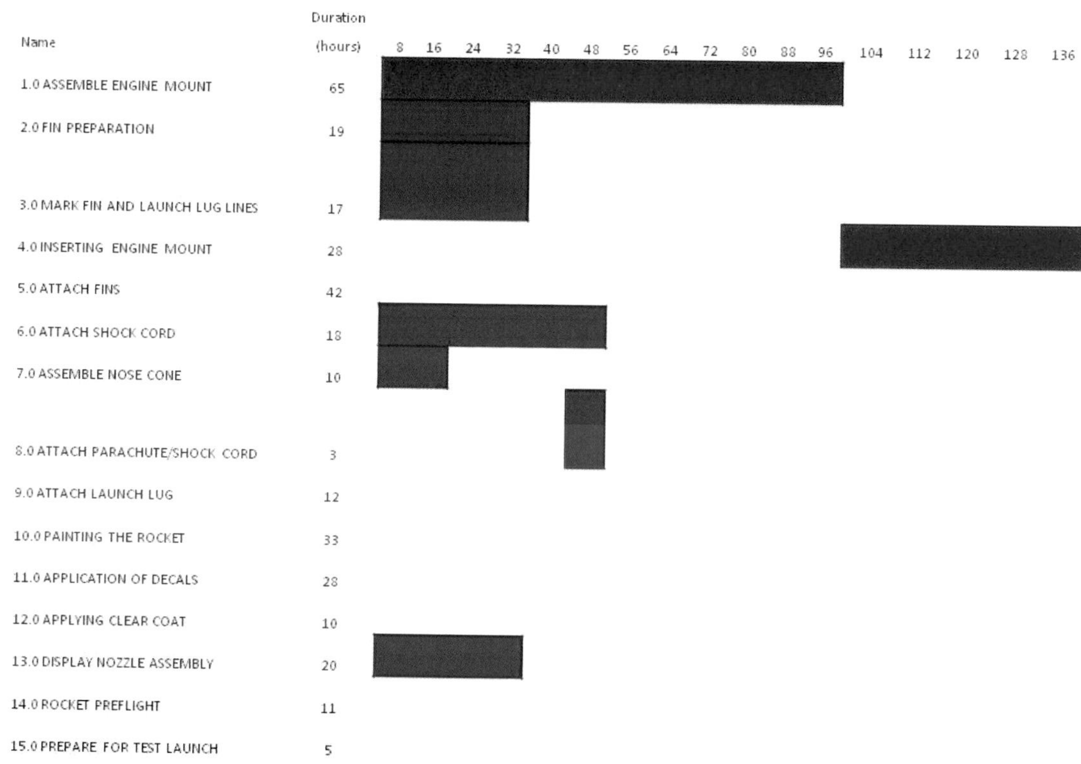

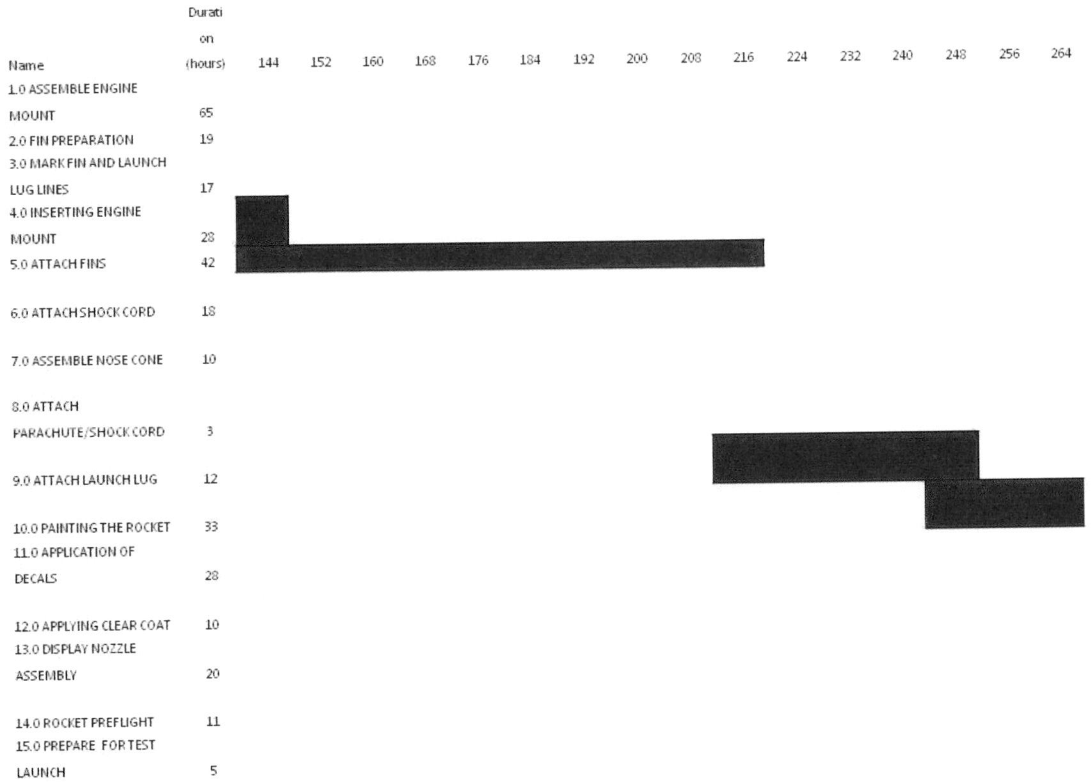
Name
Duration (hours)
144
152
160
168
176
184
192
200
208
216
224
232
240
248
256
264
1.0 ASSEMBLE ENGINE MOUNT
65
2.0 FIN PREPARATION
19
3.0 MARK FIN AND LAUNCH LUG LINES
17
4.0 INSERTING ENGINE MOUNT
28
5.0 ATTACH FINS
42
6.0 ATTACH SHOCK CORD
18
7.0 ASSEMBLE NOSE CONE
10
8.0 ATTACH PARACHUTE/SHOCK CORD
3
9.0 ATTACH LAUNCH LUG
12
10.0 PAINTING THE ROCKET
33
11.0 APPLICATION OF DECALS
28
12.0 APPLYING CLEAR COAT
10
13.0 DISPLAY NOZZLE ASSEMBLY
20
14.0 ROCKET PREFLIGHT
11
15.0 PREPARE FOR TEST LAUNCH
5

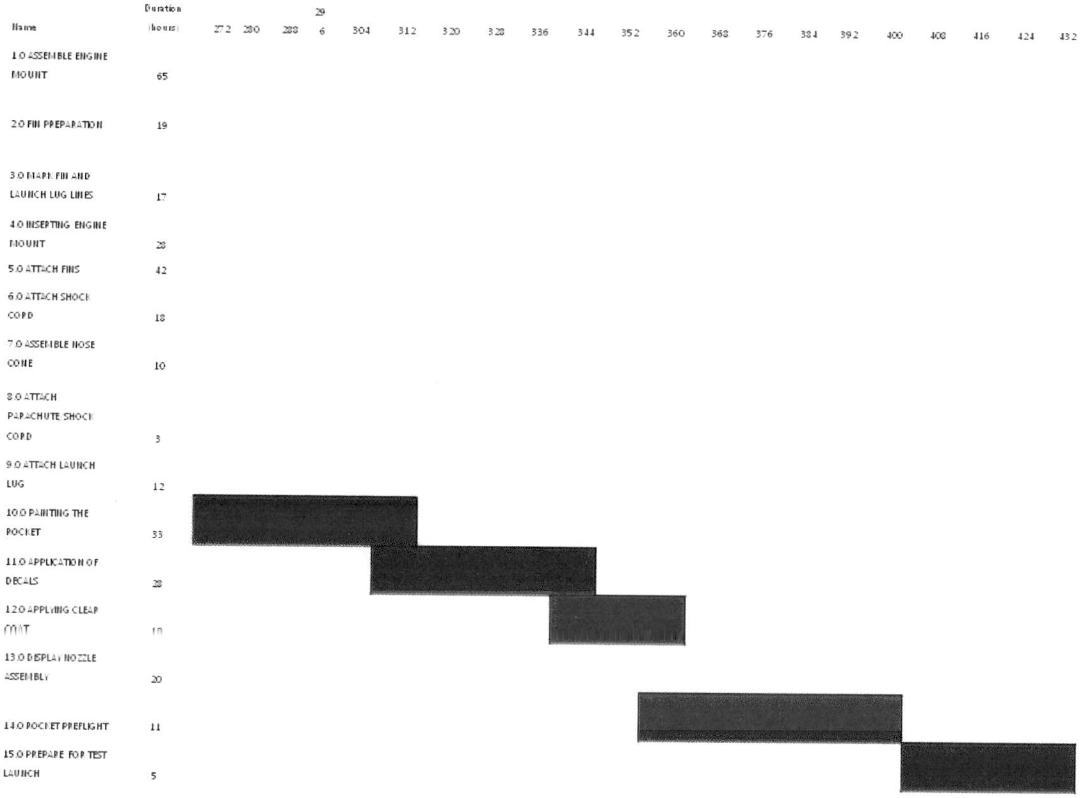

Name	Duration (hours)	272	280	288	296	304	312	320	328	336	344	352	360	368	376	384	392	400	408	416	424	432
1.0 ASSEMBLE ENGINE MOUNT	65																					
2.0 FIN PREPARATION	19																					
3.0 MARK FIN AND LAUNCH LUG LINES	17																					
4.0 INSERTING ENGINE MOUNT	28																					
5.0 ATTACH FINS	42																					
6.0 ATTACH SHOCK CORD	18																					
7.0 ASSEMBLE NOSE CONE	10																					
8.0 ATTACH PARACHUTE/SHOCK CORD	3																					
9.0 ATTACH LAUNCH LUG	12																					
10.0 PAINTING THE ROCKET	33																					
11.0 APPLICATION OF DECALS	28																					
12.0 APPLYING CLEAR COAT	10																					
13.0 DISPLAY NOZZLE ASSEMBLY	20																					
14.0 ROCKET PREFLIGHT	11																					
15.0 PREPARE FOR TEST LAUNCH	5																					

Appendix WR: WBS with resources leveled

Name	Duration	Start Date	Finish Date	Resource Names
1.0 ASSEMBLE ENGINE MOUNT	**95**	**5/22/2011**	**6/5/2011**	
1.1 Measure, Mark and Cut Engine Tube	*35*	*5/22/2011*	*5/26/2011*	
-1.1.1 Lay ruler along engine tube	5	5/22/2011	5/22/2011	Fitter #1
-1.1.2 Measure engine from left of engine tube tube @ 1/8"	5	5/22/2011	5/23/2011	Drafstman #1
-1.1.3 Mark left end of Engine Tube @ 1/8'	5	5/23/2011	5/23/2011	Drafstman #1
-1.1.4 Measure engine from left of engine tube @ 3/4"	5	5/23/2011	5/24/2011	Drafstman #1
-1.1.5 Mark from left of Engine Tube @ 3/4"	5	5/24/2011	5/25/2011	Drafstman #1
-1.1.6 Measure engine tube from left of engine tube @ 11/2"	5	5/25/2011	5/25/2011	Drafstman #1
-1.1.7 Mark from left of Engine Tube @ 1 1/2"	5	5/25/2011	5/26/2011	Drafstman #1
-1.2 Cut Engine Tube	*2*	*5/26/2011*	*5/26/2011*	
-1.2.1 Cut Slit of 1/8" @ 1 1/2 inch Mark on Engine Tube	2	5/26/2011	5/26/2011	Cutter #1
-1.3 Glue, Tube, Assemble Hook	*7*	*5/26/2011*	*5/30/2011*	
-1.3.1 Apply thin line of glue completely around engine at 3/4" mark	2	5/26/2011	5/26/2011	Gluer #1
-1.3.2 Position Hook per diagram	2	5/26/2011	5/30/2011	Fitter #1
-1.3.3 Insert Engine Hook into 1/8" Slit on Engine Mount Tube	3	5/30/2011	5/30/2011	Fitter #1
-1.4 Assemble Mylar Ring to Tube	*9*	*5/30/2011*	*5/30/2011*	
-1.4.1 Slide Mylar ring onto Engine Mount tube at 3/4" mark	1	5/30/2011	5/30/2011	Fitter #1
-1.4.2 Let Dry	8	5/30/2011	5/30/2011	
-1.5 Assemble Yellow Engine Block to Engine Mount Tube	*10*	*5/31/2011*	*5/31/2011*	
-1.5.1 Apply glue inside front of Engine Mount tube	1	5/31/2011	5/31/2011	Gluer #1
-1.5.2 Insert Yellow Engine Block flush with the right end per diagram	1	5/31/2011	5/31/2011	Fitter #1
-1.5.3 Let Dry	8	5/31/2011	5/31/2011	

-1.6 Assemble Centering Rings	*22*	*6/1/2011*	*6/2/2011*	
-1.6.1 Remove Centering rings from card with modeling knife	2	6/1/2011	6/1/2011	Cutter #1
-1.6.2 Apply thin line of Glue around engine mount tube @ 1/8" mark	1	6/1/2011	6/1/2011	Gluer #1
-1.6.3 Slide notched Centering Ring onto glued line @ 1/8" mark	1	6/1/2011	6/1/2011	Fitter #1
-1.6.4 Let Glue Set	8	6/1/2011	6/2/2011	
-1.6.5 Apply thin line of Glue to opposite side of notched center ring flush with end of engine mount tube	1	6/2/2011	6/2/2011	Gluer #1
-1.6.6 Slide unnotched Centering Ring in place over glue flush with end of engine tube mount	1	6/2/2011	6/2/2011	Fitter #1
-1.6.7 Let Dry	8	6/2/2011	6/2/2011	
-1.7 Application of Glue Fillets	*10*	*6/5/2011*	*6/5/2011*	
-1.7.1 Apply Glue Fillets to both sides of Centering Rings for reinforcement	2	6/5/2011	6/5/2011	Gluer #1
-1.7.2 Let Dry	8	6/5/2011	6/5/2011	
2.0 FIN PREPARATION	**30**	**5/22/2011**	**5/25/2011**	
-2.1 Sand/Cut fins	*8*	*5/22/2011*	*5/22/2011*	
-2.1.1 Sand Laser Cut Balsa Sheet w/Fine Sandpaper	8	5/22/2011	5/22/2011	Sander-I #1
-2.2 Cutting Out Fins	*12*	*5/23/2011*	*5/24/2011*	
2.2.1 Cut out fin #1 w/modeling knife	3	5/23/2011	5/23/2011	Cutter #2
2.2.2 Cut out fin #2 w/modeling knife	3	5/23/2011	5/23/2011	Cutter #2
2.2.3 Cut out fin #3 w/ modeling knife	3	5/23/2011	5/24/2011	Cutter #2
2.2.4 Cut out fin #4 w/modeling knife	3	5/24/2011	5/24/2011	Cutter #2
-2.3 Stack and Sand Fins	*10*	*5/24/2011*	*5/25/2011*	
-2.3.1 Stack Fins	2	5/24/2011	5/24/2011	Fitter #2
-2.3.2 Sand Edges of fins	8	5/24/2011	5/25/2011	Sander-I #1
3.0 MARK FIN AND LAUNCH LUG LINES	**33**	**5/22/2011**	**5/30/2011**	
-3.1 Cut - Tape	*13*	*5/22/2011*	*5/25/2011*	
-3.1.2 Cut out tube marking guide	2	5/22/2011	5/22/2011	Cutter #3
-3.1.2 Tape tube marking guide around body tube	3	5/23/2011	5/23/2011	Fitter #3
-3.1.3 Mark body tube at arrows	4	5/23/2011	5/23/2011	Draftsman #2
-3.1.4 Mark Launch Lug Line as LL on Body tube	4	5/24/2011	5/25/2011	Drafstman #2
-3.2 Remove guide, connect fins and lug lines, extend LL line	*16*	*5/25/2011*	*5/30/2011*	

Task	Duration	Start	Finish	Resource
-3.2.1 Remove Tube Marking guide from body tube	4	5/25/2011	5/25/2011	Fitter #3
-3.2.2 Connect Fins using door frame	4	5/25/2011	5/26/2011	Fitter #3
-3.2.3 Connect launch lug lines using door frame	8	5/26/2011	5/30/2011	Fitter #3
-3.3 Extend Launch Lug Line	*4*	*5/30/2011*	*5/30/2011*	
-3.3.1 Extend launch lug line 3 3/4" from end of tube	4	5/30/2011	5/30/2011	Drafstman #2
4.0 INSERTING ENGINE MOUNT	**43**	**6/6/2011**	**6/9/2011**	
-4.1 Mark inside of tube @ 5/8" where LL is	*7*	*6/6/2011*	*6/6/2011*	
-4.1.1 Measure inside tube to 5/8" position on tube	4	6/6/2011	6/6/2011	Drafstman #1
-4.1.2 Mark inside tube at 5/8"	3	6/6/2011	6/6/2011	Drafstman #1
-4.2 Glue Tube	*5*	*6/6/2011*	*6/7/2011*	
-4.2.1 Measure inside rear of body tube to 1 3/4' position on tube	3	6/6/2011	6/7/2011	Drafstman #1
-4.2.2 Use finger to smear glue 1 3/4" inside rear of body tube along LL.	2	6/7/2011	6/7/2011	Gluer #1
-4.3 Assemble Engine Hook	*18*	*6/7/2011*	*6/8/2011*	
-4.3.1 Align engine hook with LL line	5	6/7/2011	6/8/2011	Fitter #1
-4.3.2 Insert engine mount into body tube until centering ring is even w/the 5/8" glue mark	5	6/8/2011	6/8/2011	Fitter #1
-4.3.3 Let Dry	8	6/8/2011	6/8/2011	
-4.4 Gluing Center Body Ring	*13*	*6/9/2011*	*6/9/2011*	
-4.4.1 Locate scrap piece of balsa to apply glue	1	6/9/2011	6/9/2011	Fitter #1
-4.4.2 Apply glue to centering/body tube joint	4	6/9/2011	6/9/2011	Gluer #1
-4.4.3 Let Dry	8	6/9/2011	6/9/2011	
5.0 ATTACH FINS	**73**	**6/12/2011**	**6/16/2011**	
-5.1 Attach Fin #1	*10*	*6/12/2011*	*6/13/2011*	
-5.1.1 Apply thin layer of glue to edge of fin	3	6/12/2011	6/12/2011	Gluer #3
-5.1.2 Allow to dry (1 minute for model)	1	6/12/2011	6/12/2011	
-5.1.3 Apply second layer of glue to edge of fin	2	6/12/2011	6/12/2011	Gluer #3
-5.1.4 Attach Fin to body tube along one of fin lines flush w/end	4	6/12/2011	6/13/2011	Fitter #3
-5.2 Attach Fin #2	*10*	*6/12/2011*	*6/13/2011*	
-5.2.1 Apply thin layer of glue to edge of fin#2	3	6/12/2011	6/12/2011	Gluer #2
-5.2.2 Allow to dry (1 minute for model)	1	6/12/2011	6/12/2011	
-5.2.3 Apply second layer of glue to edge of fin #2	2	6/12/2011	6/12/2011	Gluer #2
-5.2.4 Attach Fin #2 to body tube along one of fin lines flush w/end	4	6/12/2011	6/13/2011	Fitter #2

-5.3 Attach Fin #3	*10*	*6/12/2011*	*6/13/2011*	
-5.3.1 Apply thin layer of glue to edge of fin #3	3	6/12/2011	6/12/2011	Gluer #1
-5.3.2 Allow to dry (1 minute for model)	1	6/12/2011	6/12/2011	
-5.3.3 Apply second layer of glue to edge of fin #3	2	6/12/2011	6/12/2011	Gluer #1
-5.3.4 Attach Fin #3 to body tube along one of fin lines flush w/end	4	6/12/2011	6/13/2011	Fitter #1
-5.4 Attach Fin #4	*10*	*6/12/2011*	*6/13/2011*	
-5.4.1 Apply thin layer of glue to edge of fin #4	3	6/12/2011	6/12/2011	Gluer #4
-5.4.2 Allow to dry (1 minute for model)	1	6/12/2011	6/12/2011	
-5.4.3 Apply second layer of glue to edge of fin #4	2	6/12/2011	6/12/2011	Gluer #4
-5.4.4 Attach Fin #4 to body tube along one of fin lines flush w/end	4	6/12/2011	6/13/2011	Fitter #4
-5.5 Check Fin Alignment	*16*	*6/13/2011*	*6/15/2011*	
-5.5.1 Check Fin #1 Alignment as shown in diagram	4	6/13/2011	6/13/2011	Draftsman #1
-5.5.2 Check Fin #2 Alignment as shown in diagram	4	6/13/2011	6/14/2011	Draftsman #2
-5.5.3 Check Fin #3 Alignment as shown in diagram	4	6/14/2011	6/14/2011	Draftsman #1
-5.5.4 Check Fin #4 Alignment as shown in diagram	4	6/14/2011	6/15/2011	Draftsman #2
-5.6 Allow glue to dry	*17*	*6/15/2011*	*6/16/2011*	
-5.6.1 Let Glue Set	5	6/15/2011	6/15/2011	
-5.6.2 Stand Rocket on end	4	6/15/2011	6/16/2011	Fitter #1
-5.6.3 let glue dries completely	8	6/16/2011	6/16/2011	
6.0 ATTACH SHOCK CORD	**44**	**5/22/2011**	**5/26/2011**	
-6.1 Cut out shock cord mount	*5*	*5/22/2011*	*5/22/2011*	
-6.1.1 Cut out shock cord from front page	5	5/22/2011	5/22/2011	Cutter #1
-6.2 First Glue Application	*12*	*5/22/2011*	*5/24/2011*	
-6.2.1 Attach shock cord to shock cord mount	4	5/22/2011	5/23/2011	Fitter #5
-6.2.2 Apply glue to shock cord mount	4	5/23/2011	5/23/2011	Gluer #4
-6.2.3 Fold edge of shock cord mount forward over glued shock cord	4	5/23/2011	5/24/2011	Fitter #5
-6.3 Second Glue Application	*8*	*5/24/2011*	*5/25/2011*	
-6.3.1 Apply glue to shock cord mount	4	5/24/2011	5/24/2011	Gluer #4
-6.3.2 Fold forward again-see diagram for clarification	4	5/24/2011	5/25/2011	Fitter #5
-6.4 Squeeze and Hold	*6*	*5/25/2011*	*5/25/2011*	
-6.4.1 Squeeze shock cord/shock cord mount tightly	2	5/25/2011	5/25/2011	Gluer #4
-6.4.2 Hold for 1 minute	4	5/25/2011	5/25/2011	Gluer #4

-6.5 Attaching Shock Cord Mount	*13*	*5/25/2011*	*5/26/2011*	
-6.5.1 Glue mount 1" inside body tube	4	5/25/2011	5/26/2011	Gluer #4,Fitter #5
-6.5.2 Hold until glue sets	1	5/26/2011	5/26/2011	Gluer #4
-6.5.3 Let Dry Completely	8	5/26/2011	5/26/2011	
7.0 ASSEMBLE NOSE CONE	**16**	**5/22/2011**	**5/23/2011**	
-7.1 Glue nose cone	*16*	*5/22/2011*	*5/23/2011*	
-7.1.1 Apply plastic cement to inside rim of nose cone	4	5/22/2011	5/22/2011	Gluer #5
-7.1.2 Press Nose Cone Insert into place over plastic cement inside of nose cone rim	4	5/22/2011	5/22/2011	Fitter #2
-7.1.3 Let Dry Completely	8	5/22/2011	5/23/2011	
8.0 ATTACH PARACHUTE/SHOCK CORD	**18**	**5/30/2011**	**6/2/2011**	
-8.1 Attach Lines	*7*	*5/30/2011*	*5/31/2011*	
-8.1.1 Pass shroud line on parachute through eyelet	7	5/30/2011	5/31/2011	Fitter #1
-8.2 Attach Parachute	*5*	*5/31/2011*	*6/1/2011*	
-8.2.1 Pass parachute through loop in shroud-look to diagram for clarification	5	5/31/2011	6/1/2011	Fitter #1
-8.3 Tie Lines	*6*	*6/1/2011*	*6/2/2011*	
-8.3.1 Tie shock cord to nose cone using a double knot	6	6/1/2011	6/2/2011	Fitter #1
9.0 ATTACH LAUNCH LUG	**32**	**6/19/2011**	**6/22/2011**	
-9.1 Glue launch lines	*4*	*6/19/2011*	*6/19/2011*	
-9.1.1 Glue LL centered onto LL Line on rocket body	4	6/19/2011	6/19/2011	Gluer #1
-9.2 Application of Glue Fillets	*28*	*6/19/2011*	*6/22/2011*	
-9.2.1 Apply glue fillets along launch lug	4	6/19/2011	6/19/2011	Gluer #1
-9.2.2 Apply glue fillets along fin/body tube joints	12	6/20/2011	6/21/2011	Gluer #1
-9.2.3 Smooth each fillet with finger	4	6/21/2011	6/21/2011	Gluer #1
-9.2.4 Let glue dry completely	8	6/21/2011	6/22/2011	
10.0 PAINTING THE ROCKET	**64**	**6/22/2011**	**6/29/2011**	
-10.1 Apply first coat	*16*	*6/22/2011*	*6/23/2011*	
-10.1.1 Spray rocket with white primer	8	6/22/2011	6/22/2011	Painter-I #1
-10.1.2 Let Dry	8	6/22/2011	6/23/2011	
-10.2 Sand	*8*	*6/23/2011*	*6/23/2011*	
-10.1.2 Sand entire rocket	8	6/23/2011	6/23/2011	Sander-I #1,Sander-I #2,Sander-II #1,Sander-II #2
-10.3 Apply final coat	*40*	*6/26/2011*	*6/29/2011*	
-10.3.1 Spray completed rocket with white second coat	8	6/26/2011	6/26/2011	Painter-II

of primer				#1,Painter-II #2
-10.3.2 Let Dry	8	6/26/2011	6/27/2011	
-10.3.3 Spray Nose Cone with Copper paint	16	6/27/2011	6/28/2011	Painter-II #1,Painter-II #2
-10.3.4 Let Dry	8	6/28/2011	6/29/2011	
11.0 APPLICATION OF DECALS	**35**	**6/29/2011**	**7/6/2011**	
-11.1 Apply first decal	*5*	*6/29/2011*	*6/29/2011*	
-11.1.1 Remove First decal from back sheet	1	6/29/2011	6/29/2011	Drafstman #1
-11.1.2 Place on Rocket where indicated	3	6/29/2011	6/29/2011	Drafstman #2
-11.1.3 Rub decal to remove bubbles	1	6/29/2011	6/29/2011	Drafstman #1
-11.2 Apply second decal	*5*	*6/29/2011*	*6/30/2011*	
-11.2.1 Remove second decal from backing sheet	1	6/29/2011	6/29/2011	Drafstman #1
-11.2.2 Place on Rocket where indicated	3	6/29/2011	6/30/2011	Drafstman #2
-11.2.3 Rub decal to remove bubbles	1	6/30/2011	6/30/2011	Drafstman #1
-11.3 Apply third decal	*5*	*6/30/2011*	*6/30/2011*	
-11.3.1 Remove third decal from backing sheet	1	6/30/2011	6/30/2011	Drafstman #1
-11.3.2 Place on Rocket where indicated	3	6/30/2011	6/30/2011	Drafstman #2
-11.3.3 Rub decal to remove bubbles	1	6/30/2011	6/30/2011	Drafstman #1
-11.4 Apply fourth decal	*5*	*6/30/2011*	*7/3/2011*	
-11.4.1 Remove fourth decal from backing sheet	1	6/30/2011	6/30/2011	Drafstman #1
-11.4.2 Place on Rocket where indicated	3	7/3/2011	7/3/2011	Drafstman #2
-11.4.3 Rub decal to remove bubbles	1	7/3/2011	7/3/2011	Drafstman #1
-11.5 Apply fifth decal	*5*	*7/3/2011*	*7/5/2011*	
-11.5.1 Remove fifth decal from backing sheet	1	7/3/2011	7/3/2011	Drafstman #1

-11.5.2 Place on Rocket where indicated	3	7/3/2011	7/3/2011	Drafstman #2
-11.5.3 Rub decal to remove bubbles	1	7/5/2011	7/5/2011	Drafstman #1
-11.6 Apply sixth Decal	*5*	*7/5/2011*	*7/5/2011*	
-11.6.1 Remove sixth decal from backing sheet	1	7/5/2011	7/5/2011	Drafstman #1
-11.6.2 Place on Rocket where indicated	3	7/5/2011	7/5/2011	Drafstman #2
-11.6.3 Rub decal to remove bubbles	1	7/5/2011	7/5/2011	Drafstman #1
-11.7 Apply seventh Decal	*5*	*7/5/2011*	*7/6/2011*	
-11.7.1 Remove seventh decal from backing sheet	1	7/5/2011	7/5/2011	Drafstman #1
-11.7.2 Place on Rocket where indicated	3	7/5/2011	7/6/2011	Drafstman #2
-11.7.3 Rub decal to remove bubbles	1	7/6/2011	7/6/2011	Drafstman #1
12.0 APPLYING CLEAR COAT	**16**	**7/6/2011**	**7/7/2011**	
-12.1 Apply clear coat to entire rocket	*16*	*7/6/2011*	*7/7/2011*	
-12.1.1 Apply clear coat to entire rocket	8	7/6/2011	7/7/2011	Painter-II #1
-12.1.2 Dry Completely	8	7/7/2011	7/7/2011	
13.0 DISPLAY NOZZLE ASSEMBLY	**32**	**7/10/2011**	**7/13/2011**	
-13.1 Spray Nozzle Base White	*18*	*7/10/2011*	*7/11/2011*	
-13.1.1 Paint Nozzle #1 w/Silver Paint Pen	2.5	7/10/2011	7/10/2011	Painter-I #1
-13.1.2 Paint Nozzle #2 w/ Silver Paint Pen	2.5	7/10/2011	7/10/2011	Painter-I #1
-13.1.3 Paint Nozzle #3 w/ Silver Paint Pen	2.5	7/10/2011	7/10/2011	Painter-I #1
-13.1.4 Paint Nozzle #4 w/ Silver Paint Pen	2.5	7/10/2011	7/11/2011	Painter-I #1
-13.1.5 Allow to dry	8	7/11/2011	7/11/2011	
-13.2 Apply Glue	*14*	*7/12/2011*	*7/13/2011*	
-13.2.1 Apply glue to tab on nozzle #1	1.5	7/12/2011	7/12/2011	Gluer #1
-13.2.2 Place Nozzle #1 into hole on base	2	7/12/2011	7/12/2011	Fitter #1
-13.2.3 Apply glue to tab on nozzle #2	1.5	7/12/2011	7/12/2011	Gluer #1
-13.2.4 Place Nozzle #2 into hole on base	2	7/12/2011	7/12/2011	Fitter #1
-13.2.5 Apply glue to tab on nozzle #3	1.5	7/12/2011	7/13/2011	Gluer #1
-13.2.6 Place Nozzle #3 into hole on base	2	7/13/2011	7/13/2011	Fitter #1
-13.2.7 Apply glue to tab on nozzle #4	1.5	7/13/2011	7/13/2011	Gluer #1
-13.2.8 Place Nozzle #4 into hole on base	2	7/13/2011	7/13/2011	Fitter #1
14.0 ROCKET PREFLIGHT	**42**	**7/13/2011**	**7/20/2011**	

14.1 prepare	*13*	*7/13/2011*	*7/17/2011*	
-14.1.1 Remove Nose Cone from Rocket	6	7/13/2011	7/14/2011	Fitter #1
-14.1.2 Locate recovery wadding	1	7/14/2011	7/14/2011	Fitter #1
-14.1.3 Insert 4-5 loosely crumpled squares of recovery wadding	6	7/14/2011	7/17/2011	Fitter #1
14.2 Spike	*4*	*7/17/2011*	*7/17/2011*	
-14.2.1 Pull parachute into a spike-see diagram for clarification	4	7/17/2011	7/17/2011	Fitter #1
14.3 Fold	*4*	*7/17/2011*	*7/18/2011*	
-14.3.1 Fold parachute according to diagram	4	7/17/2011	7/18/2011	Fitter #1
14.4 Roll	*4*	*7/18/2011*	*7/18/2011*	
-14.4.1 Roll parachute according to diagram	4	7/18/2011	7/18/2011	Fitter #1
14.5 Re-insert	*17*	*7/18/2011*	*7/20/2011*	
-14.5.1 Wrap lines loosely around rolled parachute-see diagram for clarification	5	7/18/2011	7/19/2011	Fitter #1
-14.5.2 Insert parachute into body tube of rocket	6	7/19/2011	7/20/2011	Fitter #1
-14.5.3 Insert shock cord into body tube of rocket	2	7/20/2011	7/20/2011	Fitter #1
-14.5.4 Insert nose cone into body tube of rocket	4	7/20/2011	7/20/2011	Fitter #1
15.0 PREPARE FOR TEST LAUNCH	**32**	**7/21/2011**	**7/26/2011**	
-15.1 Insert Engine	*32*	*7/21/2011*	*7/26/2011*	
-15.1.1 Remove engine	10	7/21/2011	7/24/2011	Engineer #1
-15.1.2 Insert tip to touch propellant	10	7/24/2011	7/25/2011	Engineer #1
-15.1.3 Insert engine into rocket	12	7/25/2011	7/26/2011	Engineer #1

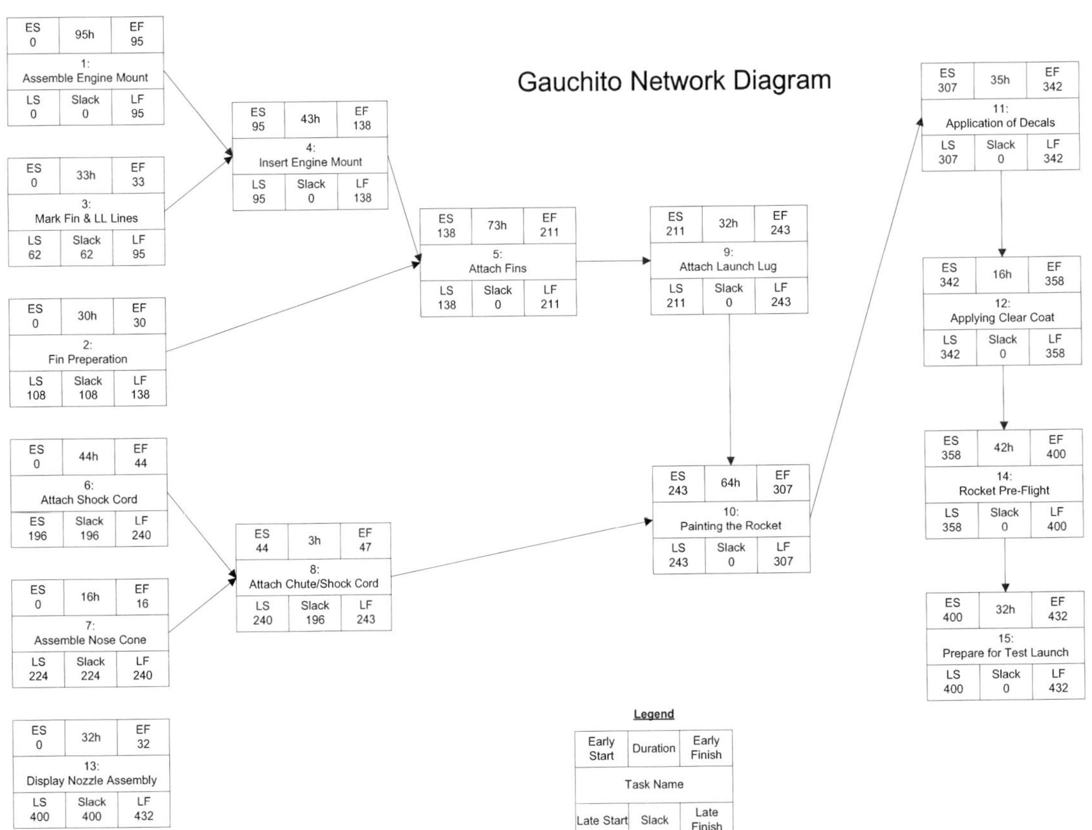
Gauchito Network Diagram
ES 0 | 95h | EF 95
1: Assemble Engine Mount
LS 0 | Slack 0 | LF 95
ES 0 | 33h | EF 33
3: Mark Fin & LL Lines
LS 62 | Slack 62 | LF 95
ES 0 | 30h | EF 30
2: Fin Preperation
LS 108 | Slack 108 | LF 138
ES 0 | 44h | EF 44
6: Attach Shock Cord
ES 196 | Slack 196 | LF 240
ES 0 | 16h | EF 16
7: Assemble Nose Cone
LS 224 | Slack 224 | LF 240
ES 0 | 32h | EF 32
13: Display Nozzle Assembly
LS 400 | Slack 400 | LF 432
ES 95 | 43h | EF 138
4: Insert Engine Mount
LS 95 | Slack 0 | LF 138
ES 44 | 3h | EF 47
8: Attach Chute/Shock Cord
LS 240 | Slack 196 | LF 243
ES 138 | 73h | EF 211
5: Attach Fins
LS 138 | Slack 0 | LF 211
ES 211 | 32h | EF 243
9: Attach Launch Lug
LS 211 | Slack 0 | LF 243
ES 243 | 64h | EF 307
10: Painting the Rocket
LS 243 | Slack 0 | LF 307
ES 307 | 35h | EF 342
11: Application of Decals
LS 307 | Slack 0 | LF 342
ES 342 | 16h | EF 358
12: Applying Clear Coat
LS 342 | Slack 0 | LF 358
ES 358 | 42h | EF 400
14: Rocket Pre-Flight
LS 358 | Slack 0 | LF 400
ES 400 | 32h | EF 432
15: Prepare for Test Launch
LS 400 | Slack 0 | LF 432
Legend
Early Start | Duration | Early Finish
Task Name
Late Start | Slack | Late Finish

3.0 Cost Management Plan

Introduction

The Gauchito Rocket Project Cost Management Plan covers defining cost estimates, creating the cost baseline, and managing the cost of the project. Since the project is of short duration, requiring intense workloads during the schedule in order to produce the deliverables, cost will be critical to manage and to control in order to meet the definitive budget.

The overall labor estimate is $19,950.

The Estimated at Completion (EAC) is $50,150 for the 10-week schedule. The EAC includes all direct labor costs, and material and equipments costs. The details of cost management for the Gauchito Project are covered below.

1. Equipment and custom parts
2. Equipment and Material order dates
3. Precision formats
4. How the cost estimate is developed
5. Precision formats
6. Personnel usage by time period labor expenditure on the project (Reference Appendix E)
7. How cost baseline and budget was developed (Reference Appendix H)
8. Identify when personnel are utilized and differences with the Cost Budget
9. Reporting formats for cost management
10. Cost control and managing process
11. Cost constraints
12. Cost assumptions

The constraints and assumptions are specific to cost management of the project. The overall project constraints and assumptions also apply to cost management.

Equipment and Custom Parts

The Gauchito Project requires a complete rocket assembly and specialty hybrid engines. These parts must be purchased and on-site no later than the Friday before the project start date to ensure work can start on schedule. The Risk Management Plan addresses response if some material and equipment is not received by that date. For example, if the paint is not received, it would have no cost impact since it is not used at project start, and can be re-ordered and delivered before it is needed. The previous order would be cancelled so double charges are not incurred.

The cost for materials, equipment and custom parts is included in the first week, as shown in the cost baseline in Appendix H pg 128. A breakout is below.

Item	Cost	Purchase date
Rocket Assembly – all standard rocket components, including rocket engine wadding, parachute, nose cone, and rocket body.	$15,000	Due at project start
Hybrid Engines – A3-4T (4 @ $2500 each)	$10,000*	Due at project start
Delivery costs	$125	
Materials as specified in the assembly construction plan, including, pens, pencils, glue, scissors, engine wadding, paint,	$5,000	Due at project start

tape measure, string, sandpaper, and modeling knife		

* The original cost estimates included the hybrid engines, but the cost increased after procurement evaluation and determining the actual cost. The difference is $5,000.00 between the scope estimated budget and the cost baseline provided in this plan.

Equipment and Material Order Dates

All equipment, including the specialty hybrid engines, is to be ordered at least 12 days prior to project start. The hybrid engines are not required until the last week of the project. However, in order to validate compatibility with the rocket, they are due at the same time as other materials and equipment, the week before project start.

The Project Plan and cost approval will include authorization to order the equipment before project start and allocate funds to the materials and equipment. Though the material and equipment will be ordered prior to project start, they are not allocated to the baseline until after receipt, so they are applied to the cost expenditures for the first week of the project. They are included in the overall EAC.

3.1 Precision Formats

3.1.1 Cost estimation for WBS by skill set:

- The cost estimates are in whole hours, rounded to the nearest hour.
- The labor rates are rounded to the nearest $5.00 increment, and are shown at the bottom of the cost estimate spreadsheet.

3.1.2 Baseline budget and EAC:

- The material and equipment cost is rounded up to the nearest $100.00.
- The labor rate for employees is a blended rate.
- The costs are reflected by week plus cumulative for all weeks to calculate the EAC.

3.2 How the cost estimate is developed

The Gauchito Project Manager and team members met to review the Product Description, Project Charter, and Preliminary Scope Statement. These documents provided an overall definition of the goal, the deliverables, initial rough order cost and budget estimates, and the project timeframe.

The team reviewed the Work Breakdown Structure, initial staffing resource needs, scheduled durations for each deliverable, milestones, and the target budget. These detailed data provided the basis upon which to refine resources needed for each WBS work package and to define costs for each type of resource skill set, e.g. Fitters, for the project.

In order to arrive at a complete cost estimate, the project manager and team met with Subject Matter Experts (SME's) for each of the disciplines, e.g. Fitters, Draftsman, and other skill types. This proved invaluable in defining the activities needed to accomplish each work package task, if it was not predefined. The SMEs' and project team reviewed the Gauchito Rocket Construction Plan (in Appendix C.) as a reference to ensure all activities were included for cost estimation.

In addition, the project manager reviewed existing cost estimates for the previously concluded Generic Estes project. While that project was not of the same size and scope of the Gauchito Project, it provided useful cost information and lessons learned for the cost estimates.

The project manager gathered the estimation of time, in man-hours, needed by each skill set to complete each work package. The total time for each Deliverable, and for all Deliverables, was calculated, as well as total time for each skill set, e.g. Fitter. The hourly rate for each skill set was applied to the resource time estimates to arrive at the total project labor cost.

No overhead resources were included in the cost estimate. Though the duration estimate number of hours includes "dummy" time for drying the glue, it is not included in any cost estimates.

Personnel usage by time period labor expenditure on project

Appendix C shows the personnel skill set needed for the project, and when they will be used on the project. The resource skill sets and time estimates for each are applied to each WBS work package. This duration estimate is part of the cost estimate spreadsheet.

Duration smoothing was not applied since the tasks are so well defined and SSTC has previous experience form the Generic Estes project. No optimistic schedule was determined. A consideration for a pessimistic schedule was that the new hybrid engines are unknown technology in conjunction with the standard rocket kit assembly. However, the team determined that the task would take no more time than installing standard rockets.

3.3 How the Cost Baseline and Budget is Developed

The total labor costs from the duration and cost estimate chart, and the material and equipment costs, were input to create the cost baseline and budget. Labor costs: The total costs from the cost estimation results – the personnel by WBS work package - have been input as part of the development of the budget and cost baseline. The resource requirements for each week were determined using resource staffing information per the Staffing Management Plan. The resources needed to complete the work packages scheduled for the week have been input to the spend plan and total costs applied to the week based on blended labor rates. The labor cost was based upon a blended rate of $35 per hour for employees. The contracted labor cost was based upon a rate of $50 per hour. The total labor cost is reflected in the appendices.

All cost of material and equipment is included in the baseline. The materials and equipment costs have been provided per the Procurement Management Plan, and will be purchased for delivery the week before project start. Therefore, those costs are reflected during the first week of the project. The difference from the preliminary budget is $5,000. However, there is no difference between the definitive budget and cost baseline since the costs are included.

The baseline budget EAC is targeted to within -5% and +10 of the Budget at Completion (BAC).

Identify when personnel are utilized and differences with the Cost Budget

The baseline is in Appendix H. The baseline is shown in increments by time period reporting, which is weekly, showing the labor costs per each week as well as the material and equipment cost per week.

The costs are reflected in an S-curve chart showing the cumulative budgeted costs weekly, and showing the total budgeted cost, EAC.

The spend plan for personnel is shown in Appendix H as part of the input to creating the cost baseline and budget. The input to the spend plan is the duration estimates and costs applied to each resource type, along with the schedule. The cost is shown weekly for each resource needed to complete the work scheduled for that week.

The differences between the spend plan costs and the original cost budget estimates reflect a slight increase due to expert evaluation of the amount of time needed to complete each task.

Reporting formats for cost reports

The project manager will report weekly on cost and schedule status for the previous week. The report will be distributed to SSTC executive management, the sponsor, finance, DeLeon and Associates customer contact, and functional managers with staff assigned to the project. The report will be briefed at the weekly project meeting. These costs are based on the Budgeted Cost of Work Scheduled (BCWS) in the baseline cost in Appendix H. An example report format is below, and will use Earned Value Management to provide actual costs and work performed against the BCWS (the Planned Value (PV)). The BCWS/ baseline costs, the actual costs, and the cost of amount of work performed will be plotted on the S-Curve chart, similar to the graphic shown. The amount of work performed may reflect either a Deliverable or the WBS tasks that should have been completed in support of a deliverable. The Cost Variance (Earned Value – Actual Cost), and the Schedule Variance (Earned value – Planned Value) are included, along with explanations for the variance.

EXAMPLE Cost Management Report: Figure 3-1

Gauchito Project Cost Management Report   Date:

The Gauchito Project EAC is ____________.

The Gauchito Project BAC is ____________.

Week #: _______

Earned Value for cost of work actually performed (BCWP or EV):

Actual Costs for the week (ACWP or AC):

Cost Variance: (EV – AC)

Explanation and corrective action, if needed:

Earned Value for cost of work actually performed (BCWP or EV):

Budgeted cost of work scheduled (BCWS or PV):

Schedule Variance: (EV – PV)

Explanation and corrective action, if needed:

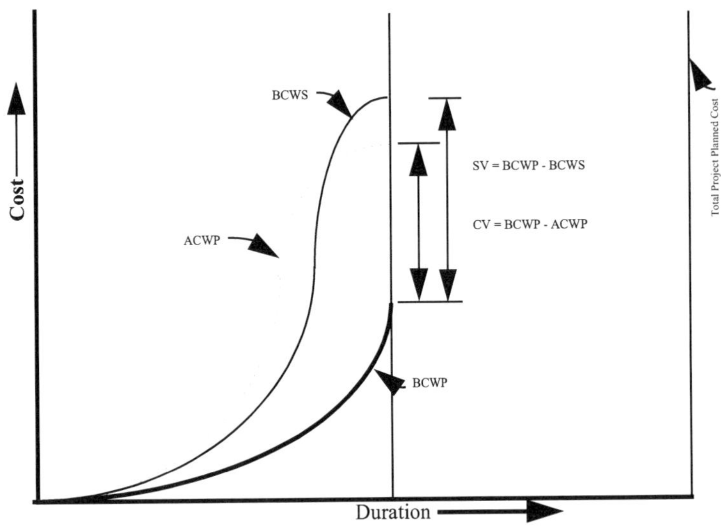

Figure 4-2 Cost baseline Cumulative S Curve (Colorado Technical University Distance Learning, Module 6 Cost Budgeting and Control, course PMGT605)

3.5 Cost Control

The project manager will use the weekly time reporting and roll up costs reported for each account/WBS to total the amount spent for the week. This amount will be calculated into the actual costs for the week. The project manager will use the weekly status reports to determine which deliverables and work packages were completed.

If the labor actual cost exceeds the value of the work completed, compared to the cost baseline, the project manager will determine reasons for the difference. For example, if Deliverable 1 is completed during Week 1 of the project, with an Earned Value of $1000, and the actual labor costs for the week total $1200, the variance is negative $200. One reason may be that may be tasks in the work packages scheduled for Week 1 took longer than expected due to unforeseen problems.

One area to examine is to ensure that additional work was not performed. If problems arose, then the project team will identify those problem areas and a course of action to see if the time can be made up, and if costs will not increase. This is especially critical if the problem could occur in future work packages for the project.

If the Earned value for Deliverable 1 completed in Week 1 is $1000, and the Planned Value was to be $1200, then there is a negative $200 in schedule. This means some tasks may be behind schedule. The project manager will use the same approach as for cost variances, in determining root cause and course of action.

All changes to scope, schedule, contracts, or purchases, will follow the overall change control process outlined in the Scope Management Plan. Proposed changes will be presented to the Configuration Control board, along with the associated cost changes to the baseline cost.

If costs are increased due to finding that the tasks take longer than expected, the project manager and contracts/procurement management will determine a course of action based on the contract type. The project manager will consult with functional managers to define alternate approaches.

As approved changes occur, updates will be applied to the cost estimates, personnel usage, material and equipment changes. The project manager will revise the baseline with a new EAC, as well as to this Cost Management Plan. The changes will be applied to other impacted plans as necessary.

To enable the project manager to track costs and changes, corporate databases for time reporting, issues and risks will be used. In addition, standard corporate guidelines for cost accounting, procurement and contracts and Earned Value Management will be followed.

Cost Constraints

1. The Fitter positions will be outsourced. This increases the labor rates to contractor rates, used in cost estimation.
2. The Memorial Day and Independence Day holidays fall within the project start/finish dates.

Cost Assumptions

1. Labor is calculated based on man-hour rates.
2. Labor rates have been provided as static for this project. No increases are planned in the 10-week project timeframe. The blended rate used is standard across the corporation. Contractor labor rates are negotiated per the outsourcing contract and are static for the project's duration.
3. No overtime hours and rates for resources are included in the cost estimates.
4. No cost estimates are applied for Memorial Day and Independence Day. Fitters are not paid for that day and employee time off is part of overhead costs.

Project Name: Ansari X Prize Gauchito Rocket

Product-Process: Quality

Prepared By: Thomas Jones

Project Quality Plan Version Control

Version	Date	Author	Change Description
1.0	4/30/06	Thomas Jones	Initial

4.0 Quality Management Plan

4.1 Project Quality Plan Purpose

The purpose of this plan is to ensure that the rocket is built to the specifications set by the customer. Customer satisfaction with the workmanship, cost, and final delivery of the final product is key to achieving the goal of follow-on work of future contracts.

Quality Management Method

The construction material used for this project has been handpicked by the costumer. It will only be inspected for damage that may have been done during shipping. The construction processes have also been written by the costumer. Quality for this project will only consist of insuring that the construction processes have been followed and if there is any room for improvement.

4.2 Quality Plan Processes

Quality Assurance

It is the policy of Space Systems Technologies Corporation (SSTC) and its elements to develop, integrate, and implement QA and QC practices to assure delivery of quality products and services that meet or exceed customer needs and expectations in accordance with applicable laws policies and technical criteria, schedules, and budgets. Adherence to quality principles and established QA and QC practices is integral to the roles and responsibilities of all SSTC's elements and functions.

Quality standards have been set by the customer in the kit assembly directions given to the Gauchito Rocket project team. The QA team will inspect each deliverable as milestones are reached. Checklists will be developed using the kit directions for each station assembling a section of the rocket. The checklist will simply ensure each step in the assembly process is done in accordance with the customer's instructions.

Quality Control

The checklists at each station will be picked up by the QA team during the inspection of the deliverable and given to the customer with training documentation.

Project Deliverables and Processes Acceptance Criteria

All deliverables will be constructed according to kit instructions.

1.0 ASSEMBLE ENGINE MOUNT

2.0 FIN PREPARATION

3.0 MARK FIN AND LAUNCH LUG LINES

4.0 INSERTING ENGINE MOUNT

5.0 ATTACH FINS

6.0 ATTACH SHOCK CORD

7.0 ASSEMBLE NOSE CONE

8.0 ATTACH PARACHUTE/SHOCK CORD

9.0 ATTACH LAUNCH LUG

10.0 PAINTING THE ROCKET

11.0 APPLICATION OF DECALS

12.0 APPLYING CLEAR COAT

13.0 DISPLAY NOZZLE ASSEMBLY

14.0 ROCKET PREFLIGHT

15.0 PREPARE FOR TEST LAUNCH

Project Overview

This project will address design consideration of the Gauchito Rocket. The rocket's design, launch and test results can be observed using a 7/8 scale of the full sized rocket. This approach provides a valid measurement of the rocket's success without the time and expense necessary to build a full-sized rocket. This will also help in the identification, mitigation and avoidance of risk to the space development program. This project is being under taken to show that our company has the ability to produce a reliable test product that accurately duplicates the final full size rocket. To do this we will deliver the completed 7/8 scale rocket 3 days after the assembly is completed to Peterson AFB test launch site.

See Appendix for WBS, schedule, risks, and cost.

Quality Standards

Rocket parts included in the kit have been inspected. These parts are of acceptable quality and grade for this project. The 4 solid fuel rockets being installed on the 7/8th scaled rocket have been engineered and tested to produce similar thrust as the 4 hybrid engines on the full scale rocket.

Quality Tools

Audits of all deliverables will be made by a QA team member. Checklists will be verified and signed by the Fitter, Draftsman, Gluer, or sander. The checklist will be verified and signed by the QA team member and turned over to the customer with the training documentation.

Quality Manager's Responsibilities

Thomas Jones has been assigned Quality Manager and has the responsibility for:

Project Quality Assurance

- Specifying how the quality assurance processes should be applied
- Specifying how the quality control procedures should be applied
- Specifying the continuous process improvement for the project
- Defining criteria for the effective execution of key project activities, processes, and deliverables
- Defining quality management responsibilities for the project
- Identifying or include any checklists or templates that should be used by project team members
- Defining how the project will be audited to ensure compliance with the quality management plan

Contractor	Reliability %	Work Quality	Mistakes
Local Fitters Union	100	100	0
ACME Fitters	40	60	25
Fitter-R-Us	25	65	25

Quality assurance helps to establish if a deliverable is acceptable based on the processes used to create it. Quality assurance processes are used to evaluate overall project performance frequently and to determine that quality reviews were held, deliverables tested, and customer acceptance acquired.

Quality Assurance Procedures

Quality has been designed into the product. All of the parts used in this rocket project have been handpicked by the customer for the 7/8th scaled rocket. Although the assembly procedures were written by the customer, they will be monitored by QA team members looking for ways to improve the process of gluing, sanding, and painting through the use of better tools or material. Staff and Subcontractor's knowledge of the processes being used will be asked for recommendations for improvement on the checklists.

Subcontract Fitters- Three of the top Fitter contracting companies in the local area have been judge on their previous job performances. The Local Fitters Union has been found to have a reputation for good reliable work with exceptional employees.

Project Monitoring Processes

A check list will be marked off for each of the measurable steps in the construction process. These check lists will be signed off by one of the staff or subcontracted fitters and a QA team member. This will ensure that all steps in the construct process was followed. Staff and Subcontractor's knowledge of the processes being used will be asked for recommendations for improvement on the checklists. These recommendations will be pasted to management and the customer for consideration in improving the construction of the full scale rocket.

Project Quality Control

	Step Completed	
ASSEMBLE ENGINE MOUNT	YES	NO
Mark left end of Engine Tube @ 1/8'		
Mark from left of Engine Tube @ ¾'		
Mark from left of Engine Tube @ 1 ½'		
Cut Slit of 1/8' @ 1 ½' inch Mark on Engine Tube		
Glue, Tube, Assemble Hook		
Apply thin line of glue completely around engine at ¾' mark		
Insert Engine Hook into 1/8' Slit on Engine Mount Tube		
Slide Mylar ring onto Engine Mount tube at 3/4"" mark "		
Glue dry at ¾' mark		
Apply glue inside front of Engine Mount tube		
Yellow Engine Block flush with the right end per diagram		
Let Dry		
Remove Centering rings from card with modeling knife		
Apply thin line of Glue around engine mount tube @ 1/8"" mark		
Slide notched Centering Ring onto glued line @ 1/8"" mark		
Glue Set		
Apply thin line of Glue to opposite side of notched center ring flush with end of engine mount tube		
Slide unnotched Centering Ring in place over glue flush with end of engine tube mount		

Centering Rings Dry		
Apply Glue Fillets to both sides of Centering Rings for reinforcement		
Centering Rings Dry		

Signatures Date

Verifier ______________________ ____________

QA Team ______________________ ____________

Suggestions for improvement (materials or processes): ____________

____

____

____

____

	Step Completed	
FIN PREPARATION	YES	NO
Sand Laser Cut Balsa Sheet w/Fine Sandpaper		
Cut out fin #1		
Cut out fin #2		
Cut out fin #3		
Cut out fin #4		
Sand Edges of fins		
FIN PREPARATION		
Sand Laser Cut Balsa Sheet w/Fine Sandpaper		
Cut out fin #1		
Cut out fin #2		
Cut out fin #3		
Cut out fin #4		
Sand Edges of fins		
FIN PREPARATION		

Signatures Date

Verifier ______________________________ ____________

QA Team ______________________________ ____________

Suggestions for improvement (materials or processes): __________________

____

____

____

____

	Step Completed	
MARK FIN AND LAUNCH LUG LINES	YES	NO
Mark body tube at arrows		
Mark Launch Lug Line as LL on Body tube		
Connect Fins		
Connect launch lug lines		
Extend launch lug line 3 ¾" from end of tube"		
MARK FIN AND LAUNCH LUG LINES		
Mark body tube at arrows		
Mark Launch Lug Line as LL on Body tube		
Connect Fins		
Connect launch lug lines		
Extend launch lug line 3 ¾" from end of tube"		
MARK FIN AND LAUNCH LUG LINES		
Mark body tube at arrows		
Mark Launch Lug Line as LL on Body tube		
Connect Fins		

Signatures Date

Verifier ______________________________ __________

QA Team ______________________________ __________

Suggestions for improvement (materials or processes): ________________

____

____

	Step Completed	
INSERTING ENGINE MOUNT	YES	NO
Mark inside tube at 5/8""""		
Glue Tube		

Smeared glue 1 3/4" inside rear of body tube along LL.		
Aligned engine hook with LL line		
Inserted engine mount into body tube until centering ring is even w/the 5/8" glue mark		
Located scrap piece of balsa		
Applied glue to centering/body tube joint		

Signatures Date

Verifier ______________________ __________

QA Team ______________________ __________

Suggestions for improvement (materials or processes): ____________

____

____

____

____

	Step Completed	
ATTACHING FINS	YES	NO
Applied thin layer of glue to edge of fin		
Allowed to dry (1 minute for model)		
Applied second layer of glue to edge of fin		
Attached Fin #1 to body tube along one of fin lines flush w/end		
Applied thin layer of glue to edge of fin#2		
Allowed to dry (1 minute for model)		
Applied second layer of glue to edge of fin #2		
Attached Fin #2 to body tube along one of fin lines flush w/end		
Applied thin layer of glue to edge of fin #3		
Allowed to dry (1 minute for model)		
Applied second layer of glue to edge of fin #3		
Attached Fin #3 to body tube along one of fin lines flush w/end		
Applied thin layer of glue to edge of fin #4		
Allowed to dry (1 minute for model)		
Applied second layer of glue to edge of fin #4		
Attached Fin #4 to body tube along one of fin lines flush w/end		
Check Fin #1 Alignment		
Check Fin #2 Alignment		
Check Fin #3 Alignment		
Check Fin #4 Alignment		
Let Glue Set		
Stood Rocket on end		
Let glue dried completely		

Signatures　　　　　　　　　　　　Date

Verifier ______________________ __________

QA Team ______________________ __________

Suggestions for improvement (materials or processes): ____________

____

____

____

____

	Step Completed	
ATTACH SHOCK CORD	YES	NO
Cut out shock cord from front page		
Attached shock cord to shock cord mount		
Applied glue to shock cord mount		
Folded edge of shock cord mount over glued shock cord		
Applied glue to shock cord mount		
Folded over shock cord second time		
Held Shock Cord for 1 minute		
Glued Shock Cord mount 1" inside body tube		
Held until glue sets		
Let Dry Completely		

Signatures Date

Verifier ______________________________ ____________

QA Team ______________________________ ____________

Suggestions for improvement (materials or processes): ____________________

____

____

____

____

	Step Completed	
ASSEMBLE NOSE CONE	YES	NO
Applied plastic cement to inside rim of nose cone		
Pressed Nose Cone Insert into place over plastic cement		
inside of nose cone rim		
Let Dry Completely		
ASSEMBLE NOSE CONE		
Applied plastic cement to inside rim of nose cone		
Pressed Nose Cone Insert into place over plastic cement		
inside of nose cone rim		
Let Dry Completely		

Signatures Date

Verifier ______________________________ ____________

QA Team ______________________________ ____________

Suggestions for improvement (materials or processes): ____________________

____

____

____

____

	Step Completed	
ATTACH PARACHUTE	YES	NO
Passed shroud line on parachute through eyelet		
Attached Parachute		
Passed parachute through loop in shroud		
Tied Lines		
Tied shock cord to nose cone using a double knot		

Signatures Date

Verifier ______________________ ________

QA Team ______________________ ________

Suggestions for improvement (materials or processes): ____________

____

____

____

____

	Step Completed	
ATTACH LAUNCH LUG	YES	NO
Glued LL centered onto LL Line on rocket body		
Applied glue fillets along launch lug		
Applied glue fillets along fin/body tube joints		
Smoothed each fillet with finger		
Let glue dry completely		

Signatures Date

Verifier ______________________ __________

QA Team ______________________ __________

Suggestions for improvement (materials or processes): ______________

____

____

____

____

	Step Completed	
APPLICATION OF DECALS	YES	NO
First decal placed on Rocket according to instructions.		
Bubbles removed from decal		
Second decal placed on Rocket according to instructions.		
Bubbles removed from decal		
Third decal placed on Rocket according to instructions.		
Bubbles removed from third decal		
Fourth decal placed on Rocket according to instructions.		
Bubbles removed from decal.		
Fifth decal placed on Rocket according to instructions.		
Bubbles removed from decal.		
Sixth decal placed on Rocket according to instructions.		
Bubbles removed from decal.		
Seventh decal placed on Rocket according to instructions.		
Bubbles removed from decal.		

Signatures Date

Verifier ______________________________ ____________

QA Team ______________________________ ____________

Suggestions for improvement (materials or processes): ________________

____

____

	Step Completed	
PAINTING THE ROCKET	YES	NO
Sprayed rocket with white primer		
Let Dry		
Sanded entire rocket		
Sprayed completed rocket with white second coat of primer		
Let Dry		
Sprayed Nose Cone with Copper paint		
Let Dry		

Signatures Date

Inspector ______________________________ ____________

QA Team ______________________________ ____________

Suggestions for improvement (materials or processes): ____________________

____

____

____

____

	Step Completed	
APPLYING CLEAR COAT	YES	NO
Applied clear coat to entire rocket		
Dry Completely		

Signatures Date

Verifier ______________________________ ____________

QA Team ______________________________ ____________

Suggestions for improvement (materials or processes): __________________

____

____

____

____

DISPLAY NOZZLE ASSEMBLY	Step Completed	
	YES	NO
Nozzle #1 painted w/Silver Paint		
Nozzle #2 painted w/ Silver Paint		
Nozzle #3 painted w/ Silver Paint		
Nozzle #4 painted w/ Silver Paint		
Nozzles allowed to dry		
Apply glue to tab on nozzle #1		
Nozzle #1 was placed into hole on base		
Apply glue to tab on nozzle #2		
Nozzle #2 was placed into hole on base		
Apply glue to tab on nozzle #3		
Nozzle #3 was placed into hole on base		
Apply glue to tab on nozzle #4		
Nozzle #4 was placed into hole on base		

Signatures Date

Verifier ______________________________ ____________

QA Team ______________________________ ____________

Suggestions for improvement (materials or processes): ________________

____

____

____

____

	Step Completed	
ROCKET PREFLIGHT	YES	NO
Removed Nose Cone from Rocket		
Inserted 4-5 loosely crumpled squares of recovery wadding		
Parachute folded accordingly		
Parachute lines wrap loosely around rolled parachute		
Parachute inserted into body tube of rocket		
Shock cord inserted into body tube of rocket		
Nose cone inserted onto body tube of rocket		

Signatures Date

Verifier ______________________________ ____________

QA Team ______________________________ ____________

Suggestions for improvement (materials or processes): ____________________

____

____

____

____

	Step Completed	
PREPARE FOR TEST LAUNCH	YES	NO
Engine installed		
Remove engine		
Insert tip to touch propellant		
Insert engine into rocket		
PREPARE FOR TEST LAUNCH		
Engine installed		

Signatures Date

Verifier ______________________________ ____________

QA Team ______________________________ ____________

Suggestions for improvement (materials or processes): ________________

____

____

____

____

Project Deliverables

Checklist signed by a verifier and a QA team member. The checklist will also include suggestions by the staff member or subcontracted fitter who did the construction of the rocket deliverable.

Project Deliverables Test & Acceptance Process

The construction material used for this project has been handpicked by the costumer.

Project Deliverables Acceptance Criteria

All deliverables will be constructed according to kit instructions.

01-Assembling of the Engine Mount:

The engine mount will pass inspection and be accepted if:

- Three marks are on the engine tube marked at 1/8, ¾, and 1 ½ inches.
- 1/8th inch slit has been cut 1 ½ inches on the engine tube
- The assembly hook has been inserted into 1/8th inch slit and glued at the ¾ inch mark.
- The yellow engine block is glued into the front of the mount tube and flush with the end of the mount tube.
- The notched centering ring is glued into place at the 1/8th inch mark.
- The un-notched centering ring is glued flush with the tube end.
- The glue has dried completely.

02-Fin Preparation

The Fin Preparation will pass inspection and be accepted if:

- The Fins have been carefully cut from the balsa sheet.
- The edges of the fins have been sanded smooth.

03-Marking of Fin and Lug Lines

The Fin and Lug line markings will pass inspection and be accepted if:

- Check that the Fin and lug lines have been mark on the body tube using the guide.

04-Insertion of Engine Mount

- The Engine Mount will pass inspection and be accepted if:
- The engine hook and launch lug are aligned.
- The engine mount has been inserted into the body tube and the centering ring is flush with the 5/8th inch mark.
- Extra glue has been added to the 5/8th inch mark inside the body tube.

The glue has dried completely.

05-Fin Attachment

The Fin Attachment will pass inspection and be accepted if:

- The four fins should project straight out from the body tube.
- Each fin should be on the fin lines flush with the end.
- The glue has dried completely.

06-Shock Cord Attachment

The shock cord attachment will pass inspection and be accepted if:

- The shock cord has been attached one inch to the inside of the body tube.
- The glue has died completely

07-Nose Cone Assembly

The nose cone attachment will pass inspection and be accepted if:

- The tube type cement has been used to connect the nose cone and the nose cone insert.
- The glue has died completely.

08-Parachute and Shock Cord Attachment

The Parachute and Shock Cord attachment will pass inspection and be accepted if:

- The shroud line has been connected through the eyelet on the nose cone insert.
- The parachute has been passed through the parachute line loop.
- The shock cord has been tied to the nose cone with a double knot.

09-Launch Lug Attachment

The Launch Lug attachment will pass inspection and be accepted if:

- The launch lug has been centered on the LL line and double glued.
- The glue has dried completely.

10-Paint the Rocket

The paint job will pass inspection and be accepted if:

- The rocket is painted and the surface is smooth.

11- Decal Application

The decal application will pass inspection and be accepted if:

- Apply all decals.
- All Decals will be smooth

12-Clear Coat Application

The clear coat application will pass inspection and be accepted if:

- The rocket is smooth.
- The clear coat is completely dry.

13-Display Nozzle Assembly

The display nozzle assembly will pass inspection and be accepted if:

- The base is painted white.
- The nozzles are painted silver.
- The base plate and the silver nozzles are completely dry.

The silver nozzles are glued into place on the base plate.

14-Rocket Pre-Flight

- The rocket preflight assembly will pass inspection and be accepted if:
- The rocket will have four or five sheets of recovery wadding loosely packed in the top section.
- The parachute will be folded with the parachute lines loosely wrapped around it.
- The parachute will be placed into the top section of the rocket.
- The cone will be placed onto the top of the rocket.

15-Prepare for Test Launch

- The engine will be inserted into the rocket

Project Audits & Quality Reviews

Project Quality Audit Review	Planned Date	Quality Review Auditor	Comments
Assembling of the Engine Mount Audit	Completion of Deliverable	QA Team member	
Fin Preparation Audit	Completion of Deliverable	QA Team member	
Marking of Fin and Lug Lines Audit	Completion of Deliverable	QA Team member	
Insertion of Engine Mount Audit	Completion of Deliverable	QA Team member	
Fin Attachment Audit	Completion of Deliverable	QA Team member	
Shock Cord Attachment Audit	Completion of Deliverable	QA Team member	
Nose Cone Assembly Audit	Completion of Deliverable	QA Team member	
Parachute and Shock Cord Attachment Audit	Completion of Deliverable	QA Team member	
Launch Lug Attachment Audit	Completion of Deliverable	QA Team member	
Paint the Rocket Audit	Completion of Deliverable	QA Team member	
Decal Application Audit	Completion of Deliverable	QA Team member	
Clear Coat Application Audit	Completion of Deliverable	QA Team member	
Display Nozzle Assembly Audit	Completion of Deliverable	QA Team member	
Rocket Pre-Flight Audit	Completion of Deliverable	QA Team member	

Quality Plan Approvals

Prepared by ______________________________

Project Manager

Approved by ______________________________

Project Sponsor

____

Executive Sponsor

____

Client Sponsor

5.0 Staffing Management Plan

Project Name: Ansari X Prize Gauchito Rocket

Project Manager: Julie Davis Space Systems Technologies Corporation

Project Tracking Number: PMGT 605-0001 **Date: May 8, 2011, 2011**

Project Justification: In developing the 7/8 scaled down model of the Ansari X Gauchito Rocket, the opportunity to address needed modifications identified through quality analysis and testing on the design is invaluable to the Pablo de Leon & Associates space development program. This will also help in the identification, mitigation and avoidance of risk to the space development program.

Overview of Staff requirements:

01 - Fitters (Not generic to the organlzation)

02 - Draftsmen

03 - Painter(s)

04 - Gluer/Assembler

05 - Cutter

06 - Sander Level I

07 -..Sander Level II (5.1.4/13.1.1)

08 - Engineer

5.1 Key Constraints:

Fitters are not generic to the organization; there is a requirement for fitters on this project.

Fitters will be outsourced through a staffing organization and employed based on requirements identified in the WBS and further matched to the Histogram .

5.2 Key Assumptions:

Resources are properly allocated to ensure load balancing throughout the project.

5.3 Staff Requirements

1. The Gauchito Scaled Demo Project is a project that will utilize much of the expertise within De Leon Enterprises (DLE). This is a precision project that calls upon many skills and skill sets housed under the De Leon logo. As usual we will rise to the task, asking the best of the best to step forward in anticipation of a well produced and structurally sound product.

The below are specific job requirements in support of the Gauchito project; individuals volunteering

to support this undertaking will be screened by the project manager Julie Davis as it is her responsibility to ensure team success. The primary criteria used in selection will be:

- ✓ Attendance and performance
- ✓ Special knowledge and skills

- ✓ Work history
- ✓ Current project workload
- ✓ Authorization and costing to work overtime
- ✓ Interest in the project

5.4 CTU, Staff Acquisition and Team Development

Selected individuals will be detailed to support this project as an addendum to ongoing requirements. Specific position requirements are listed below. A team building activity will be scheduled after selection and prior to the beginning of the project. This project has an expected completion date of not later than 10 may 2011.

Job Description for: STRUCTURAL DRAFTSMEN

This position requires a Bachelor's Degree in civil engineering, or a closely related field; or five years of experience in rocketry and structural design work including six-months of CADD operation, and an Associate's Degree in Civil engineering, drafting, or design technology. This candidate must have experience with ESTES plans. The person assigned to this position will perform other duties as assigned.

Job Description for: CUTTER

This position requires a Bachelor's Degree in knife or scissors use. Selected individual will be able to cut read and interpret simple instructions. Individual will be able to cut out, with an appropriate tool, any patterns; within one-millimeter of specifications. The person assigned to this position will perform other duties as assigned.

Job Description for: PAINTER I

1. Must possess a High school diploma or GED equivalent with three years journey level experience.
2. Will scrape, sandpaper, prime, or seal surfaces prior to painting.
3. Must be able to Mix, match, and apply paint, varnish, shellac, enamel, and other finishes.
4. Will clean and care for brushes, spray guns, and other equipment.

Job Description for: PAINTER II (Supervisor)

1. Must possess a High school diploma or GED equivalent with five years master level experience.
2. Responsible for the preparation of all surfaces prior to painting.
3. Ensures proper application and adherence to surfaces of all kinds
4. Responsible for checking the condition of woodwork, reporting any carpentry needs, clean-up, and ensuring completeness and customer satisfaction with assigned projects.

Job Description for: Test Engineer (Rocket Scientist)

Review test specifications. Develop product test plans and identify and procure test equipment as needed.

Interface with local Project Managers and worldwide customers. Follow NAR guidelines and procedures.

Participate in design reviews. Support lab accreditation efforts. General requirements: Bachelor degree in Rocket Engineering required, Masters Degree in Engineering preferred, Minimum of 3 years of experience in Product Verification Testing. Knowledge of Rocket specifications and Quality systems preferred. Strong computer and communication skills required. Experience with NAR Rocket testing methods and Equipment Experience in electronic hardware and software design methods.

Job Description for: Sander I

1. Must possess a High school diploma or GED equivalent with three years journey level experience.
2. Uses a machine or hand sands any surface until surface is smooth.
3. Applies filler compound to surfaces to seal wood.

Job Description for: Sander II

1. Must possess a High school diploma or GED equivalent with five years master level experience.
2. Uses a machine or hands sands to "fine" specifications.
3. Responsible for selection of proper "grit" sandpaper and or sanding appliances.
4. Verifies adherence to requirements using applicable tools and or experience.

Job Description for: GLUER/ ASSEMBLER

Applies glue between seams in order to bind parts wooden of rockets or other items to make them airtight by either of following methods: (1) Guides gluing tool that automatically forces gluing material into seam. Fills glue runner (funnel) with glue and guides runner along seam to fill seam with glue. Removes excess glue, using scraper or towel.

5.5 Constraints

2. This project has a requirement for staff; fitters, that are not organic to DLE. Authorization has been secured from management for external recruitment.

Job Description for: STRUCTURAL FITTER

This position requires an Associate's Degree in fitter sciences, or a closely related field; or five years of experience in performing duties including part or equipment location, assembly and or construction. Additional requirements for this position include the ability to read and follow simple instructions. The person assigned to this position will perform other duties as assigned.

Recruitment

3. Project team A will immediately begin recruitment actions through the DLE recruitment section to recruit and hire a qualified candidate(s) to meet these staffing needs. After initial selection by recruitment, candidates will be interviewed by "Team A," and will need to secure a two-thirds majority vote in order to secure the position(s). This is a process that is now, and will remain germane to DLE enterprises.

5.6 Continued Employment

4. Under the general terms of this project and based on the past performance of DLE, this firm anticipates continued contracts in support of this parent project; as such, DLE will support the uninterrupted employment of a minimum of two (2) fitters. Hired individuals will remain under the functional control/management of the assembly section. Re-evaluation of this policy will occur not later than one calendar year from the final date of this document.

5. Sufficient resources are available to support this undertaking. Resource allocation has been formally studied and supporting documentation (enclosed) is available for review by functional managers. These requirements will be continually evaluated throughout the life of the project and adjustments made as required.

6.0 Communications Management Plan

6.1 Effective communication, internally and externally, is the most overlooked resource in the project management arena. As we delve into yet another project; this will not become a stumbling block for SSTC. We are not reinventing the wheel; we will continue to communicate in a manner that has been proven to work in support of other projects. The procedures listed below have been designed to build communication at all levels, and to ease the supporting processes while continuing to capitalize on its inherent benefit.

6.2 The Project Manager is responsible for disseminating any and all information to concerned parties. This responsibility includes information of the type indicated in the chart below as well as other information deemed pertinent by any interested party. Items not covered in this chart (Enclosure II) will, at a minimum, be posted in the Gauchito Project Website daily (by close of business).

Note: The project secretary will post weekly status meeting minutes to the company Gauchito Project Website weekly.

6.3 Information becomes such when it is inclusive of the components who, what, when where, why and how; effective communication includes these components and addresses the specific subject of interest. Information communicated about this or any project will be as detailed as possible initially, and will be followed up in writing or in an e-mail to all concerned parties. Any input, as a contributor to the successful outcome of this project, will be welcomed.

6.4 When seeking answers or addressing concerns, a response in writing will be provided to the initiating party within 24 hours (work hours). If this timeframe is violated or is not sufficient, escalation will follow the below listed path:

a. Functional Department Manager

b. Project Manager

c. Project Sponsor

NOTE: Information will not be communicated directly to the customer except through the personnel listed above.

Escalation to any of the above listed parties will be in writing or through e-mail. Additionally, a copy of this correspondence must be maintained by the initiating party.

6.5 The chart below, shown as Enclosure I, is a guide to be used in support of this communications plan; concerned parties have been broken into teams to ensure that information flows are consistent with the needs of both Stakeholders and management. This list may not be inclusive and provisions for the update of it, Enclosure II, or this communications plan are detailed in the paragraph below.

6.6 Organizational feedback is always welcome. As DLA strives to satisfy the needs of both its customer and employees, concerned individuals should feel free to offer suggestions for improvement, update or refinement of this or any other policies. Requests for modification of this plan or communication chart(s) will be voiced in writing through the hierarchal structure as specified above. Failure to comply with this minimal communication guidance will result in disciplinary action or termination.

TEAM A		
Title	Name	Organization
Sponsor	Jeff Tyler	SSTC
Project Manager	Julie Davis	SSTC
Cost Financing	Gwen Edward	SSTC

TEAM B		
Title	Name	Organization
Quality Assessment	Brian Kirouac	SSTC
Quality Assessment	Tom Jones	SSTC

TEAM C		
Title	Name	Organization

Functional Mgr. (Drafting)	B. Jose Alonzo	SSTC
Functional Mgr. (Painting)	Robert Muse	SSTC
Functional Mgr. (Finishing/Sanding)	Buford T. Linking	SSTC
Functional Mgr. (Assembly/Gluer)	J. Christian Bose	SSTC
Functional Mgr. (Fitters)	Charles Gooding	SSTC

TEAM D

Title	Name	Organization
Procurement	Jeanea Brown	SSTC

Enclosure I

Project Communications Planner

Who?	What Information?	When?	How? (Form/Medium)
Team A	Supplies confirmation	Upon receipt	E-mail/Weekly meeting
	Fitters assignment	Contract signing	E-mail/Weekly meeting
	Change Modification Request Change Mod. Confirmation	Upon receipt	Telephonic
		Prior to implementation	Telephonic/E-mail
	Schedule modification	48 hours prior	Weekly meeting
	Personnel change (impact) Personnel change (no-impact)	Prior to change	Telephonic/E-mail
		Weekly status meeting	Weekly meeting
	Facilities (impact)	Immediate	Telephonic/E-mail
	Weather (impact)	Immediate	Telephonic/E-mail
	Weekly status	Weekly	Weekly meeting
	Stage completion	Upon completion	E-mail/Weekly meeting
	Project completion	One-day prior	E-mail
Team B	Change Mod. Confirmation	After completion	E-mail
	Schedule modification	After implementation	E-mail
	Stage completion	Upon completion	E-mail

Team C	Supplies confirmation	Upon receipt	E-mail
	Supplies requests/mod.	Immediately	E-mail/weekly meeting
	Supplies lost or damaged	Immediately	E-mail/weekly meeting
	Budgetary changes	Immediately	E-mail/telephonic
	Change Mod. Confirmation Schedule modification	Immediately	E-mail
Team D	Personnel change (impact)	Immediately	E-mail
	Personnel change (no-impact)	Immediately	E-mail
	Facilities (impact) Weather (impact)	Immediately	E-mail
	Stage completion	Immediately	E-mail
Project Manager	Project completion	Immediately	E-mail
		Upon completion	E-mail
		One-day prior	E-mail
All	Schedule/Costs Reports	Weekly	E-mail/Database update
Recruitment	Weekly status meeting minutes	Within 24 hours	E-mail/Project Web site
	Time-cards (Fitters)	Fridays by 5:00 p.m.	Fax/E-mail

http:www.hrdpress.com/Files/worksheets.doc

7.0 Risk Management Plan

After holding a risk planning meeting, the Gauchito Rocket project team focused on all the of the possible project risks and their ramifications, and determined that it would be imperative to seek out a risk management plan in order to prepare for risk events and lay out mitigation plans for this risks that seemed the most likely to affect the project's scope, quality, or schedule.

7.1 Methodology

The Gauchito Project team determined that the best way to approach risk determination and definition would be to bring the entire team together, including all of the individuals of the various skill sets involved in project construction, and brainstorm. It seemed using everyone's ideas, and narrowing the risk events down from there was the most accurate way to determine all of the risks involved from every perspective of this project. Data from previous projects completed by the SSTC team members were used as input to risk definition.

7.2 Roles and Responsibilities

It was decided among the project team that the roles and responsibilities would be laid out as shown in the Appendix labeled Risk Roles and Responsibilities. The bulk of the responsibility will be placed on the Project Manager, as they have the authority within the team to approve or deny any mitigation plans that are developed as well as the authority to alter the scope statement, the budget, or the quality plan as may be required if any of the determined risk events occurs.

7.3 Budgeting

The Gauchito Rocket Project team discussed the budget, and what effects there would be, if any, according to each risk event. It was determined that, while certain risks could have an effect on the schedule and quality of the project, corrective costs would be negligible unless the risk event went unnoticed and thus uncorrected for an extended time period. Therefore, the Project Manager, along with the Cost and Risk managers, determined it would be feasible to allocate roughly 10% of the budget to Risk Management and Mitigation. This percentage will be reevaluated weekly for the life of the project, but it is not necessary to "re-baseline" for this project.

7.4 Timing

After conferring with the rest of the project team, the Risk Manager, along with the other team managers, attempted to determine precisely how critically the project schedule might be affected should any of the risk events occur. It was determined that, with the mitigation plans that were approved by the project manager, the schedule would take a minimal hit if any one event occurred. Buffers were already written into the schedule should any unforeseen overtures occur, in order to prevent the project going past its scheduled end date, and the team feels these buffers will be appropriate for the Risk Management Plan, and rewriting the project schedule will be unnecessary.

7.5 Risk Categories

It seemed most appropriate, according to the Gauchito Rocket Project team, to categorize the risks by the three major constraints of any project. These three constraints are, of course, Cost, Quality, and Schedule. The reasons for selecting these three particular categories are as follows: Cost, as any risk event that occurs will inevitably affect the project's budget in some form or another; Quality, because it often happens that, in order to mitigate a risk event or alter a project plan after an unexpected risk occurs that effects cost or schedule, time and money have to be reallocated and that often alters the quality of a product; and Schedule, due to the fact that many risk events on any project alter the schedule in some way or other, be it a large or small change.

7.6 Definition of Risk Probability and Impact

After careful consideration and collaboration between all of the plan managers on the project, it was determined that a project of this scale needed impact and probably measurements to signify low, moderate, and high. Very low and very high were deemed unnecessary. Numeric values were assigned to each of these levels as follows:

Probability –

Low / 0.05	Medium / 0.1	High / 0.5

Impact –

Low / 0.1	Medium / 0.3	High / 0.5

The determined risk events were scored on their probability and impact in a risk assessment table, prior to being placed into the Probability Impact Matrix (Appendix C). The total ratings in the table, which were determined by taking Probability times Impact, can be used to determine the organization's sensitivity to each risk event listed.

		Probability of Risk			Magnitude of Damage			Planned Action	
Activity	**Rank**	**Low/0.05**	**Med./0.1**	**High/0.5**	**Low/0.1**	**Med./ 0.3**	**High/0.5**	**Total Rating**	**Type of Action**
Key Personnel Un-available.	**3**		**X**				**X**	0.05	**Insure contractors are available if necessary.**
Delayed delivery of materials and equipment	**1**		**X**				**X**	0.05	**Make delivery a requirement in supplier contracts.**
Weather	**5**		**X**		**X**			0.01	**Change Schedule if necessary**
Materials Shortages	**4**	**X**				**X**		0.03	**Contract with current supplier, and Identify alternate suppliers if needed.**
Damage to original parts provided in kit.	**2**	**X**				**X**		0.03	**Insurance & Liability Waiver**

Revised Stakeholder Tolerances

After determining the risk categories, the specific risk events, their probability and impact, and their total ratings, all of this information was put together and brought before the project sponsor for approval before it was presented to the primary stakeholders. The risk events were laid out before the project stakeholders, as well as the mitigation plans that had been approved for each event, and after careful consideration and discussions between themselves, the project sponsor, and the project manager, the primary stakeholders informed the PM that they would tolerate the risk events as they were laid out and were more than willing to allow SSTC to continue with the project. The Stakeholder Tolerances did not have to be altered in this instance, but as the project is monitored for risks, the stakeholders will be kept abreast of any changes, and should their risk tolerance change it will be documented for this project and for future reference.

7.7 Reporting Formats for Risk Register

The risk registry, as shown in the example below, lays out the definition of the risk, what category it fits into, the root cause of the risk event (if the root cause has been determined and is relevant to the project), the triggers for the risk, and how SSTC will respond to the risk event. There will be weekly quality assessments, and at this time the Risk Manager will go along with the Quality Manager, and the RM will be assessing the progress of the project and any occurrences that could be considered a risk. The assessments, as well as any and all reports from the construction staff and/or the functional managers will all be used to determine risk occurrences, which will all go into the register, be they big or small.

Risk Register

Project

Revision: Date

Risk #	Risk Description	Risk Root Cause	Risk Category	Trigger	Risk Response
1					
2					
3					
4					

7.8 Tracking

It is imperative that any risk events be tracked throughout the life of this project, be they big or small, as a small risk is likely to become a big risk and a detriment to the project if it goes unchecked for a length of time. As this information can be important to any member of the project, it needs to be easily accessible, therefore each plan manager as well as the project manager has copies of the Risk Register and the weekly assessments available for viewing upon request.

8.0 Procurement Management Plan

8.1 Contract Types

There are several different contracts to choose from, so it was left to the Procurement Manager to determine what contracts would be the most beneficial for the Gauchito Rocket Project team, in order to ensure that all necessary materials and equipment were delivered in a timely fashion without it becoming a huge expense to the organization. The Procurement Manager, after discussing all of the materials and equipment to be purchased, determined that the best form of contract to use for materials and equipment (M&E) purchases was firm fixed price.

These contracts were entered into with a clear understanding that all of the M&E purchased was to be delivered no later than a week prior to the project start. This was agreed upon by the organization and the suppliers, and the legal documents were filed with legal, with copies being distributed to the Project Manager, the project sponsor, and a copy to go on file in the procurement office.

There was also a need to outsource the fitters for this project, as that skill set is no longer available on-staff within the organization. After a discussion with the HR and using the Quality Manager's research it was determined that the fitters would be contracted from the Local Fitter's Union. This means that contracts will be drawn up specifying their pay per hour, their breaks and lunches, and all other requirements necessary to meet Union requirements. Since these fitters are unionized, and will have a specific hourly wage for their skill set and experience, it was decided that a fixed price contract would be best in this instance as well. The fitters will receive their hourly wage, and that will be all, ass there will not be any overtime or extraneous costs where the outsourced staff is involved.

8.2 Uses of Organizational Procurement, Contracting or Purchasing Departments

The Procurement Manager, along with the rest of the procurement department, was responsible for; determining what suppliers to contact, drawing up all of the Requests for Proposals (RFP's), creating the benchmark to determine the best supplier to meet the project team's needs, determining what types of contracts to enter into with suppliers, and managing those contracts throughout the life of this project.

8.3 Standardized Procurement Documents

There are several forms of standardized documents used in procurement, many of which were used for this project. These documents include: the firm fixed price contracts entered into with the suppliers, the Requests for Proposal sent out to several suppliers, and the benchmark.

8.4 Constraints and Assumptions

There are a number of constraints and assumptions that have to be considered with any project, and this one is no exception. The assumptions and constraints for this project are as follows:

Constraints:

- There are no available fitters within the organization.
- Trained fitters have to be outsourced for this project
- Delayed delivery of materials and/or equipment will result in a schedule delay

Assumptions:

- The materials and equipment will arrive one week prior to project start date
- All necessary personnel will be available at the time of the project start
- The contracts will be followed as written without any delays or difficulties

8.5 Purchase and Acquisition Lead Times

The suppliers for all of the necessary materials and equipment are in the United States and provide rush delivery, but that is no reason to delay the purchase of the necessary M&E. It was determined that the wisest time to place the purchase orders was 12 days prior to project start, and ensure that the suppliers had the necessary materials and equipment in stock and ready to ship in order to ensure it all arrived promptly on the designated delivery date.

8.6 Types of Warranties

It was clearly stated upon the purchase of the materials and equipment necessary for this project that everything came with a manufacturer warranty, and the stakeholders and project sponsor all deemed these warranties sufficient for this project, since this rocket is a test product and will not be used repeatedly, but rather for data gathering.

8.7 Probability and Impact Matrix

Probability and Impact Matrix			
Probability			
0.5			
0.1	Risk 5		Risk 1 Risk 3
0.01		Risk 2 Risk 4	
Impact	0.1	0.3	0.5

= High Level Risk - Resolve immediately

= Moderate Risk - Track through the life of the project

= Minimal Risk - Be aware of it, but no tracking necessary

Benchmark

Benchmark

Suppliers	Ballard Power	Quantum Tech	Cordant Tech	Pratt & Whitney
Cost Of Hybrid Engines (4)	$12,000	$10,000	$10, 750	$11, 000
Cost of M&E	$4,500	$5,000	$5,000	$5,500
Delivery Time	1.5 weeks	1 week	2 weeks	2.5 weeks
Delivery Cost	$200	$125	$175	$195
RFP Score	8	10	9	10

Quantum Tech has the most criteria matching what the Gauchito Project team is looking for

Therefore, they will be the obvious choice for the supplier for the necessary specialty hybrid engines.

APPENDIX A

Space Systems Technologies Corporation

Ansari X Prize Cup-Gauchito Rocket

Project Charter

Project Name: Ansari X Prize Cup Gauchito Rocket

Project Manager: Julie Davis

Project Tracking Number: PMGT 605-0001 **Date: May 7, 2011**

Project Justification:

This project will address design consideration of the Gauchito Rocket. The rocket's design, launch and test results can be observed using a 7/8 scale of the full sized rocket. This approach provides a valid measurement of the rocket's success without the time and expense necessary to build a full-sized rocket. This will also help in the identification, mitigation and avoidance of risk to the Pablo de Leon X Prize entry. This project is being under taken to show that our company has the ability to produce a reliable test product that accurately duplicates the final full size rocket.

Overview of Deliverables:

1.0 ASSEMBLE ENGINE MOUNT
2.0 FIN PREPARATION
3.0 MARK FIN AND LAUNCH LUG LINES
4.0 INSERTING ENGINE MOUNT
5.0 ATTACH FINS
6.0 ATTACH SHOCK CORD
7.0 ASSEMBLE NOSE CONE
8.0 ATTACH PARACHUTE/SHOCK CORD
9.0 ATTACH LAUNCH LUG
10.0 PAINTING THE ROCKET
11.0 APPLICATION OF DECALS
12.0 APPLYING CLEAR COAT
13.0 DISPLAY NOZZLE ASSEMBLY
14.0 ROCKET PREFLIGHT
15.0 PREPARE FOR TEST LAUNCH

Specific Project Objectives and Success Criteria:

A. The project goal is to build a functional model rocket at 7/8 the actual size within three months from the start date of the project.

B. The SSTC Project Manager "PM" Julie Davis will be responsible for providing the sponsor Jeff Tyler with the scheduling status on a daily to weekly basis as this is a short duration project.

1. Cost

   A. The Gauchito Rocket 7/8 model rocket will be built on the estimated funding of $63,000.00 dollars.

   B. The cost will be further defined as the project resources and cost estimates progress using SSTC existing templates. The budget status shall be provided to the project sponsor on a weekly basis.

2. Quality

   A. The Gauchito Rocket is to be built as a 7/8 scale model of the planned full size rocket the Delta II.

   B. The Gauchito Rocket will be built according to all specifications in the kit.

   C. Length 39.37 ft, Diameter 7.28 ft, GTOW 17,637 lb, DRY WT 5291 lb.

D. All deliverables stated be inspected by QA staff before completion of rocket.

E. Risk Management shall be addressed by the SSTC team in tandem with QA.

F. Testing will be done by the test staff to gather metrics during the test launch.

G. Goal is an altitude of 67 miles with a max speed of 2,684 mph.

Primary Stakeholders and Roles:

The primary stakeholders are

Name	Role	Responsibilities / Authority
SSTC- Mr. Jeff Tyler	Pablo de Leon & Associates / Signoff charter	Fulfill customer contract, e.g. funding; monitor contract fulfillment, coordinating test site and rocket test launch demonstration. Approval of project completion and closure.
SSTC- Mr. Jeff Tyler	Pablo de Leon & Associates Project Sponsor / Signoff charter	Communicate with stakeholders and commitment of personnel resources.
SSTC Ms. Julie Davis	Pablo De Leon & Associates-Ansari X Prize Gauchito Rocket Project Manager / Signoff Charter/Scope	<u>Responsibilities:</u> Coordinate the project planning, executing, monitoring and controlling, and closing, following DOD's processes based on the PMI. Ensure project deliverables are completed on time and in budget. Report progress of project to stakeholders to cover critical path schedule, deliverables, and any identified risks updated during weekly status meetings. Coordinate training for outsourced Fitters, Coordinate and lead project meetings. <u>Authority:</u> Communicate with DOD contact on any issues. Communicate directly with project sponsor Major T.J. Stone and DOD executives on status and issues. Communicate with resource officer and affected functional managers regarding resource allocation and scheduling.

		Authorize changes and any corrections to be taken, to include DOD activities. <u>Limitations</u>: The PM will not manage HR activities regarding DOD personnel.
SSTC Julie Davis	Scope	-Project Charter*-Julie -Project Preliminary Scope-Tom -Product Description*-Gwen -WBS*-Julie -Constraints*-Julie -Assumptions*-Julie
SSTC Brian Kirouac	Schedule	-Scheduled start dates for WBS tasks -Major Milestones and target dates
SSTC Tom Jones	Quality	-Provide Quality Assurance Staff for the project to validate each deliverable.
SSTC Gwen Edwards	Cost/Financing	-Preparation of Cost Estimates - Performance Measurement Baseline
SSTC Kevin LaSalle	Staffing	Responsibility Assignment Matrix -Key or Required Staff
SSTC Jeanea Brown	Risk Manager	Identify -Key risks and provide risk management resources to the project to facilitate identifying risks and planning for contingencies.
SSTC Kevin LaSalle	Communications	Description of how the communication for the project is going to proceed.
SSTC	Procurement	Coordination of resources with resource officer and any functional managers affected.

Key Constraints:

1. SSTC does not currently have the employee resources available during our project start to finish dates for the Fitter positions. If the materials are not delivered in the time frame which the project was based on there will be a change to the project delivery date which we do not have available to us.

2. The materials must be delivered the Friday before project start.

3. Project must be completed in 3 months time.

4. Estimated Budget is not to exceed $63,000.00.

Key Assumptions:

1. All materials for the rocket will have been purchased by SSTC and received no later than the Friday before project start. (Recommended engines are as follows: 1/2A3-2T, A3-4T, A10-3T.)

2. All activities associated to building the model rocket will follow the National Association of Rocketry (NAR) Safety Code.

3. All Project Management activities will use SSTC's project tools, templates and processes, based on PMI standards.

4. That the project can be completed in 3 months time and within an estimated budget of $63,000.00

Signatures—The following people agree that the above information is accurate:

- SSTC project team members:

Ms. Julie Davis ______________________________

Ms. Gwen Edwards ______________________________

Ms. Jeanea Brown ______________________________

Mr. Tom Jones ______________________________

Mr. Kevin LaSalle ______________________________

Mr. Brian Kirouac ______________________________

- Project sponsor and/or authorizing manager(s):

Mr. Jeff Tyler ______________________________

APPENDIX B

Gauchito Rocket Scaled Demonstration

Product Description

Project Name: Ansari X Prize Gauchito Rocket **Date: May 8, 2011**

Project Overview:

Rocket Components and Steps:

The components of the rocket will be built following the steps in the provided Construction Plan. The steps are below.

01-Assembling of the Engine Mount

02-Fin Preparation

03-Marking of Fin and Lug Lines

04-Insertion of Engine Mount

05-Fin Attachment

06-Shock Cord Attachment

07-Nose Cone Assembly

08-Parachute and Shock Cord Attachment

09-Launch Lug Attachment

10-Paint the rocket

11- Decal Application

12-Clear Coat Application

13-Display Nozzle Assembly

14-Rocket Pre-Flight

15-Prepare for Rocket Test Launch

Specific Product Specifications:

The Gauchito Rocket will be built according to following specifications:

1. 7/8 scale model of the planned full size rocket the Delta II

2. The rocket will be assembled with materials and equipment in the assembly kit. All rocket components in the construction kit will be assembled as part of the rocket or launch setup.

3. Recommended hybrid engines are as follows: 1/2A3-2T, A3-4T, A10-3T to replace the standard engines in the construction kit. The construction company will select the best engine to meet the performance requirements.

4. Length = 39.37 ft, Diameter = 7.28 ft, GTOW 17,637 lb, DRY WT 5291 lb.

Performance: The Gauchito Rocket performance will be based upon the following

1. Reaching a launch altitude of 67 miles in less than 17 seconds total flying time
2. Total thrust of 52,910 pounds
3. The maximum speed capable of being reached is 2,684 mph, and will be part of metrics gathered during test. It is not a determination in measuring if the rocket performance is acceptable. It is, however, a factor in obtaining the launch altitude specified. A reduced speed may make the rocket incapable of reaching the required altitude.
4. Payload capacity of three crewmembers or 300 kg.
5. Crew environment: Nitrogen-Oxygen using pressurized suites in a pure oxygen atmosphere

Quality:

1. The Gauchito Rocket will be built according to all instructions in the Construction Plan.
2. All activities associated to building the model rocket will follow the National Association of Rocketry (NAR) Safety Code.

Product Assumptions:

1. Pablo de Leon & Associates will take possession of the rocket upon completion of assembly following the above steps and meeting the requirements.

APPENDIX C

Scope Statement

Gauchito Rocket

Project Name: Ansari X Prize Gauchito Rocket

Project Manager: Julie Davis

Project Tracking Number: PMGT 605-0001 Date: April 19, 2011

Project Justification: This project will address design consideration of the Gauchito Rocket. The rocket's design, launch and test results can be observed using a 7/8 scale of the full sized rocket. This approach provides a valid measurement of the rocket's success without the time and expense necessary to build a full-sized rocket. This will also help in the identification, mitigation and avoidance of risk to the space development program. This project is being under taken to show that our company has the ability to produce a reliable test product that accurately duplicates the final full size rocket. To do this we will deliver the completed 7/8 scale rocket 3 days after the assembly is completed to Peterson AFB test launch site.

I. Overview of Deliverables:

Reference the Work Breakdown Structure (WBS), prepared as a separate document and an example included in Appendix A, for details on each deliverable.

All deliverables will be constructed according to kit instructions.

1.0 ASSEMBLE ENGINE MOUNT

2.0 FIN PREPARATION

3.0 MARK FIN AND LAUNCH LUG LINES

4.0 INSERTING ENGINE MOUNT

5.0 ATTACH FINS

6.0 ATTACH SHOCK CORD

7.0 ASSEMBLE NOSE CONE

8.0 ATTACH PARACHUTE/SHOCK CORD

9.0 ATTACH LAUNCH LUG

10.0 PAINTING THE ROCKET

11.0 APPLICATION OF DECALS

12.0 APPLYING CLEAR COAT

13.0 DISPLAY NOZZLE ASSEMBLY

14.0 ROCKET PREFLIGHT

15.0 PREPARE FOR TEST LAUNCH

II. Specific Project Objectives and Success Criteria:

1. The project objective is to develop, build, and test a working model rocket at 7/8 the actual size within two months from the start date of the project.

2. The initial milestones are as follows and can be changed utilizing already implemented change management templates as the project progresses toward completion.

3. Schedule

   a. The project goal is to build a working model within three months from project start.

   b. The demonstration rocket testing will be scheduled within one week of completion of the model rocket, at the test launch facility. The test launch will be scheduled with an alternate date in case the wind speed is over 10 miles per hour on the target date, since high wind speed may negatively impact the rocket success.

   c. The preliminary schedule in Appendix B shows milestones for each deliverable, based on the WBS. The schedule will be further refined during project planning, and milestones may be moved, depending on factors such as concurrent work activities.

   d. Each resource assigned to the project will provide weekly status reports to include issues.

   e. The project manager will provide schedule status to the project sponsor and the customer on a weekly basis, given the project short duration.

4. Cost

   a. The build of the rocket will be built based on an agreed upon funding of $50,000.

   b. The project planning will further refine the preliminary resource and cost estimates provided in Appendix C. This process will use existing templates and procedures. The project manager will provide budget status to the project sponsor and the customer on a weekly basis, given the project short duration.

   c. Engineering resources assigned to the project will support refining requirements and cost estimates.

5. Quality

    a. The Scaled composite Gauchito rocket will be a 7/8 scale model of the planned full sized rocket model.

    b. The demonstration rocket will be built to the specifications in the kit, including optional steps, such as fin sanding to optimize performance.

    c. All fins available in the kit will be installed, per the Fin Preparation step, to ensure rocket stability.

    d. Quality Assurance personnel assigned to the project will prepare a Quality Assurance Plan input to the PM to gather necessary approvals.

    e. Quality Assurance personnel assigned to the project will examine each individual component produced by a deliverable before attaching each component as part of the rocket. QA will also inspect the rocket prior to launch.

    f. Configuration Management personnel assigned to the project will support the PM in preparation of a Configuration Management Plan, and support definition of activities for defect correction.

    g. Configuration Management personnel assigned to the project will maintain a list of issues and resolutions.

    h. Risk Management personnel assigned to the project will support the PM in preparation of a Risk Management plan to identify risks, level of risk and contingencies if the risks should occur.

    i. Test personnel assigned to the project will support the PM to provide input to the Test Plan.

    j. The rocket will be launched using the purchased four hybrid rocket engines.

    k. The rocket body will remain intact through the test launch, without breaking up before reaching the target altitude and return safely.

III. Scope Management Issues:

The project scope will be maintained by entering all requirements and work activities into existing program tools for tracking requirements (WBS, Scope Management Plan, Project Charter etc…). The activities will meet the project objectives and the contract requirements.

<u>1. Defects:</u>

If defects are identified by QA during construction, they will document and provide the data to the PM. The PM and project team will identify options for correcting the defects and present them, along with the most effective option. Any schedule, cost, risk, and performance impacts will be identified. The Change Control Board "CCB" will approve the corrective action and associated impacts.

The Finance personnel assigned to the project will work contract changes as need due to changes to cost and schedule.

Configuration Management will maintain a list of defects and resolutions, and CCB minutes.

2. Change requests:

If requests for additional materials or changes in construction from those provided in the installation kit, they will complete a Change Request form and provide it the PM.

(Note: Changes may be requested due to identifying a better installation technique.)

The request, along with cost, schedule, and risk impacts, will be presented to the CCB for evaluation and approval or denial.

If the Change Request is approved, the PM will update cost and schedule to incorporate the change. Finance personnel assigned to the project will work contract changes as need due to changes to cost and schedule. Engineering, CM, QA, Risk and Technical documentation will be updated accordingly. This includes updates to the kit instructions.

If the Change Request is denied, no changes will be made to the project scope.

Any additional materials needed due to a Change Request will be procured by Space Systems Technologies Corporation "SSTC" and provided to the project test site.

Primary Stakeholders and Roles:

Name	Role	Responsibilities
SSTC	Customer	Fulfill customer contract, e.g. funding; monitor contract fulfillment, including participation in Configuration Control Board (CCB), coordinating test site and rocket test launch demonstration.
Mr. Jeff Tyler	Project Sponsor / Signoff Scope Statement	Communicate with stakeholders and commitment of personnel resources.
Ms. Julie Davis	Project Manager / Signoff Scope Statement	Coordinate the project planning, executing, monitoring and controlling, and closing. Responsible for the project budget, cost and schedule. Provide schedule, define risks, report status, task personnel resources, coordinate any necessary training, coordinate and lead CCB and project meetings. The PM will provide input to line managers on staff performance, but will not manage HR activities. (Reference full responsibilities and authority in the Project Charter.)
Mr. Tom Jones	Quality Assurance (QA) and Signoff Scope Statement	Provide QA resources to the project to validate each deliverable. Participate in CM processes for possible defect correction in deliverables.
Mr. Kevin LaSalle	Staffing Manager / Signoff Scope Statement	Provide staffing resources to the project to coordinate support as specified in the Statement of Work (SOW).
Ms. Gwen Edwards	Cost Management / Signoff Scope Statement	Provide financial resources for contract activities and closure.
Mr. Brian	Schedule Management Plan / Signoff Scope Statement	Defining severity levels of potential schedule impacts. Identifying who needs to be involved at each level. Determining how changes will be incorporated into the project schedule. Determining how

		schedule changes will be communicated to key project stakeholders.
Ms. Jeanea Brown	Risk Manager / Signoff Scope Statement	Provide risk management resources to the project to facilitate identifying risks and planning for contingencies.

IV. Key Constraints:

1. SSTC does not currently have the employee resources available during our project start to finish dates for the Fitter positions. If the materials are not delivered in the time frame which the project was based on there will be a change to the project delivery date which we do not have available to us.
2. The materials must be delivered the Friday before project start.
3. Project must be completed in 3 months time.
4. Estimated Budget is not to exceed $63,000.00.

Key Assumptions:

5. All materials for the rocket will have been purchased by SSTC and received no later than the Friday before project start. (Recommended engines are as follows: 1/2A3-2T, A3-4T, A10-3T.)
6. All activities associated to building the model rocket will follow the National Association of Rocketry (NAR) Safety Code.
7. All Project Management activities will use SSTC's project tools, templates and processes, based on PMI standards.
8. That the project can be completed in 3 months time and within an estimated budget of $63,000.00

Signatures— The following people agree that the above information is accurate:

- Project team members:

Ms. Julie Davis, Project Manager ______________________

Ms. Gwen Edwards, Finance ______________________

Mr. Brain, Engineering Manager ______________________

Mr. Kevin LaSalle, Staffing Manager ______________________

Ms. Jeannea Brown, Risk Manager ______________________

Mr. Tom Jones, Quality Manager ______________________

- Project sponsor and/or authorizing manager(s):

Mr. Jeff Tyler, Sponsor ______________________________

APPENDIX D

WORK BREAKDOWN STRUCTURE

1.0 ASSEMBLE ENGINE MOUNT

- 1.1 Measure, Mark and Cut Engine Tube "
  - 1.1.1 Lay ruler along engine tube
  - 1.1.2 Measure engine from left of engine tube @ 1/8""""
  - 1.1.3 Mark left end of engine Tube @ 1/8'
  - 1.1.4 Measure engine from left of engine tube @ 3/4""""
  - 1.1.5 Mark from left of engine tube @ 3/4"" "
  - 1.1.6 Measure engine tube from left of engine tube @ 11/2""""
  - 1.1.7 Mark from left of engine tube @ 1 1/2""""
- 1.2 Cut Engine Tube
  - 1.2.1 Cut Slit of 1/8"" @ 1 1/2 inch Mark on Engine Tube"
- 1.3 Glue, Tube, Assemble Hook "
  - 1.3.1 Apply thin line of glue completely around engine at 3/4"" mark"
  - 1.3.2 Position Hook per diagram
  - 1.3.3 Insert Engine Hook into 1/8"" Slit on Engine Mount Tube"
- 1.4 Assemble Mylar Ring to Tube
  - 1.4.1 Slide Mylar ring onto Engine Mount tube at 3/4"" mark "
  - 1.4.2 Let Dry
- 1.5 Assemble Yellow Engine Block to Engine Mount Tube
  - 1.5.1 Apply glue inside front of Engine Mount tube
  - 1.5.2 Insert Yellow Engine Block flush with the right end per diagram
  - 1.5.3 Let Dry
- 1.6 Assemble Centering Rings
  - 1.6.1 Remove Centering rings from card with modeling knife
  - 1.6.2 Apply thin line of Glue around engine mount tube @ 1/8"" mark"
  - 1.6.3 Slide notched Centering Ring onto glued line @ 1/8"" mark"
  - 1.6.4 Let Glue Set
  - 1.6.5 Apply thin line of Glue to opposite side of notched center ring flush with end of engine mount tube
  - 1.6.6 Slide un-notched Centering Ring in place over glue flush with end of engine tube mount
  - 1.6.7 Let Dry
- 1.7 Application of Glue Fillets
  - 1.7.1 Apply Glue Fillets to both sides of Centering Rings for reinforcement
  - 1.7.2 Let Dry

2.0 FIN PREPARATION

2.1 Sand/Cut fins

2.1.1 Sand Laser Cut Balsa Sheet w/Fine Sandpaper

2.2 Cutting Out Fins

2.2.1 Cut out fin #1 w/modeling knife

2.2.2 Cut out fin #2 w/modeling knife

2.2.3 Cut out fin #3 w/ modeling knife

2.2.4 Cut out fin #4 w/modeling knife

2.3 Stack and Sand Fins

2.3.1 Stack Fins

2.3.2 Sand Edges of fins

3.0 MARK FIN AND LAUNCH LUG LINES

3.1 Cut - Tape

3.1.2 Cut out tube marking guide

3.1.2 Tape tube marking guide around body tube

3.1.3 Mark body tube at arrows

3.1.4 Mark Launch Lug Line as LL on Body tube

3.2 Remove guide, connect fins and lug lines, extend LL line"

3.2.1 Remove Tube Marking guide from body tube

3.2.2 Connect Fins using door frame

3.2.3 Connect launch lug lines using door frame

3.3 Extend Launch Lug Line

3.3.1 Extend launch lug line 3 3/4"" from end of tube"

4.0 INSERTING ENGINE MOUNT

4.1 Mark inside of tube @ 5/8"" where LL is"

4.1.1 Measure inside tube to 5/8"" position on tube"

4.1.2 Mark inside tube at 5/8"""

4.2 Glue Tube

4.2.1 Measure inside rear of body tube to 1 3/4' position on tube

4.2.2 Use finger to smear glue 1 3/4"" inside rear of body tube along LL."

4.3 Assemble Engine Hook

4.3.1 Align engine hook with LL line

4.3.2 Insert engine mount into body tube until centering ring is even w/the 5/8"" glue mark"

4.3.3 Let Dry

4.4 Gluing Center Body Ring

4.4.1 Locate scrap piece of balsa to apply glue

4.4.2 Apply glue to centering/body tube joint

4.4.3 Let Dry

5.0 ATTACH FINS

5.1 Attach Fin #1

5.1.1 Apply thin layer of glue to edge of fin

5.1.2 Allow to dry (1 minute for model)

5.1.3 Apply second layer of glue to edge of fin

5.1.4 Attach Fin to body tube along one of fin lines flush w/end

5.2 Attach Fin #2

5.2.1 Apply thin layer of glue to edge of fin#2

5.2.2 Allow to dry (1 minute for model)

5.2.3 Apply second layer of glue to edge of fin #2

5.2.4 Attach Fin #2 to body tube along one of fin lines flush w/end

5.3 Attach Fin #3

5.3.1 Apply thin layer of glue to edge of fin #3

5.3.2 Allow to dry (1 minute for model)

5.3.3 Apply second layer of glue to edge of fin #3

5.3.4 Attach Fin #3 to body tube along one of fin lines flush w/end

5.4 Attach Fin #4

5.4.1 Apply thin layer of glue to edge of fin #4

5.4.2 Allow to dry (1 minute for model)

5.4.3 Apply second layer of glue to edge of fin #4

5.4.4 Attach Fin #4 to body tube along one of fin lines flush w/end

5.5 Check Fin Alignment

5.5.1 Check Fin #1 Alignment as shown in diagram

5.5.2 Check Fin #2 Alignment as shown in diagram

5.5.3 Check Fin #3 Alignment as shown in diagram

5.5.4 Check Fin #4 Alignment as shown in diagram

5.6 Allow glue to dry

5.6.1 Let Glue Set

5.6.2 Stand Rocket on end

5.6.3 let glue dries completely

6.0 ATTACH SHOCK CORD

6.1 Cut out shock cord mount

6.1.1 Cut out shock cord from front page

6.2 First Glue Application

6.2.1 Attach shock cord to shock cord mount

6.2.2 Apply glue to shock cord mount

6.2.3 Fold edge of shock cord mount forward over glued shock cord

6.3 Second Glue Application

6.3.1 Apply glue to shock cord mount

6.3.2 Fold forward again-see diagram for clarification

6.4 Squeeze and Hold

6.4.1 Squeeze shock cord/shock cord mount tightly

6.4.2 Hold for 1 minute

6.5 Attaching Shock Cord Mount

6.5.1 Glue mount 1"" inside body tube"

6.5.2 Hold until glue sets

6.5.3 Let Dry Completely

7.0 ASSEMBLE NOSE CONE

7.1 Glue nose cone

7.1.1 Apply plastic cement to inside rim of nose cone

7.1.2 Press Nose Cone Insert into place over plastic cement inside of nose cone rim

7.1.3 Let Dry Completely

8.0 ATTACH PARACHUTE/SHOCK CORD

8.1 Attach Lines

8.1.1 Pass shroud line on parachute through eyelet

8.2 Attach Parachute

8.2.1 Pass parachute through loop in shroud-look to diagram for clarification

8.3 Tie Lines

8.3.1 Tie shock cord to nose cone using a double knot

9.0 ATTACH LAUNCH LUG

9.1 Glue launch lines

9.1.1 Glue LL centered onto LL Line on rocket body

9.2 Application of Glue Fillets

9.2.1 Apply glue fillets along launch lug

9.2.2 Apply glue fillets along fin/body tube joints

9.2.3 Smooth each fillet with finger

9.2.4 Let glue dry completely

10.0 PAINTING THE ROCKET

10.1 Apply first coat

10.1.1 Spray rocket with white primer

10.1.2 Let Dry

10.2 Sand

10.1.2 Sand entire rocket

10.3 Apply final coat

10.3.1 Spray completed rocket with white second coat of primer

10.3.2 Let Dry

10.3.3 Spray Nose Cone with Copper paint

10.3.4 Let Dry

11.0 APPLICATION OF DECALS

11.1 Apply first decal

11.1.1 Remove First decal from back sheet

11.1.2 Place on Rocket where indicated

11.1.3 Rub decal to remove bubbles

11.2 Apply second decal

11.2.1 Remove second decal from backing sheet

11.2.2 Place on Rocket where indicated

11.2.3 Rub decal to remove bubbles

11.3 Apply third decal

11.3.1 Remove third decal from backing sheet

11.3.2 Place on Rocket where indicated

11.3.3 Rub decal to remove bubbles

11.4 Apply fourth decal

11.4.1 Remove fourth decal from backing sheet

11.4.2 Place on Rocket where indicated

11.4.3 Rub decal to remove bubbles

11.5 Apply fifth decal

11.5.1 Remove fifth decal from backing sheet

11.5.2 Place on Rocket where indicated

11.5.3 Rub decal to remove bubbles

11.6 Apply sixth Decal

11.6.1 Remove sixth decal from backing sheet

11.6.2 Place on Rocket where indicated

11.6.3 Rub decal to remove bubbles

11.7 Apply seventh Decal

11.7.1 Remove seventh decal from backing sheet

11.7.2 Place on Rocket where indicated

11.7.3 Rub decal to remove bubbles

12.0 APPLYING CLEAR COAT

12.1 Apply clear coat to entire rocket

12.1.1 Apply clear coat to entire rocket

12.1.2 Dry Completely

13.0 DISPLAY NOZZLE ASSEMBLY

13.1 Spray Nozzle Base White

13.1.1 Paint Nozzle #1 w/Silver Paint Pen

13.1.2 Paint Nozzle #2 w/ Silver Paint Pen

13.1.3 Paint Nozzle #3 w/ Silver Paint Pen

13.1.4 Paint Nozzle #4 w/ Silver Paint Pen

13.1.5 Allow to dry

13.2 Apply Glue

13.2.1 Apply glue to tab on nozzle #1

13.2.2 Place Nozzle #1 into hole on base

13.2.3 Apply glue to tab on nozzle #2

13.2.4 Place Nozzle #2 into hole on base

13.2.5 Apply glue to tab on nozzle #3

13.2.6 Place Nozzle #3 into hole on base

13.2.7 Apply glue to tab on nozzle #4

13.2.8 Place Nozzle #4 into hole on base

14.0 ROCKET PREFLIGHT

14.1 prepare

14.1.1 Remove Nose Cone from Rocket

14.1.2 Locate recovery wadding

14.1.3 Insert 4-5 loosely crumpled squares of recovery wadding

14.2 Spike

14.2.1 Pull parachute into a spike-see diagram for clarification

14.3 Fold

14.3.1 Fold parachute according to diagram

14.4 Roll

14.4.1 Roll parachute according to diagram

14.5 Re-insert

14.5.1 Wrap lines loosely around rolled parachute-see diagram for clarification

14.5.2 Insert parachute into body tube of rocket

14.5.3 Insert shock cord into body tube of rocket

14.5.4 Insert nose cone into body tube of rocket

15.0 PREPARE FOR TEST LAUNCH

15.1 Insert Engine

15.1.1 Remove engine

15.1.2 Insert tip to touch propellant

15.1.3 Insert engine into rocket

APPENDIX E

COST ROLLUP ESTIMATES

(see next page)

APPENDIX F

Resource types - estimates in man-hours for Duration Estimate

TASKS	Fitter	Draftsman	Gluer	Cutter	SanderI	SanderII	Painter I	Painter II	Engineer	Dummy	
1.0 ASSEMBLE ENGINE MOUNT	14	30	7	4	0	0	0	0	0	40	95
1.1 Measure, Mark and Cut Engine Tube	5	30	0	0	0	0	0	0	0	0	
-1.1.1 Lay ruler along engine tube	5										
-1.1.2 Measure engine from left of engine tube tube @ 1/8"		5									
-1.1.3 Mark left end of Engine Tube @ 1/8'		5									
-1.1.4 Measure engine from left of engine tube @ 3/4"		5									
-1.1.5 Mark from left of EngineTube @ 3/4"		5									
-1.1.6 Measure engine tube from left of engine tube @ 11/2"		5									
-1.1.7 Mark from left of Engine Tube @ 1 1/2"		5									
-1.2 Cut Engine Tube	0	0	0	2	0	0	0	0	0	0	
-1.2.1 Cut Slit of 1/8" @ 1 1/2 inch Mark on Engine Tube				2							
-1.3 Glue, Tube, Assemble Hook	5	0	2	0	0	0	0	0	0	0	
-1.3.1 Apply thin line of glue completely around engine at 3/4" mark			2								
-1.3.2 Position Hook per diagram	2										
-1.3.3 Insert Engine Hook into 1/8" Slit on Engine Mount Tube	3										
-1.4 Assemble Mylar Ring to Tube	1	0	0	0	0	0	0	0	0	8	
-1.4.1 Slide Mylar ring onto Engline Mount tube at 3/4" mark	1										
-1.4.2 Let Dry										8	
-1.5 Assemble Yellow Engine Block to Engine Mount Tube	1	0	1	0	0	0	0	0	0	8	
-1.5.1 Apply glue inside front of Engine Mount tube			1								
-1.5.2 Insert Yellow Engine Block flush with the right end per diagram	1										
-1.5.3 Let Dry										8	
-1.6 Assemble Centering Rings	2	0	2	2	0	0	0	0	0	16	
-1.6.1 Remove Centering rings from card with modeling knife				2							
-1.6.2 Apply thin line of Glue around engine mount tube @ 1/8" mark			1								
-1.6.3 Slide notched Centering Ring onto glued line @ 1/8" mark	1										
-1.6.4 Let Glue Set										8	
-1.6.5 Apply thin line of Glue to opposite side of notched center ring flush with end of engine mount tube			1								
-1.6.6 Slide unnotched Centering Ring in place over glue flush with end of engine tube mount	1										
-1.6.7 Let Dry										8	
-1.7 Application of Glue Fillets	0	0	2	0	0	0	0	0	0	8	
-1.7.1 Apply Glue Fillets to both sides of Centering Rings for reinforcement			2								
-1.7.2 Let Dry										8	
2.0 FIN PREPARATION	2	0	0	12	16	0	0	0	0	0	30
-2.1 Sand/Cut fins	0	0	0	0	8	0	0	0	0	0	
-2.1.1 Sand Laser Cut Balsa Sheet w/Fine Sandpaper					8						
-2.2 Cutting Out Fins	0	0	0	12	0	0	0	0	0	0	

2.2.1 Cut out fin #1 w/modeling knife				3							
2.2.2 Cut out fin #2 w/modeling knife				3							
2.2.3 Cut out fin #3 w/ modeling knife				3							
2.2.4 Cut out fin #4 w/modeling knife				3							
-2.3 Stack and Sand Fins	2	0	0	0	8	0	0	0	0	0	
-2.3.1 Stack Fins	2										
-2.3.2 Sand Edges of fins					8						
3.0 MARK FIN AND LAUNCH LUG LINES	19	12	0	2	0	0	0	0	0	0	33
-3.1 Cut - Tape	3	8	0	2	0	0	0	0	0	0	
3.1.1 Cut out tube marking guide				2							
-3.1.2 Tape tube marking guide around body tube	3										
-3.1.3 Mark body tube at arrows		4									
-3.1.4 Mark Launch Lug Line as LL on Body tube		4									
-3.2 Remove guide, connect fins and lug lines, extend LL line	16	0	0	0	0	0	0	0	0	0	
-3.2.1 Remove Tube Marking guide from body tube	4										
-3.2.2 Connect Fins using door frame	4										
-3.2.3 Connect launch lug lines using door frame	8										
-3.3 Extend Launch Lug Line	0	4	0	0	0	0	0	0	0	0	
-3.3.1 Extend launch lug line 3 3/4" from end of tube		4									
4.0 INSERTING ENGINE MOUNT	11	10	6	0	0	0	0	0	0	16	43
-4.1 Mark inside of tube @ 5/8" where LL is	0	7	0	0	0	0	0	0	0	0	
-4.1.1 Measure inside tube to 5/8" position on tube		4									
-4.1.2 Mark inside tube at 5/8"		3									
-4.2 Glue Tube	0	3	2	0	0	0	0	0	0	0	
-4.2.1 Measure inside rear of body tube to 1 3/4' position on tube		3									
-4.2.2 Use finger to smear glue 1 3/4" inside rear of body tube along LL.			2								
-4.3 Assemble Engine Hook	10	0	0	0	0	0	0	0	0	8	
-4.3.1 Align engine hook with LL line	5										
-4.3.2 Insert engine mount into body tube until centering ring is even w/the 5/8" glue mark	5										
-4.3.3 Let Dry										8	
-4.4 Gluing Center Body Ring	1	0	4	0	0	0	0	0	0	8	
-4.4.1 Locate scrap piece of balsa to apply glue	1										
-4.4.2 Apply glue to centering/body tube joint			4								
-4.4.3 Let Dry										8	
5.0 ATTACH FINS	20	16	20	0	0	0	0	0	0	17	73
-5.1 Attach Fin #1	4	0	5	0	0	0	0	0	0	1	
-5.1.1 Apply thin layer of glue to edge of fin			3								
-5.1.2 Allow to dry (1 minute for model)										1	
-5.1.3 Apply second layer of glue to edge of fin			2								
-5.1.4 Attach Fin to body tube along one of fin lines flush w/end	4										
-5.2 Attach Fin #2	4	0	5	0	0	0	0	0	0	1	
-5.2.1 Apply thin layer of glue to edge of fin#2			3								
-5.2.2 Allow to dry (1 minute for model)										1	
-5.2.3 Apply second layer of glue to edge of fin #2			2								
-5.2.4 Attach Fin #2 to body tube along one of fin lines flush w/end	4										
-5.3 Attach Fin #3	4	0	5	0	0	0	0	0	0	1	
-5.3.1 Apply thin layer of glue to edge of fin #3			3								
-5.3.2 Allow to dry (1 minute for model)										1	
-5.3.3 Apply second layer of glue to edge of fin #3			2								
-5.3.4 Attach Fin #3 to body tube along one of fin lines flush w/end	4										
-5.4 Attach Fin #4	4	0	5	0	0	0	0	0	0	1	
-5.4.1 Apply thin layer of glue to edge of fin #4			3								
-5.4.2 Allow to dry (1 minute for model)										1	

-5.4.3 Apply second layer of glue to edge of fin #4			2								
-5.4.4 Attach Fin #4 to body tube along one of fin lines flush w/end	4										
-5.5 Check Fin Alignment	0	16	0	0	0	0	0	0	0	0	
-5.5.1 Check Fin #1 Alignment as shown in diagram		4									
-5.5.2 Check Fin #2 Alignment as shown in diagram		4									
-5.5.3 Check Fin #3 Alignment as shown in diagram		4									
-5.5.4 Check Fin #4 Alignment as shown in diagram		4									
-5.6 Allow glue to dry	4	0	0	0	0	0	0	0	0	13	
-5.6.1 Let Glue Set										5	
-5.6.2 Stand Rocket on end	4										
-5.6.3 let glue dries completely										8	
6.0 ATTACH SHOCK CORD	16	0	19	5	0	0	0	0	0	8	48
-6.1 Cut out shock cord mount	0	0	0	5	0	0	0	0	0	0	
-6.1.1 Cut out shock cord from front page				5							
-6.2 First Glue Application	8	0	4	0	0	0	0	0	0	0	
-6.2.1 Attach shock cord to shock cord mount	4										
-6.2.2 Apply glue to shock cord mount			4								
-6.2.3 Fold edge of shock cord mount forward over glued shock cord	4										
-6.3 Second Glue Application	4	0	4	0	0	0	0	0	0	0	
-6.3.1 Apply glue to shock cord mount			4								
-6.3.2 Fold forward again-see diagram for clarification	4										
-6.4 Squueze and Hold	0	0	6	0	0	0	0	0	0	0	
-6.4.1 Squeeze shock cord/shock cord mount tightly			2								
-6.4.2 Hold for 1 minute			4								
-6.5 Attaching Shock Cord Mount	4	0	5	0	0	0	0	0	0	8	
-6.5.1 Glue mount 1" inside body tube	4		4								
-6.5.2 Hold until glue sets			1								
-6.5.3 Let Dry Completely										8	
7.0 ASSEMBLE NOSE CONE	4	0	4	0	0	0	0	0	0	8	16
-7.1 Glue nose cone	4	0	4	0	0	0	0	0	0	8	
-7.1.1 Apply plastic cement to inside rim of nose cone			4								
-7.1.2 Press Nose Cone Insert into place over plastic cement inside of nose cone rim	4										
-7.1.3 Let Dry Completely										8	
8.0 ATTACH PARACHUTE/SHOCK CORD	18	0	0	0	0	0	0	0	0	0	18
-8.1 Attach Lines	7	0	0	0	0	0	0	0	0	0	
-8.1.1 Pass shroud line on parachute through eyelit	7										
-8.2 Attach Parachute	5	0	0	0	0	0	0	0	0	0	
-8.2.1 Pass parachute through loop in shroud-look to diagram for clarification	5										
-8.3 Tie Lines	6	0	0	0	0	0	0	0	0	0	
-8.3.1 Tie shock cord to nose cone using a double knot	6										
9.0 ATTACH LAUNCH LUG	0	0	24	0	0	0	0	0	0	8	32
-9.1 Glue launch lines	0	0	4	0	0	0	0	0	0	0	
-9.1.1 Glue LL centerd onto LL Line on rocket body			4								
-9.2 Application of Glue Fillets	0	0	20	0	0	0	0	0	0	8	
-9.2.1 Apply glue fillets along launch lug			4								
-9.2.2 Apply glue fillets along fin/body tube joints			12								
-9.2.3 Smooth each fillet with finger			4								
-9.2.4 Let glue dry completely										8	
10.0 PAINTING THE ROCKET	0	0	0	0	1	16	8	48	0	24	97
-10.1 Apply first coat	0	0	0	0	0	0	8	0	0	8	
-10.1.1 Spray rocket with white primer							8				
-10.1.2 Let Dry										8	
-10.2 Sand	0	0	0	0	1	16	0	0	0	0	

-10.1.2 Sand entire rocket					1	16					
-10.3 Apply final coat	0	0	0	0	0	0	0	48	0	16	
-10.3.1 Spray completed rocket with white second coat of primer								16			
-10.3.2 Let Dry										8	
-10.3.3 Spray Nose Cone with Copper paint								32			
-10.3.4 Let Dry										8	
11.0 APPLICATION OF DECALS	0	35	0	0	0	0	0	0	0	0	35
-11.1 Apply first decal	0	5	0	0	0	0	0	0	0	0	
-11.1.1 Remove First decal from back sheet		1									
-11.1.2 Place on Rocket where indicated		3									
-11.1.3 Rub decal to remove bubbles		1									
-11.2 Apply second decal	0	5	0	0	0	0	0	0	0	0	
-11.2.1 Remove second decal from backing sheet		1									
-11.2.2 Place on Rocket where indicated		3									
-11.2.3 Rub decal to remove bubbles		1									
-11.3 Apply third decal	0	5	0	0	0	0	0	0	0	0	
-11.3.1 Remove third decal from backing sheet		1									
-11.3.2 Place on Rocket where indicated		3									
-11.3.3 Rub decal to remove bubbles		1									
-11.4 Apply fourth decal	0	5	0	0	0	0	0	0	0	0	
-11.4.1 Remove fourth decal from backing sheet		1									
-11.4.2 Place on Rocket where indicated		3									
-11.4.3 Rub decal to remove bubbles		1									
-11.5 Apply fifth decal	0	5	0	0	0	0	0	0	0	0	
-11.5.1 Remove fifth decal from backing sheet		1									
-11.5.2 Place on Rocket where indicated		3									
-11.5.3 Rub decal to remove bubbles		1									
-11.6 Apply sixth Decal	0	5	0	0	0	0	0	0	0	0	
-11.6.1 Remove sixth decal from backing sheet		1									
-11.6.2 Place on Rocket where indicated		3									
-11.6.3 Rub decal to remove bubbles		1									
-11.7 Apply seventh Decal	0	5	0	0	0	0	0	0	0	0	
-11.7.1 Remove seventh decal from backing sheet		1									
-11.7.2 Place on Rocket where indicated		3									
-11.7.3 Rub decal to remove bubbles		1									
12.0 APPLYING CLEAR COAT	0	0	0	0	0	0	0	8	0	8	16
-12.1 Apply clear coat to entire rocket	0	0	0	0	0	0	0	8	0	8	
12.1.1 Apply clear coat to entire rocket								8			
12.1.2 Dry Completely										8	
13.0 DISPLAY NOZZLE ASSEMBLY	8	0	8	0	0	0	9	0	0	8	33
-13.1 Spray Nozzle Base White	0	0	0	0	0	0	9	0	0	8	
-13.1.1 Paint Nozzle #1 w/Silver Paint Pen							2				
-13.1.2 Paint Nozzle #2 w/ Silver Paint Pen							2				
-13.1.3 Paint Nozzle #3 w/ Silver Paint Pen							2				
-13.1.4 Paint Nozzle #4 w/ Silver Paint Pen							3				
-13.1.5 Allow to dry										8	
-13.2 Apply Glue	8	0	8	0	0	0	0	0	0	0	
-13.2.1 Apply glue to tab on nozzle #1			2								
-13.2.2 Place Nozzle #1 into hole on base	2										
-13.2.3 Apply glue to tab on nozzle #2			2								
-13.2.4 Place Nozzle #2 into hole on base	2										
-13.2.5 Apply glue to tab on nozzle #3			2								
-13.2.6 Place Nozzle #3 into hole on base	2										
-13.2.7 Apply glue to tab on nozzle #4			2								
-13.2.8 Place Nozzle #4 into hole on base	2										
14.0 ROCKET PREFLIGHT	42	0	0	0	0	0	0	0	0	0	42
14.1 prepare	13	0	0	0	0	0	0	0	0	0	
-14.1.1 Remove Nose Cone from Rocket	6										
-14.1.2 Locate recovery wadding	1										
-14.1.3 Insert 4-5 loosely crumpled squares of recovery wadding	6										
14.2 Spike	4	0	0	0	0	0	0	0	0	0	

-14.2.1 Pull parachute into a spike-see diagram for clarification	4										
14.3 Fold	4	0	0	0	0	0	0	0	0	0	
-14.3.1 Fold parachute according to diagram	4										
14.4 Roll	4	0	0	0	0	0	0	0	0	0	
-14.4.1 Roll parachute according to diagram	4										
14.5 Re-insert	17	0	0	0	0	0	0	0	0	0	
-14.5.1 Wrap lines loosely around rolled parachute-see diagram for clarification	5										
-14.5.2 Insert parachute into body tube of rocket	6										
-14.5.3 Insert shock cord into body tube of rocket	2										
-14.5.4 Insert nose cone into body tube of rocket	4										
15.0 PREPARE FOR TEST LAUNCH	0	0	0	0	0	0	0	0	32	0	32
-15.1 Insert Engine	0	0	0	0	0	0	0	0	32	0	
-15.1.1 Remove engine									10		
-15.1.2 Insert tip to touch propellant									10		
-15.1.3 Insert engine into rocket									12		
RESOURCE TOTALS	154	103	88	23	17	16	17	56	32	137	643
Add resource totals as cross check											643
RESOURCE HOURLY RATES	$50.00	$40.00	$25.00	$40.00	$25.00	$30.00	$25.00	$30.00	$55.00		
RESOURCE COSTS	$7,700.00	$4,120.00	$2,200.00	$920.00	$425.00	$480.00	$425.00	$1,680.00	$1,760.00		$19,710.00

SCHEDULED START DATES

Name	Duration	Start Date	Finish Date
1.0 ASSEMBLE ENGINE MOUNT	95	5/22/2011	6/5/2011
1.1 Measure, Mark and Cut Engine Tube	35	5/22/2011	5/26/2011
-1.2 Cut Engine Tube	2	5/26/2011	5/26/2011
-1.3 Glue, Tube, Assemble Hook	7	5/26/2011	5/30/2011
-1.4 Assemble Mylar Ring to Tube	9	5/30/2011	5/30/2011
-1.5 Assemble Yellow Engine Block to Engine Mount Tube	10	5/31/2011	5/31/2011
-1.6 Assemble Centering Rings	22	6/1/2011	6/2/2011
-1.7 Application of Glue Fillets	10	6/5/2011	6/5/2011
2.0 FIN PREPARATION	30	5/22/2011	5/25/2011
-2.1 Sand/Cut fins	8	5/22/2011	5/22/2011
-2.2 Cutting Out Fins	12	5/23/2011	5/24/2011
-2.3 Stack and Sand Fins	10	5/24/2011	5/25/2011
3.0 MARK FIN AND LAUNCH LUG LINES	33	5/22/2011	5/30/2011
-3.1 Cut - Tape	13	5/22/2011	5/25/2011
-3.2 Remove guide, connect fins and lug lines, extend LL line	16	5/25/2011	5/30/2011
-3.3 Extend Launch Lug Line	4	5/30/2011	5/30/2011
4.0 INSERTING ENGINE MOUNT	43	6/6/2011	6/9/2011
-4.1 Mark inside of tube @ 5/8" where LL is	7	6/6/2011	6/6/2011
-4.2 Glue Tube	5	6/6/2011	6/7/2011
-4.3 Assemble Engine Hook	18	6/7/2011	6/8/2011
-4.4 Gluing Center Body Ring	13	6/9/2011	6/9/2011

5.0 ATTACH FINS	73	6/12/2011	6/16/2011
-5.1 Attach Fin #1	10	6/12/2011	6/13/2011
-5.2 Attach Fin #2	10	6/12/2011	6/13/2011
-5.3 Attach Fin #3	10	6/12/2011	6/13/2011
-5.4 Attach Fin #4	10	6/12/2011	6/13/2011
-5.5 Check Fin Alignment	16	6/13/2011	6/15/2011
-5.6 Allow glue to dry	17	6/15/2011	6/16/2011
6.0 ATTACH SHOCK CORD	44	5/22/2011	5/26/2011
-6.1 Cut out shock cord mount	5	5/22/2011	5/22/2011
-6.2 First Glue Application	12	5/22/2011	5/24/2011
-6.3 Second Glue Application	8	5/24/2011	5/25/2011
-6.4 Squeeze and Hold	6	5/25/2011	5/25/2011
-6.5 Attaching Shock Cord Mount	13	5/25/2011	5/26/2011
7.0 ASSEMBLE NOSE CONE	16	5/22/2011	5/23/2011
-7.1 Glue nose cone	16	5/22/2011	5/23/2011
8.0 ATTACH PARACHUTE/SHOCK CORD	18	5/30/2011	6/2/2011
-8.1 Attach Lines	7	5/30/2011	5/31/2011
-8.2 Attach Parachute	5	5/31/2011	6/1/2011
-8.3 Tie Lines	6	6/1/2011	6/2/2011
9.0 ATTACH LAUNCH LUG	32	6/19/2011	6/22/2011
-9.1 Glue launch lines	4	6/19/2011	6/19/2011
-9.2 Application of Glue Fillets	28	6/19/2011	6/22/2011
10.0 PAINTING THE ROCKET	64	6/22/2011	6/29/2011
-10.1 Apply first coat	16	6/22/2011	6/23/2011
-10.2 Sand	8	6/23/2011	6/23/2011
-10.3 Apply final coat	40	6/26/2011	6/29/2011
11.0 APPLICATION OF DECALS	35	6/29/2011	7/6/2011
-11.1 Apply first decal	5	6/29/2011	6/29/2011
-11.2 Apply second decal	5	6/29/2011	6/30/2011
-11.3 Apply third decal	5	6/30/2011	6/30/2011
-11.4 Apply fourth decal	5	6/30/2011	7/3/2011
-11.5 Apply fifth decal	5	7/3/2011	7/5/2011
-11.6 Apply sixth Decal	5	7/5/2011	7/5/2011
-11.7 Apply seventh Decal	5	7/5/2011	7/6/2011
12.0 APPLYING CLEAR COAT	16	7/6/2011	7/7/2011
-12.1 Apply clear coat to entire rocket	16	7/6/2011	7/7/2011
13.0 DISPLAY NOZZLE ASSEMBLY	32	7/10/2011	7/13/2011
-13.1 Spray Nozzle Base White	18	7/10/2011	7/11/2011
-13.2 Apply Glue	14	7/12/2011	7/13/2011
14.0 ROCKET PREFLIGHT	42	7/13/2011	7/20/2011
14.1 prepare	13	7/13/2011	7/17/2011
14.2 Spike	4	7/17/2011	7/17/2011
14.3 Fold	4	7/17/2011	7/18/2011
14.4 Roll	4	7/18/2011	7/18/2011

14.5 Re-insert	17	7/18/2011	7/20/2011
15.0 PREPARE FOR TEST LAUNCH	32	7/21/2011	7/26/2011
-15.1 Insert Engine	32	7/21/2011	7/26/2011

APPENDIX G

RESPONSIBILITY ASSIGNMENT MATRIX

	Member Teams (Deliverables Owners)						
Deliverable(s)	Stage Name	Team A	Team B	Team C	Team D	Core Team	Alternate
1.0	Assemble Engine Mount					CORE	N/A
	Quality Check		Brian Kirouac				DoD Rep.
2.0	Fin Preparation					CORE	N/A
	Quality Check		Tom Jones				DoD Rep.
3.0	Mark Fin & Launch Lug Lines					CORE	N/A
	Quality Check		Brian Kirouac				DoD Rep.
4.0	Inserting Engine Mount					CORE	N/A
	Quality Check		Tom Jones				DoD Rep.
5.0	Attach Fins					CORE	N/A
	Quality Check		Brian Kirouac				DoD Rep.
6.0	Attach Shock Cord					CORE	N/A
	Quality Check		Tom Jones				DoD Rep.

7.0	Assemble Nose Cone			J.C. Bose		B.T. Linking
	Quality Check		Brian Kirouac			DoD Rep.
8.0	Attach Parachute & Shock Cord Assembly			J.C. Bose		B.T. Linking
	Quality Check		Tom Jones			DoD Rep.
9.0	Attach Launch Lug			J.C. Bose		B.T. Linking
	Quality Check		Brian Kirouac			DoD Rep.
10.00	Painting the Rocket			Robert Muse		J.C. Bose
10.2	Sand			B.T. Linking		J.C. Bose
10.3	Apply White Primer			Robert Muse		J.C. Bose
11.00	Application of Decals			J.C. Bose		B.T. Linking
	Quality Check		Brian Kirouac			DoD Rep.
12.00	Applying Clear Coat			Robert Muse		J.C. Bose
	Quality Check		Tom Jones			DoD Rep.
13.00	Display Nozzle Assembly				CORE	N/A
	Quality Check		Brian Kirouac			DoD Rep.
14.00	Rocket Pre-Flight		Tom Jones		CORE	N/A
	Quality Check	Team A				N/A
15.00	Prepare for Test Launch	Team A	Brian Kirouac		CORE	N/A
	Quality Check	Team A	Tom Jones		CORE	N/A

APPENDIX H

SPEND PLAN - BASELINE

CATEGORY	Week 1	Week 2	Week 3	Week 4	Week 5	Week 6	Week 7	Week 8
Labor	7,350.00	7,350.00	7,350.00	11,550.00	4,200.00	4,200.00	12,600.00	15,400.00
Material	10,900.00	0.00	0.00	100.00	5,800.00	0.00	365.00	4,320.00
Equipment/ parts	175.00	0.00	0.00	625.00	0.00	0.00	225.00	0.00
TOTAL	18,425.00	7,350.00	7,350.00	12,275.00	10,000.00	4,200.00	13,190.00	19,720.00
CUMULATIVE	18,425.00	25,775.00	33,125.00	45,400.00	55,400.00	59,600.00	72,790.00	92,510.00

CATEGORY	Week 9	Week 10	Week 11	Week 12	Week 13	Week 14	Week 15	Week 16	
Labor	2,800.00	5,600.00	5,600.00	5,600.00	1,400.00	2,800.00	2,800.00	1400	98,000.00
Material	2,875.00	645.00	0.00	2,400.00	0.00	300.00	0.00	50000	77,705.00
Equipment/ parts	0.00	0.00	0.00	0.00	0.00	0.00	0.00	0	1,025.00
TOTAL	5,675.00	6,245.00	5,600.00	8,000.00	1,400.00	3,100.00	2,800.00	51,400.00	176,730.00
CUMULATIVE	98,185.00	104,430.00	110,030.00	118,030.00	119,430.00	122,530.00	125,330.00	176,730.00	

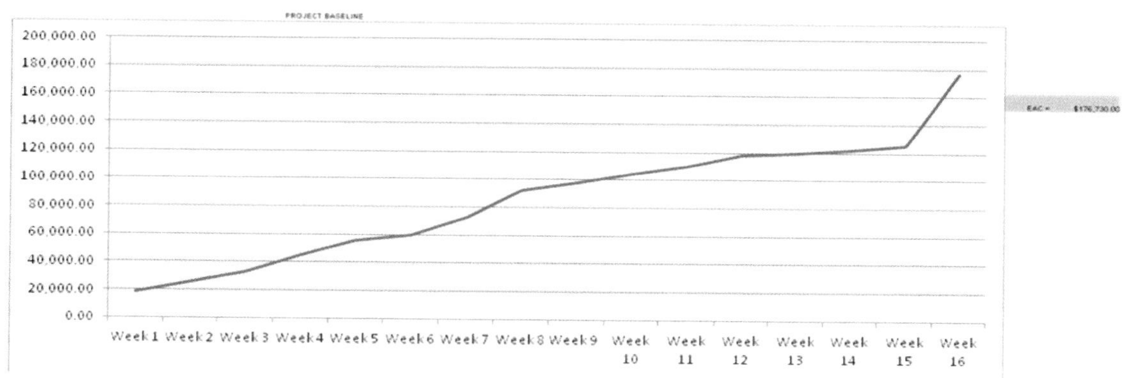

APPENDIX I

MAJOR MILESTONES

Name	**Finish Date**
1.0 ASSEMBLE ENGINE MOUNT	6/5/2011
2.0 FIN PREPARATION	5/25/2011
3.0 MARK FIN AND LAUNCH LUG LINES	5/30/2011
4.0 INSERTING ENGINE MOUNT	6/9/2011
5.0 ATTACH FINS	6/16/2011
6.0 ATTACH SHOCK CORD	5/26/2011
7.0 ASSEMBLE NOSE CONE	5/23/2011
8.0 ATTACH PARACHUTE/SHOCK CORD	6/2/2011
9.0 ATTACH LAUNCH LUG	6/22/2011
10.0 PAINTING THE ROCKET	6/29/2011
11.0 APPLICATION OF DECALS	7/6/2011
12.0 APPLYING CLEAR COAT	7/7/2011
13.0 DISPLAY NOZZLE ASSEMBLY	7/13/2011
14.0 ROCKET PREFLIGHT	7/20/2011
15.0 PREPARE FOR TEST LAUNCH	7/26/2011

APPENDIX J

KEY OR REQUIRED STAFF

TEAM A		
Title	Name	Organization
Customer		Pablo De Leon & Associates
Sponsor	Jeff Tyler	Pablo De Leon & Associates
Cost Financing	Jeanea Brown	Space Systems Technologies Corporation
Engineer	N/A	Space Systems Technologies Corporation
Project Manager	Julie Davis	Space Systems Technologies Corporation

TEAM B		
Title	Name	Organization
Quality Assessment	Brian Kirouac	Space Systems Technologies Corporation
Quality Assessment	Tom Jones	Space Systems Technologies Corporation

TEAM C		
Title	Name	Organization
Functional Mgr. (Drafting)	B. Jose Alonzo	Space Systems Technologies Corporation
Functional Mgr. (Painting)	Robert Muse	Space Systems Technologies Corporation
Functional Mgr. (Finishing/Sanding)	Buford T. Linking	Space Systems Technologies Corporation
Functional Mgr (Cutting)	Ben E. Blades	Space Systems Technologies Corporation
Functional Mgr. (Assembly/Gluer)	J. Christian Bose	Space Systems Technologies Corporation
Functional Mgr. (Fitters/Cutters)	Charles Gooding	Space Systems Technologies Corporation

TEAM D		
Title	Name	Organization
Procurement	I.B. Buying	Space Systems Technologies Corporation

APPENDIX K

KEY RISKS

		Probability of Risk			Magnitude of Damage			Planned Action	
Activity	**Rank**	**Low/0.05**	**Med./0.1**	**High/0.5**	**Low/0.1**	**Med./ 0.3**	**High/0.5**	**Total Rating**	**Type of Action**
Key Personnel Un-available.	**3**		**X**				**X**	0.05	**Insure contractors are available if necessary.**
Delayed delivery of materials and equipment	**1**		**X**				**X**	0.05	**Make delivery a requirement in supplier contracts.**
Weather	**5**		**X**		**X**			0.01	**Change Schedule if necessary**
Materials Shortages	**4**	**X**				**X**		0.03	**Contract with current supplier, and Identify alternate suppliers if needed.**
Damage to original parts provided in kit.	**2**	**X**				**X**		0.03	**Insurance & Liability Waiver**

APPENDIX L

CONSTRAINTS

1. SSTC does not currently have the employee resources available during our project start to finish dates for the Fitter positions. If the materials are not delivered in the time frame which the project was based on there will be a change to the project delivery date which we do not have available to us. This affects the Project Human Resource Management knowledge area.

2. The materials must be delivered the Friday before project start. This affects the Project Procurement Management knowledge area.

3. Project must be completed in 3 months time. This affects the Project Time Management knowledge area.

4. Estimated Budget is not to exceed $63,000.00. This affects the Project Cost Management knowledge area.

APPENDIX M

ASSUMPTIONS

1. All materials for the rocket will have been purchased by SSTC and received no later than the Friday before project start. (Recommended engines are as follows: 1/2A3-2T, A3-4T, A10-3T.) This is an external event that must occur for the project to be successful.

2. All activities associated to building the model rocket will follow the National Association of Rocketry (NAR) Safety Code. This covers implicit and explicit instructions.

3. All Project Management activities will use SSTC's project tools, templates and processes, based on PMI standards. This covers implicit and explicit instructions.

4. That the project can be completed in 3 months time and within an estimated budget of $63,000.00. This is covered by explicit and implicit instructions as well as a cost baseline analysis and the WBS and schedule.

APPENDIX N

CONSTRUCTION PLANS

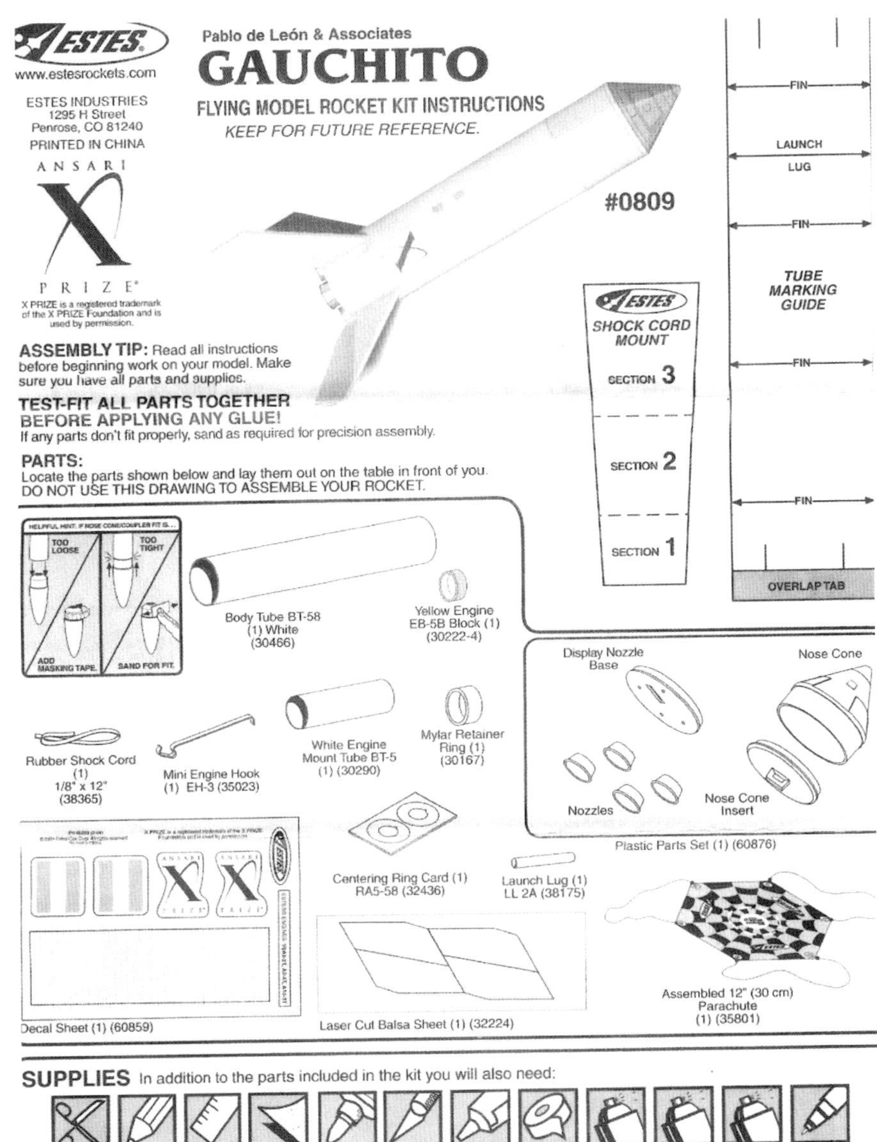

USED WITH PERMISSION

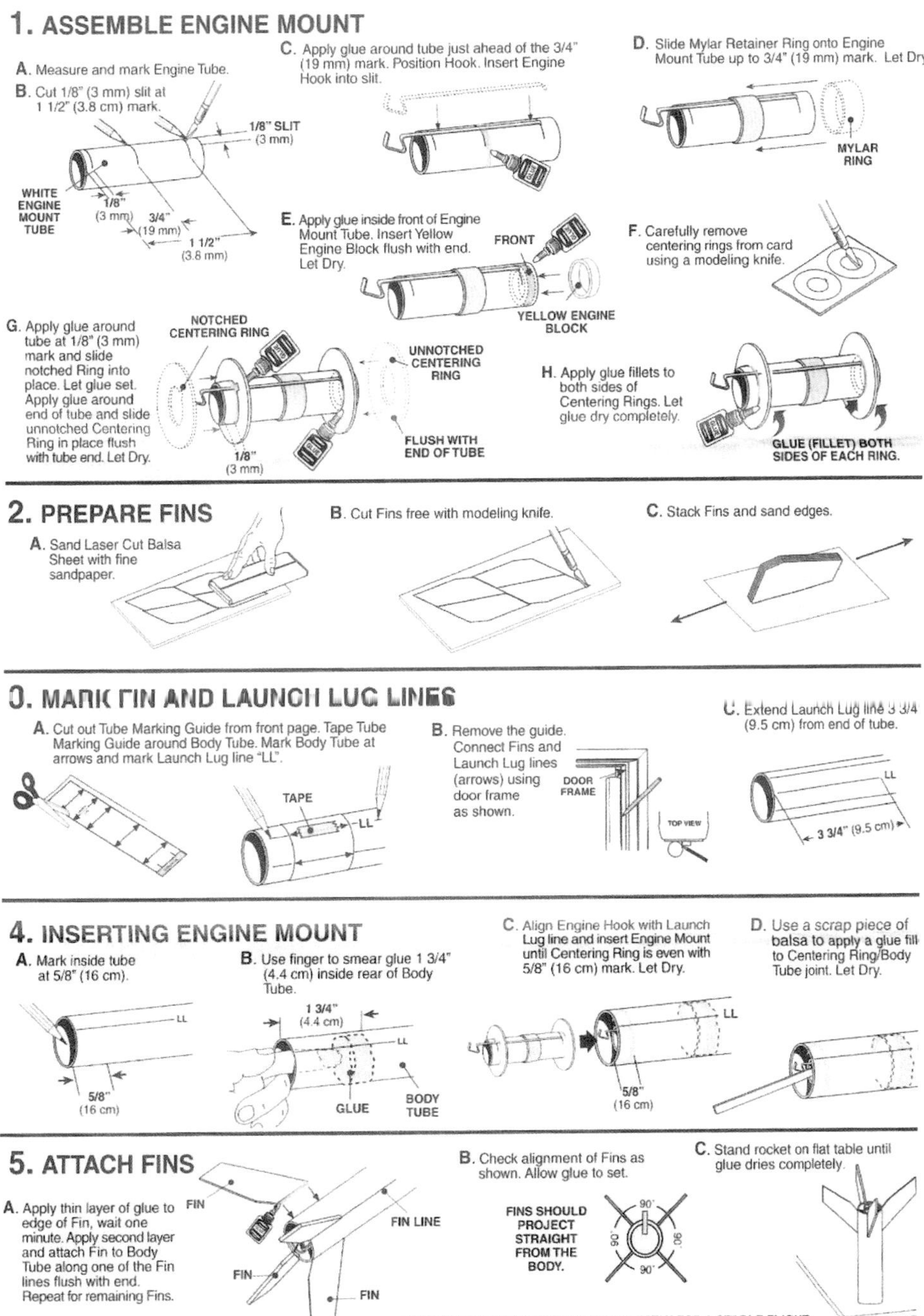
1. ASSEMBLE ENGINE MOUNT
A. Measure and mark Engine Tube.
B. Cut 1/8" (3 mm) slit at 1 1/2" (3.8 cm) mark.
1/8" SLIT (3 mm)
WHITE ENGINE MOUNT TUBE
1/8" (3 mm)
3/4" (19 mm)
1 1/2" (3.8 mm)
C. Apply glue around tube just ahead of the 3/4" (19 mm) mark. Position Hook. Insert Engine Hook into slit.
D. Slide Mylar Retainer Ring onto Engine Mount Tube up to 3/4" (19 mm) mark. Let Dry
MYLAR RING
E. Apply glue inside front of Engine Mount Tube. Insert Yellow Engine Block flush with end. Let Dry.
FRONT
YELLOW ENGINE BLOCK
F. Carefully remove centering rings from card using a modeling knife.
G. Apply glue around tube at 1/8" (3 mm) mark and slide notched Ring into place. Let glue set. Apply glue around end of tube and slide unnotched Centering Ring in place flush with tube end. Let Dry.
NOTCHED CENTERING RING
UNNOTCHED CENTERING RING
FLUSH WITH END OF TUBE
1/8" (3 mm)
H. Apply glue fillets to both sides of Centering Rings. Let glue dry completely.
GLUE (FILLET) BOTH SIDES OF EACH RING.
2. PREPARE FINS
A. Sand Laser Cut Balsa Sheet with fine sandpaper.
B. Cut Fins free with modeling knife.
C. Stack Fins and sand edges.
3. MARK FIN AND LAUNCH LUG LINES
A. Cut out Tube Marking Guide from front page. Tape Tube Marking Guide around Body Tube. Mark Body Tube at arrows and mark Launch Lug line "LL".
TAPE
LL
B. Remove the guide. Connect Fins and Launch Lug lines (arrows) using door frame as shown.
DOOR FRAME
TOP VIEW
C. Extend Launch Lug line 3 3/4 (9.5 cm) from end of tube.
LL
3 3/4" (9.5 cm)
4. INSERTING ENGINE MOUNT
A. Mark inside tube at 5/8" (16 cm).
LL
5/8" (16 cm)
B. Use finger to smear glue 1 3/4" (4.4 cm) inside rear of Body Tube.
1 3/4" (4.4 cm)
LL
GLUE
BODY TUBE
C. Align Engine Hook with Launch Lug line and insert Engine Mount until Centering Ring is even with 5/8" (16 cm) mark. Let Dry.
LL
5/8" (16 cm)
D. Use a scrap piece of balsa to apply a glue fill to Centering Ring/Body Tube joint. Let Dry.
5. ATTACH FINS
A. Apply thin layer of glue to edge of Fin, wait one minute. Apply second layer and attach Fin to Body Tube along one of the Fin lines flush with end. Repeat for remaining Fins.
FIN
FIN LINE
FIN
FIN
B. Check alignment of Fins as shown. Allow glue to set.
FINS SHOULD PROJECT STRAIGHT FROM THE BODY.
90°
90°
90°
90°
C. Stand rocket on flat table until glue dries completely.
NOTE: FINS MUST BE ATTACHED CORRECTLY FOR A STABLE FLIGHT.

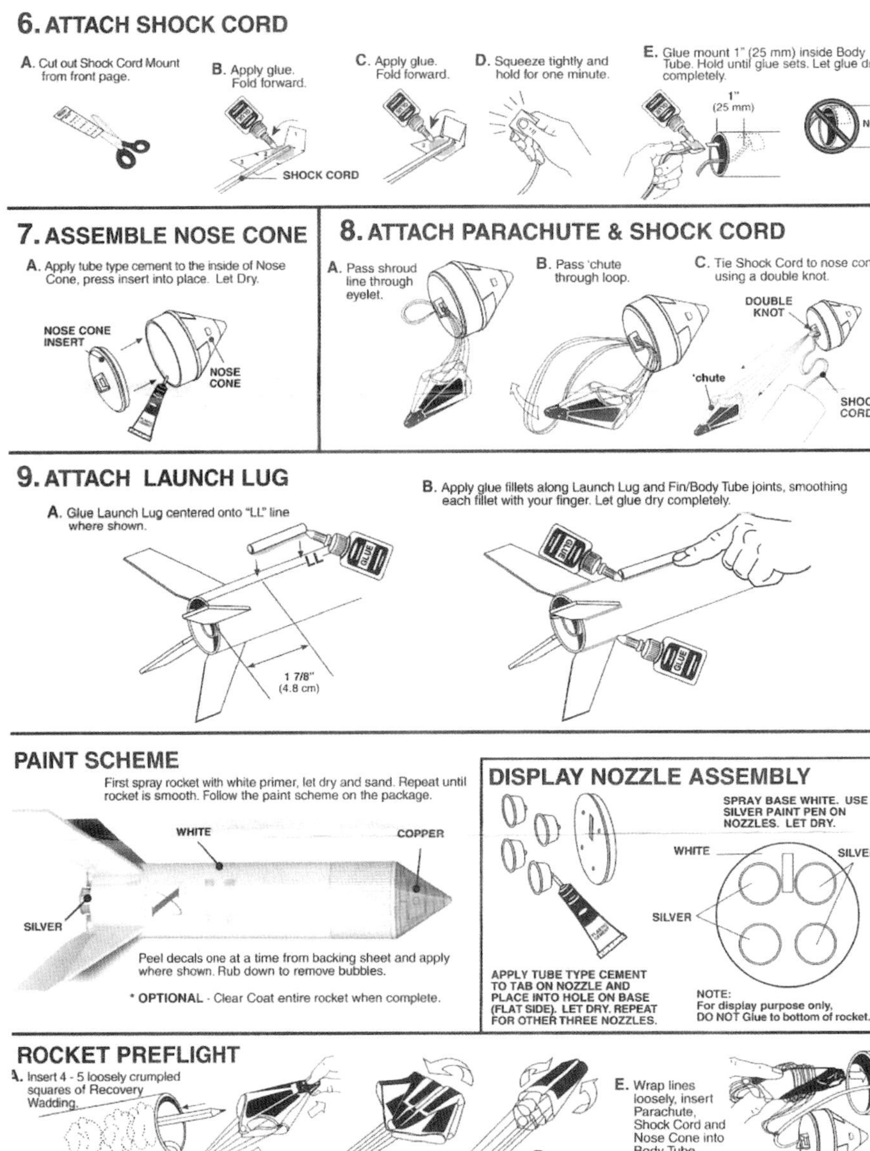

6. ATTACH SHOCK CORD
A. Cut out Shock Cord Mount from front page.
B. Apply glue. Fold forward.
SHOCK CORD
C. Apply glue. Fold forward.
D. Squeeze tightly and hold for one minute.
E. Glue mount 1" (25 mm) inside Body Tube. Hold until glue sets. Let glue dr completely.
1" (25 mm)
7. ASSEMBLE NOSE CONE
A. Apply tube type cement to the inside of Nose Cone, press insert into place. Let Dry.
NOSE CONE INSERT
NOSE CONE
8. ATTACH PARACHUTE & SHOCK CORD
A. Pass shroud line through eyelet.
B. Pass 'chute through loop.
C. Tie Shock Cord to nose con using a double knot.
DOUBLE KNOT
'chute
SHOC CORD
9. ATTACH LAUNCH LUG
A. Glue Launch Lug centered onto "LL" line where shown.
LL
1 7/8" (4.8 cm)
B. Apply glue fillets along Launch Lug and Fin/Body Tube joints, smoothing each fillet with your finger. Let glue dry completely.
PAINT SCHEME
First spray rocket with white primer, let dry and sand. Repeat until rocket is smooth. Follow the paint scheme on the package.
WHITE
COPPER
SILVER
Peel decals one at a time from backing sheet and apply where shown. Rub down to remove bubbles.
* OPTIONAL - Clear Coat entire rocket when complete.
DISPLAY NOZZLE ASSEMBLY
SPRAY BASE WHITE. USE SILVER PAINT PEN ON NOZZLES. LET DRY.
WHITE
SILVER
SILVER
APPLY TUBE TYPE CEMENT TO TAB ON NOZZLE AND PLACE INTO HOLE ON BASE (FLAT SIDE). LET DRY. REPEAT FOR OTHER THREE NOZZLES.
NOTE:
For display purpose only, DO NOT Glue to bottom of rocket.
ROCKET PREFLIGHT
A. Insert 4 - 5 loosely crumpled squares of Recovery Wadding.
OTE: Only Estes wadding 302274) recommended.
B. Spike.
C. Fold.
D. Roll.
E. Wrap lines loosely, insert Parachute, Shock Cord and Nose Cone into Body Tube.

USED WITH PERMISSION

ANSARI X PRIZE®

TEAM OVERVIEW

Pablo de León and Associates

Pablo de León and Associates is an Argentine company formed to design, build and operate a space suborbital transportation system and to compete in the X PRIZE competition. Pablo de León and Associates is formed by Argentine aerospace specialists in the branches of propulsion, mechanical design, thermal systems, and life support and computer systems among other disciplines. The company is based in Buenos Aires, Argentina and has an office in Cape Canaveral, Florida, USA.

Name: Pablo de León & Associates
Website: www.pablodeleon.com
Country of Origin: Buenos Aires, Argentina

VEHICLE SPECIFICATIONS:
Name: Gauchito
Length: 39.37 feet (12 m). Diameter: 7.28 feet (2.20 m). GTOW: 17,637 lb (8,000 kg). DRY WT: 5,291 lb (2400 kg).
Engines: Four hybrid engines. Total Thrust: 52,910 lb. (250,000 N). Payload Capacity: 3 crewmembers or 300 kg.
Crew Environment: Nitrogen-Oxygen using pressurized suits in a pure oxygen atmosphere.

MISSION SPECIFICATIONS:
Launch Method: Vertical take-off from ground. Max Accel. Force: 3 G's. Max Speed: 2,684 mph (1200 m/s).
Max. Altitude: 67 miles (108 km). Time in Weightless Conditions: 240 seconds. Landing Method: Parachute landing into water. Total Flight Duration: ~17minutes.

WARNING: FLAMMABLE

To avoid serious injury, read instructions & NAR Safety Code included with engines.
PREPARE YOUR ENGINE ONLY WHEN YOU ARE OUTSIDE AT THE LAUNCH SITE PREPARING TO LAUNCH!
If you do not use your prepared engine, remove the igniter before storing your engine.

A.

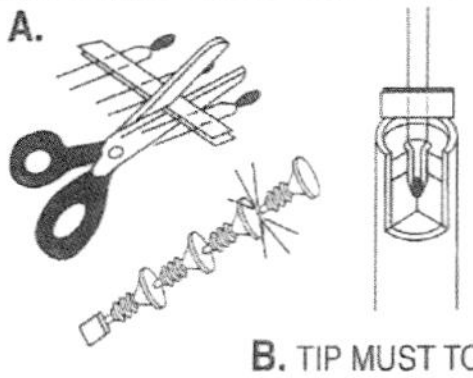

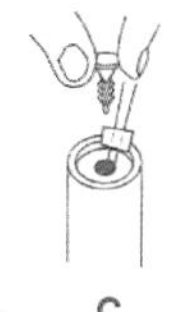

B. TIP MUST TOUCH PROPELLANT.

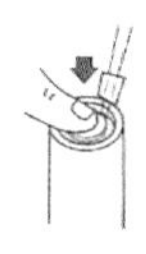

C.

D.

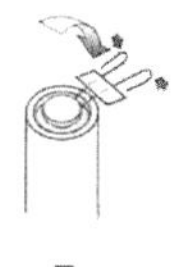

E.

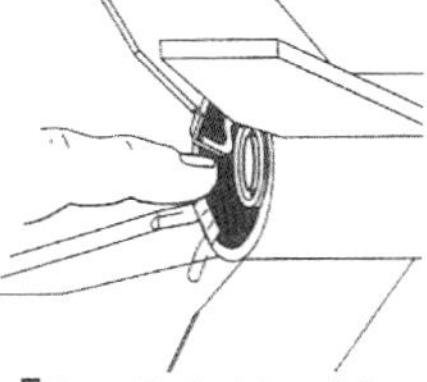

F. Insert Engine into rocket.

COUNTDOWN AND LAUNCH

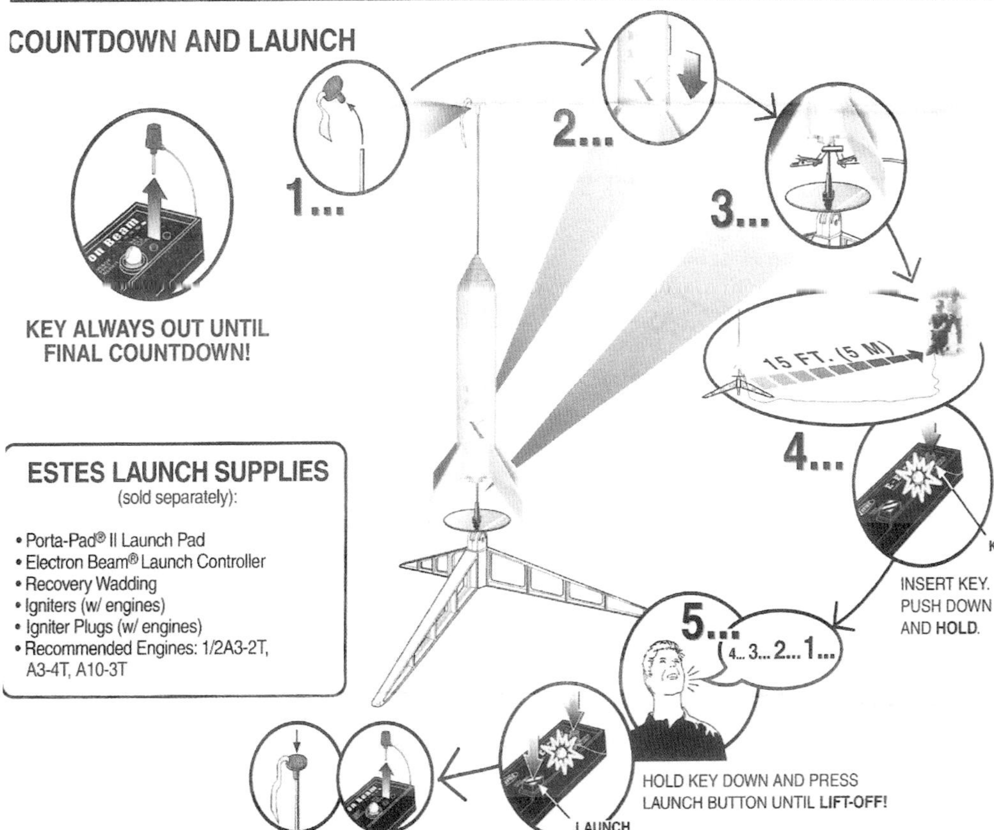
KEY ALWAYS OUT UNTIL FINAL COUNTDOWN!
1...
2...
3...
15 FT. (5 M)
4...
INSERT KEY. PUSH DOWN AND HOLD.
5...
4... 3... 2... 1...
HOLD KEY DOWN AND PRESS LAUNCH BUTTON UNTIL LIFT-OFF!
LAUNCH BUTTON

ESTES LAUNCH SUPPLIES

(sold separately):

- Porta-Pad® II Launch Pad
- Electron Beam® Launch Controller
- Recovery Wadding
- Igniters (w/ engines)
- Igniter Plugs (w/ engines)
- Recommended Engines: 1/2A3-2T, A3-4T, A10-3T

PRECAUTIONS

NAR Safety Code

NO DRY GRASS OR WEEDS

FLYING YOUR ROCKET

Choose a large field (250 ft. [76 m] square) free of dry weeds and brown grass. The larger the launch area, the better your chance of recovering your rocket. Football fields and playgrounds are great. Launch only with little or no wind and good visibility.

Always follow the National Association of Rocketry (NAR) SAFETY CODE.

MISFIRES

TAKE THE KEY OUT OF THE CONTROLLER. WAIT ONE MINUTE BEFORE GOING NEAR THE ROCKET! Disconnect the igniter clips and remove the engine. Take the plug and igniter out of the engine. If the igniter has burned, it worked but did not ignite the engine because it was not touching the propellant inside the engine. Put a new igniter all the way inside the engine without bending it. Push the plug in place. Repeat the steps under Countdown and Launch.

Appendix-B: The Gauchito Rocket Assembly Project Excel® Workbook©

Tab Deliverables-Project deliverables become tasks to be completed.

	A
1	1.0 ASSEMBLE ENGINE MOUNT
2	2.0 FIN PREPARATION
3	3.0 MARK FIN AND LAUNCH LUG LINES
4	4.0 INSERTING ENGINE MOUNT
5	5.0 ATTACH FINS
6	6.0 ATTACH SHOCK CORD
7	7.0 ASSEMBLE NOSE CONE
8	8.0 ATTACH PARACHUTE/SHOCK CORD
9	9.0 ATTACH LAUNCH LUG
10	10.0 PAINTING THE ROCKET
11	11.0 APPLICATION OF DECALS
12	12.0 APPLYING CLEAR COAT
13	13.0 DISPLAY NOZZLE ASSEMBLY
14	14.0 ROCKET PREFLIGHT
15	15.0 PREPARE FOR TEST LAUNCH

Tab Hi-Level WBS-SME's identify the major activities needed to accomplish the tasks.

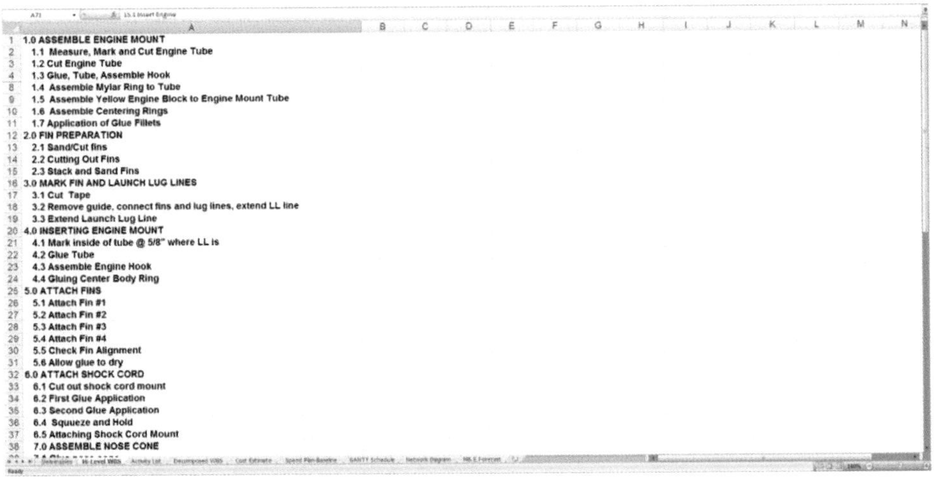

	A
1	**1.0 ASSEMBLE ENGINE MOUNT**
2	1.1 Measure, Mark and Cut Engine Tube
3	1.2 Cut Engine Tube
4	1.3 Glue, Tube, Assemble Hook
8	1.4 Assemble Mylar Ring to Tube
9	1.5 Assemble Yellow Engine Block to Engine Mount Tube
10	1.6 Assemble Centering Rings
11	1.7 Application of Glue Fillets
12	**2.0 FIN PREPARATION**
13	2.1 Sand/Cut fins
14	2.2 Cutting Out Fins
15	2.3 Stack and Sand Fins
16	**3.0 MARK FIN AND LAUNCH LUG LINES**
17	3.1 Cut Tape
18	3.2 Remove guide, connect fins and lug lines, extend LL line
19	3.3 Extend Launch Lug Line
20	**4.0 INSERTING ENGINE MOUNT**
21	4.1 Mark inside of tube @ 5/8" where LL is
22	4.2 Glue Tube
23	4.3 Assemble Engine Hook
24	4.4 Gluing Center Body Ring
25	**5.0 ATTACH FINS**
26	5.1 Attach Fin #1
27	5.2 Attach Fin #2
28	5.3 Attach Fin #3
29	5.4 Attach Fin #4
30	5.5 Check Fin Alignment
31	5.6 Allow glue to dry
32	**6.0 ATTACH SHOCK CORD**
33	6.1 Cut out shock cord mount
34	6.2 First Glue Application
35	6.3 Second Glue Application
36	6.4 Squueze and Hold
37	6.5 Attaching Shock Cord Mount
38	**7.0 ASSEMBLE NOSE CONE**

Tab Hi-Level WBS-Continued.

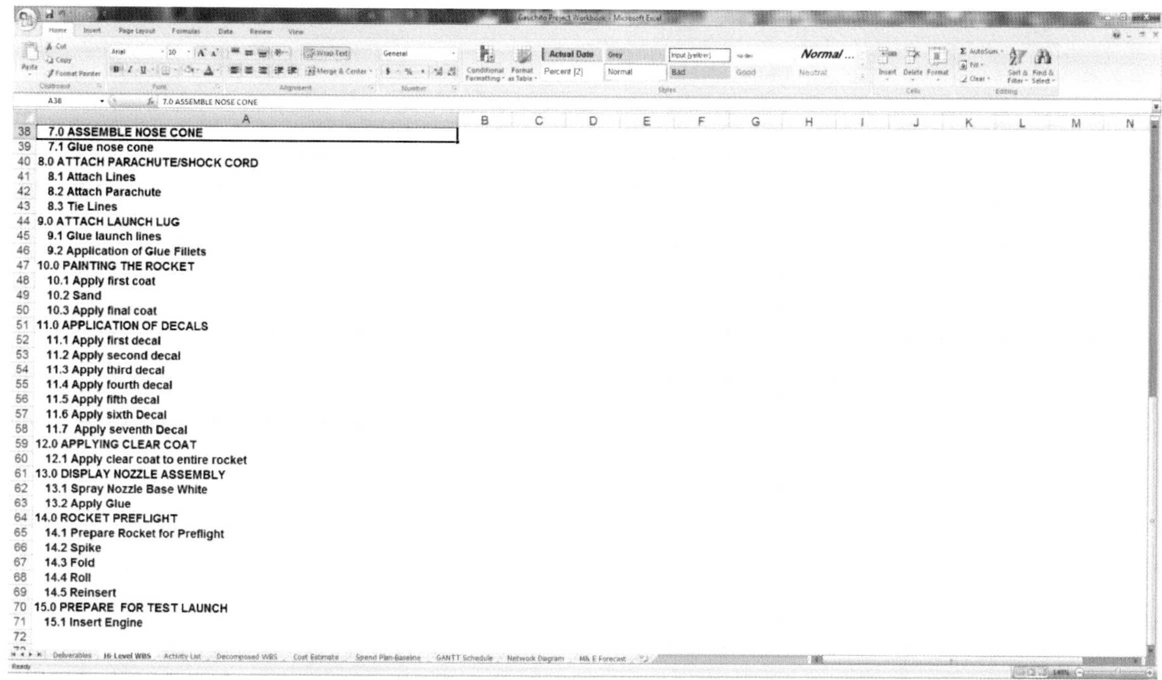

	A
38	7.0 ASSEMBLE NOSE CONE
39	7.1 Glue nose cone
40	8.0 ATTACH PARACHUTE/SHOCK CORD
41	8.1 Attach Lines
42	8.2 Attach Parachute
43	8.3 Tie Lines
44	9.0 ATTACH LAUNCH LUG
45	9.1 Glue launch lines
46	9.2 Application of Glue Fillets
47	10.0 PAINTING THE ROCKET
48	10.1 Apply first coat
49	10.2 Sand
50	10.3 Apply final coat
51	11.0 APPLICATION OF DECALS
52	11.1 Apply first decal
53	11.2 Apply second decal
54	11.3 Apply third decal
55	11.4 Apply fourth decal
56	11.5 Apply fifth decal
57	11.6 Apply sixth Decal
58	11.7 Apply seventh Decal
59	12.0 APPLYING CLEAR COAT
60	12.1 Apply clear coat to entire rocket
61	13.0 DISPLAY NOZZLE ASSEMBLY
62	13.1 Spray Nozzle Base White
63	13.2 Apply Glue
64	14.0 ROCKET PREFLIGHT
65	14.1 Prepare Rocket for Preflight
66	14.2 Spike
67	14.3 Fold
68	14.4 Roll
69	14.5 Reinsert
70	15.0 PREPARE FOR TEST LAUNCH
71	15.1 Insert Engine
72	

Tab Activity List-SME's further decompose activities down to the lowest level activities that are individual activities and less than 80 hours or 10 days to complete.

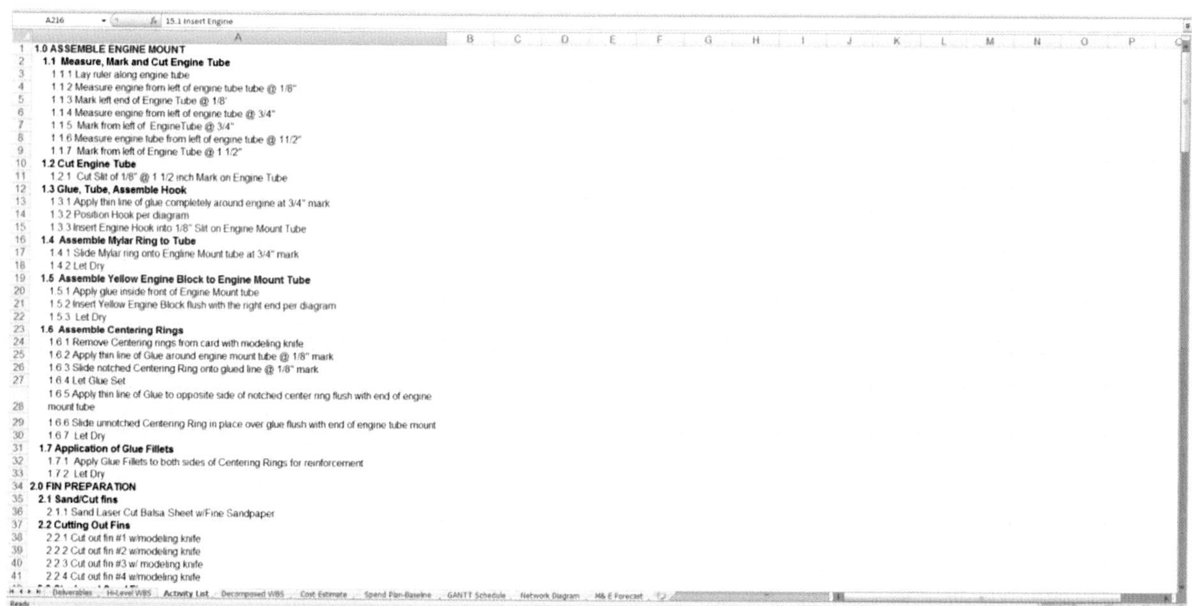

	A
1	1.0 ASSEMBLE ENGINE MOUNT
2	1.1 Measure, Mark and Cut Engine Tube
3	1.1.1 Lay ruler along engine tube
4	1.1.2 Measure engine from left of engine tube tube @ 1/8"
5	1.1.3 Mark left end of Engine Tube @ 1/8'
6	1.1.4 Measure engine from left of engine tube @ 3/4"
7	1.1.5 Mark from left of EngineTube @ 3/4"
8	1.1.6 Measure engine tube from left of engine tube @ 11/2"
9	1.1.7 Mark from left of Engine Tube @ 1 1/2"
10	1.2 Cut Engine Tube
11	1.2.1 Cut Slit of 1/8" @ 1 1/2 inch Mark on Engine Tube
12	1.3 Glue, Tube, Assemble Hook
13	1.3.1 Apply thin line of glue completely around engine at 3/4" mark
14	1.3.2 Position Hook per diagram
15	1.3.3 Insert Engine Hook into 1/8" Slit on Engine Mount Tube
16	1.4 Assemble Mylar Ring to Tube
17	1.4.1 Slide Mylar ring onto Engine Mount tube at 3/4" mark
18	1.4.2 Let Dry
19	1.5 Assemble Yellow Engine Block to Engine Mount Tube
20	1.5.1 Apply glue inside front of Engine Mount tube
21	1.5.2 Insert Yellow Engine Block flush with the right end per diagram
22	1.5.3 Let Dry
23	1.6 Assemble Centering Rings
24	1.6.1 Remove Centering rings from card with modeling knife
25	1.6.2 Apply thin line of Glue around engine mount tube @ 1/8" mark
26	1.6.3 Slide notched Centering Ring onto glued line @ 1/8" mark
27	1.6.4 Let Glue Set
28	1.6.5 Apply thin line of Glue to opposite side of notched center ring flush with end of engine mount tube
29	1.6.6 Slide unnotched Centering Ring in place over glue flush with end of engine tube mount
30	1.6.7 Let Dry
31	1.7 Application of Glue Fillets
32	1.7.1 Apply Glue Fillets to both sides of Centering Rings for reinforcement
33	1.7.2 Let Dry
34	2.0 FIN PREPARATION
35	2.1 Sand/Cut fins
36	2.1.1 Sand Laser Cut Balsa Sheet w/Fine Sandpaper
37	2.2 Cutting Out Fins
38	2.2.1 Cut out fin #1 w/modeling knife
39	2.2.2 Cut out fin #2 w/modeling knife
40	2.2.3 Cut out fin #3 w/ modeling knife
41	2.2.4 Cut out fin #4 w/modeling knife

Tab Activity List-Continued.

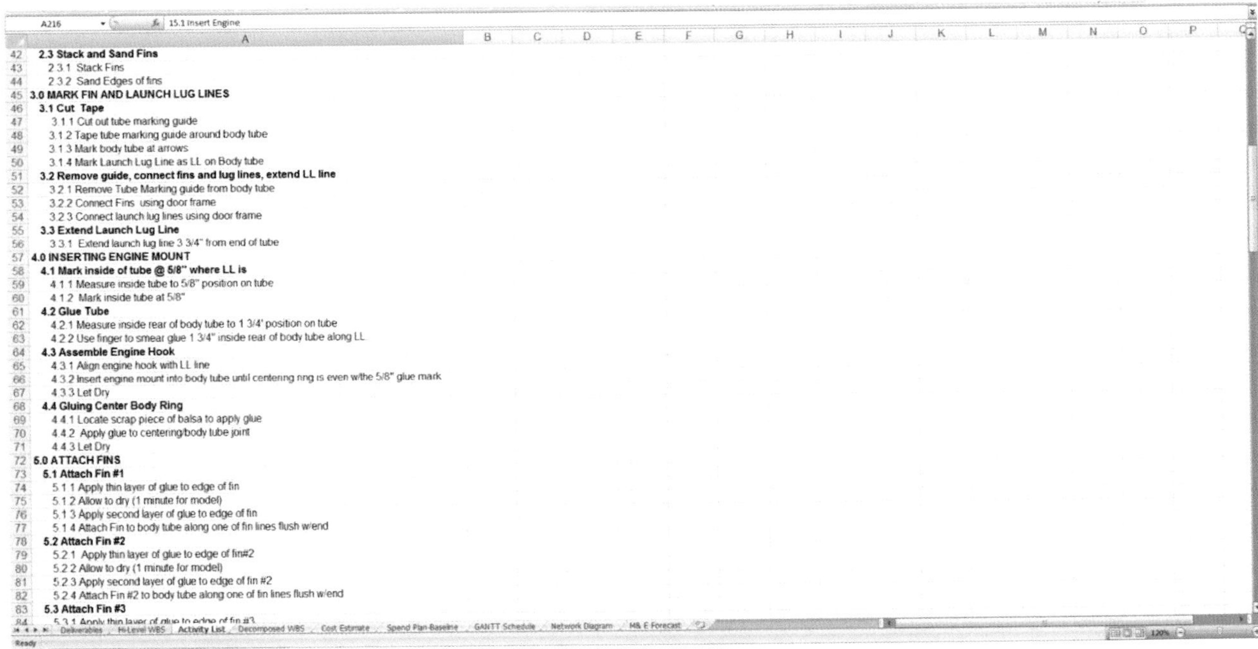

A216 | 15.1 Insert Engine

2.3 Stack and Sand Fins
2.3.1 Stack Fins
2.3.2 Sand Edges of fins
3.0 MARK FIN AND LAUNCH LUG LINES
3.1 Cut Tape
3.1.1 Cut out tube marking guide
3.1.2 Tape tube marking guide around body tube
3.1.3 Mark body tube at arrows
3.1.4 Mark Launch Lug Line as LL on Body tube
3.2 Remove guide, connect fins and lug lines, extend LL line
3.2.1 Remove Tube Marking guide from body tube
3.2.2 Connect Fins using door frame
3.2.3 Connect launch lug lines using door frame
3.3 Extend Launch Lug Line
3.3.1 Extend launch lug line 3 3/4" from end of tube
4.0 INSERTING ENGINE MOUNT
4.1 Mark inside of tube @ 5/8" where LL is
4.1.1 Measure inside tube to 5/8" position on tube
4.1.2 Mark inside tube at 5/8"
4.2 Glue Tube
4.2.1 Measure inside rear of body tube to 1 3/4' position on tube
4.2.2 Use finger to smear glue 1 3/4" inside rear of body tube along LL
4.3 Assemble Engine Hook
4.3.1 Align engine hook with LL line
4.3.2 Insert engine mount into body tube until centering ring is even w/the 5/8" glue mark
4.3.3 Let Dry
4.4 Gluing Center Body Ring
4.4.1 Locate scrap piece of balsa to apply glue
4.4.2 Apply glue to centering/body tube joint
4.4.3 Let Dry
5.0 ATTACH FINS
5.1 Attach Fin #1
5.1.1 Apply thin layer of glue to edge of fin
5.1.2 Allow to dry (1 minute for model)
5.1.3 Apply second layer of glue to edge of fin
5.1.4 Attach Fin to body tube along one of fin lines flush w/end
5.2 Attach Fin #2
5.2.1 Apply thin layer of glue to edge of fin#2
5.2.2 Allow to dry (1 minute for model)
5.2.3 Apply second layer of glue to edge of fin #2
5.2.4 Attach Fin #2 to body tube along one of fin lines flush w/end
5.3 Attach Fin #3

Deliverables | Hi-Level WBS | Activity List | Decomposed WBS | Cost Estimate | Spend Plan-Baseline | GANTT Schedule | Network Diagram | M& E Forecast

Ready

Tab Activity List-Continued.

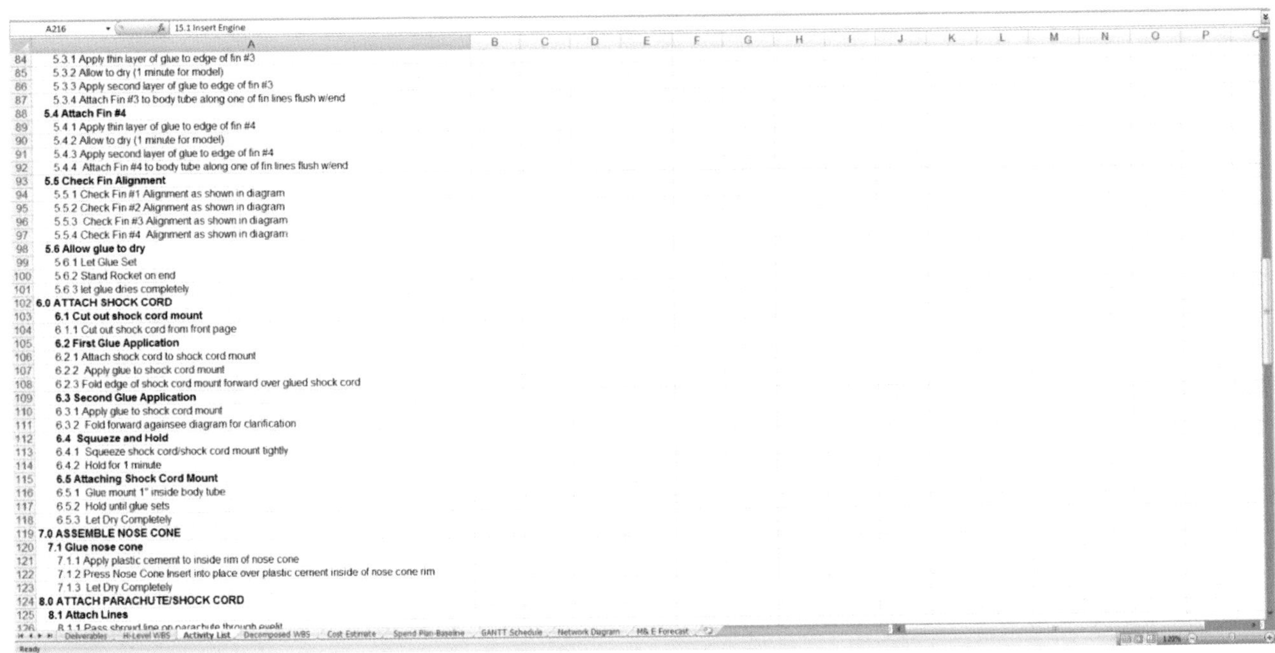

A216 | 15.1 Insert Engine

5.3.1 Apply thin layer of glue to edge of fin #3
5.3.2 Allow to dry (1 minute for model)
5.3.3 Apply second layer of glue to edge of fin #3
5.3.4 Attach Fin #3 to body tube along one of fin lines flush w/end
5.4 Attach Fin #4
5.4.1 Apply thin layer of glue to edge of fin #4
5.4.2 Allow to dry (1 minute for model)
5.4.3 Apply second layer of glue to edge of fin #4
5.4.4 Attach Fin #4 to body tube along one of fin lines flush w/end
5.5 Check Fin Alignment
5.5.1 Check Fin #1 Alignment as shown in diagram
5.5.2 Check Fin #2 Alignment as shown in diagram
5.5.3 Check Fin #3 Alignment as shown in diagram
5.5.4 Check Fin #4 Alignment as shown in diagram
5.6 Allow glue to dry
5.6.1 Let Glue Set
5.6.2 Stand Rocket on end
5.6.3 let glue dries completely
6.0 ATTACH SHOCK CORD
6.1 Cut out shock cord mount
6.1.1 Cut out shock cord from front page
6.2 First Glue Application
6.2.1 Attach shock cord to shock cord mount
6.2.2 Apply glue to shock cord mount
6.2.3 Fold edge of shock cord mount forward over glued shock cord
6.3 Second Glue Application
6.3.1 Apply glue to shock cord mount
6.3.2 Fold forward againsee diagram for clarification
6.4 Squueze and Hold
6.4.1 Squeeze shock cord/shock cord mount tightly
6.4.2 Hold for 1 minute
6.5 Attaching Shock Cord Mount
6.5.1 Glue mount 1" inside body tube
6.5.2 Hold until glue sets
6.5.3 Let Dry Completely
7.0 ASSEMBLE NOSE CONE
7.1 Glue nose cone
7.1.1 Apply plastic cememt to inside rim of nose cone
7.1.2 Press Nose Cone Insert into place over plastic cement inside of nose cone rim
7.1.3 Let Dry Completely
8.0 ATTACH PARACHUTE/SHOCK CORD
8.1 Attach Lines

Deliverables | Hi-Level WBS | Activity List | Decomposed WBS | Cost Estimate | Spend Plan-Baseline | GANTT Schedule | Network Diagram | M& E Forecast

Ready

Tab Activity List-Continued.

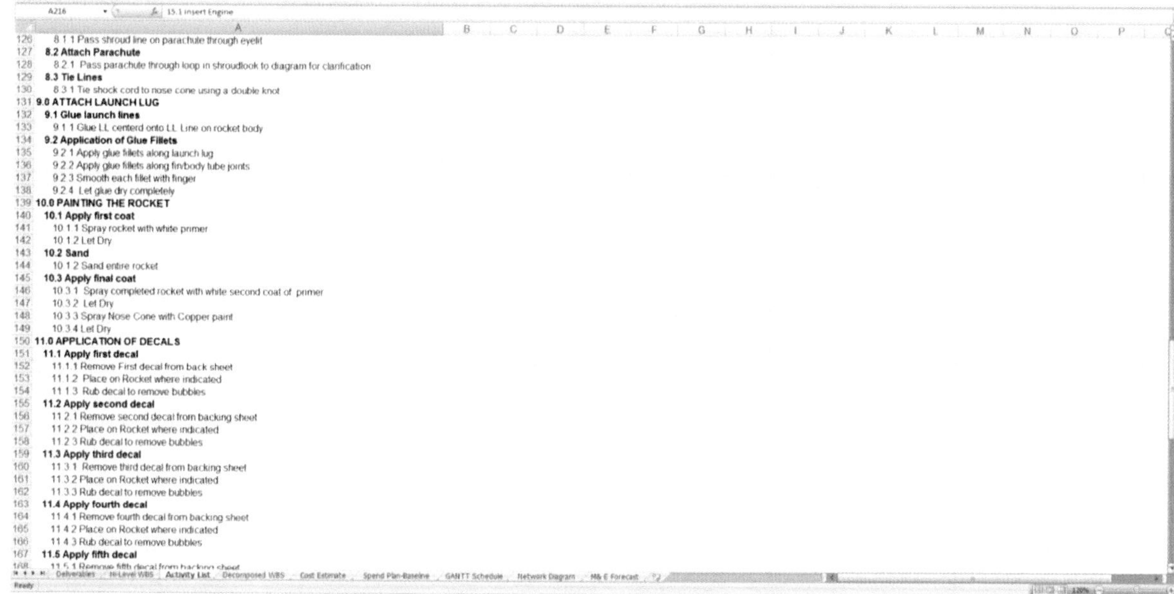

A216 | 15.1 Insert Engine

	A
126	8.1.1 Pass shroud line on parachute through eyelit
127	**8.2 Attach Parachute**
128	8.2.1 Pass parachute through loop in shroudlook to diagram for clarification
129	**8.3 Tie Lines**
130	8.3.1 Tie shock cord to nose cone using a double knot
131	**9.0 ATTACH LAUNCH LUG**
132	**9.1 Glue launch lines**
133	9.1.1 Glue LL centerd onto LL Line on rocket body
134	**9.2 Application of Glue Fillets**
135	9.2.1 Apply glue fillets along launch lug
136	9.2.2 Apply glue fillets along fin/body tube joints
137	9.2.3 Smooth each fillet with finger
138	9.2.4 Let glue dry completely
139	**10.0 PAINTING THE ROCKET**
140	**10.1 Apply first coat**
141	10.1.1 Spray rocket with white primer
142	10.1.2 Let Dry
143	**10.2 Sand**
144	10.1.2 Sand entire rocket
145	**10.3 Apply final coat**
146	10.3.1 Spray completed rocket with white second coat of primer
147	10.3.2 Let Dry
148	10.3.3 Spray Nose Cone with Copper paint
149	10.3.4 Let Dry
150	**11.0 APPLICATION OF DECALS**
151	**11.1 Apply first decal**
152	11.1.1 Remove First decal from back sheet
153	11.1.2 Place on Rocket where indicated
154	11.1.3 Rub decal to remove bubbles
155	**11.2 Apply second decal**
156	11.2.1 Remove second decal from backing sheet
157	11.2.2 Place on Rocket where indicated
158	11.2.3 Rub decal to remove bubbles
159	**11.3 Apply third decal**
160	11.3.1 Remove third decal from backing sheet
161	11.3.2 Place on Rocket where indicated
162	11.3.3 Rub decal to remove bubbles
163	**11.4 Apply fourth decal**
164	11.4.1 Remove fourth decal from backing sheet
165	11.4.2 Place on Rocket where indicated
166	11.4.3 Rub decal to remove bubbles
167	**11.5 Apply fifth decal**
168	11.5.1 Remove fifth decal from backing sheet

Deliverables | Hi-Level WBS | Activity List | Decomposed WBS | Cost Estimate | Spend Plan-Baseline | GANTT Schedule | Network Diagram | M& E Forecast

Tab Activity List-Continued.

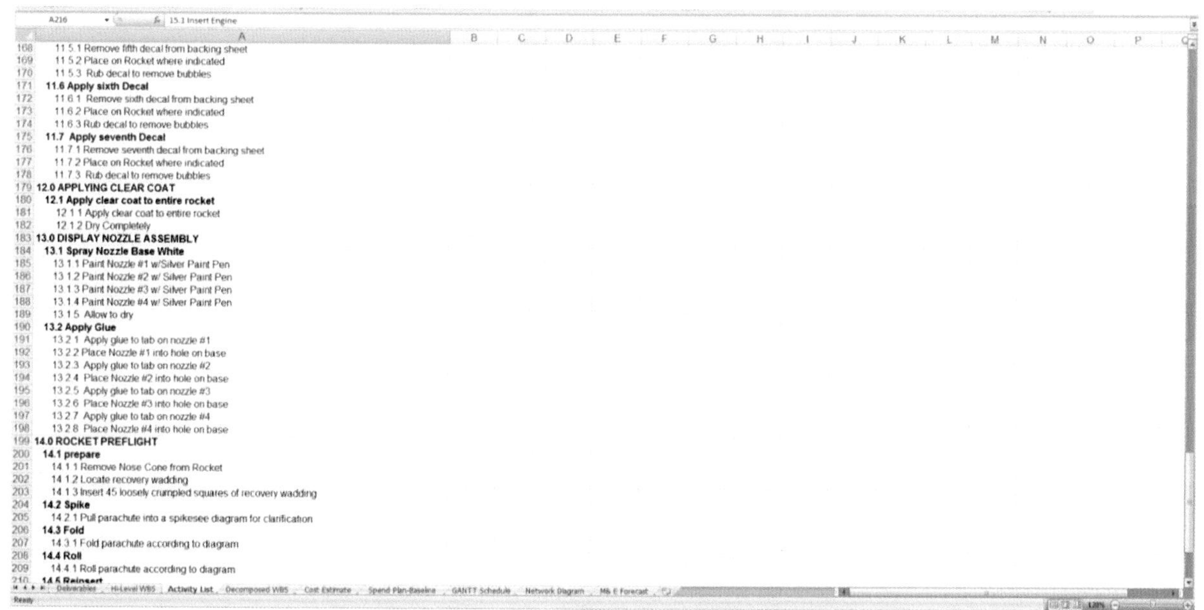

A216 | 15.1 Insert Engine

	A
168	11.5.1 Remove fifth decal from backing sheet
169	11.5.2 Place on Rocket where indicated
170	11.5.3 Rub decal to remove bubbles
171	**11.6 Apply sixth Decal**
172	11.6.1 Remove sixth decal from backing sheet
173	11.6.2 Place on Rocket where indicated
174	11.6.3 Rub decal to remove bubbles
175	**11.7 Apply seventh Decal**
176	11.7.1 Remove seventh decal from backing sheet
177	11.7.2 Place on Rocket where indicated
178	11.7.3 Rub decal to remove bubbles
179	**12.0 APPLYING CLEAR COAT**
180	**12.1 Apply clear coat to entire rocket**
181	12.1.1 Apply clear coat to entire rocket
182	12.1.2 Dry Completely
183	**13.0 DISPLAY NOZZLE ASSEMBLY**
184	**13.1 Spray Nozzle Base White**
185	13.1.1 Paint Nozzle #1 w/Silver Paint Pen
186	13.1.2 Paint Nozzle #2 w/ Silver Paint Pen
187	13.1.3 Paint Nozzle #3 w/ Silver Paint Pen
188	13.1.4 Paint Nozzle #4 w/ Silver Paint Pen
189	13.1.5 Allow to dry
190	**13.2 Apply Glue**
191	13.2.1 Apply glue to tab on nozzle #1
192	13.2.2 Place Nozzle #1 into hole on base
193	13.2.3 Apply glue to tab on nozzle #2
194	13.2.4 Place Nozzle #2 into hole on base
195	13.2.5 Apply glue to tab on nozzle #3
196	13.2.6 Place Nozzle #3 into hole on base
197	13.2.7 Apply glue to tab on nozzle #4
198	13.2.8 Place Nozzle #4 into hole on base
199	**14.0 ROCKET PREFLIGHT**
200	**14.1 prepare**
201	14.1.1 Remove Nose Cone from Rocket
202	14.1.2 Locate recovery wadding
203	14.1.3 Insert 45 loosely crumpled squares of recovery wadding
204	**14.2 Spike**
205	14.2.1 Pull parachute into a spikesee diagram for clarification
206	**14.3 Fold**
207	14.3.1 Fold parachute according to diagram
208	**14.4 Roll**
209	14.4.1 Roll parachute according to diagram
210	**14.5 Reinsert**

Deliverables | Hi-Level WBS | Activity List | Decomposed WBS | Cost Estimate | Spend Plan-Baseline | GANTT Schedule | Network Diagram | M& E Forecast

Tab Activity List-Continued.

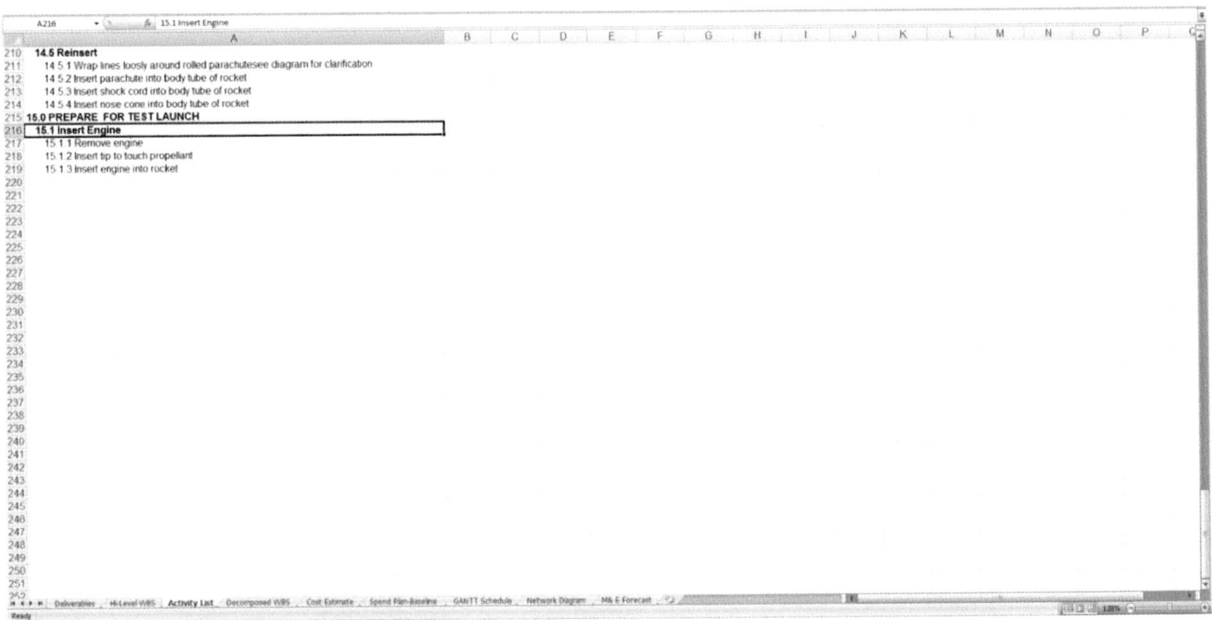

14.5 Reinsert
14 5 1 Wrap lines loosly around rolled parachutesee diagram for clarification
14 5 2 Insert parachute into body tube of rocket
14 5 3 Insert shock cord into body tube of rocket
14 5 4 Insert nose cone into body tube of rocket
15.0 PREPARE FOR TEST LAUNCH
15.1 Insert Engine
15 1 1 Remove engine
15 1 2 Insert tip to touch propellant
15 1 3 Insert engine into rocket

Tab Decomposed WBS-A completed activity list becomes a fully decomposed (broken-down) WBS.

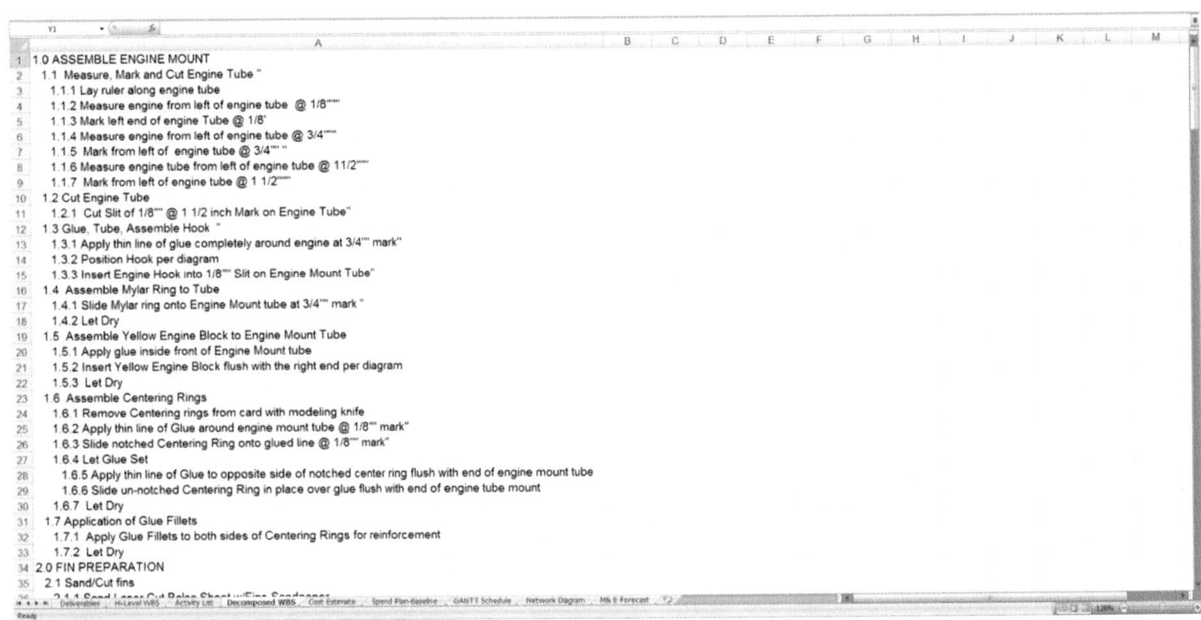

1.0 ASSEMBLE ENGINE MOUNT
1.1 Measure, Mark and Cut Engine Tube "
1.1.1 Lay ruler along engine tube
1.1.2 Measure engine from left of engine tube @ 1/8""""
1.1.3 Mark left end of engine Tube @ 1/8'
1.1.4 Measure engine from left of engine tube @ 3/4""""
1.1.5 Mark from left of engine tube @ 3/4""" "
1.1.6 Measure engine tube from left of engine tube @ 11/2""""
1.1.7 Mark from left of engine tube @ 1 1/2""""
1.2 Cut Engine Tube
1.2.1 Cut Slit of 1/8""" @ 1 1/2 inch Mark on Engine Tube"
1.3 Glue, Tube, Assemble Hook "
1.3.1 Apply thin line of glue completely around engine at 3/4""" mark"
1.3.2 Position Hook per diagram
1.3.3 Insert Engine Hook into 1/8""" Slit on Engine Mount Tube"
1.4 Assemble Mylar Ring to Tube
1.4.1 Slide Mylar ring onto Engine Mount tube at 3/4""" mark "
1.4.2 Let Dry
1.5 Assemble Yellow Engine Block to Engine Mount Tube
1.5.1 Apply glue inside front of Engine Mount tube
1.5.2 Insert Yellow Engine Block flush with the right end per diagram
1.5.3 Let Dry
1.6 Assemble Centering Rings
1.6.1 Remove Centering rings from card with modeling knife
1.6.2 Apply thin line of Glue around engine mount tube @ 1/8""" mark"
1.6.3 Slide notched Centering Ring onto glued line @ 1/8""" mark"
1.6.4 Let Glue Set
1.6.5 Apply thin line of Glue to opposite side of notched center ring flush with end of engine mount tube
1.6.6 Slide un-notched Centering Ring in place over glue flush with end of engine tube mount
1.6.7 Let Dry
1.7 Application of Glue Fillets
1.7.1 Apply Glue Fillets to both sides of Centering Rings for reinforcement
1.7.2 Let Dry
2.0 FIN PREPARATION
2.1 Sand/Cut fins

Tab Decomposed WBS-Continued.

2.1.1 Sand Laser Cut Balsa Sheet w/Fine Sandpaper
2.2 Cutting Out Fins
2.2.1 Cut out fin #1 w/modeling knife
2.2.2 Cut out fin #2 w/modeling knife
2.2.3 Cut out fin #3 w/ modeling knife
2.2.4 Cut out fin #4 w/modeling knife
2.3 Stack and Sand Fins
2.3.1 Stack Fins
2.3.2 Sand Edges of fins
3.0 MARK FIN AND LAUNCH LUG LINES
3.1 Cut - Tape
3.1.2 Cut out tube marking guide
3.1.2 Tape tube marking guide around body tube
3.1.3 Mark body tube at arrows
3.1.4 Mark Launch Lug Line as LL on Body tube
3.2 Remove guide, connect fins and lug lines, extend LL line"
3.2.1 Remove Tube Marking guide from body tube
3.2.2 Connect Fins using door frame
3.2.3 Connect launch lug lines using door frame
3.3 Extend Launch Lug Line
3.3.1 Extend launch lug line 3 3/4"" from end of tube"
4.0 INSERTING ENGINE MOUNT
4.1 Mark inside of tube @ 5/8"" where LL is"
4.1.1 Measure inside tube to 5/8"" position on tube"
4.1.2 Mark inside tube at 5/8"""
4.2 Glue Tube
4.2.1 Measure inside rear of body tube to 1 3/4' position on tube
4.2.2 Use finger to smear glue 1 3/4"" inside rear of body tube along LL "
4.3 Assemble Engine Hook
4.3.1 Align engine hook with LL line
4.3.2 Insert engine mount into body tube until centering ring is even w/the 5/8"" glue mark"
4.3.3 Let Dry
4.4 Gluing Center Body Ring
4.4.1 Locate scrap piece of balsa to apply glue
4.4.2 Apply glue to centering/body tube joint

Deliverables | Hi-Level WBS | Activity List | Decomposed WBS | Cost Estimate | Spend Plan-Baseline | GANTT Schedule | Network Diagram | M& E Forecast

Tab Decomposed WBS-Continued.

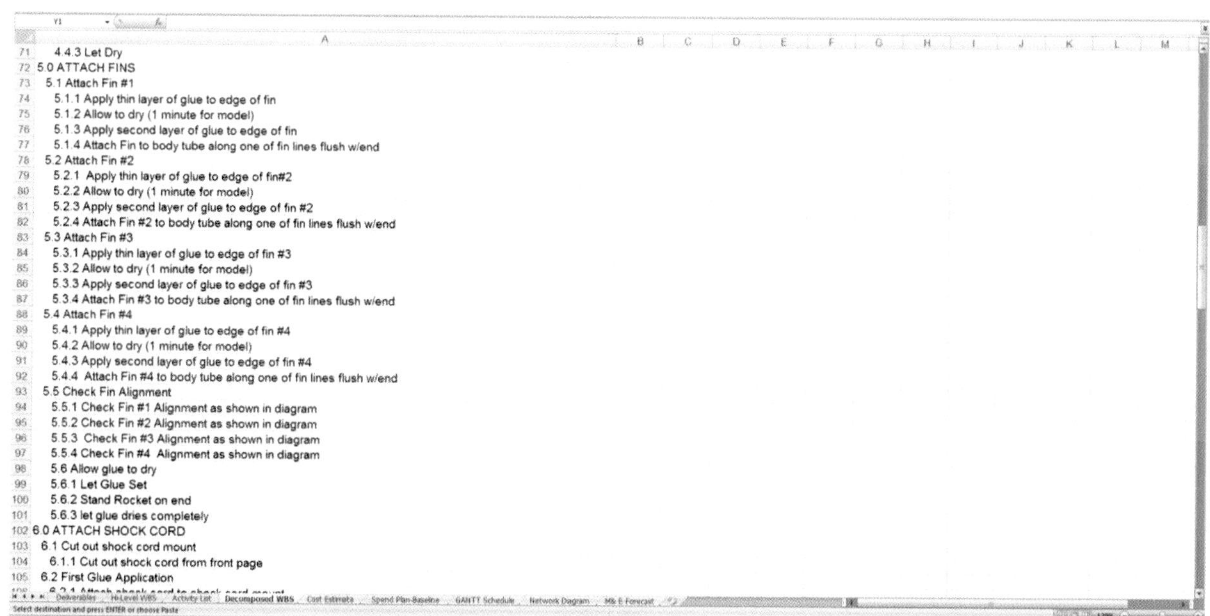

4.4.3 Let Dry
5.0 ATTACH FINS
5.1 Attach Fin #1
5.1.1 Apply thin layer of glue to edge of fin
5.1.2 Allow to dry (1 minute for model)
5.1.3 Apply second layer of glue to edge of fin
5.1.4 Attach Fin to body tube along one of fin lines flush w/end
5.2 Attach Fin #2
5.2.1 Apply thin layer of glue to edge of fin#2
5.2.2 Allow to dry (1 minute for model)
5.2.3 Apply second layer of glue to edge of fin #2
5.2.4 Attach Fin #2 to body tube along one of fin lines flush w/end
5.3 Attach Fin #3
5.3.1 Apply thin layer of glue to edge of fin #3
5.3.2 Allow to dry (1 minute for model)
5.3.3 Apply second layer of glue to edge of fin #3
5.3.4 Attach Fin #3 to body tube along one of fin lines flush w/end
5.4 Attach Fin #4
5.4.1 Apply thin layer of glue to edge of fin #4
5.4.2 Allow to dry (1 minute for model)
5.4.3 Apply second layer of glue to edge of fin #4
5.4.4 Attach Fin #4 to body tube along one of fin lines flush w/end
5.5 Check Fin Alignment
5.5.1 Check Fin #1 Alignment as shown in diagram
5.5.2 Check Fin #2 Alignment as shown in diagram
5.5.3 Check Fin #3 Alignment as shown in diagram
5.5.4 Check Fin #4 Alignment as shown in diagram
5.6 Allow glue to dry
5.6.1 Let Glue Set
5.6.2 Stand Rocket on end
5.6.3 let glue dries completely
6.0 ATTACH SHOCK CORD
6.1 Cut out shock cord mount
6.1.1 Cut out shock cord from front page
6.2 First Glue Application

Deliverables | Hi-Level WBS | Activity List | Decomposed WBS | Cost Estimate | Spend Plan-Baseline | GANTT Schedule | Network Diagram | M& E Forecast

Tab Decomposed WBS-Continued.

6.2.1 Attach shock cord to shock cord mount
6.2.2 Apply glue to shock cord mount
6.2.3 Fold edge of shock cord mount forward over glued shock cord
6.3 Second Glue Application
6.3.1 Apply glue to shock cord mount
6.3.2 Fold forward again-see diagram for clarification
6.4 Squeeze and Hold
6.4.1 Squeeze shock cord/shock cord mount tightly
6.4.2 Hold for 1 minute
6.5 Attaching Shock Cord Mount
6.5.1 Glue mount 1"" inside body tube"
6.5.2 Hold until glue sets
6.5.3 Let Dry Completely
7.0 ASSEMBLE NOSE CONE
7.1 Glue nose cone
7.1.1 Apply plastic cement to inside rim of nose cone
7.1.2 Press Nose Cone Insert into place over plastic cement inside of nose cone rim
7.1.3 Let Dry Completely
8.0 ATTACH PARACHUTE/SHOCK CORD
8.1 Attach Lines
8.1.1 Pass shroud line on parachute through eyelet
8.2 Attach Parachute
8.2.1 Pass parachute through loop in shroud-look to diagram for clarification
8.3 Tie Lines
8.3.1 Tie shock cord to nose cone using a double knot
9.0 ATTACH LAUNCH LUG
9.1 Glue launch lines
9.1.1 Glue LL centered onto LL Line on rocket body
9.2 Application of Glue Fillets
9.2.1 Apply glue fillets along launch lug
9.2.2 Apply glue fillets along fin/body tube joints
9.2.3 Smooth each fillet with finger
9.2.4 Let glue dry completely
10.0 PAINTING THE ROCKET
10.1 Apply first coat

Tab Decomposed WBS-Continued.

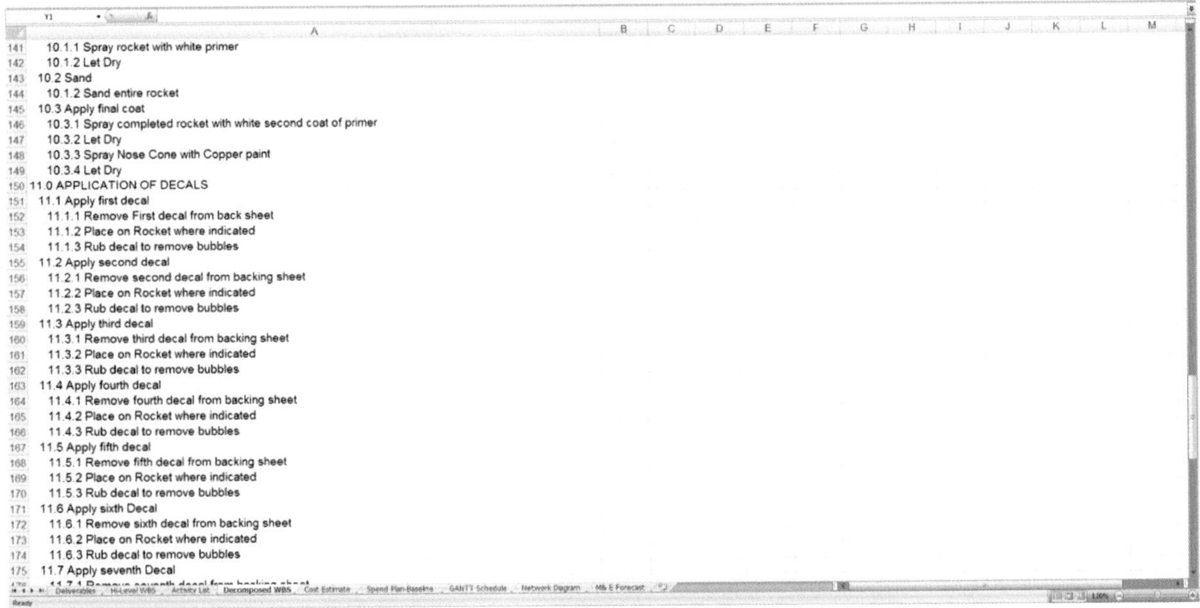
10.1.1 Spray rocket with white primer
10.1.2 Let Dry
10.2 Sand
10.1.2 Sand entire rocket
10.3 Apply final coat
10.3.1 Spray completed rocket with white second coat of primer
10.3.2 Let Dry
10.3.3 Spray Nose Cone with Copper paint
10.3.4 Let Dry
11.0 APPLICATION OF DECALS
11.1 Apply first decal
11.1.1 Remove First decal from back sheet
11.1.2 Place on Rocket where indicated
11.1.3 Rub decal to remove bubbles
11.2 Apply second decal
11.2.1 Remove second decal from backing sheet
11.2.2 Place on Rocket where indicated
11.2.3 Rub decal to remove bubbles
11.3 Apply third decal
11.3.1 Remove third decal from backing sheet
11.3.2 Place on Rocket where indicated
11.3.3 Rub decal to remove bubbles
11.4 Apply fourth decal
11.4.1 Remove fourth decal from backing sheet
11.4.2 Place on Rocket where indicated
11.4.3 Rub decal to remove bubbles
11.5 Apply fifth decal
11.5.1 Remove fifth decal from backing sheet
11.5.2 Place on Rocket where indicated
11.5.3 Rub decal to remove bubbles
11.6 Apply sixth Decal
11.6.1 Remove sixth decal from backing sheet
11.6.2 Place on Rocket where indicated
11.6.3 Rub decal to remove bubbles
11.7 Apply seventh Decal

Tab Decomposed WBS-Continued.

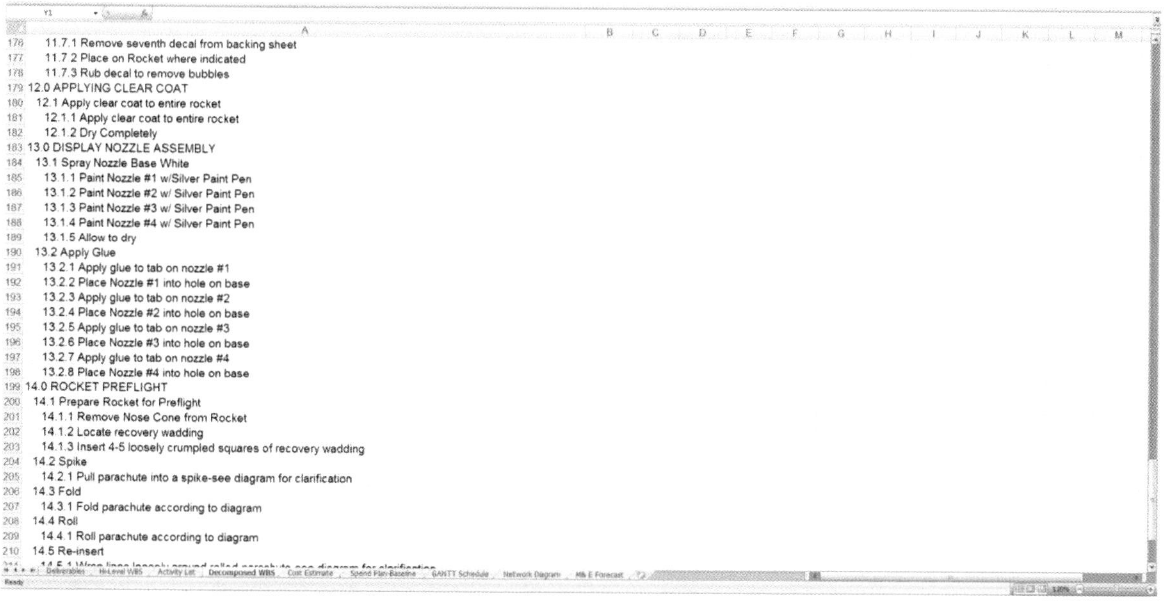

11.7.1 Remove seventh decal from backing sheet
11.7.2 Place on Rocket where indicated
11.7.3 Rub decal to remove bubbles
12.0 APPLYING CLEAR COAT
12.1 Apply clear coat to entire rocket
12.1.1 Apply clear coat to entire rocket
12.1.2 Dry Completely
13.0 DISPLAY NOZZLE ASSEMBLY
13.1 Spray Nozzle Base White
13.1.1 Paint Nozzle #1 w/Silver Paint Pen
13.1.2 Paint Nozzle #2 w/ Silver Paint Pen
13.1.3 Paint Nozzle #3 w/ Silver Paint Pen
13.1.4 Paint Nozzle #4 w/ Silver Paint Pen
13.1.5 Allow to dry
13.2 Apply Glue
13.2.1 Apply glue to tab on nozzle #1
13.2.2 Place Nozzle #1 into hole on base
13.2.3 Apply glue to tab on nozzle #2
13.2.4 Place Nozzle #2 into hole on base
13.2.5 Apply glue to tab on nozzle #3
13.2.6 Place Nozzle #3 into hole on base
13.2.7 Apply glue to tab on nozzle #4
13.2.8 Place Nozzle #4 into hole on base
14.0 ROCKET PREFLIGHT
14.1 Prepare Rocket for Preflight
14.1.1 Remove Nose Cone from Rocket
14.1.2 Locate recovery wadding
14.1.3 Insert 4-5 loosely crumpled squares of recovery wadding
14.2 Spike
14.2.1 Pull parachute into a spike-see diagram for clarification
14.3 Fold
14.3.1 Fold parachute according to diagram
14.4 Roll
14.4.1 Roll parachute according to diagram
14.5 Re-insert

Tab Decomposed WBS-Continued.

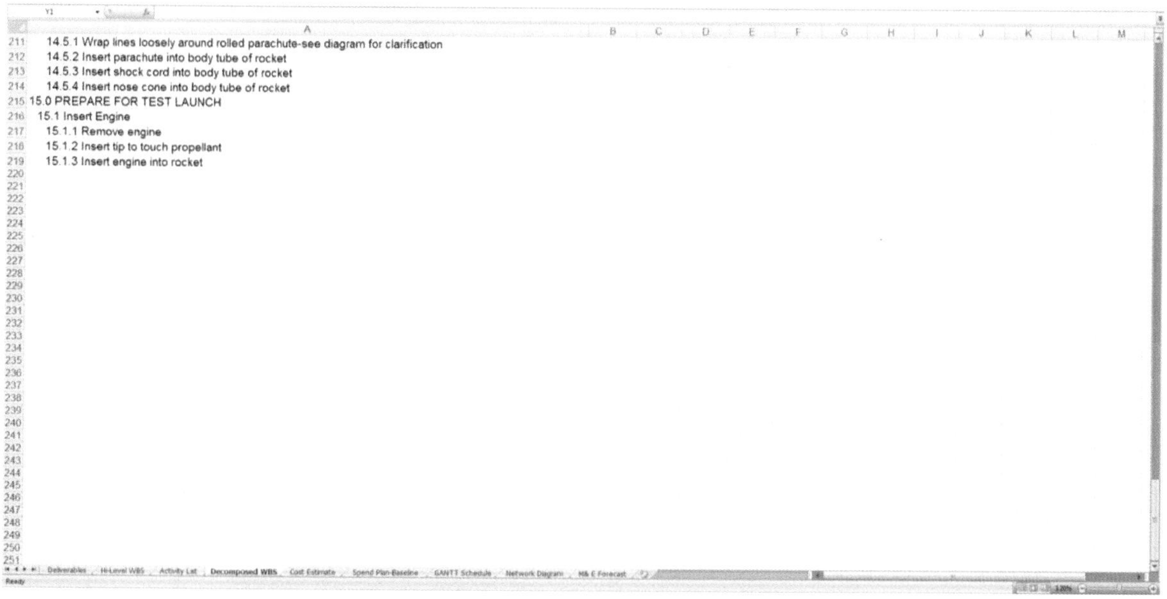

14.5.1 Wrap lines loosely around rolled parachute-see diagram for clarification
14.5.2 Insert parachute into body tube of rocket
14.5.3 Insert shock cord into body tube of rocket
14.5.4 Insert nose cone into body tube of rocket
15.0 PREPARE FOR TEST LAUNCH
15.1 Insert Engine
15.1.1 Remove engine
15.1.2 Insert tip to touch propellant
15.1.3 Insert engine into rocket

Tab Resource Allocation (Matrix) or RAM- Notice that the "X's" identify where labor is needed for a work package. Notice that "0's" ate the totals of the next indented activities below that totaled activity.

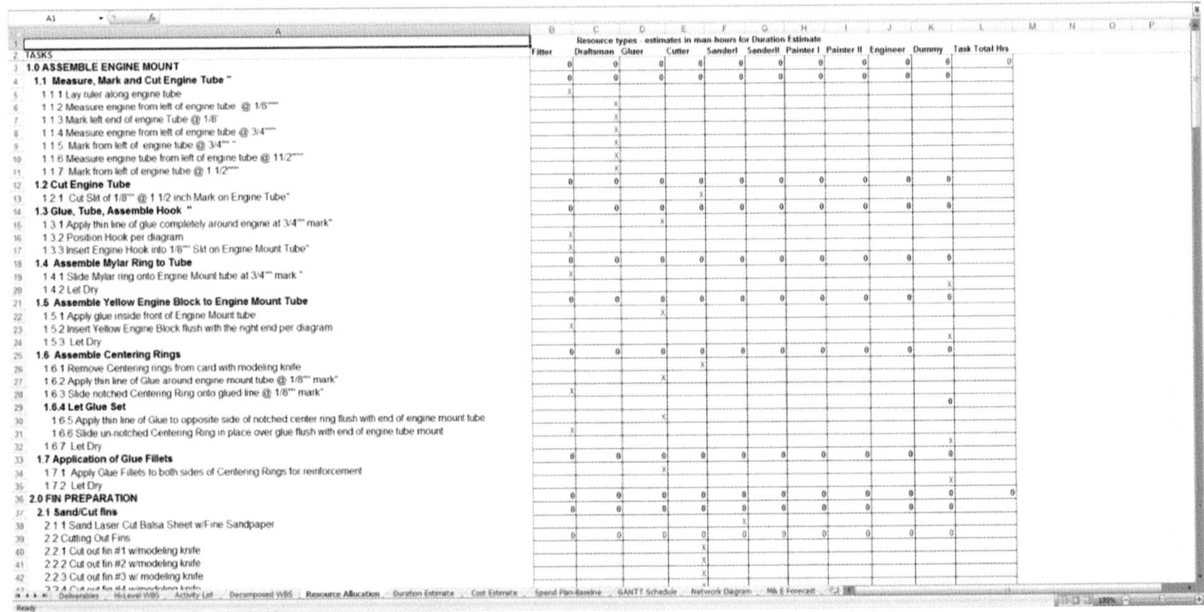

Resource types - estimates in man-hours for Duration Estimate

	TASKS	Fitter	Draftsman	Gluer	Cutter	SanderI	SanderII	Painter I	Painter II	Engineer	Dummy	Task Total Hrs
3	**1.0 ASSEMBLE ENGINE MOUNT**	0	0	0	0	0	0	0	0	0	0	0
4	**1.1 Measure, Mark and Cut Engine Tube "**	0	0	0	0	0	0	0	0	0	0	
5	1.1.1 Lay ruler along engine tube	X										
6	1.1.2 Measure engine from left of engine tube @ 1/8"""		X									
7	1.1.3 Mark left end of engine Tube @ 1/8'		X									
8	1.1.4 Measure engine from left of engine tube @ 3/4"""		X									
9	1.1.5 Mark from left of engine tube @ 3/4"" "		X									
10	1.1.6 Measure engine tube from left of engine tube @ 11/2"""		X									
11	1.1.7 Mark from left of engine tube @ 1 1/2"""		X									
12	**1.2 Cut Engine Tube**	0	0	0	0	0	0	0	0	0	0	
13	1.2.1 Cut Slit of 1/8"" @ 1 1/2 inch Mark on Engine Tube"				X							
14	**1.3 Glue, Tube, Assemble Hook "**	0	0	0	0	0	0	0	0	0	0	
15	1.3.1 Apply thin line of glue completely around engine at 3/4"" mark"			X								
16	1.3.2 Position Hook per diagram	X										
17	1.3.3 Insert Engine Hook into 1/8"" Slit on Engine Mount Tube"	X										
18	**1.4 Assemble Mylar Ring to Tube**	0	0	0	0	0	0	0	0	0	0	
19	1.4.1 Slide Mylar ring onto Engine Mount tube at 3/4"" mark "	X										
20	1.4.2 Let Dry										X	
21	**1.5 Assemble Yellow Engine Block to Engine Mount Tube**	0	0	0	0	0	0	0	0	0	0	
22	1.5.1 Apply glue inside front of Engine Mount tube			X								
23	1.5.2 Insert Yellow Engine Block flush with the right end per diagram	X										
24	1.5.3 Let Dry										X	
25	**1.6 Assemble Centering Rings**	0	0	0	0	0	0	0	0	0	0	
26	1.6.1 Remove Centering rings from card with modeling knife				X							
27	1.6.2 Apply thin line of Glue around engine mount tube @ 1/8"" mark"			X								
28	1.6.3 Slide notched Centering Ring onto glued line @ 1/8"" mark"	X										
29	**1.6.4 Let Glue Set**										0	
30	1.6.5 Apply thin line of Glue to opposite side of notched center ring flush with end of engine mount tube			X								
31	1.6.6 Slide un-notched Centering Ring in place over glue flush with end of engine tube mount	X										
32	1.6.7 Let Dry										X	
33	**1.7 Application of Glue Fillets**	0	0	0	0	0	0	0	0	0	0	
34	1.7.1 Apply Glue Fillets to both sides of Centering Rings for reinforcement			X								
35	1.7.2 Let Dry										X	
36	**2.0 FIN PREPARATION**	0	0	0	0	0	0	0	0	0	0	0
37	**2.1 Sand/Cut fins**	0	0	0	0	0	0	0	0	0	0	
38	2.1.1 Sand Laser Cut Balsa Sheet w/Fine Sandpaper					X						
39	2.2 Cutting Out Fins	0	0	0	0	0	0	0	0	0	0	
40	2.2.1 Cut out fin #1 w/modeling knife				X							
41	2.2.2 Cut out fin #2 w/modeling knife				X							
42	2.2.3 Cut out fin #3 w/ modeling knife				X							

Tab Resource Allocation-Continued.

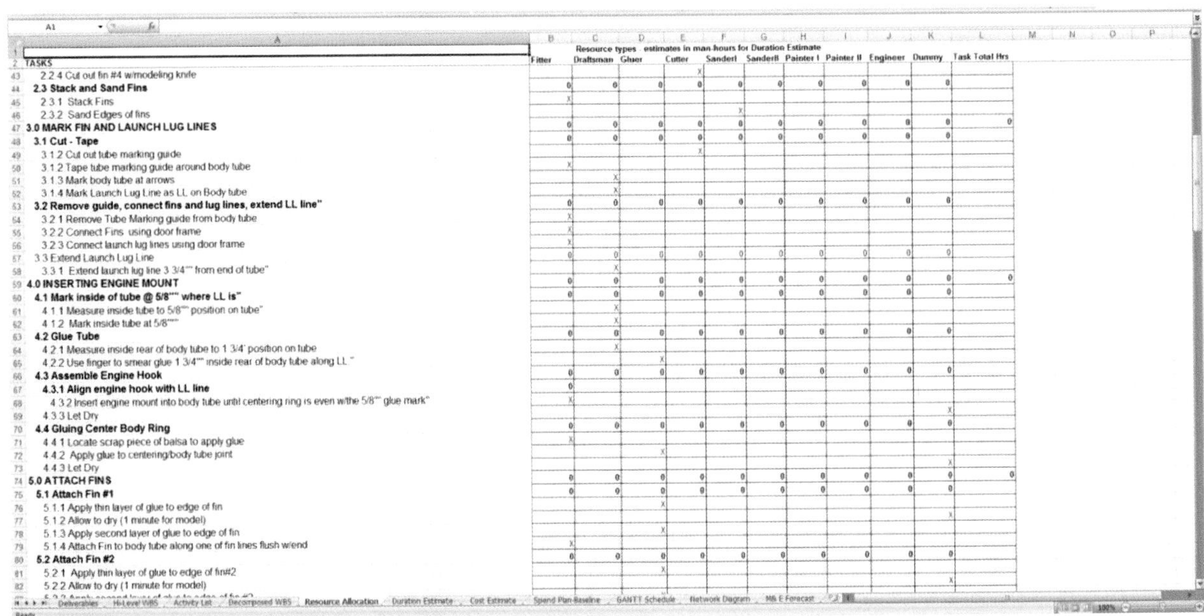

Resource types - estimates in man-hours for Duration Estimate

	TASKS	Fitter	Draftsman	Gluer	Cutter	SanderI	SanderII	Painter I	Painter II	Engineer	Dummy	Task Total Hrs
43	2.2.4 Cut out fin #4 w/modeling knife				X							
44	**2.3 Stack and Sand Fins**	0	0	0	0	0	0	0	0	0	0	
45	2.3.1 Stack Fins	X										
46	2.3.2 Sand Edges of fins					X						
47	**3.0 MARK FIN AND LAUNCH LUG LINES**	0	0	0	0	0	0	0	0	0	0	0
48	**3.1 Cut - Tape**	0	0	0	0	0	0	0	0	0	0	
49	3.1.2 Cut out tube marking guide				X							
50	3.1.2 Tape tube marking guide around body tube	X										
51	3.1.3 Mark body tube at arrows		X									
52	3.1.4 Mark Launch Lug Line as LL on Body tube		X									
53	**3.2 Remove guide, connect fins and lug lines, extend LL line"**	0	0	0	0	0	0	0	0	0	0	
54	3.2.1 Remove Tube Marking guide from body tube	X										
55	3.2.2 Connect Fins using door frame	X										
56	3.2.3 Connect launch lug lines using door frame	X										
57	3.3 Extend Launch Lug Line	0	0	0	0	0	0	0	0	0	0	
58	3.3.1 Extend launch lug line 3 3/4"" from end of tube"		X									
59	**4.0 INSERTING ENGINE MOUNT**	0	0	0	0	0	0	0	0	0	0	0
60	**4.1 Mark inside of tube @ 5/8""" where LL is"**	0	0	0	0	0	0	0	0	0	0	
61	4.1.1 Measure inside tube to 5/8"" position on tube"		X									
62	4.1.2 Mark inside tube at 5/8"""		X									
63	**4.2 Glue Tube**	0	0	0	0	0	0	0	0	0	0	
64	4.2.1 Measure inside rear of body tube to 1 3/4' position on tube		X									
65	4.2.2 Use finger to smear glue 1 3/4"" inside rear of body tube along LL "			X								
66	**4.3 Assemble Engine Hook**	0	0	0	0	0	0	0	0	0	0	
67	**4.3.1 Align engine hook with LL line**	0										
68	4.3.2 Insert engine mount into body tube until centering ring is even w/the 5/8"" glue mark"	X										
69	4.3.3 Let Dry										X	
70	**4.4 Gluing Center Body Ring**	0	0	0	0	0	0	0	0	0	0	
71	4.4.1 Locate scrap piece of balsa to apply glue	X										
72	4.4.2 Apply glue to centering/body tube joint			X								
73	4.4.3 Let Dry										X	
74	**5.0 ATTACH FINS**	0	0	0	0	0	0	0	0	0	0	0
75	**5.1 Attach Fin #1**	0	0	0	0	0	0	0	0	0	0	
76	5.1.1 Apply thin layer of glue to edge of fin			X								
77	5.1.2 Allow to dry (1 minute for model)										X	
78	5.1.3 Apply second layer of glue to edge of fin			X								
79	5.1.4 Attach Fin to body tube along one of fin lines flush w/end	X										
80	**5.2 Attach Fin #2**	0	0	0	0	0	0	0	0	0	0	
81	5.2.1 Apply thin layer of glue to edge of fin#2			X								
82	5.2.2 Allow to dry (1 minute for model)										X	

Tab Resource Allocation-Continued.

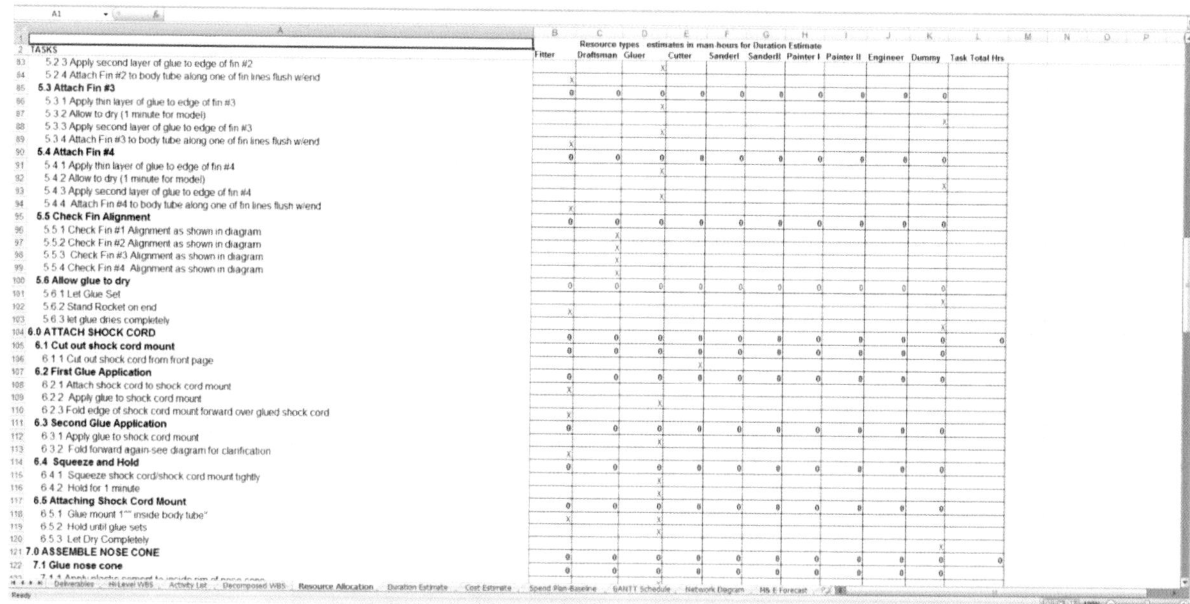

Row	TASKS	Fitter	Draftsman	Gluer	Cutter	SanderI	SanderII	Painter I	Painter II	Engineer	Dummy	Task Total Hrs
		Resource types estimates in man hours for Duration Estimate										
83	5.2.3 Apply second layer of glue to edge of fin #2			X								
84	5.2.4 Attach Fin #2 to body tube along one of fin lines flush w/end	X										
85	**5.3 Attach Fin #3**	0	0	0	0	0	0	0	0	0	0	
86	5.3.1 Apply thin layer of glue to edge of fin #3			X								
87	5.3.2 Allow to dry (1 minute for model)										X	
88	5.3.3 Apply second layer of glue to edge of fin #3			X								
89	5.3.4 Attach Fin #3 to body tube along one of fin lines flush w/end	X										
90	**5.4 Attach Fin #4**	0	0	0	0	0	0	0	0	0	0	
91	5.4.1 Apply thin layer of glue to edge of fin #4			X								
92	5.4.2 Allow to dry (1 minute for model)										X	
93	5.4.3 Apply second layer of glue to edge of fin #4			X								
94	5.4.4 Attach Fin #4 to body tube along one of fin lines flush w/end	X										
95	**5.5 Check Fin Alignment**	0	0	0	0	0	0	0	0	0	0	
96	5.5.1 Check Fin #1 Alignment as shown in diagram		X									
97	5.5.2 Check Fin #2 Alignment as shown in diagram		X									
98	5.5.3 Check Fin #3 Alignment as shown in diagram		X									
99	5.5.4 Check Fin #4 Alignment as shown in diagram		X									
100	**5.6 Allow glue to dry**	0	0	0	0	0	0	0	0	0	0	
101	5.6.1 Let Glue Set										X	
102	5.6.2 Stand Rocket on end	X										
103	5.6.3 let glue dries completely										X	
104	**6.0 ATTACH SHOCK CORD**	0	0	0	0	0	0	0	0	0	0	0
105	**6.1 Cut out shock cord mount**	0	0	0	0	0	0	0	0	0	0	
106	6.1.1 Cut out shock cord from front page				X							
107	**6.2 First Glue Application**	0	0	0	0	0	0	0	0	0	0	
108	6.2.1 Attach shock cord to shock cord mount	X										
109	6.2.2 Apply glue to shock cord mount			X								
110	6.2.3 Fold edge of shock cord mount forward over glued shock cord	X										
111	**6.3 Second Glue Application**	0	0	0	0	0	0	0	0	0	0	
112	6.3.1 Apply glue to shock cord mount			X								
113	6.3.2 Fold forward again-see diagram for clarification	X										
114	**6.4 Squeeze and Hold**	0	0	0	0	0	0	0	0	0	0	
115	6.4.1 Squeeze shock cord/shock cord mount tightly			X								
116	6.4.2 Hold for 1 minute			X								
117	**6.5 Attaching Shock Cord Mount**	0	0	0	0	0	0	0	0	0	0	
118	6.5.1 Glue mount 1"" inside body tube"	X		X								
119	6.5.2 Hold until glue sets			X								
120	6.5.3 Let Dry Completely										X	
121	**7.0 ASSEMBLE NOSE CONE**	0	0	0	0	0	0	0	0	0	0	0
122	**7.1 Glue nose cone**	0	0	0	0	0	0	0	0	0	0	

Tab Resource Allocation-Continued.

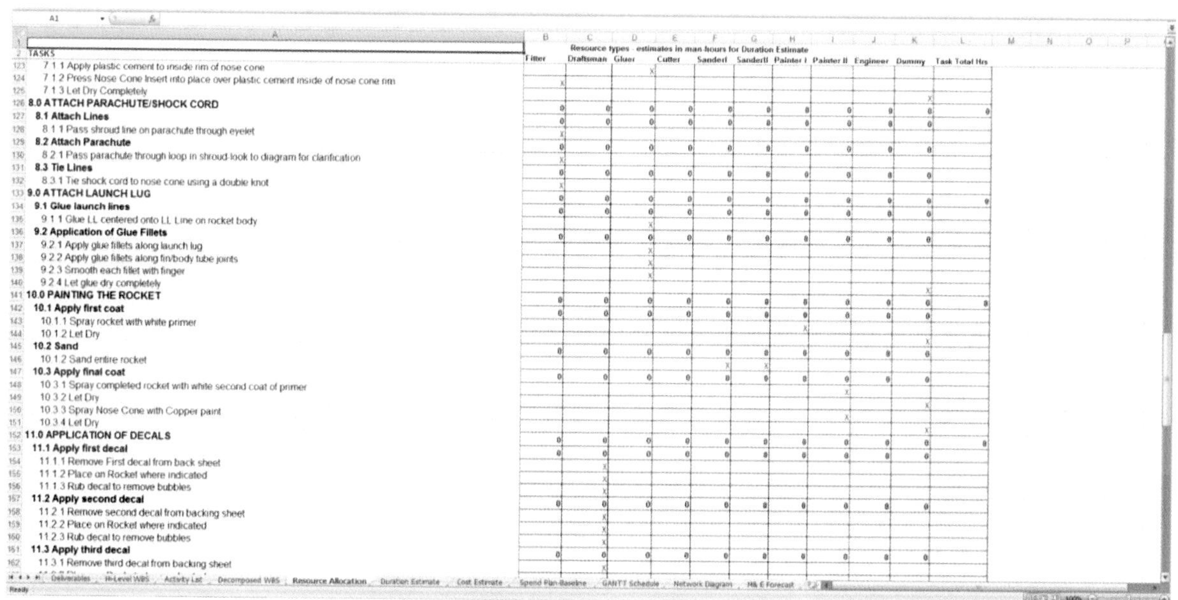

Row	TASKS	Fitter	Draftsman	Gluer	Cutter	SanderI	SanderII	Painter I	Painter II	Engineer	Dummy	Task Total Hrs
		Resource types estimates in man hours for Duration Estimate										
123	7.1.1 Apply plastic cement to inside rim of nose cone			X								
124	7.1.2 Press Nose Cone Insert into place over plastic cement inside of nose cone rim	X										
125	7.1.3 Let Dry Completely										X	
126	**8.0 ATTACH PARACHUTE/SHOCK CORD**	0	0	0	0	0	0	0	0	0	0	0
127	**8.1 Attach Lines**	0	0	0	0	0	0	0	0	0	0	
128	8.1.1 Pass shroud line on parachute through eyelet	X										
129	**8.2 Attach Parachute**	0	0	0	0	0	0	0	0	0	0	
130	8.2.1 Pass parachute through loop in shroud-look to diagram for clarification	X										
131	**8.3 Tie Lines**	0	0	0	0	0	0	0	0	0	0	
132	8.3.1 Tie shock cord to nose cone using a double knot	X										
133	**9.0 ATTACH LAUNCH LUG**	0	0	0	0	0	0	0	0	0	0	0
134	**9.1 Glue launch lines**	0	0	0	0	0	0	0	0	0	0	
135	9.1.1 Glue LL centered onto LL Line on rocket body			X								
136	**9.2 Application of Glue Fillets**	0	0	0	0	0	0	0	0	0	0	
137	9.2.1 Apply glue fillets along launch lug			X								
138	9.2.2 Apply glue fillets along fin/body tube joints			X								
139	9.2.3 Smooth each fillet with finger			X								
140	9.2.4 Let glue dry completely										X	
141	**10.0 PAINTING THE ROCKET**	0	0	0	0	0	0	0	0	0	0	0
142	**10.1 Apply first coat**	0	0	0	0	0	0	0	0	0	0	
143	10.1.1 Spray rocket with white primer							X				
144	10.1.2 Let Dry										X	
145	**10.2 Sand**	0	0	0	0	0	0	0	0	0	0	
146	10.1.2 Sand entire rocket					X	X					
147	**10.3 Apply final coat**	0	0	0	0	0	0	0	0	0	0	
148	10.3.1 Spray completed rocket with white second coat of primer								X			
149	10.3.2 Let Dry										X	
150	10.3.3 Spray Nose Cone with Copper paint								X			
151	10.3.4 Let Dry										X	
152	**11.0 APPLICATION OF DECALS**	0	0	0	0	0	0	0	0	0	0	0
153	**11.1 Apply first decal**	0	0	0	0	0	0	0	0	0	0	
154	11.1.1 Remove First decal from back sheet		X									
155	11.1.2 Place on Rocket where indicated		X									
156	11.1.3 Rub decal to remove bubbles		X									
157	**11.2 Apply second decal**	0	0	0	0	0	0	0	0	0	0	
158	11.2.1 Remove second decal from backing sheet		X									
159	11.2.2 Place on Rocket where indicated		X									
160	11.2.3 Rub decal to remove bubbles		X									
161	**11.3 Apply third decal**	0	0	0	0	0	0	0	0	0	0	
162	11.3.1 Remove third decal from backing sheet		X									

Tab Resource Allocation-Continued.

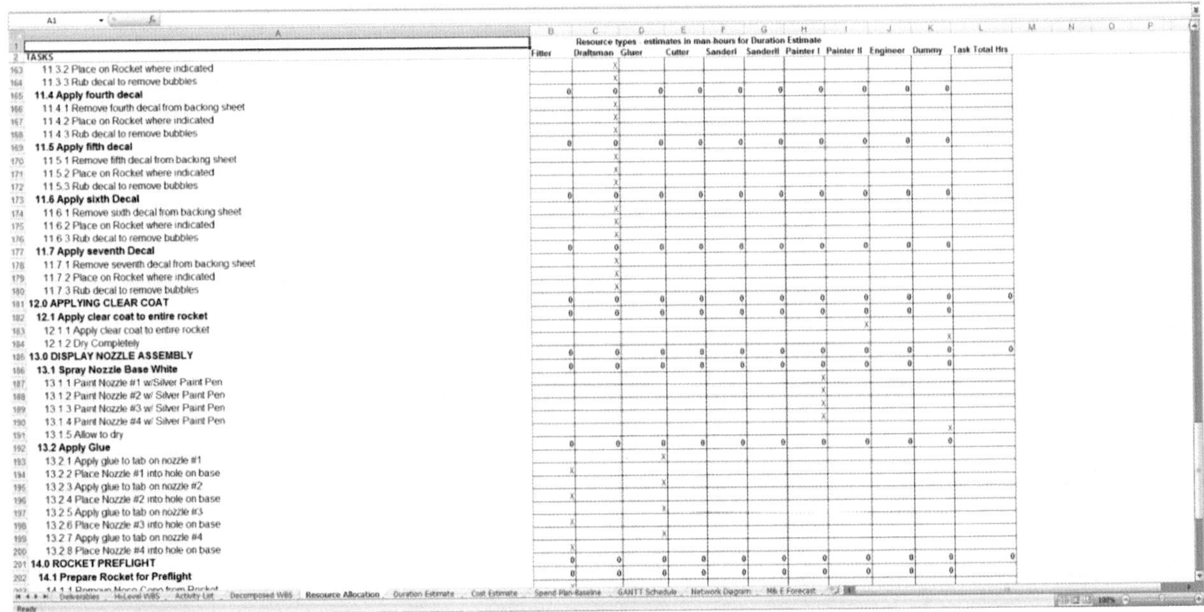

Resource types - estimates in man-hours for Duration Estimate

	TASKS	Fitter	Draftsman	Gluer	Cutter	SanderI	SanderII	Painter I	Painter II	Engineer	Dummy	Task Total Hrs
163	11.3.2 Place on Rocket where indicated		X									
164	11.3.3 Rub decal to remove bubbles		X									
165	**11.4 Apply fourth decal**	0	0	0	0	0	0	0	0	0	0	
166	11.4.1 Remove fourth decal from backing sheet		X									
167	11.4.2 Place on Rocket where indicated		X									
168	11.4.3 Rub decal to remove bubbles		X									
169	**11.5 Apply fifth decal**	0	0	0	0	0	0	0	0	0	0	
170	11.5.1 Remove fifth decal from backing sheet		X									
171	11.5.2 Place on Rocket where indicated		X									
172	11.5.3 Rub decal to remove bubbles		X									
173	**11.6 Apply sixth Decal**	0	0	0	0	0	0	0	0	0	0	
174	11.6.1 Remove sixth decal from backing sheet		X									
175	11.6.2 Place on Rocket where indicated		X									
176	11.6.3 Rub decal to remove bubbles		X									
177	**11.7 Apply seventh Decal**	0	0	0	0	0	0	0	0	0	0	
178	11.7.1 Remove seventh decal from backing sheet		X									
179	11.7.2 Place on Rocket where indicated		X									
180	11.7.3 Rub decal to remove bubbles		X									
181	**12.0 APPLYING CLEAR COAT**	0	0	0	0	0	0	0	0	0	0	0
182	**12.1 Apply clear coat to entire rocket**	0	0	0	0	0	0	0	0	0	0	
183	12.1.1 Apply clear coat to entire rocket								X			
184	12.1.2 Dry Completely										X	
185	**13.0 DISPLAY NOZZLE ASSEMBLY**	0	0	0	0	0	0	0	0	0	0	0
186	**13.1 Spray Nozzle Base White**	0	0	0	0	0	0	0	0	0	0	
187	13.1.1 Paint Nozzle #1 w/Silver Paint Pen							X				
188	13.1.2 Paint Nozzle #2 w/ Silver Paint Pen							X				
189	13.1.3 Paint Nozzle #3 w/ Silver Paint Pen							X				
190	13.1.4 Paint Nozzle #4 w/ Silver Paint Pen							X				
191	13.1.5 Allow to dry										X	
192	**13.2 Apply Glue**	0	0	0	0	0	0	0	0	0	0	
193	13.2.1 Apply glue to tab on nozzle #1			X								
194	13.2.2 Place Nozzle #1 into hole on base	X										
195	13.2.3 Apply glue to tab on nozzle #2			X								
196	13.2.4 Place Nozzle #2 into hole on base	X										
197	13.2.5 Apply glue to tab on nozzle #3			X								
198	13.2.6 Place Nozzle #3 into hole on base	X										
199	13.2.7 Apply glue to tab on nozzle #4			X								
200	13.2.8 Place Nozzle #4 into hole on base	X										
201	**14.0 ROCKET PREFLIGHT**	0	0	0	0	0	0	0	0	0	0	0
202	**14.1 Prepare Rocket for Preflight**	0	0	0	0	0	0	0	0	0	0	

Deliverables | Hi-Level WBS | Activity List | Decomposed WBS | Resource Allocation | Duration Estimate | Cost Estimate | Spend Plan-Baseline | GANTT Schedule | Network Diagram | M& E Forecast

Ready

Tab Resource Allocation-Continued.

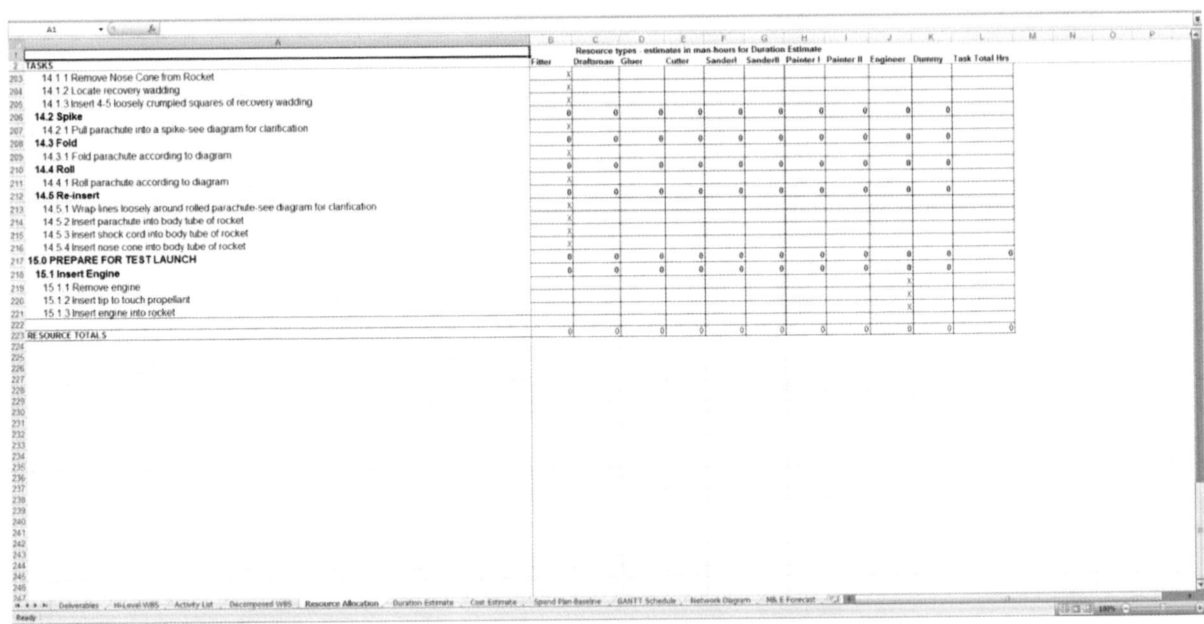

Resource types - estimates in man-hours for Duration Estimate

	TASKS	Fitter	Draftsman	Gluer	Cutter	SanderI	SanderII	Painter I	Painter II	Engineer	Dummy	Task Total Hrs
203	14.1.1 Remove Nose Cone from Rocket	X										
204	14.1.2 Locate recovery wadding	X										
205	14.1.3 Insert 4-5 loosely crumpled squares of recovery wadding	X										
206	**14.2 Spike**	0	0	0	0	0	0	0	0	0	0	
207	14.2.1 Pull parachute into a spike-see diagram for clarification	X										
208	**14.3 Fold**	0	0	0	0	0	0	0	0	0	0	
209	14.3.1 Fold parachute according to diagram	X										
210	**14.4 Roll**	0	0	0	0	0	0	0	0	0	0	
211	14.4.1 Roll parachute according to diagram	X										
212	**14.5 Re-insert**	0	0	0	0	0	0	0	0	0	0	
213	14.5.1 Wrap lines loosely around rolled parachute-see diagram for clarification	X										
214	14.5.2 Insert parachute into body tube of rocket	X										
215	14.5.3 Insert shock cord into body tube of rocket	X										
216	14.5.4 Insert nose cone into body tube of rocket	X										
217	**15.0 PREPARE FOR TEST LAUNCH**	0	0	0	0	0	0	0	0	0	0	0
218	**15.1 Insert Engine**	0	0	0	0	0	0	0	0	0	0	
219	15.1.1 Remove engine									X		
220	15.1.2 Insert tip to touch propellant									X		
221	15.1.3 Insert engine into rocket									X		
222												
223	RESOURCE TOTALS	0	0	0	0	0	0	0	0	0	0	0

Deliverables | Hi-Level WBS | Activity List | Decomposed WBS | Resource Allocation | Duration Estimate | Cost Estimate | Spend Plan-Baseline | GANTT Schedule | Network Diagram | M& E Forecast

Ready

Tab Duration Estimate.

	TASKS	Fitter	Draftsman	Gluer	Cutter	SanderI	SanderII	Painter I	Painter II	Engineer	Dummy	
1			Resource types - estimates in man-hours for Duration Estimate									
3	1.0 ASSEMBLE ENGINE MOUNT	14	30	7	4	0	0	0	0	0	40	95
4	1.1 Measure, Mark and Cut Engine Tube "	5	30	0	0	0	0	0	0	0	0	
5	1.1.1 Lay ruler along engine tube	5										
6	1.1.2 Measure engine from left of engine tube @ 1/8""		5									
7	1.1.3 Mark left end of engine Tube @ 1/8'		5									
8	1.1.4 Measure engine from left of engine tube @ 3/4""		5									
9	1.1.5 Mark from left of engine tube @ 3/4"" "		5									
10	1.1.6 Measure engine tube from left of engine tube @ 11/2""		5									
11	1.1.7 Mark from left of engine tube @ 1 1/2""		5									
12	1.2 Cut Engine Tube	0	0	0	2	0	0	0	0	0	0	
13	1.2.1 Cut Slit of 1/8"" @ 1 1/2 inch Mark on Engine Tube"				2							
14	1.3 Glue, Tube, Assemble Hook "	5	0	2	0	0	0	0	0	0	0	
15	1.3.1 Apply thin line of glue completely around engine at 3/4"" mark"			2								
16	1.3.2 Position Hook per diagram	2										
17	1.3.3 Insert Engine Hook into 1/8"" Slit on Engine Mount Tube"	3										
18	1.4 Assemble Mylar Ring to Tube	1	0	0	0	0	0	0	0	0	8	
19	1.4.1 Slide Mylar ring onto Engine Mount tube at 3/4"" mark "	1										
20	1.4.2 Let Dry										8	
21	1.5 Assemble Yellow Engine Block to Engine Mount Tube	1	0	1	0	0	0	0	0	0	8	
22	1.5.1 Apply glue inside front of Engine Mount tube			1								
23	1.5.2 Insert Yellow Engine Block flush with the right end per diagram	1										
24	1.5.3 Let Dry										8	
25	1.6 Assemble Centering Rings	2	0	2	2	0	0	0	0	0	16	
26	1.6.1 Remove Centering rings from card with modeling knife				2							
27	1.6.2 Apply thin line of Glue around engine mount tube @ 1/8"" mark"			1								
28	1.6.3 Slide notched Centering Ring onto glued line @ 1/8"" mark"	1										
29	1.6.4 Let Glue Set										8	
30	1.6.5 Apply thin line of Glue to opposite side of notched center ring flush with end of engine mount tube			1								
31	1.6.6 Slide un-notched Centering Ring in place over glue flush with end of engine tube mount	1										
32	1.6.7 Let Dry										8	
33	1.7 Application of Glue Fillets	0	0	2	0	0	0	0	0	0	8	
34	1.7.1 Apply Glue Fillets to both sides of Centering Rings for reinforcement			2								
35	1.7.2 Let Dry										8	
36	2.0 FIN PREPARATION	2	0	0	12	16	0	0	0	0	0	30
37	2.1 Sand/Cut fins	0	0	0	0	8	0	0	0	0	0	
38	2.1.1 Sand Laser Cut Balsa Sheet w/Fine Sandpaper					8						
39	2.2 Cutting Out Fins	0	0	0	12	0	0	0	0	0	0	

Deliverables | Hi-Level WBS | Activity List | Decomposed WBS | Resource Allocation | Duration Estimate | Cost Estimate | Spend Plan-Baseline | GANTT Schedule | Network Diagram | M& E Forecast

Tab Duration Estimate-Continued.

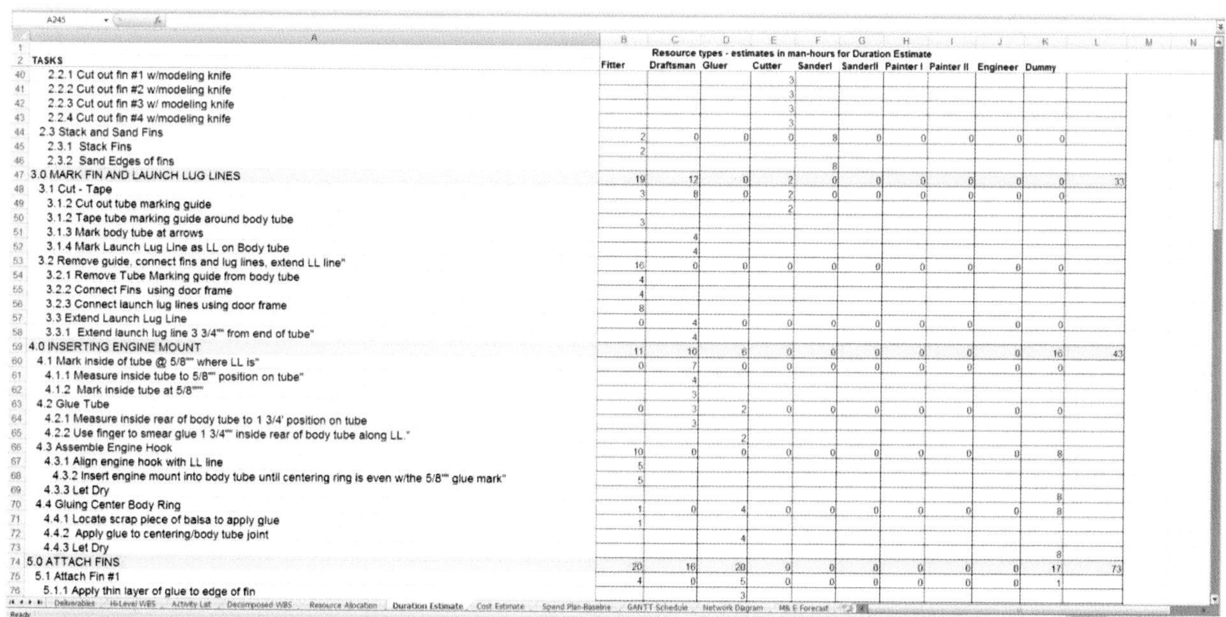

	TASKS	Fitter	Draftsman	Gluer	Cutter	SanderI	SanderII	Painter I	Painter II	Engineer	Dummy	
1			Resource types - estimates in man-hours for Duration Estimate									
40	2.2.1 Cut out fin #1 w/modeling knife				3							
41	2.2.2 Cut out fin #2 w/modeling knife				3							
42	2.2.3 Cut out fin #3 w/ modeling knife				3							
43	2.2.4 Cut out fin #4 w/modeling knife				3							
44	2.3 Stack and Sand Fins	2	0	0	0	8	0	0	0	0	0	
45	2.3.1 Stack Fins	2										
46	2.3.2 Sand Edges of fins					8						
47	3.0 MARK FIN AND LAUNCH LUG LINES	19	12	0	2	0	0	0	0	0	0	33
48	3.1 Cut - Tape	3	8	0	2	0	0	0	0	0	0	
49	3.1.2 Cut out tube marking guide				2							
50	3.1.2 Tape tube marking guide around body tube	3										
51	3.1.3 Mark body tube at arrows		4									
52	3.1.4 Mark Launch Lug Line as LL on Body tube		4									
53	3.2 Remove guide, connect fins and lug lines, extend LL line"	16	0	0	0	0	0	0	0	0	0	
54	3.2.1 Remove Tube Marking guide from body tube	4										
55	3.2.2 Connect Fins using door frame	4										
56	3.2.3 Connect launch lug lines using door frame	8										
57	3.3 Extend Launch Lug Line	0	4	0	0	0	0	0	0	0	0	
58	3.3.1 Extend launch lug line 3 3/4"" from end of tube"		4									
59	4.0 INSERTING ENGINE MOUNT	11	10	6	0	0	0	0	0	0	16	43
60	4.1 Mark inside of tube @ 5/8"" where LL is"	0	7	0	0	0	0	0	0	0	0	
61	4.1.1 Measure inside tube to 5/8"" position on tube"		4									
62	4.1.2 Mark inside tube at 5/8""		3									
63	4.2 Glue Tube	0	3	2	0	0	0	0	0	0	0	
64	4.2.1 Measure inside rear of body tube to 1 3/4' position on tube		3									
65	4.2.2 Use finger to smear glue 1 3/4"" inside rear of body tube along LL."			2								
66	4.3 Assemble Engine Hook	10	0	0	0	0	0	0	0	0	8	
67	4.3.1 Align engine hook with LL line	5										
68	4.3.2 Insert engine mount into body tube until centering ring is even w/the 5/8"" glue mark"	5										
69	4.3.3 Let Dry										8	
70	4.4 Gluing Center Body Ring	1	0	4	0	0	0	0	0	0	8	
71	4.4.1 Locate scrap piece of balsa to apply glue	1										
72	4.4.2 Apply glue to centering/body tube joint			4								
73	4.4.3 Let Dry										8	
74	5.0 ATTACH FINS	20	16	20	0	0	0	0	0	0	17	73
75	5.1 Attach Fin #1	4	0	5	0	0	0	0	0	0	1	
76	5.1.1 Apply thin layer of glue to edge of fin			3								

Deliverables | Hi-Level WBS | Activity List | Decomposed WBS | Resource Allocation | Duration Estimate | Cost Estimate | Spend Plan-Baseline | GANTT Schedule | Network Diagram | M& E Forecast

Tab Duration Estimate-Continued.

Row	TASKS	Fitter	Draftsman	Gluer	Cutter	SanderI	SanderII	Painter I	Painter II	Engineer	Dummy	
		Resource types - estimates in man-hours for Duration Estimate										
77	5.1.2 Allow to dry (1 minute for model)										1	
78	5.1.3 Apply second layer of glue to edge of fin			2								
79	5.1.4 Attach Fin to body tube along one of fin lines flush w/end	4										
80	5.2 Attach Fin #2	4	0	5	0	0	0	0	0	0	1	
81	5.2.1 Apply thin layer of glue to edge of fin#2			3								
82	5.2.2 Allow to dry (1 minute for model)										1	
83	5.2.3 Apply second layer of glue to edge of fin #2			2								
84	5.2.4 Attach Fin #2 to body tube along one of fin lines flush w/end	4										
85	5.3 Attach Fin #3	4	0	5	0	0	0	0	0	0	1	
86	5.3.1 Apply thin layer of glue to edge of fin #3			3								
87	5.3.2 Allow to dry (1 minute for model)										1	
88	5.3.3 Apply second layer of glue to edge of fin #3			2								
89	5.3.4 Attach Fin #3 to body tube along one of fin lines flush w/end	4										
90	5.4 Attach Fin #4	4	0	5	0	0	0	0	0	0	1	
91	5.4.1 Apply thin layer of glue to edge of fin #4			3								
92	5.4.2 Allow to dry (1 minute for model)										1	
93	5.4.3 Apply second layer of glue to edge of fin #4			2								
94	5.4.4 Attach Fin #4 to body tube along one of fin lines flush w/end	4										
95	5.5 Check Fin Alignment	0	16	0	0	0	0	0	0	0	0	
96	5.5.1 Check Fin #1 Alignment as shown in diagram		4									
97	5.5.2 Check Fin #2 Alignment as shown in diagram		4									
98	5.5.3 Check Fin #3 Alignment as shown in diagram		4									
99	5.5.4 Check Fin #4 Alignment as shown in diagram		4									
100	5.6 Allow glue to dry	4	0	0	0	0	0	0	0	0	13	
101	5.6.1 Let Glue Set										5	
102	5.6.2 Stand Rocket on end	4										
103	5.6.3 let glue dries completely										8	
104	6.0 ATTACH SHOCK CORD	16	0	19	5	0	0	0	0	0	8	48
105	6.1 Cut out shock cord mount	0	0	0	5	0	0	0	0	0	0	
106	6.1.1 Cut out shock cord from front page				5							
107	6.2 First Glue Application	8	0	4	0	0	0	0	0	0	0	
108	6.2.1 Attach shock cord to shock cord mount	4										
109	6.2.2 Apply glue to shock cord mount			4								
110	6.2.3 Fold edge of shock cord mount forward over glued shock cord	4										
111	6.3 Second Glue Application	4	0	4	0	0	0	0	0	0	0	
112	6.3.1 Apply glue to shock cord mount			4								
113	6.3.2 Fold forward again-see diagram for clarification	4										

Tab Duration Estimate-Continued.

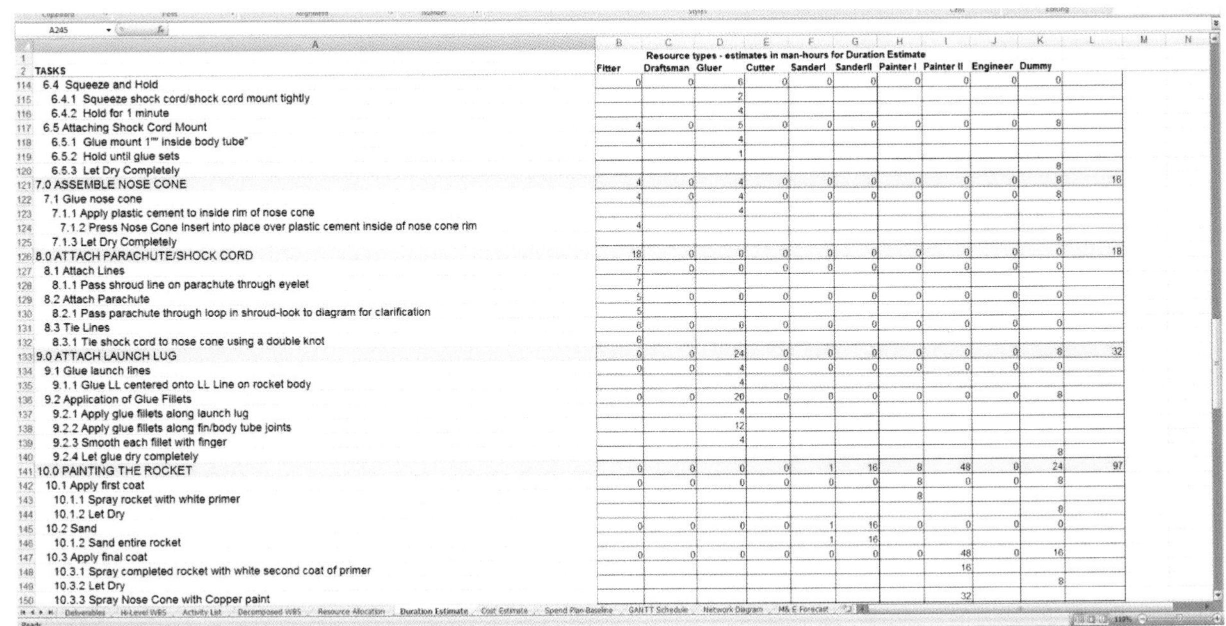

Row	TASKS	Fitter	Draftsman	Gluer	Cutter	SanderI	SanderII	Painter I	Painter II	Engineer	Dummy	
		Resource types - estimates in man-hours for Duration Estimate										
114	6.4 Squeeze and Hold	0	0	6	0	0	0	0	0	0	0	
115	6.4.1 Squeeze shock cord/shock cord mount tightly			2								
116	6.4.2 Hold for 1 minute			4								
117	6.5 Attaching Shock Cord Mount	4	0	5	0	0	0	0	0	0	8	
118	6.5.1 Glue mount 1"" inside body tube"	4		4								
119	6.5.2 Hold until glue sets			1								
120	6.5.3 Let Dry Completely										8	
121	7.0 ASSEMBLE NOSE CONE	4	0	4	0	0	0	0	0	0	8	16
122	7.1 Glue nose cone	4	0	4	0	0	0	0	0	0	8	
123	7.1.1 Apply plastic cement to inside rim of nose cone			4								
124	7.1.2 Press Nose Cone Insert into place over plastic cement inside of nose cone rim	4										
125	7.1.3 Let Dry Completely										8	
126	8.0 ATTACH PARACHUTE/SHOCK CORD	18	0	0	0	0	0	0	0	0	0	18
127	8.1 Attach Lines	7	0	0	0	0	0	0	0	0	0	
128	8.1.1 Pass shroud line on parachute through eyelet	7										
129	8.2 Attach Parachute	5	0	0	0	0	0	0	0	0	0	
130	8.2.1 Pass parachute through loop in shroud-look to diagram for clarification	5										
131	8.3 Tie Lines	6	0	0	0	0	0	0	0	0	0	
132	8.3.1 Tie shock cord to nose cone using a double knot	6										
133	9.0 ATTACH LAUNCH LUG	0	0	24	0	0	0	0	0	0	8	32
134	9.1 Glue launch lines	0	0	4	0	0	0	0	0	0	0	
135	9.1.1 Glue LL centered onto LL Line on rocket body			4								
136	9.2 Application of Glue Fillets	0	0	20	0	0	0	0	0	0	8	
137	9.2.1 Apply glue fillets along launch lug			4								
138	9.2.2 Apply glue fillets along fin/body tube joints			12								
139	9.2.3 Smooth each fillet with finger			4								
140	9.2.4 Let glue dry completely										8	
141	10.0 PAINTING THE ROCKET	0	0	0	0	1	16	8	48	0	24	97
142	10.1 Apply first coat	0	0	0	0	0	0	8	0	0	8	
143	10.1.1 Spray rocket with white primer							8				
144	10.1.2 Let Dry										8	
145	10.2 Sand	0	0	0	0	1	16	0	0	0	0	
146	10.1.2 Sand entire rocket					1	16					
147	10.3 Apply final coat	0	0	0	0	0	0	0	48	0	16	
148	10.3.1 Spray completed rocket with white second coat of primer								16			
149	10.3.2 Let Dry										8	
150	10.3.3 Spray Nose Cone with Copper paint								32			

Tab Duration Estimate-Continued.

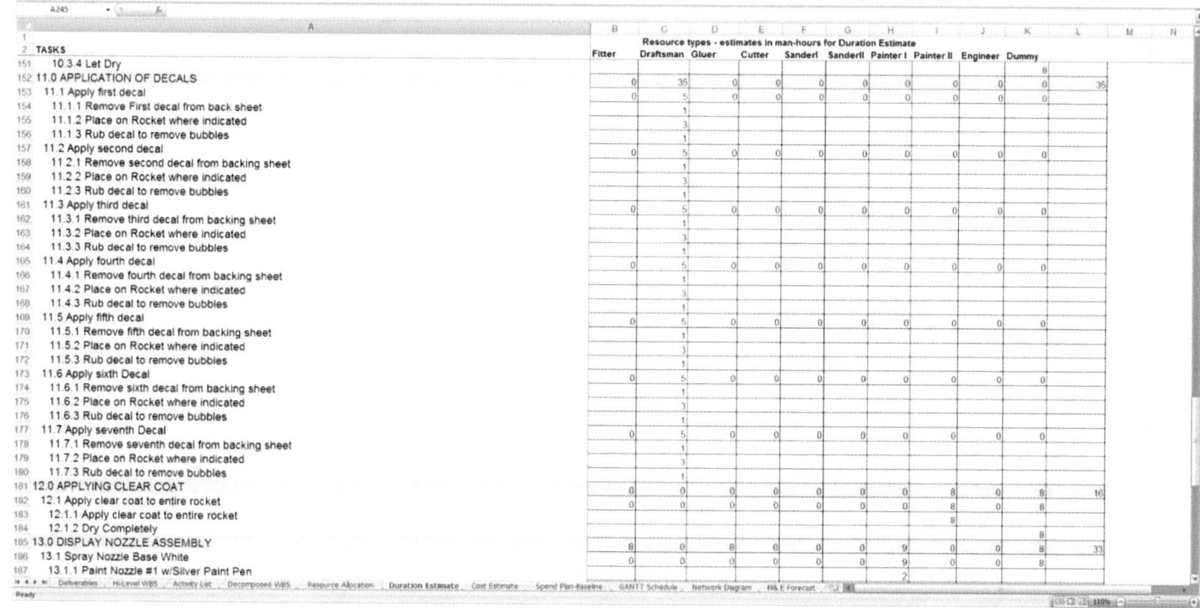

Resource types - estimates in man-hours for Duration Estimate

	TASKS	Fitter	Draftsman	Gluer	Cutter	SanderI	SanderII	Painter I	Painter II	Engineer	Dummy	
151	10.3.4 Let Dry										8	
152	11.0 APPLICATION OF DECALS	0	35	0	0	0	0	0	0	0	0	35
153	11.1 Apply first decal	0	5	0	0	0	0	0	0	0	0	
154	11.1.1 Remove First decal from back sheet		1									
155	11.1.2 Place on Rocket where indicated		3									
156	11.1.3 Rub decal to remove bubbles		1									
157	11.2 Apply second decal	0	5	0	0	0	0	0	0	0	0	
158	11.2.1 Remove second decal from backing sheet		1									
159	11.2.2 Place on Rocket where indicated		3									
160	11.2.3 Rub decal to remove bubbles		1									
161	11.3 Apply third decal	0	5	0	0	0	0	0	0	0	0	
162	11.3.1 Remove third decal from backing sheet		1									
163	11.3.2 Place on Rocket where indicated		3									
164	11.3.3 Rub decal to remove bubbles		1									
165	11.4 Apply fourth decal	0	5	0	0	0	0	0	0	0	0	
166	11.4.1 Remove fourth decal from backing sheet		1									
167	11.4.2 Place on Rocket where indicated		3									
168	11.4.3 Rub decal to remove bubbles		1									
169	11.5 Apply fifth decal	0	5	0	0	0	0	0	0	0	0	
170	11.5.1 Remove fifth decal from backing sheet		1									
171	11.5.2 Place on Rocket where indicated		3									
172	11.5.3 Rub decal to remove bubbles		1									
173	11.6 Apply sixth Decal	0	5	0	0	0	0	0	0	0	0	
174	11.6.1 Remove sixth decal from backing sheet		1									
175	11.6.2 Place on Rocket where indicated		3									
176	11.6.3 Rub decal to remove bubbles		1									
177	11.7 Apply seventh Decal	0	5	0	0	0	0	0	0	0	0	
178	11.7.1 Remove seventh decal from backing sheet		1									
179	11.7.2 Place on Rocket where indicated		3									
180	11.7.3 Rub decal to remove bubbles		1									
181	12.0 APPLYING CLEAR COAT	0	0	0	0	0	0	0	8	0	8	16
182	12.1 Apply clear coat to entire rocket	0	0	0	0	0	0	0	8	0	8	
183	12.1.1 Apply clear coat to entire rocket								8			
184	12.1.2 Dry Completely										8	
185	13.0 DISPLAY NOZZLE ASSEMBLY	8	0	8	0	0	0	9	0	0	8	33
186	13.1 Spray Nozzle Base White	0	0	0	0	0	0	9	0	0	8	
187	13.1.1 Paint Nozzle #1 w/Silver Paint Pen							2				

Tab Duration Estimate-Continued.

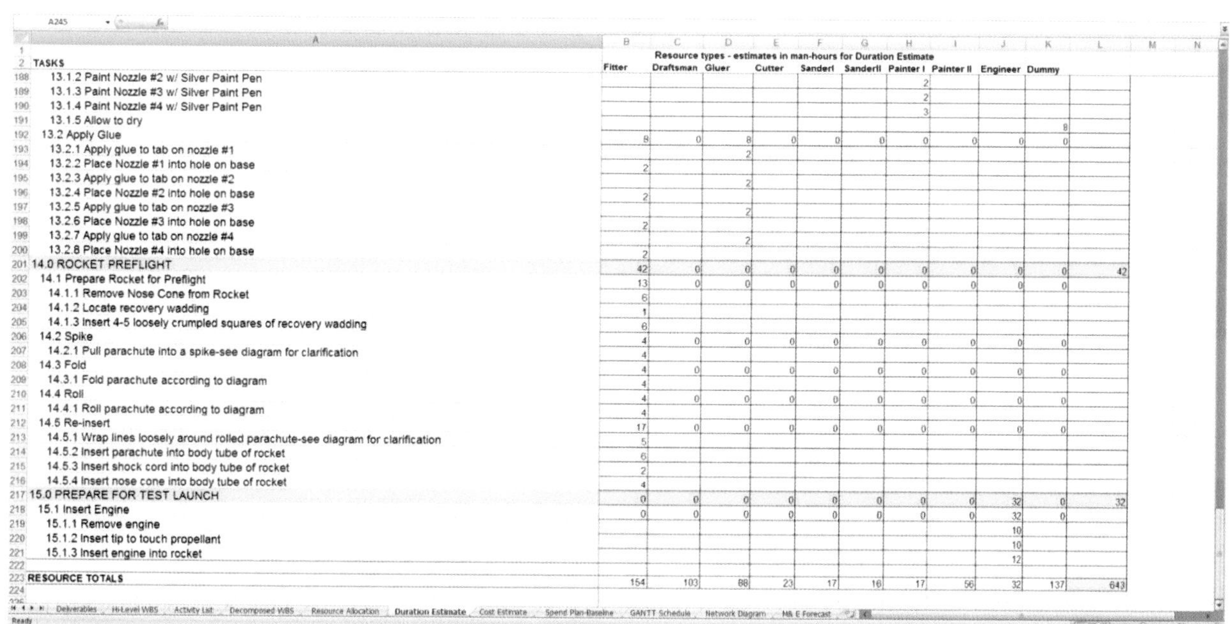

Resource types - estimates in man-hours for Duration Estimate

	TASKS	Fitter	Draftsman	Gluer	Cutter	SanderI	SanderII	Painter I	Painter II	Engineer	Dummy	
188	13.1.2 Paint Nozzle #2 w/ Silver Paint Pen							2				
189	13.1.3 Paint Nozzle #3 w/ Silver Paint Pen							2				
190	13.1.4 Paint Nozzle #4 w/ Silver Paint Pen							3				
191	13.1.5 Allow to dry										8	
192	13.2 Apply Glue	8	0	8	0	0	0	0	0	0	0	
193	13.2.1 Apply glue to tab on nozzle #1			2								
194	13.2.2 Place Nozzle #1 into hole on base	2										
195	13.2.3 Apply glue to tab on nozzle #2			2								
196	13.2.4 Place Nozzle #2 into hole on base	2										
197	13.2.5 Apply glue to tab on nozzle #3			2								
198	13.2.6 Place Nozzle #3 into hole on base	2										
199	13.2.7 Apply glue to tab on nozzle #4			2								
200	13.2.8 Place Nozzle #4 into hole on base	2										
201	14.0 ROCKET PREFLIGHT	42	0	0	0	0	0	0	0	0	0	42
202	14.1 Prepare Rocket for Preflight	13	0	0	0	0	0	0	0	0	0	
203	14.1.1 Remove Nose Cone from Rocket	6										
204	14.1.2 Locate recovery wadding	1										
205	14.1.3 Insert 4-5 loosely crumpled squares of recovery wadding	6										
206	14.2 Spike	4	0	0	0	0	0	0	0	0	0	
207	14.2.1 Pull parachute into a spike-see diagram for clarification	4										
208	14.3 Fold	4	0	0	0	0	0	0	0	0	0	
209	14.3.1 Fold parachute according to diagram	4										
210	14.4 Roll	4	0	0	0	0	0	0	0	0	0	
211	14.4.1 Roll parachute according to diagram	4										
212	14.5 Re-insert	17	0	0	0	0	0	0	0	0	0	
213	14.5.1 Wrap lines loosely around rolled parachute-see diagram for clarification	5										
214	14.5.2 Insert parachute into body tube of rocket	6										
215	14.5.3 Insert shock cord into body tube of rocket	2										
216	14.5.4 Insert nose cone into body tube of rocket	4										
217	15.0 PREPARE FOR TEST LAUNCH	0	0	0	0	0	0	0	0	32	0	32
218	15.1 Insert Engine	0	0	0	0	0	0	0	0	32	0	
219	15.1.1 Remove engine									10		
220	15.1.2 Insert tip to touch propellant									10		
221	15.1.3 Insert engine into rocket									12		
222												
223	RESOURCE TOTALS	154	103	88	23	17	16	17	56	32	137	643

Tab Cost Estimate-This is just a completed duration estimate with the labor rate formulae set up at the bottom.

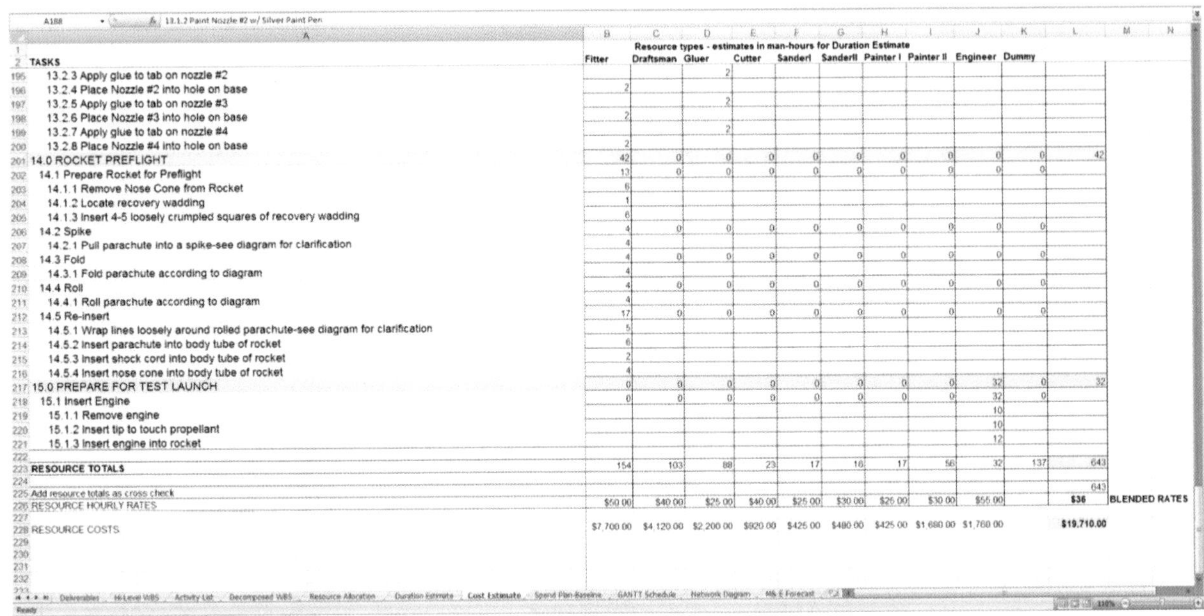

TASKS	Fitter	Draftsman	Gluer	Cutter	SanderI	SanderII	Painter I	Painter II	Engineer	Dummy	
	Resource types - estimates in man-hours for Duration Estimate										
13.2.3 Apply glue to tab on nozzle #2			2								
13.2.4 Place Nozzle #2 into hole on base	2										
13.2.5 Apply glue to tab on nozzle #3			2								
13.2.6 Place Nozzle #3 into hole on base	2										
13.2.7 Apply glue to tab on nozzle #4			2								
13.2.8 Place Nozzle #4 into hole on base	2										
14.0 ROCKET PREFLIGHT	42	0	0	0	0	0	0	0	0	0	42
14.1 Prepare Rocket for Preflight	13	0	0	0	0	0	0	0	0	0	
14.1.1 Remove Nose Cone from Rocket	6										
14.1.2 Locate recovery wadding	1										
14.1.3 Insert 4-5 loosely crumpled squares of recovery wadding	6										
14.2 Spike	4	0	0	0	0	0	0	0	0	0	
14.2.1 Pull parachute into a spike-see diagram for clarification	4										
14.3 Fold	4	0	0	0	0	0	0	0	0	0	
14.3.1 Fold parachute according to diagram	4										
14.4 Roll	4	0	0	0	0	0	0	0	0	0	
14.4.1 Roll parachute according to diagram	4										
14.5 Re-insert	17	0	0	0	0	0	0	0	0	0	
14.5.1 Wrap lines loosely around rolled parachute-see diagram for clarification	5										
14.5.2 Insert parachute into body tube of rocket	6										
14.5.3 Insert shock cord into body tube of rocket	2										
14.5.4 Insert nose cone into body tube of rocket	4										
15.0 PREPARE FOR TEST LAUNCH	0	0	0	0	0	0	0	0	32	0	32
15.1 Insert Engine	0	0	0	0	0	0	0	0	32	0	
15.1.1 Remove engine									10		
15.1.2 Insert tip to touch propellant									10		
15.1.3 Insert engine into rocket									12		
RESOURCE TOTALS	154	103	88	23	17	16	17	56	32	137	643
Add resource totals as cross check											643
RESOURCE HOURLY RATES	$50.00	$40.00	$25.00	$40.00	$25.00	$30.00	$25.00	$30.00	$55.00		**$36** BLENDED RATES
RESOURCE COSTS	$7,700.00	$4,120.00	$2,200.00	$920.00	$425.00	$480.00	$425.00	$1,680.00	$1,760.00		**$19,710.00**

Tab Spend Plan-Baseline- Delineates the incremental expenditures over time and their cumulative costs. Project Baseline is an Excel chart with data taken from the yellow highlighted cells.

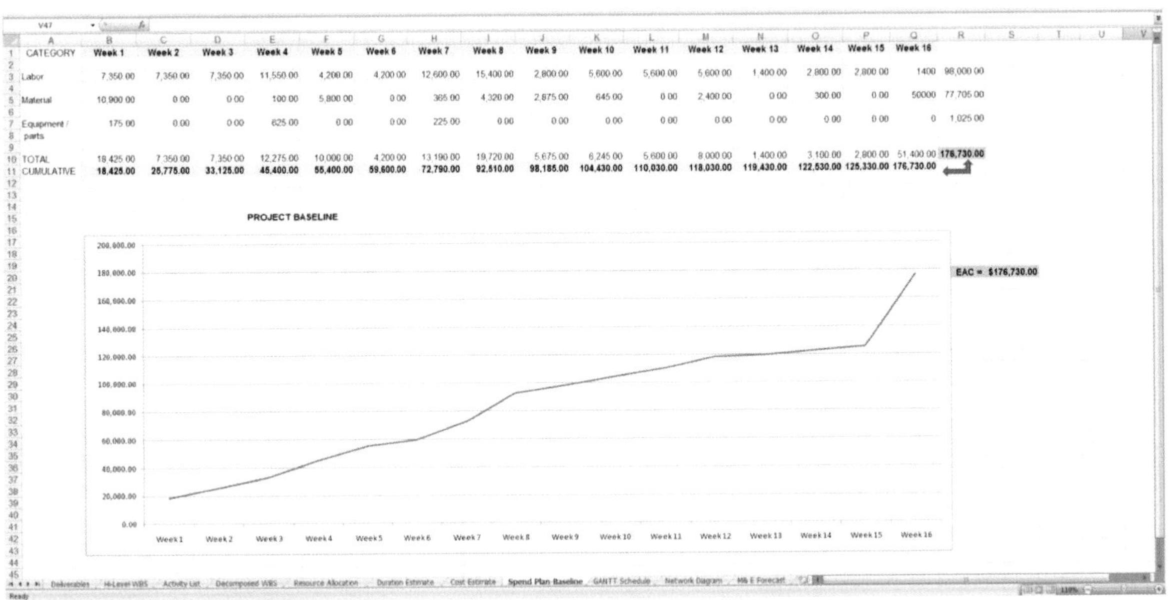

CATEGORY	Week 1	Week 2	Week 3	Week 4	Week 5	Week 6	Week 7	Week 8
Labor	7,350.00	7,350.00	7,350.00	11,550.00	4,200.00	4,200.00	12,600.00	15,400.00
Material	10,900.00	0.00	0.00	100.00	5,800.00	0.00	365.00	4,320.00
Equipment / parts	175.00	0.00	0.00	625.00	0.00	0.00	225.00	0.00
TOTAL	18,425.00	7,350.00	7,350.00	12,275.00	10,000.00	4,200.00	13,190.00	19,720.00
CUMULATIVE	**18,425.00**	**25,775.00**	**33,125.00**	**45,400.00**	**55,400.00**	**59,600.00**	**72,790.00**	**92,510.00**

CATEGORY	Week 9	Week 10	Week 11	Week 12	Week 13	Week 14	Week 15	Week 16	
Labor	2,800.00	5,600.00	5,600.00	5,600.00	1,400.00	2,800.00	2,800.00	1400	98,000.00
Material	2,875.00	645.00	0.00	2,400.00	0.00	300.00	0.00	50000	77,705.00
Equipment / parts	0.00	0.00	0.00	0.00	0.00	0.00	0.00	0	1,025.00
TOTAL	5,675.00	6,245.00	5,600.00	8,000.00	1,400.00	3,100.00	2,800.00	51,400.00	**176,730.00**
CUMULATIVE	**98,185.00**	**104,430.00**	**110,030.00**	**118,030.00**	**119,430.00**	**122,530.00**	**125,330.00**	**176,730.00**	

Tab Gantt Schedule.

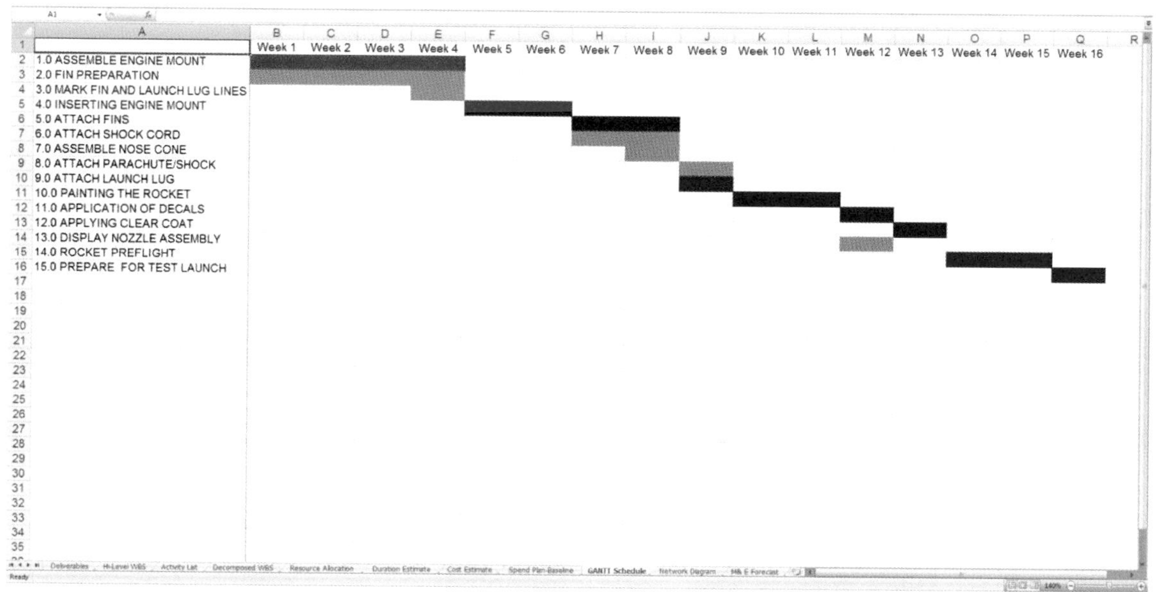

Tab Network Diagram- Showing the Precedence Diagramming Method (PDM).

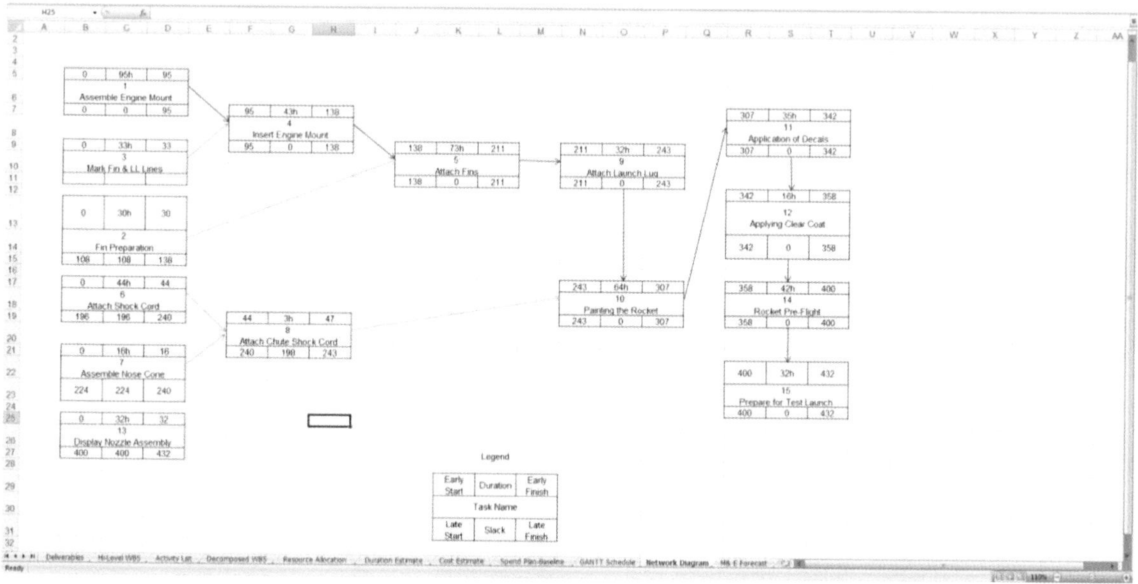

Tab M&E Forecast- The incremental expenditure of material and equipment. All M&E expenditures are forecasted to be spent the first time the material and equipment is needed on project even if that material or equipment is scheduled to be needed at repeated times over the life of the project.

Code	Item	Cost	Week 1	Week 2	Week 3	Week 4	Week 5	Week 6	Week 7	Week 8	Week 9	Week 10	Week 11	Week 12	Week 13	Week 14	Week 15	Week 16
	Equipment	**$1,025**	**$175**	**$0**	**$0**	**$625**	**$0**	**$0**	**$225**	**$0**	**$0**	**$0**	**$0**	**$0**	**$0**	**$0**	**$0**	**$0**
	Scissors x 10	$100							$100									
	Pencil x10	$25	$25															
	Ruler x10	$50	$50															
	Modeling Knife x 5	$100	$100															
	Guide, Tube Marking	$500				$500												
	Tool, Framing x 1	$125				$125												
	Tool, Fin Alignment x 1	$125							$125									
	Material	**$77,705**	**$10,900**	**$0**	**$0**	**$100**	**$5,800**	**$0**	**$365**	**$4,320**	**$2,875**	**$645**	**$0**	**$2,400**	**$0**	**$300**	**$0**	**$50,000**
	Guide, Shock Cord Mount	$250							$250									
	Sand Paper (Course)	$75	$75															
	Sand Paper (Fine)	$75	$75															
	Glue	$150	$150															
	Cement	$120								$120								
	Tape, Masking	$100				$100												
	Primer, Spray	$110										$110						
	Paint, Spray (White)	$160										$160						
	Paint, Spray (Clear)	$125										$125						
	Pen, Paint (Silver)	$250										$250						
	Tube, Body BT-58	$5,800					$5,800											
	Block, Engine EB-5B	$5,000	$5,000															
	Cord, Shock, Rubber	$115							$115									
	Hook, Mini Engine EH-3	$300	$300															
	Tube, Engine Mount BT-5	$500	$500															
	Ring, Retainer (Mylar)	$250	$250															
	Sheet, Decal #60859	$650												$650				
	Card, Centering Ring RA5-58	$550	$550															
	Lug Launch LL-2A	$375									$375							
	Fins, Laser Cut x4	$4,000	$4,000															
	Parachute Assembly 12' x 1	$2,500									$2,500							
	Base, Nozzle, Display x 1	$750												$750				
	Nozzles x 4	$1,000												$1,000				
	Cone, Nose x 1	$3,000								$3,000								
	Insert, Nose Cone x 1	$1,200								$1,200								
	Wadding, Recovery x 1pk	$300														$300		
	Engine Assembly, A10-3T x 1	$50,000																$50,000
		TOTAL	**$22,150**	**$0**	**$0**	**$1,450**	**$11,600**	**$0**	**$1,180**	**$8,640**	**$5,750**	**$1,290**	**$0**	**$4,800**	**$0**	**$600**	**$0**	**$100,000**

Deliverables | Hi-Level WBS | Activity List | Decomposed WBS | Resource Allocation | Duration Estimate | Cost Estimate | Spend Plan Baseline | GANTT Schedule | Network Diagram | H& L Forecast

Appendix-C: Gauchito Project WBS

1.0 ASSEMBLE ENGINE MOUNT

1.1 Measure, Mark and Cut Engine Tube

1.1.1 Lay ruler along engine tube

1.1.3 Mark left end of engine Tube @ 1/8'

1.1.4 Measure engine from left of engine tube @ 3/4"

1.1.5 Mark from left of engine tube @ 3/4"

1.1.6 Measure engine tube from left of engine tube @ 11/2"

1.1.7 Mark from left of engine tube @ 1 1/2"

1.2 Cut Engine Tube

1.2.1 Cut Slit of 1/8" @ 1 1/2 inch Mark on Engine Tube

1.3 Glue, Tube, Assemble Hook

1.3.1 Apply thin line of glue completely around engine at 3/4" mark

1.3.2 Position Hook per diagram

1.3.3 Insert Engine Hook into 1/8" Slit on Engine Mount Tube

1.4 Assemble Mylar Ring to Tube

1.4.1 Slide Mylar ring onto Engine Mount tube at 3/4" mark

1.4.2 Let Dry

1.5 Assemble Yellow Engine Block to Engine Mount Tube

1.5.1 Apply glue inside front of Engine Mount tube

1.5.2 Insert Yellow Engine Block flush with the right end per diagram

1.5.3 Let Dry

1.6 Assemble Centering Rings

1.6.1 Remove Centering rings from card with modeling knife

1.6.2 Apply thin line of Glue around engine mount tube @ 1/8" mark

1.6.3 Slide notched Centering Ring onto glued line @ 1/8" mark

1.6.4 Let Glue Set

1.6.5 Apply thin line of Glue to opposite side of notched center ring flush with end of engine mount tube

1.6.6 Slide un-notched Centering Ring in place over glue flush with end of engine tube mount

1.6.7 Let Dry

1.7 Application of Glue Fillets

1.7.1 Apply Glue Fillets to both sides of Centering Rings for reinforcement

1.7.2 Let Dry

2.0 FIN PREPARATION

2.1 Sand/Cut fins

2.1.1 Sand Laser Cut Balsa Sheet w/Fine Sandpaper

2.2 Cutting Out Fins

2.2.1 Cut out fin #1 w/modeling knife

2.2.2 Cut out fin #2 w/modeling knife

2.2.3 Cut out fin #3 w/ modeling knife

2.2.4 Cut out fin #4 w/modeling knife

2.3 Stack and Sand Fins

2.3.1 Stack Fins

2.3.2 Sand Edges of fins

3.0 MARK FIN AND LAUNCH LUG LINES

3.1 Cut - Tape

3.1.2 Cut out tube marking guide

3.1.2 Tape tube marking guide around body tube

3.1.3 Mark body tube at arrows

3.1.4 Mark Launch Lug Line as LL on Body tube

3.2 Remove guide, connect fins and lug lines, extend LL line

3.2.1 Remove Tube Marking guide from body tube

3.2.2 Connect Fins using door frame

3.2.3 Connect launch lug lines using door frame

3.3 Extend Launch Lug Line

3.3.1 Extend launch lug line 3 3/4" from end of tube

4.0 INSERTING ENGINE MOUNT

4.1 Mark inside of tube @ 5/8" where LL is

4.1.1 Measure inside tube to 5/8" position on tube

4.1.2 Mark inside tube at 5/8"

4.2 Glue Tube

4.2.1 Measure inside rear of body tube to 1 3/4' position on tube

4.2.2 Use finger to smear glue 1 3/4" inside rear of body tube along LL.

4.3 Assemble Engine Hook

4.3.1 Align engine hook with LL line

4.3.2 Insert engine mount into body tube until centering ring is even w/the 5/8" glue mark

4.3.3 Let Dry

4.4 Gluing Center Body Ring

4.4.1 Locate scrap piece of balsa to apply glue

4.4.2 Apply glue to centering/body tube joint

4.4.3 Let Dry

5.0 ATTACH FINS

5.1 Attach Fin #1

5.1.1 Apply thin layer of glue to edge of fin

5.1.2 Allow to dry (1 minute for model)

5.1.3 Apply second layer of glue to edge of fin

5.1.4 Attach Fin to body tube along one of fin lines flush w/end

5.2 Attach Fin #2

5.2.1 Apply thin layer of glue to edge of fin#2

5.2.2 Allow to dry (1 minute for model)

5.2.3 Apply second layer of glue to edge of fin #2

5.2.4 Attach Fin #2 to body tube along one of fin lines flush w/end

5.3 Attach Fin #3

5.3.1 Apply thin layer of glue to edge of fin #3

5.3.2 Allow to dry (1 minute for model)

5.3.3 Apply second layer of glue to edge of fin #3

5.3.4 Attach Fin #3 to body tube along one of fin lines flush w/end

5.4 Attach Fin #4

5.4.1 Apply thin layer of glue to edge of fin #4

5.4.2 Allow to dry (1 minute for model)

5.4.3 Apply second layer of glue to edge of fin #4

5.4.4 Attach Fin #4 to body tube along one of fin lines flush w/end

5.5 Check Fin Alignment

5.5.1 Check Fin #1 Alignment as shown in diagram

5.5.2 Check Fin #2 Alignment as shown in diagram

5.5.3 Check Fin #3 Alignment as shown in diagram

5.5.4 Check Fin #4 Alignment as shown in diagram

5.6 Allow glue to dry

5.6.1 Let Glue Set

5.6.2 Stand Rocket on end

5.6.3 let glue dries completely

6.0 ATTACH SHOCK CORD

6.1 Cut out shock cord mount

6.1.1 Cut out shock cord from front page

6.2 First Glue Application

6.2.1 Attach shock cord to shock cord mount

6.2.2 Apply glue to shock cord mount

6.2.3 Fold edge of shock cord mount forward over glued shock cord

6.3 Second Glue Application

6.3.1 Apply glue to shock cord mount

6.3.2 Fold forward again-see diagram for clarification

6.4 Squeeze and Hold

6.4.1 Squeeze shock cord/shock cord mount tightly

6.4.2 Hold for 1 minute

6.5 Attaching Shock Cord Mount

6.5.1 Glue mount 1" inside body tube

6.5.2 Hold until glue sets

6.5.3 Let Dry Completely

7.0 ASSEMBLE NOSE CONE

7.1 Glue nose cone

7.1.1 Apply plastic cement to inside rim of nose cone

7.1.2 Press Nose Cone Insert into place over plastic cement inside of nose cone rim

7.1.3 Let Dry Completely

8.0 ATTACH PARACHUTE/SHOCK CORD

8.1 Attach Lines

8.1.1 Pass shroud line on parachute through eyelet

8.2 Attach Parachute

8.2.1 Pass parachute through loop in shroud-look to diagram for clarification

8.3 Tie Lines

8.3.1 Tie shock cord to nose cone using a double knot

9.0 ATTACH LAUNCH LUG

9.1 Glue launch lines

9.1.1 Glue LL centered onto LL Line on rocket body

9.2 Application of Glue Fillets

9.2.1 Apply glue fillets along launch lug

9.2.2 Apply glue fillets along fin/body tube joints

9.2.3 Smooth each fillet with finger

9.2.4 Let glue dry completely

10.0 PAINTING THE ROCKET

10.1 Apply first coat

10.1.1 Spray rocket with white primer

10.1.2 Let Dry

10.2 Sand

10.2.1 Sand entire rocket

10.3 Apply final coat

10.3.1 Spray completed rocket with white second coat of primer

10.3.2 Let Dry

10.3.3 Spray Nose Cone with Copper paint

10.3.4 Let Dry

11.0 APPLICATION OF DECALS

11.1 Apply first decal

11.1.1 Remove First decal from back sheet

11.1.2 Place on Rocket where indicated

11.1.3 Rub decal to remove bubbles

11.2 Apply second decal

11.2.1 Remove second decal from backing sheet

11.2.2 Place on Rocket where indicated

11.2.3 Rub decal to remove bubbles

11.3 Apply third decal

11.3.1 Remove third decal from backing sheet

11.3.2 Place on Rocket where indicated

11.3.3 Rub decal to remove bubbles

11.4 Apply fourth decal

11.4.1 Remove fourth decal from backing sheet

11.4.2 Place on Rocket where indicated

11.4.3 Rub decal to remove bubbles

11.5 Apply fifth decal

11.5.1 Remove fifth decal from backing sheet

11.5.2 Place on Rocket where indicated

11.5.3 Rub decal to remove bubbles

11.6 Apply sixth Decal

11.6.1 Remove sixth decal from backing sheet

11.6.2 Place on Rocket where indicated

11.6.3 Rub decal to remove bubbles

11.7 Apply seventh Decal

11.7.1 Remove seventh decal from backing sheet

11.7.2 Place on Rocket where indicated

11.7.3 Rub decal to remove bubbles

12.0 APPLYING CLEAR COAT

12.1 Apply clear coat to entire rocket

12.1.1 Apply clear coat to entire rocket

12.1.2 Dry Completely

13.0 DISPLAY NOZZLE ASSEMBLY

13.1 Spray Nozzle Base White

13.1.1 Paint Nozzle #1 w/Silver Paint Pen

13.1.2 Paint Nozzle #2 w/ Silver Paint Pen

13.1.3 Paint Nozzle #3 w/ Silver Paint Pen

13.1.4 Paint Nozzle #4 w/ Silver Paint Pen

13.1.5 Allow to dry

13.2 Apply Glue

13.2.1 Apply glue to tab on nozzle #1

13.2.2 Place Nozzle #1 into hole on base

13.2.3 Apply glue to tab on nozzle #2

13.2.4 Place Nozzle #2 into hole on base

13.2.5 Apply glue to tab on nozzle #3

13.2.6 Place Nozzle #3 into hole on base

13.2.7 Apply glue to tab on nozzle #4

13.2.8 Place Nozzle #4 into hole on base

14.0 ROCKET PREFLIGHT

14.1 Prepare Rocket

14.1.1 Remove Nose Cone from Rocket

14.1.2 Locate recovery wadding

14.1.3 Insert 4-5 loosely crumpled squares of recovery wadding

14.2 Spike

14.2.1 Pull parachute into a spike-see diagram for clarification

14.3 Fold

14.3.1 Fold parachute according to diagram

14.4 Roll

14.4.1 Roll parachute according to diagram

14.5 Re-insert

14.5.1 Wrap lines loosely around rolled parachute-see diagram for clarification

14.5.2 Insert parachute into body tube of rocket

14.5.3 Insert shock cord into body tube of rocket

14.5.4 Insert nose cone into body tube of rocket

15.0 PREPARE FOR TEST LAUNCH

15.1 Insert Engine

15.1.1 Remove engine

15.1.2 Insert tip to touch propellant

15.1.3 Insert engine into rocket

Appendix-D: Gauchito Assembly Project

ID	WBS	Task Name	Duration	Start	Finish	Predecessors	Resource Names
0	**0**	**Gauchito Assembly Project**	**1 day?**	**Wed 6/30/10**	**Wed 6/30/10**		
1	**1**	**ASSEMBLE ENGINE MOUNT**	**1 day?**	**Wed 6/30/10**	**Wed 6/30/10**		
2	**1.1**	**Measure, Mark and Cut Engine Tube**	**1 day?**	**Wed 6/30/10**	**Wed 6/30/10**		
3	1.1.1	Lay ruler along engine tube	1 day?	Wed 6/30/10	Wed 6/30/10		
4	1.1.2	Mark left end of engine Tube @ 1/8	1 day?	Wed 6/30/10	Wed 6/30/10		
5	1.1.3	Measure engine from left of engine tube @ 3/4"	1 day?	Wed 6/30/10	Wed 6/30/10		
6	1.1.4	Mark from left of engine tube @ 3/4"	1 day?	Wed 6/30/10	Wed 6/30/10		
7	1.1.5	Measure engine tube from left of engine tube @ 1 1/2"	1 day?	Wed 6/30/10	Wed 6/30/10		
8	1.1.6	Mark from left of engine tube @ 1 1/2"	1 day?	Wed 6/30/10	Wed 6/30/10		
9	**1.2**	**Cut Engine Tube**	**1 day?**	**Wed 6/30/10**	**Wed 6/30/10**		
10	1.2.1	Cut Slit of 1/8" @ 1 1/2 inch Mark on Engine Tube	1 day?	Wed 6/30/10	Wed 6/30/10		
11	**1.3**	**Glue, Tube, Assemble Hook**	**1 day?**	**Wed 6/30/10**	**Wed 6/30/10**		
12	1.3.1	Apply thin line of glue completely around engine at 3/4" mark	1 day?	Wed 6/30/10	Wed 6/30/10		
13	1.3.2	Position Hook per diagram	1 day?	Wed 6/30/10	Wed 6/30/10		
14	1.3.3	Insert Engine Hook into 1/8" Slit on Engine Mount Tube	1 day?	Wed 6/30/10	Wed 6/30/10		
15	**1.4**	**Assemble Mylar Ring to Tube**	**1 day?**	**Wed 6/30/10**	**Wed 6/30/10**		
16	1.4.1	Slide Mylar ring onto Engine Mount tube at 3/4" mark	1 day?	Wed 6/30/10	Wed 6/30/10		
17	1.4.2	Let Dry	1 day?	Wed 6/30/10	Wed 6/30/10		
18	**1.5**	**Assemble Yellow Engine Block to Engine Mount Tube**	**1 day?**	**Wed 6/30/10**	**Wed 6/30/10**		
19	1.5.1	Apply glue inside front of Engine Mount tube	1 day?	Wed 6/30/10	Wed 6/30/10		
20	1.5.2	Insert Yellow Engine Block flush with the right end per diagram	1 day?	Wed 6/30/10	Wed 6/30/10		
21	1.5.3	Let Dry	1 day?	Wed 6/30/10	Wed 6/30/10		
22	**1.6**	**Assemble Centering Rings**	**1 day?**	**Wed 6/30/10**	**Wed 6/30/10**		
23	1.6.1	Remove Centering rings from card with modeling knife	1 day?	Wed 6/30/10	Wed 6/30/10		
24	1.6.2	Apply thin line of Glue around engine mount tube @ 1/8" mark	1 day?	Wed 6/30/10	Wed 6/30/10		
25	1.6.3	Slide notched Centering Ring onto glued line @ 1/8" mark	1 day?	Wed 6/30/10	Wed 6/30/10		
26	1.6.4	Let Glue Set	1 day?	Wed 6/30/10	Wed 6/30/10		
27	1.6.5	Apply thin line of Glue to opposite side of notched center ring flush with end of engine mount tube	1 day?	Wed 6/30/10	Wed 6/30/10		
28	1.6.6	Slide un-notched Centering Ring in place over glue flush with end of engine tube mount	1 day?	Wed 6/30/10	Wed 6/30/10		
29	1.6.7	Let Dry	1 day?	Wed 6/30/10	Wed 6/30/10		
30	**1.7**	**Application of Glue Fillets**	**1 day?**	**Wed 6/30/10**	**Wed 6/30/10**		
31	1.7.1	Apply Glue Fillets to both sides of Centering Rings for reinforcement	1 day?	Wed 6/30/10	Wed 6/30/10		
32	1.7.2	Let Dry	1 day?	Wed 6/30/10	Wed 6/30/10		
33	**2**	**FIN PREPARATION**	**1 day?**	**Wed 6/30/10**	**Wed 6/30/10**		
34	**2.1**	**Sand/Cut fins**	**1 day?**	**Wed 6/30/10**	**Wed 6/30/10**		
35	2.1.1	Sand Laser Cut Balsa Sheet w/Fine Sandpaper	1 day?	Wed 6/30/10	Wed 6/30/10		
36	**2.2**	**Cutting Out Fins**	**1 day?**	**Wed 6/30/10**	**Wed 6/30/10**		
37	2.2.1	Cut out fin #1 w/modeling knife	1 day?	Wed 6/30/10	Wed 6/30/10		
38	2.2.2	Cut out fin #2 w/modeling knife	1 day?	Wed 6/30/10	Wed 6/30/10		
39	2.2.3	Cut out fin #3 w/ modeling knife	1 day?	Wed 6/30/10	Wed 6/30/10		
40	2.2.4	Cut out fin #4 w/modeling knife	1 day?	Wed 6/30/10	Wed 6/30/10		
41	**2.3**	**Stack and Sand Fins**	**1 day?**	**Wed 6/30/10**	**Wed 6/30/10**		
42	2.3.1	Stack Fins	1 day?	Wed 6/30/10	Wed 6/30/10		
43	2.3.2	Sand Edges of fins	1 day?	Wed 6/30/10	Wed 6/30/10		

Ready | New Tasks : Auto Scheduled

ID	WBS	Task Name	Duration	Start	Finish	Predecessors	Resource Names
44	**3**	**MARK FIN AND LAUNCH LUG LINES**	**1 day?**	**Wed 6/30/10**	**Wed 6/30/10**		
45	**3.1**	**Cut - Tape**	**1 day?**	**Wed 6/30/10**	**Wed 6/30/10**		
46	3.1.1	Cut out tube marking guide	1 day?	Wed 6/30/10	Wed 6/30/10		
47	3.1.2	Tape tube marking guide around body tube	1 day?	Wed 6/30/10	Wed 6/30/10		
48	3.1.3	Mark body tube at arrows	1 day?	Wed 6/30/10	Wed 6/30/10		
49	3.1.4	Mark Launch Lug Line as LL on Body tube	1 day?	Wed 6/30/10	Wed 6/30/10		
50	**3.2**	**Remove guide, connect fins and lug lines, extend LL line**	**1 day?**	**Wed 6/30/10**	**Wed 6/30/10**		
51	3.2.1	Remove Tube Marking guide from body tube	1 day?	Wed 6/30/10	Wed 6/30/10		
52	3.2.2	Connect Fins using door frame	1 day?	Wed 6/30/10	Wed 6/30/10		
53	3.2.3	Connect launch lug line using door frame	1 day?	Wed 6/30/10	Wed 6/30/10		
54	**3.3**	**Extend Launch Lug Line**	**1 day?**	**Wed 6/30/10**	**Wed 6/30/10**		
55	3.3.1	Extend launch lug line 1 3/4" from end of tube	1 day?	Wed 6/30/10	Wed 6/30/10		
56	**4**	**INSERTING ENGINE MOUNT**	**1 day?**	**Wed 6/30/10**	**Wed 6/30/10**		
57	**4.1**	**Mark inside of tube @ 5/8" where LL is**	**1 day?**	**Wed 6/30/10**	**Wed 6/30/10**		
58	4.1.1	Measure inside tube to 5/8" position on tube	1 day?	Wed 6/30/10	Wed 6/30/10		
59	4.1.2	Mark inside tube at 5/8"	1 day?	Wed 6/30/10	Wed 6/30/10		
60	**4.2**	**Glue Tube**	**1 day?**	**Wed 6/30/10**	**Wed 6/30/10**		
61	4.2.1	Measure inside rear of body tube to 1 3/4" position on tube	1 day?	Wed 6/30/10	Wed 6/30/10		
62	4.2.2	Use finger to smear glue 1 3/4" inside rear of body tube along LL	1 day?	Wed 6/30/10	Wed 6/30/10		
63	**4.3**	**Assemble Engine Hook**	**1 day?**	**Wed 6/30/10**	**Wed 6/30/10**		
64	4.3.1	Align engine hook with LL line	1 day?	Wed 6/30/10	Wed 6/30/10		
65	4.3.2	Insert engine mount into body tube until centering ring is even with the 5/8" glue mark	1 day?	Wed 6/30/10	Wed 6/30/10		
66	4.3.3	Let Dry	1 day?	Wed 6/30/10	Wed 6/30/10		
67	**4.4**	**Gluing Center Body Ring**	**1 day?**	**Wed 6/30/10**	**Wed 6/30/10**		
68	4.4.1	Locate scrap piece of balsa to apply glue	1 day?	Wed 6/30/10	Wed 6/30/10		
69	4.4.2	Apply glue to centering/body tube joint	1 day?	Wed 6/30/10	Wed 6/30/10		
70	4.4.3	Let Dry	1 day?	Wed 6/30/10	Wed 6/30/10		
71	**5**	**ATTACH FINS**	**1 day?**	**Wed 6/30/10**	**Wed 6/30/10**		
72	**5.1**	**Attach Fin #1**	**1 day?**	**Wed 6/30/10**	**Wed 6/30/10**		
73	5.1.1	Apply thin layer of glue to edge of fin	1 day?	Wed 6/30/10	Wed 6/30/10		
74	5.1.2	Allow to dry (1 minute for model)	1 day?	Wed 6/30/10	Wed 6/30/10		
75	5.1.3	Apply second layer of glue to edge of fin	1 day?	Wed 6/30/10	Wed 6/30/10		
76	5.1.4	Attach Fin to body tube along one of fin lines flush w/end	1 day?	Wed 6/30/10	Wed 6/30/10		
77	**5.2**	**Attach Fin #2**	**1 day?**	**Wed 6/30/10**	**Wed 6/30/10**		
78	5.2.1	Apply thin layer of glue to edge of fin#2	1 day?	Wed 6/30/10	Wed 6/30/10		
79	5.2.2	Allow to dry (1 minute for model)	1 day?	Wed 6/30/10	Wed 6/30/10		
80	5.2.3	Apply second layer of glue to edge of fin #2	1 day?	Wed 6/30/10	Wed 6/30/10		
81	5.2.4	Attach Fin #2 to body tube along one of fin lines flush w/end	1 day?	Wed 6/30/10	Wed 6/30/10		
82	**5.3**	**Attach Fin #3**	**1 day?**	**Wed 6/30/10**	**Wed 6/30/10**		
83	5.3.1	Apply thin layer of glue to edge of fin #3	1 day?	Wed 6/30/10	Wed 6/30/10		
84	5.3.2	Allow to dry (1 minute for model)	1 day?	Wed 6/30/10	Wed 6/30/10		
85	5.3.3	Apply second layer of glue to edge of fin #3	1 day?	Wed 6/30/10	Wed 6/30/10		
86	5.3.4	Attach Fin #3 to body tube along one of fin lines flush w/end	1 day?	Wed 6/30/10	Wed 6/30/10		
87	**5.4**	**Attach Fin #4**	**1 day?**	**Wed 6/30/10**	**Wed 6/30/10**		
88	5.4.1	Apply thin layer of glue to edge of fin #4	1 day?	Wed 6/30/10	Wed 6/30/10		

Ready | New Tasks : Auto Scheduled

ID	WBS	Task Name	Duration	Start	Finish	Predecessors	Resource Names
88	5.4.1	Apply thin layer of glue to edge of fin #4	1 day?	Wed 6/30/10	Wed 6/30/10		
89	5.4.2	Allow to dry (1 minute for model)	1 day?	Wed 6/30/10	Wed 6/30/10		
90	5.4.3	Apply second layer of glue to edge of fin #4	1 day?	Wed 6/30/10	Wed 6/30/10		
91	5.4.4	Attach Fin #4 to body tube along one of fin lines flush w/end	1 day?	Wed 6/30/10	Wed 6/30/10		
92	**5.5**	**Check Fin Alignment**	**1 day?**	**Wed 6/30/10**	**Wed 6/30/10**		
93	5.5.1	Check Fin #1 Alignment as shown in diagram	1 day?	Wed 6/30/10	Wed 6/30/10		
94	5.5.2	Check Fin #2 Alignment as shown in diagram	1 day?	Wed 6/30/10	Wed 6/30/10		
95	5.5.3	Check Fin #3 Alignment as shown in diagram	1 day?	Wed 6/30/10	Wed 6/30/10		
96	5.5.4	Check Fin #4 Alignment as shown in diagram	1 day?	Wed 6/30/10	Wed 6/30/10		
97	**5.6**	**Allow glue to dry**	**1 day?**	**Wed 6/30/10**	**Wed 6/30/10**		
98	5.6.1	Let Glue Set	1 day?	Wed 6/30/10	Wed 6/30/10		
99	5.6.2	Stand Rocket on end	1 day?	Wed 6/30/10	Wed 6/30/10		
100	5.6.3	Let glue dry completely	1 day?	Wed 6/30/10	Wed 6/30/10		
101	**6**	**ATTACH SHOCK CORD**	**1 day?**	**Wed 6/30/10**	**Wed 6/30/10**		
102	**6.1**	**Cut out shock cord mount**	**1 day?**	**Wed 6/30/10**	**Wed 6/30/10**		
103	6.1.1	Cut out shock cord from front page	1 day?	Wed 6/30/10	Wed 6/30/10		
104	**6.2**	**First Glue Application**	**1 day?**	**Wed 6/30/10**	**Wed 6/30/10**		
105	6.2.1	Attach shock cord to shock cord mount	1 day?	Wed 6/30/10	Wed 6/30/10		
106	6.2.2	Apply glue to shock cord mount	1 day?	Wed 6/30/10	Wed 6/30/10		
107	6.2.3	Fold edge of shock cord mount forward over glued shock cord	1 day?	Wed 6/30/10	Wed 6/30/10		
108	**6.3**	**Second Glue Application**	**1 day?**	**Wed 6/30/10**	**Wed 6/30/10**		
109	6.3.1	Apply glue to shock cord mount	1 day?	Wed 6/30/10	Wed 6/30/10		
110	6.3.2	Fold forward again-see diagram for clarification	1 day?	Wed 6/30/10	Wed 6/30/10		
111	**6.4**	**Squeeze and Hold**	**1 day?**	**Wed 6/30/10**	**Wed 6/30/10**		
112	6.4.1	Squeeze shock cord/shock cord mount tightly	1 day?	Wed 6/30/10	Wed 6/30/10		
113	6.4.2	Hold for 1 minute	1 day?	Wed 6/30/10	Wed 6/30/10		
114	**6.5**	**Attaching Shock Cord Mount**	**1 day?**	**Wed 6/30/10**	**Wed 6/30/10**		
115	6.5.1	Glue mount 1" inside body tube	1 day?	Wed 6/30/10	Wed 6/30/10		
116	6.5.2	Hold until glue sets	1 day?	Wed 6/30/10	Wed 6/30/10		
117	6.5.3	Let Dry Completely	1 day?	Wed 6/30/10	Wed 6/30/10		
118	**7**	**ASSEMBLE NOSE CONE**	**1 day?**	**Wed 6/30/10**	**Wed 6/30/10**		
119	**7.1**	**Glue nose cone**	**1 day?**	**Wed 6/30/10**	**Wed 6/30/10**		
120	7.1.1	Apply plastic cement to inside rim of nose cone	1 day?	Wed 6/30/10	Wed 6/30/10		
121	7.1.2	7. Press Nose Cone Insert into place over plastic cement inside of nose cone rim	1 day?	Wed 6/30/10	Wed 6/30/10		
122	7.1.3	Let Dry Completely	1 day?	Wed 6/30/10	Wed 6/30/10		
123	**8**	**ATTACH PARACHUTE/SHOCK CORD**	**1 day?**	**Wed 6/30/10**	**Wed 6/30/10**		
124	**8.1**	**Attach Lines**	**1 day?**	**Wed 6/30/10**	**Wed 6/30/10**		
125	8.1.1	Pass shroud line on parachute through eyelet	1 day?	Wed 6/30/10	Wed 6/30/10		
126	**8.2**	**Attach Parachute**	**1 day?**	**Wed 6/30/10**	**Wed 6/30/10**		
127	8.2.1	Pass parachute through loop in shroud-look at diagram for clarification	1 day?	Wed 6/30/10	Wed 6/30/10		
128	**8.3**	**Tie Lines**	**1 day?**	**Wed 6/30/10**	**Wed 6/30/10**		
129	8.3.1	Tie shock cord to nose cone using a double knot	1 day?	Wed 6/30/10	Wed 6/30/10		
130	**9**	**ATTACH LAUNCH LUG**	**1 day?**	**Wed 6/30/10**	**Wed 6/30/10**		
131	**9.1**	**Glue launch lines**	**1 day?**	**Wed 6/30/10**	**Wed 6/30/10**		
132	9.1.1	Glue LL centered onto LL Line on rocket body	1 day?	Wed 6/30/10	Wed 6/30/10		

Ready | New Tasks : Auto Scheduled

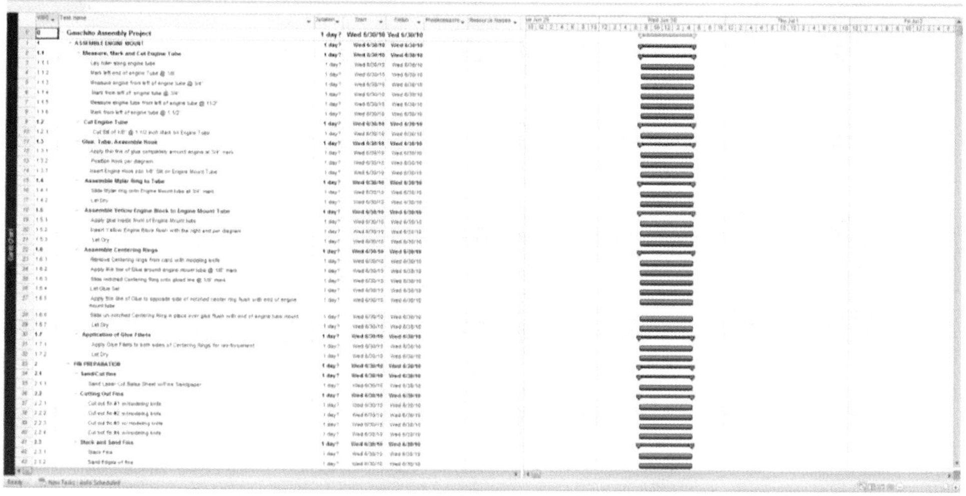

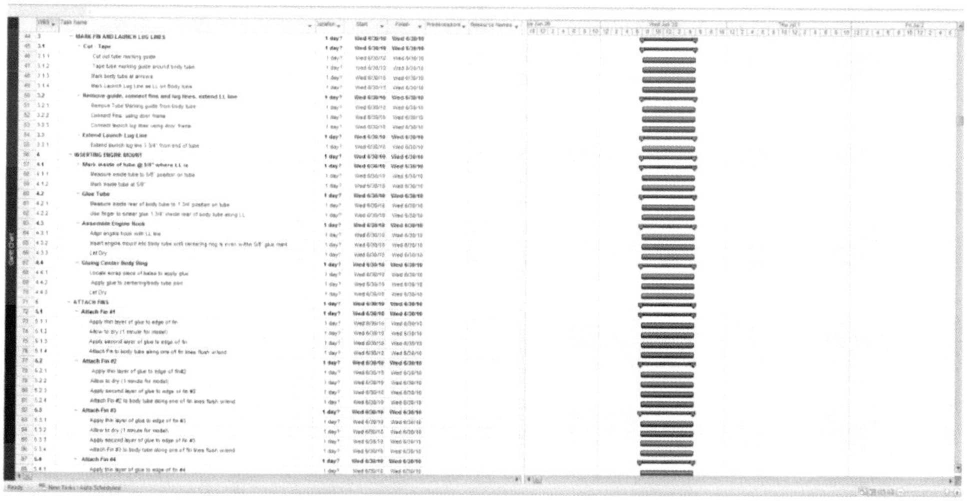

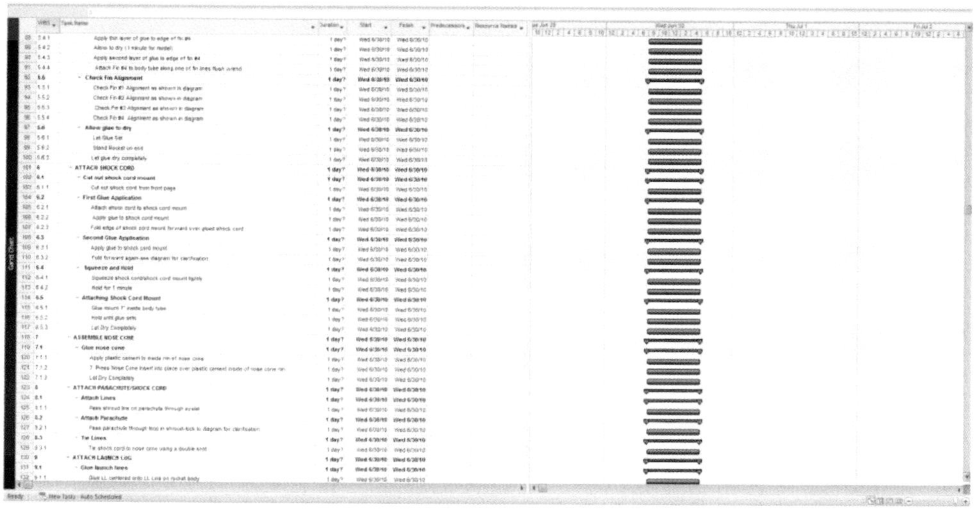

ID	WBS	Task Name	Duration	Start	Finish	Predecessors	Resource Names
132	9.1.1	Glue LL centered onto LL Line on rocket body	1 day?	Wed 6/30/10	Wed 6/30/10		
133	**9.2**	**Application of Glue Fillets**	**1 day?**	**Wed 6/30/10**	**Wed 6/30/10**		
134	9.2.1	Apply glue fillets along launch lug	1 day?	Wed 6/30/10	Wed 6/30/10		
135	9.2.2	Apply glue fillets along fin/body tube joints	1 day?	Wed 6/30/10	Wed 6/30/10		
136	9.2.3	Smooth each fillet with finger	1 day?	Wed 6/30/10	Wed 6/30/10		
137	9.2.4	Let glue dry completely	1 day?	Wed 6/30/10	Wed 6/30/10		
138	**10**	**PAINTING THE ROCKET**	**1 day?**	**Wed 6/30/10**	**Wed 6/30/10**		
139	**10.1**	**Apply first coat**	**1 day?**	**Wed 6/30/10**	**Wed 6/30/10**		
140	10.1.1	Spray rocket with white primer	1 day?	Wed 6/30/10	Wed 6/30/10		
141	10.1.2	Let Dry	1 day?	Wed 6/30/10	Wed 6/30/10		
142	**10.2**	**Sand**	**1 day?**	**Wed 6/30/10**	**Wed 6/30/10**		
143	10.2.1	Sand entire rocket	1 day?	Wed 6/30/10	Wed 6/30/10		
144	**10.3**	**Apply final coat**	**1 day?**	**Wed 6/30/10**	**Wed 6/30/10**		
145	10.3.1	Spray completed rocket with white second coat of primer	1 day?	Wed 6/30/10	Wed 6/30/10		
146	10.3.2	Let Dry	1 day?	Wed 6/30/10	Wed 6/30/10		
147	10.3.3	Spray Nose Cone with Copper paint	1 day?	Wed 6/30/10	Wed 6/30/10		
148	10.3.4	Let Dry	1 day?	Wed 6/30/10	Wed 6/30/10		
149	**11**	**APPLICATION OF DECALS**	**1 day?**	**Wed 6/30/10**	**Wed 6/30/10**		
150	**11.1**	**Apply first decal**	**1 day?**	**Wed 6/30/10**	**Wed 6/30/10**		
151	11.1.1	Remove First decal from back sheet	1 day?	Wed 6/30/10	Wed 6/30/10		
152	11.1.2	Place on Rocket where indicated	1 day?	Wed 6/30/10	Wed 6/30/10		
153	11.1.3	Rub decal to remove bubbles	1 day?	Wed 6/30/10	Wed 6/30/10		
154	**11.2**	**Apply second decal**	**1 day?**	**Wed 6/30/10**	**Wed 6/30/10**		
155	11.2.1	Remove second decal from backing sheet	1 day?	Wed 6/30/10	Wed 6/30/10		
156	11.2.2	Place on Rocket where indicated	1 day?	Wed 6/30/10	Wed 6/30/10		
157	11.2.3	Rub decal to remove bubbles	1 day?	Wed 6/30/10	Wed 6/30/10		
158	**11.3**	**Apply third decal**	**1 day?**	**Wed 6/30/10**	**Wed 6/30/10**		
159	11.3.1	Remove third decal from backing sheet	1 day?	Wed 6/30/10	Wed 6/30/10		
160	11.3.2	Place on Rocket where indicated	1 day?	Wed 6/30/10	Wed 6/30/10		
161	11.3.3	Rub decal to remove bubbles	1 day?	Wed 6/30/10	Wed 6/30/10		
162	**11.4**	**Apply fourth decal**	**1 day?**	**Wed 6/30/10**	**Wed 6/30/10**		
163	11.4.1	Remove fourth decal from backing sheet	1 day?	Wed 6/30/10	Wed 6/30/10		
164	11.4.2	Place on Rocket where indicated	1 day?	Wed 6/30/10	Wed 6/30/10		
165	11.4.3	Rub decal to remove bubbles	1 day?	Wed 6/30/10	Wed 6/30/10		
166	**11.5**	**Apply fifth decal**	**1 day?**	**Wed 6/30/10**	**Wed 6/30/10**		
167	11.5.1	Remove fifth decal from backing sheet	1 day?	Wed 6/30/10	Wed 6/30/10		
168	11.5.2	Place on Rocket where indicated	1 day?	Wed 6/30/10	Wed 6/30/10		
169	11.5.3	Rub decal to remove bubbles	1 day?	Wed 6/30/10	Wed 6/30/10		
170	**11.6**	**Apply sixth Decal**	**1 day?**	**Wed 6/30/10**	**Wed 6/30/10**		
171	11.6.1	Remove sixth decal from backing sheet	1 day?	Wed 6/30/10	Wed 6/30/10		
172	11.6.2	Place on Rocket where indicated	1 day?	Wed 6/30/10	Wed 6/30/10		
173	11.6.3	Rub decal to remove bubbles	1 day?	Wed 6/30/10	Wed 6/30/10		
174	**11.7**	**Apply seventh Decal**	**1 day?**	**Wed 6/30/10**	**Wed 6/30/10**		
175	11.7.1	Remove seventh decal from backing sheet	1 day?	Wed 6/30/10	Wed 6/30/10		
176	11.7.2	Place on Rocket where indicated	1 day?	Wed 6/30/10	Wed 6/30/10		

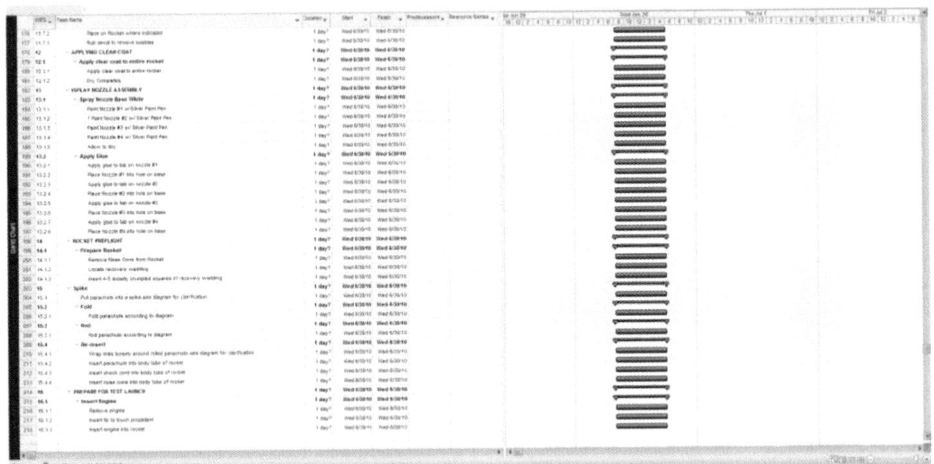

ID	WBS	Task Name	Duration	Start	Finish	Predecessors	Resource Names
176	11.7.2	Place on Rocket where indicated	1 day?	Wed 6/30/10	Wed 6/30/10		
177	11.7.3	Rub decal to remove bubbles	1 day?	Wed 6/30/10	Wed 6/30/10		
178	**12**	**APPLYING CLEAR COAT**	**1 day?**	**Wed 6/30/10**	**Wed 6/30/10**		
179	**12.1**	**Apply clear coat to entire rocket**	**1 day?**	**Wed 6/30/10**	**Wed 6/30/10**		
180	12.1.1	Apply clear coat to entire rocket	1 day?	Wed 6/30/10	Wed 6/30/10		
181	12.1.2	Dry Completely	1 day?	Wed 6/30/10	Wed 6/30/10		
182	**13**	**DISPLAY NOZZLE ASSEMBLY**	**1 day?**	**Wed 6/30/10**	**Wed 6/30/10**		
183	**13.1**	**Spray Nozzle Base White**	**1 day?**	**Wed 6/30/10**	**Wed 6/30/10**		
184	13.1.1	Paint Nozzle #1 w/Silver Paint Pen	1 day?	Wed 6/30/10	Wed 6/30/10		
185	13.1.2	Paint Nozzle #2 w/ Silver Paint Pen	1 day?	Wed 6/30/10	Wed 6/30/10		
186	13.1.3	Paint Nozzle #3 w/ Silver Paint Pen	1 day?	Wed 6/30/10	Wed 6/30/10		
187	13.1.4	Paint Nozzle #4 w/ Silver Paint Pen	1 day?	Wed 6/30/10	Wed 6/30/10		
188	13.1.5	Allow to dry	1 day?	Wed 6/30/10	Wed 6/30/10		
189	**13.2**	**Apply Glue**	**1 day?**	**Wed 6/30/10**	**Wed 6/30/10**		
190	13.2.1	Apply glue to tab on nozzle #1	1 day?	Wed 6/30/10	Wed 6/30/10		
191	13.2.2	Place Nozzle #1 into hole on base	1 day?	Wed 6/30/10	Wed 6/30/10		
192	13.2.3	Apply glue to tab on nozzle #2	1 day?	Wed 6/30/10	Wed 6/30/10		
193	13.2.4	Place Nozzle #2 into hole on base	1 day?	Wed 6/30/10	Wed 6/30/10		
194	13.2.5	Apply glue to tab on nozzle #3	1 day?	Wed 6/30/10	Wed 6/30/10		
195	13.2.6	Place Nozzle #3 into hole on base	1 day?	Wed 6/30/10	Wed 6/30/10		
196	13.2.7	Apply glue to tab on nozzle #4	1 day?	Wed 6/30/10	Wed 6/30/10		
197	13.2.8	Place Nozzle #4 into hole on base	1 day?	Wed 6/30/10	Wed 6/30/10		
198	**14**	**ROCKET PREFLIGHT**	**1 day?**	**Wed 6/30/10**	**Wed 6/30/10**		
199	**14.1**	**Prepare Rocket**	**1 day?**	**Wed 6/30/10**	**Wed 6/30/10**		
200	14.1.1	Remove Nose Cone from Rocket	1 day?	Wed 6/30/10	Wed 6/30/10		
201	14.1.2	Locate recovery wadding	1 day?	Wed 6/30/10	Wed 6/30/10		
202	14.1.3	Insert 4-5 loosely crumpled squares of recovery wadding	1 day?	Wed 6/30/10	Wed 6/30/10		
203	**15**	**Spike**	**1 day?**	**Wed 6/30/10**	**Wed 6/30/10**		
204	15.1	Pull parachute into a spike-see diagram for clarification	1 day?	Wed 6/30/10	Wed 6/30/10		
205	**15.2**	**Fold**	**1 day?**	**Wed 6/30/10**	**Wed 6/30/10**		
206	15.2.1	Fold parachute according to diagram	1 day?	Wed 6/30/10	Wed 6/30/10		
207	**15.3**	**Roll**	**1 day?**	**Wed 6/30/10**	**Wed 6/30/10**		
208	15.3.1	Roll parachute according to diagram	1 day?	Wed 6/30/10	Wed 6/30/10		
209	**15.4**	**Re-insert**	**1 day?**	**Wed 6/30/10**	**Wed 6/30/10**		
210	15.4.1	Wrap lines loosely around rolled parachute-see diagram for clarification	1 day?	Wed 6/30/10	Wed 6/30/10		
211	15.4.2	Insert parachute into body tube of rocket	1 day?	Wed 6/30/10	Wed 6/30/10		
212	15.4.3	Insert shock cord into body tube of rocket	1 day?	Wed 6/30/10	Wed 6/30/10		
213	15.4.4	Insert nose cone into body tube of rocket	1 day?	Wed 6/30/10	Wed 6/30/10		
214	**16**	**PREPARE FOR TEST LAUNCH**	**1 day?**	**Wed 6/30/10**	**Wed 6/30/10**		
215	**16.1**	**Insert Engine**	**1 day?**	**Wed 6/30/10**	**Wed 6/30/10**		
216	16.1.1	Remove engine	1 day?	Wed 6/30/10	Wed 6/30/10		
217	16.1.2	Insert tip to touch propellant	1 day?	Wed 6/30/10	Wed 6/30/10		
218	16.1.3	Insert engine into rocket	1 day?	Wed 6/30/10	Wed 6/30/10		

Appendix-E: A Program EVM Example

Tab Summary.

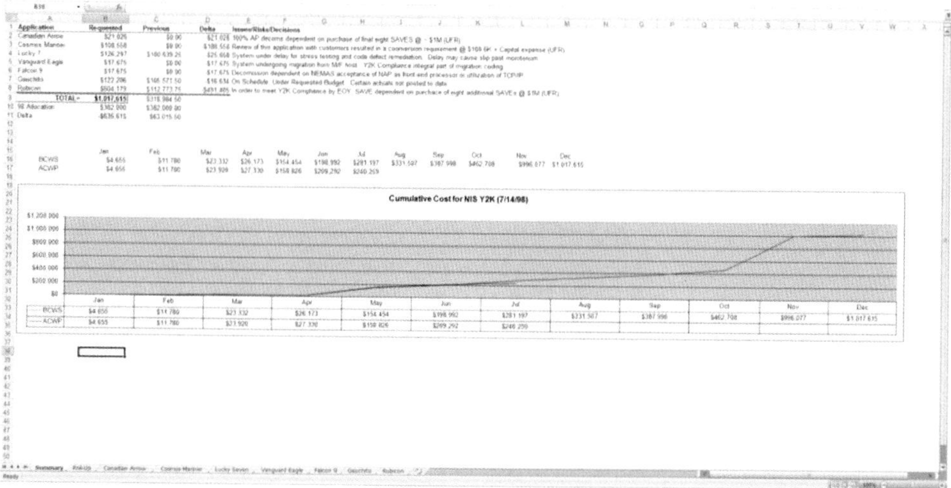

Tab Roll-Up.

A63 | Material

BCWS 6/6/98

		Jan	Feb	Mar	Apr	May	Jun	Jul (2011)	Aug	Sep	Oct	Nov	Dec	Total
Internal (SSTC Staff)	**Hours**	122.5	187.5	304	74.75	1148	881	1206	622	790	732	332	205	6,605
	Rate	38	38	38	38	38	38	38	38	38	38	38	38	
	$	4,655	7,125.00	11,552.00	2,840.50	43,624.00	33,478.00	45,828.00	23,636.00	30,020.00	27,816.00	12,616.00	7,790.00	250,981
External (Contractors)														
Grade	**Hours**	0	0	0	0	120	176	212	253	294	248	183	174	1,660
	Rate	56	56	56	56	56	56	56	56	56	56	56	56	
	$	-	-	-	-	6,722.86	9,860.19	11,877.05	14,174.02	16,471.00	13,893.90	10,252.36	9,748.14	93,000
Grade	**Hours**	0	0	0	0	0	0	70	125	100	290	65	0	650
	Rate	100	100	100	100	100	100	100	100	100	100	100	100	
	$	-	-	-	-	-	-	7,000.00	12,500.00	10,000.00	29,000.00	6,500.00	-	65,000
Grade	**Hours**													
	Rate		-	-	-	-	-	-	-	-	-	-	-	-
	$	-	-	-	-	-	-	-	-	-	-	-	-	
														-
Total Contractor	**Hours**	-	-	-	-	120	176	282	378	394	538	248	174	2,310
	$	-	-	-	-	6,723	9,860	18,877	26,674	26,471	42,894	16,752	9,748	158,000
Equipment														
Hardware	**$**	0	0	0	0	0	1200	15000	0	0	1000	501000	1000	519,200
Software	**$**	0	0	0	0	0	0	0	0	0	0	0	0	-
Material														
Team/Factory Costs	**$**	0	0	0	0	77934.84	0	0	0	0	0	0	0	77,935
Travel	**$**	0	0	0	0	0	0	2500	0	0	3000	3000	3000	11,500
	$	0	0	0	0	0	0	0	0	0	0	0	0	-
Total 1998	**$**	4,655	7,125	11,552	2,841	128,282	44,538	82,205	50,310	56,491	74,710	533,368	21,538	1,017,615

ACWP 6/2/98

		Jan	Feb	Mar	Apr	May	Jun	Jul (2011)	Aug	Sep	Oct	Nov	Dec	Total
Internal (SSTC Staff)	**Hours**	122.5	187.5	174	89.75	784.5	963.5	638	0	0	0	0	0	2,960
	Rate	38	38	38	38	38	38	38	38	38	38	38	38	
	$	4,655	7,125.00	6,612.00	3,410.50	29,811.00	36,613.00	24,244.00	-	-	-	-	-	112,471
External (Contractors)														
Grade	**Hours**	0	0	0	0	160	160	120	0	0	0	0	0	440
	Rate	56	56	56	56	56	56	56	56	56	56	56	56	
	$	-	-	-	-	8,963.81	8,963.81	6,722.86	-	-	-	-	-	24,650
Grade	**Hours**	0	0	130	0	82.5	115	0	0	0	0	0	0	328
	Rate	43	43	43	43	43	43	43	43	43	43	43	43	
	$	-	-	5,527.60	-	3,507.90	4,889.80	-	-	-	-	-	-	13,925
Grade	**Hours**													
	Rate		-	-	-	-	-	-	-	-	-	-	-	-
	$	-	-	-	-	-	-	-	-	-	-	-	-	
														-
Total Contractor	**Hours**	-	-	130	-	243	275	120	-	-	-	-	-	768
	$	-	-	5,528	-	12,472	13,854	6,723	-	-	-	-	-	38,576
Equipment														
Hardware	**$**	0	0	0	0	0	0	0	0	0	0	0	0	-
Software	**$**	0	0	0	0	0	0	0	0	0	0	0	0	-
Material														
Team/Factory Costs	**$**	0	0	0	0	89212.83	0	0	0	0	0	0	0	89,213
Travel	**$**	0	0	0	0	0	0	0	0	0	0	0	0	-
	$													-
Total 1998	**$**	4,655	7,125	12,140	3,411	131,496	50,467	30,967	-	-	-	-	-	240,259

Summary | Roll-Up | Canadian Arrow | Cosmos Mariner | Lucky Seven | Vanguard Eagle | Falcon 9 | Gauchito | Rubicon

Ready

Tab Canadian Arrow.

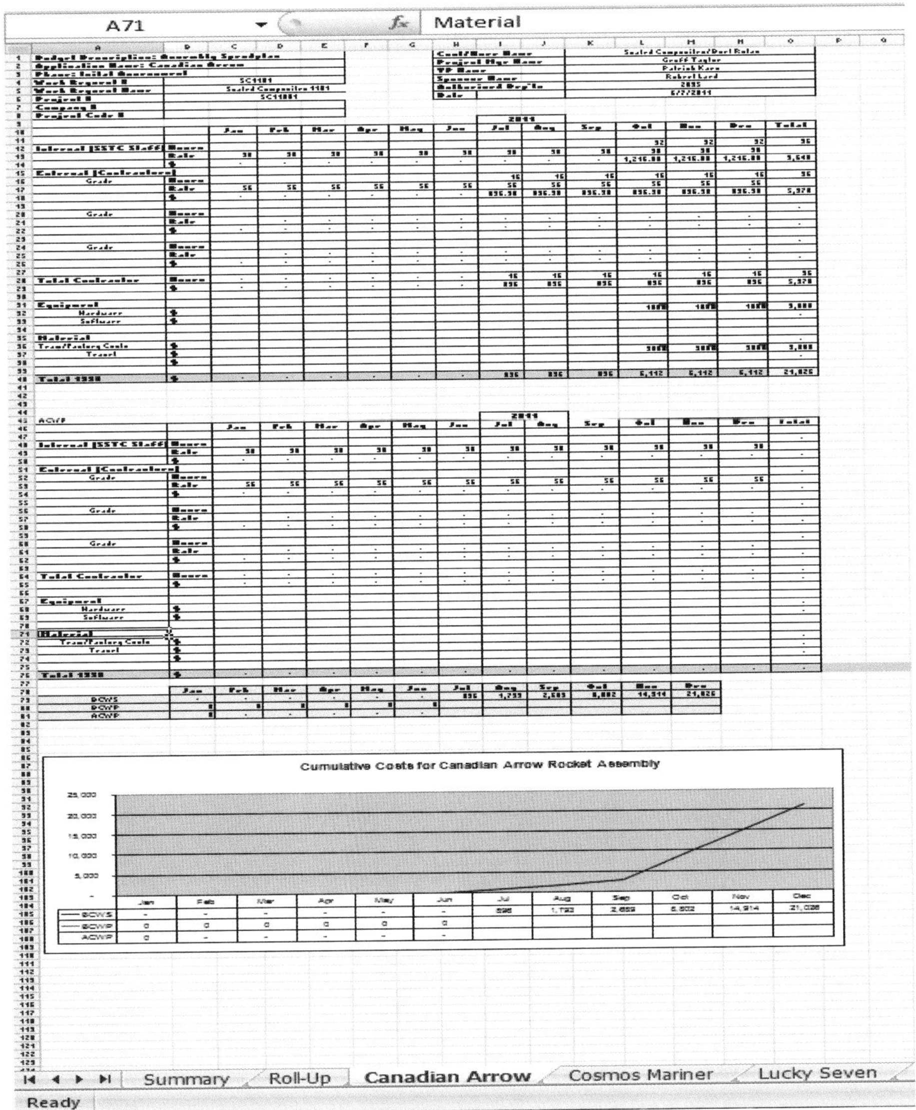

Tab Cosmos Mariner.

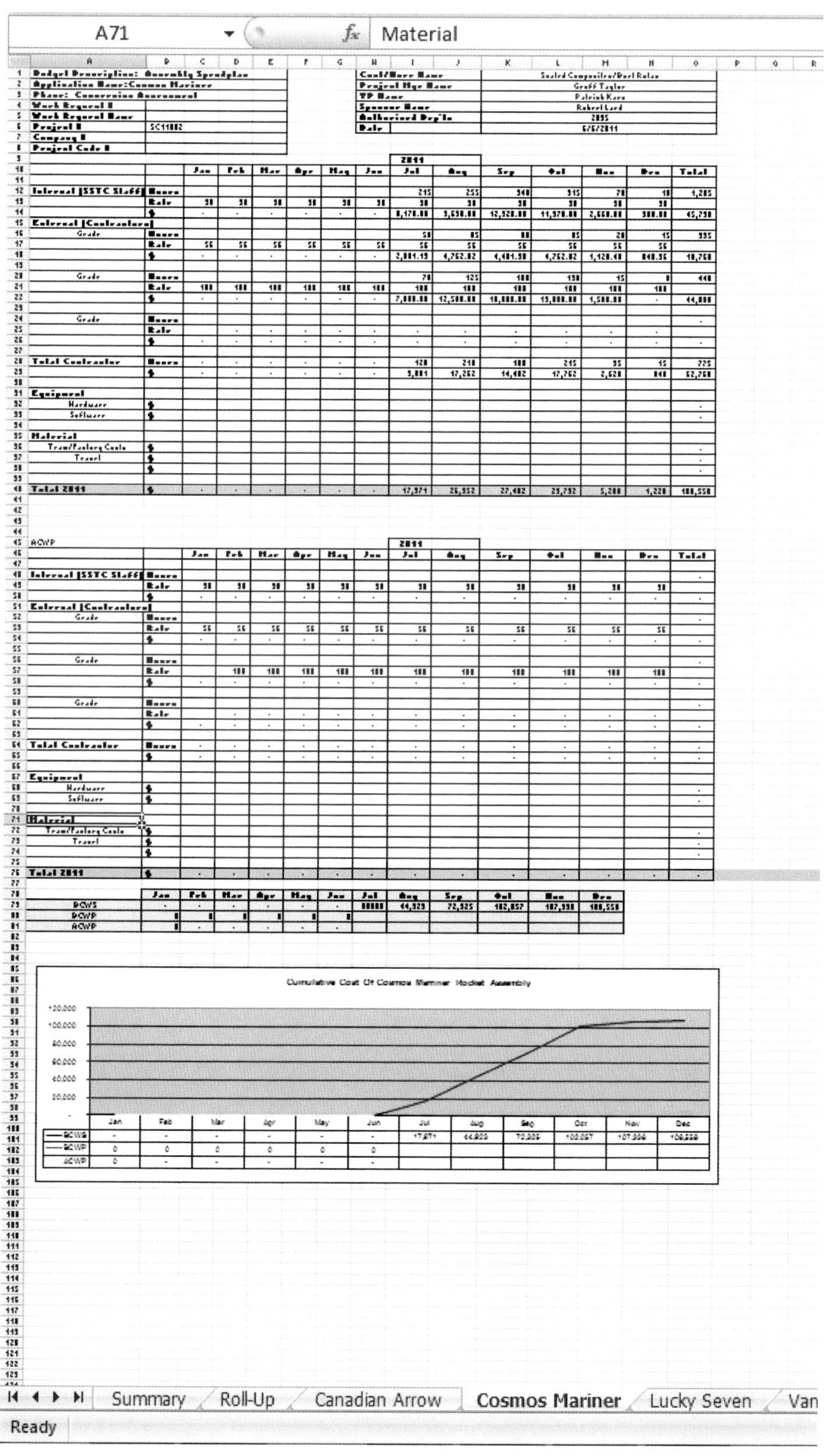

A71 | Material

Budget Description: Assembly Spreadplan		Cost/Mgr Name	Sealed Composites/Carl Rolan
Application Name:Cosmos Mariner		Project Mgr Name	Geoff Taylor
Phase: Conversion Assessment		VP Name	Patrick Kane
Work Request #		Sponsor Name	Robert Lord
Work Request Name		Authorized Dep't	2095
Project #	SC11002	Date	6/6/2011
Company #			
Project Code #			

		Jan	Feb	Mar	Apr	May	Jun	2011 Jul	Aug	Sep	Oct	Nov	Dec	Total
Internal (SSTC Staff)	Hours							215	255	340	315	70	10	1,285
	Rate	38	38	38	38	38	38	38	38	38	38	38	38	
	$	-	-	-	-	-	-	8,170.00	9,690.00	12,920.00	11,970.00	2,660.00	380.00	45,790
External (Contractors)														
Grade	Hours							50	85	80	85	20	15	335
	Rate	56	56	56	56	56	56	56	56	56	56	56	56	
	$	-	-	-	-	-	-	2,801.15	4,762.02	4,481.30	4,762.02	1,120.40	840.56	18,760
Grade	Hours							70	125	100	150	15	0	440
	Rate	100	100	100	100	100	100	100	100	100	100	100	100	
	$	-	-	-	-	-	-	7,000.00	12,500.00	10,000.00	15,000.00	1,500.00	-	44,000
Grade	Hours													-
	Rate		-	-	-	-	-	-	-	-	-	-	-	
	$	-	-	-	-	-	-	-	-	-	-	-	-	-
Total Contractor	Hours	-	-	-	-	-	-	120	210	180	235	35	15	775
	$	-	-	-	-	-	-	9,801	17,262	14,482	17,762	2,620	840	62,760
Equipment														
Hardware	$													-
Software	$													-
Material														
Tram/Factory Costs	$													-
Travel	$													-
	$													-
Total 2011	$	-	-	-	-	-	-	17,971	26,952	27,402	29,292	5,280	1,220	108,558

ACWP

		Jan	Feb	Mar	Apr	May	Jun	2011 Jul	Aug	Sep	Oct	Nov	Dec	Total
Internal (SSTC Staff)	Hours													-
	Rate	38	38	38	38	38	38	38	38	38	38	38	38	
	$	-	-	-	-	-	-	-	-	-	-	-	-	-
External (Contractors)														
Grade	Hours													-
	Rate	56	56	56	56	56	56	56	56	56	56	56	56	
	$	-	-	-	-	-	-	-	-	-	-	-	-	-
Grade	Hours													-
	Rate		100	100	100	100	100	100	100	100	100	100	100	
	$	-	-	-	-	-	-	-	-	-	-	-	-	-
Grade	Hours													-
	Rate		-	-	-	-	-	-	-	-	-	-	-	
	$	-	-	-	-	-	-	-	-	-	-	-	-	-
Total Contractor	Hours	-	-	-	-	-	-	-	-	-	-	-	-	-
	$	-	-	-	-	-	-	-	-	-	-	-	-	-
Equipment														
Hardware	$													-
Software	$													-
Material														
Tram/Factory Costs	$													-
Travel	$													-
	$													-
Total 2011	$	-	-	-	-	-	-	-	-	-	-	-	-	-

	Jan	Feb	Mar	Apr	May	Jun	Jul	Aug	Sep	Oct	Nov	Dec
BCWS	-	-	-	-	-	-	#####	44,923	72,325	102,057	107,338	108,558
BCWP	0	0	0	0	0	0						
ACWP	0	-	-	-	-	-						

Summary | Roll-Up | Canadian Arrow | Cosmos Mariner | Lucky Seven | Van

Ready

Tab Lucky Seven.

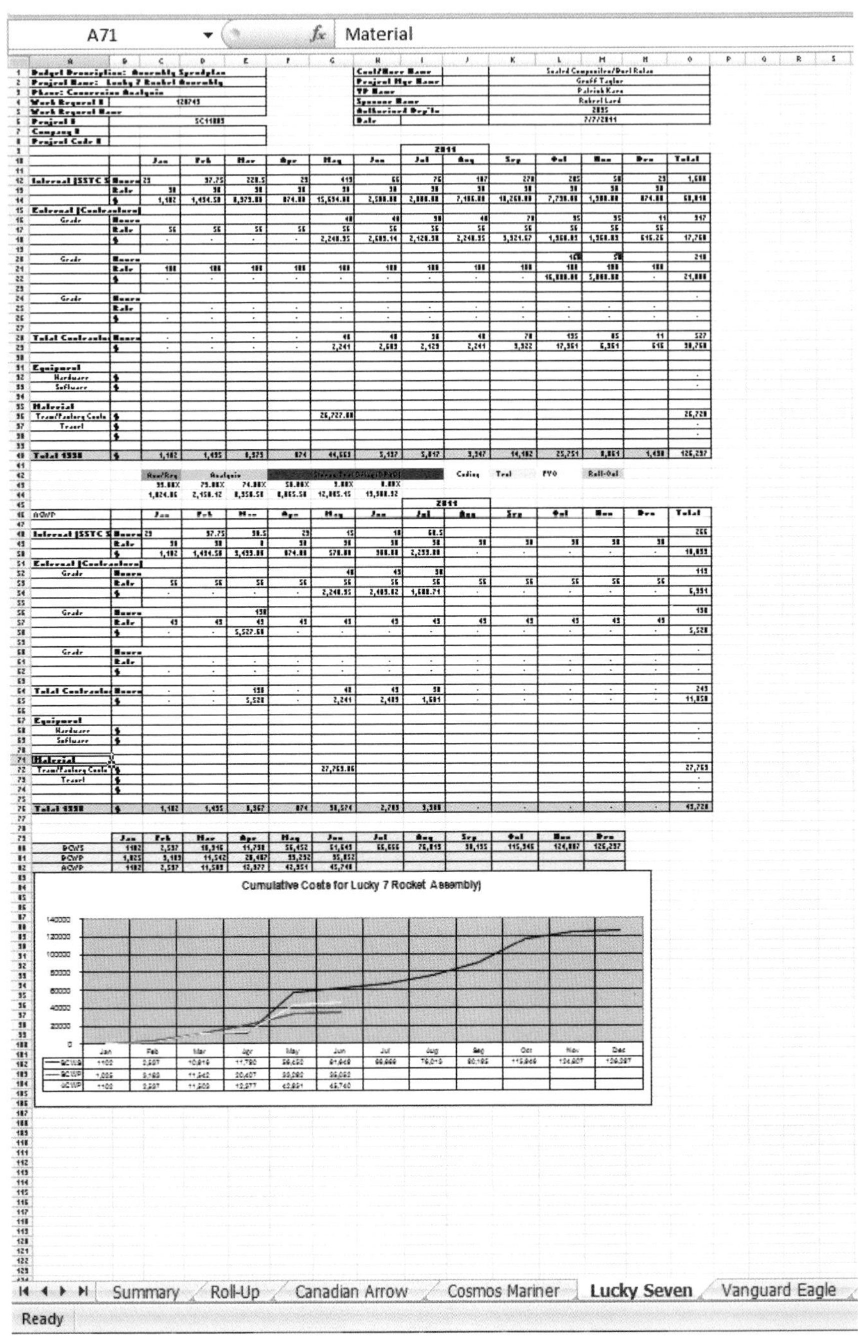

A71 | Material

	Jan	Feb	Mar	Apr	May	Jun	Jul	Aug	Sep	Oct	Nov	Dec
BCWS	1182	2,597	10,916	11,790	56,452	61,649	66,666	76,019	90,195	115,946	124,807	126,257
BCWP	1,025	3,183	11,542	20,407	33,292	35,052						
ACWP	1182	2,597	11,509	12,977	42,951	45,740						

Tab Vanguard Eagle.

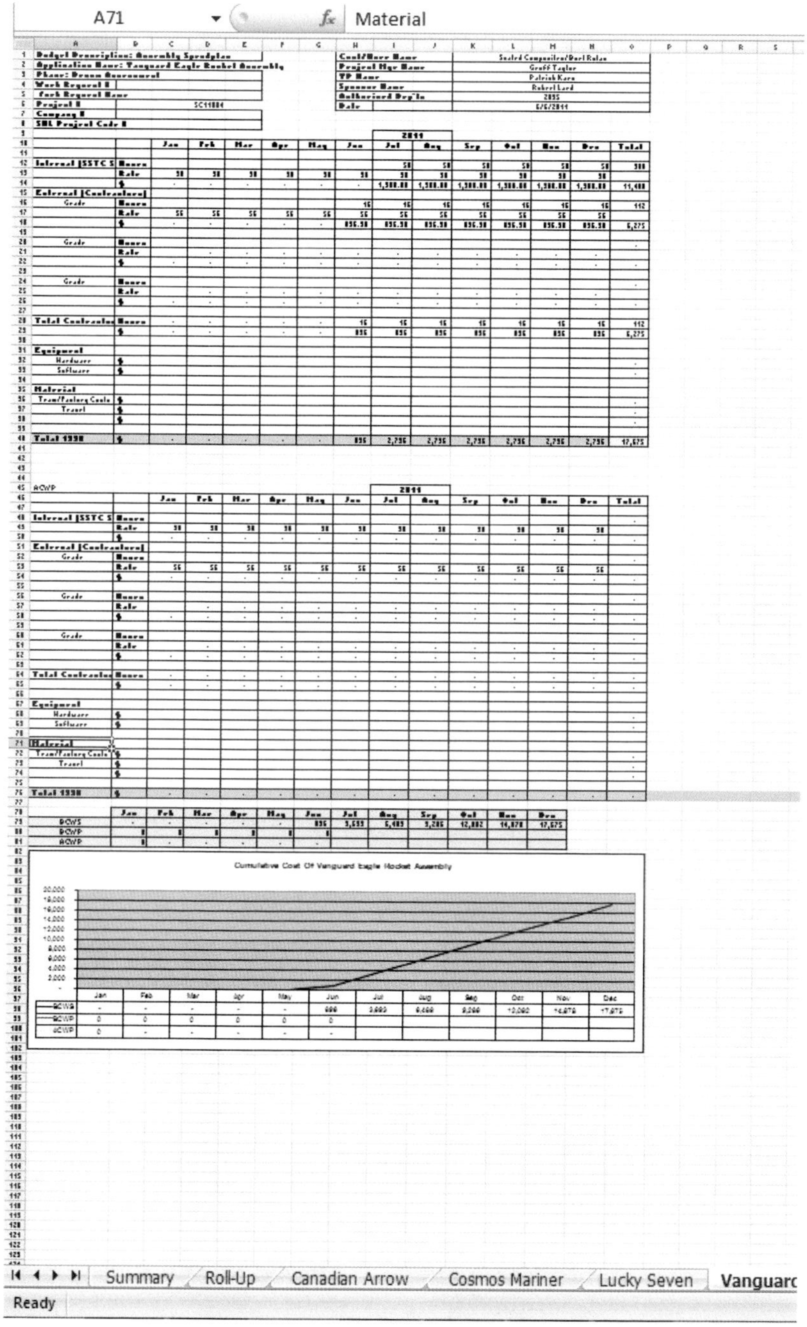

A71 | Material

Budget Description: Assembly Spreadplan		Cost/Base Name	Sealed Composites/Dart Rolas
Application Name: Vanguard Eagle Rocket Assembly		Project Mgr Name	Graff Taylor
Phase: Dream Assessment		VP Name	Patrick Karo
Work Request #		Sponsor Name	Robert Lord
Work Request Name		Authorized Dep't	2895
Project #	SC11004	Date	6/6/2011
Company #			
SBL Project Code #			

		Jan	Feb	Mar	Apr	May	Jun	Jul (2011)	Aug	Sep	Oct	Nov	Dec	Total
Internal [SSTC S	Hours							50	50	50	50	50	50	300
	Rate	38	38	38	38	38	38	38	38	38	38	38	38	
	$	-	-	-	-	-	-	1,900.00	1,900.00	1,900.00	1,900.00	1,900.00	1,900.00	11,400
External [Contractors]														
Grade	Hours						16	16	16	16	16	16	16	112
	Rate	56	56	56	56	56	56	56	56	56	56	56	56	
	$	-	-	-	-	-	896.00	896.00	896.00	896.00	896.00	896.00	896.00	6,275
Grade	Hours													-
	Rate		-	-	-	-	-	-	-	-	-	-	-	
	$	-	-	-	-	-	-	-	-	-	-	-	-	-
Grade	Hours													-
	Rate		-	-	-	-	-	-	-	-	-	-	-	
	$	-	-	-	-	-	-	-	-	-	-	-	-	-
Total Contractor	Hours	-	-	-	-	-	16	16	16	16	16	16	16	112
	$	-	-	-	-	-	896	896	896	896	896	896	896	6,275
Equipment														
Hardware	$													-
Software	$													-
Material														
Tram/Factory Costs	$													-
Travel	$													-
	$													-
														-
Total 1998	$	-	-	-	-	-	896	2,796	2,796	2,796	2,796	2,796	2,796	17,675

ACWP

		Jan	Feb	Mar	Apr	May	Jun	Jul (2011)	Aug	Sep	Oct	Nov	Dec	Total
Internal [SSTC S	Hours													-
	Rate	38	38	38	38	38	38	38	38	38	38	38	38	
	$	-	-	-	-	-	-	-	-	-	-	-	-	-
External [Contractors]														
Grade	Hours													-
	Rate	56	56	56	56	56	56	56	56	56	56	56	56	
	$	-	-	-	-	-	-	-	-	-	-	-	-	-
Grade	Hours													-
	Rate		-	-	-	-	-	-	-	-	-	-	-	
	$	-	-	-	-	-	-	-	-	-	-	-	-	-
Grade	Hours													-
	Rate		-	-	-	-	-	-	-	-	-	-	-	
	$	-	-	-	-	-	-	-	-	-	-	-	-	-
Total Contractor	Hours	-	-	-	-	-	-	-	-	-	-	-	-	-
	$	-	-	-	-	-	-	-	-	-	-	-	-	-
Equipment														
Hardware	$													-
Software	$													-
Material														
Tram/Factory Costs	$													-
Travel	$													-
	$													-
Total 1998	$	-	-	-	-	-	-	-	-	-	-	-	-	-

	Jan	Feb	Mar	Apr	May	Jun	Jul	Aug	Sep	Oct	Nov	Dec
BCWS	-	-	-	-	-	896	3,693	6,489	9,286	12,082	14,878	17,675
BCWP	0	0	0	0	0	0						
ACWP	0	-	-	-	-	-						

Cumulative Cost Of Vanguard Eagle Rocket Assembly

	Jan	Feb	Mar	Apr	May	Jun	Jul	Aug	Sep	Oct	Nov	Dec
BCWS	-	-	-	-	-	896	3,692	6,488	9,288	12,082	14,878	17,675
BCWP	0	0	0	0	0	0						
ACWP	0	-	-	-	-	-						

Summary | Roll-Up | Canadian Arrow | Cosmos Mariner | Lucky Seven | Vanguard

Ready

Tab Falcon 9.

A71 | Material

Cumulative Cost of Falcon 9 Rocket Assembly

Summary | Roll-Up | Canadian Arrow | Cosmos Mariner | Lucky Seven | Va

Ready

Tab Gauchito.

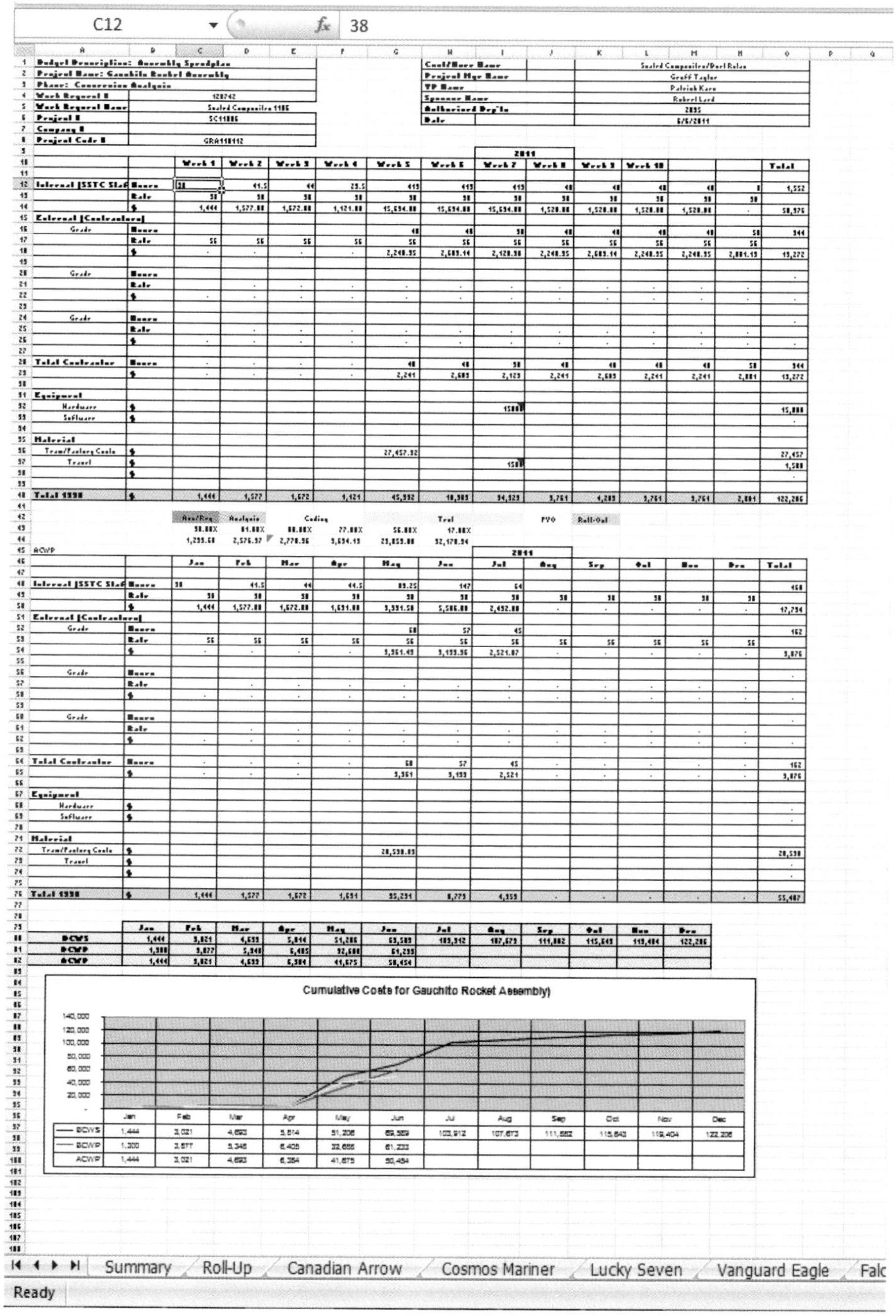

C12 | f_x 38

	A	B	C
1	Budget Description: Assembly Spreadplan		
2	Project Name: Gauchito Rocket Assembly		
3	Phase: Conversion Analysis		
4	Work Request #	128742	
5	Work Request Name	Sealed Composites 1185	
6	Project #	SC11886	
7	Company #		
8	Project Code #	GRA118112	

Cost/Base Name	Sealed Composites/Duct Rules
Project Mgr Name	Graff Taylor
VP Name	Patrick Kane
Sponsor Name	Robert Lord
Authorized Dep'ts	2835
Date	6/6/2011

Row	A	B	Week 1	Week 2	Week 3	Week 4	Week 5	Week 6	Week 7 (2011)	Week 8	Week 9	Week 10			Total
12	Internal [SSTC Staff]	Hours	38	41.5	44	29.5	413	413	413	40	40	40	40	0	1,552
13		Rate	38	38	38	38	38	38	38	38	38	38	38	38	
14		$	1,444	1,577.00	1,672.00	1,121.00	15,694.00	15,694.00	15,694.00	1,520.00	1,520.00	1,520.00	1,520.00	-	58,976
15	External [Contractors]														
16	Grade	Hours					40	48	38	40	48	40	40	50	344
17		Rate	56	56	56	56	56	56	56	56	56	56	56	56	
18		$	-	-	-	-	2,240.95	2,689.14	2,128.98	2,240.95	2,689.14	2,240.95	2,240.95	2,801.19	19,272
19															
20	Grade	Hours													-
21		Rate		-	-	-	-	-	-	-	-	-	-	-	
22		$	-	-	-	-	-	-	-	-	-	-	-	-	-
23															
24	Grade	Hours													-
25		Rate		-	-	-	-	-	-	-	-	-	-	-	
26		$	-	-	-	-	-	-	-	-	-	-	-	-	-
27															
28	Total Contractor	Hours	-	-	-	-	40	48	38	40	48	40	40	50	344
29		$	-	-	-	-	2,241	2,689	2,129	2,241	2,689	2,241	2,241	2,801	19,272
30															
31	Equipment														
32	Hardware	$							15000						15,000
33	Software	$													-
34															
35	Material														
36	Tran/Factory Costs	$					27,457.92								27,457
37	Travel	$							1500						1,500
38		$													-
39															
40	Total 1998	$	1,444	1,577	1,672	1,121	45,392	18,383	34,323	3,761	4,209	3,761	3,761	2,801	122,206

Row		Ana/Req	Analysis	Coding		Test			FVO	Roll-Out
43		90.00%	81.00%	88.00%	77.00%	56.00%	47.00%			
44		1,299.60	2,576.97	2,770.56	3,634.13	23,859.00	52,170.94			

45 ACWP

Row	A	B	Jan	Feb	Mar	Apr	May	Jun	Jul (2011)	Aug	Sep	Oct	Nov	Dec	Total
48	Internal [SSTC Staff]	Hours	38	41.5	44	44.5	89.25	147	64						468
49		Rate	38	38	38	38	38	38	38	38	38	38	38	38	
50		$	1,444	1,577.00	1,672.00	1,691.00	3,391.50	5,586.00	2,432.00	-	-	-	-	-	17,794
51	External [Contractors]														
52	Grade	Hours					60	57	45						162
53		Rate	56	56	56	56	56	56	56	56	56	56	56	56	
54		$	-	-	-	-	3,361.49	3,193.56	2,521.07	-	-	-	-	-	9,076
55															
56	Grade	Hours													-
57		Rate		-	-	-	-	-	-	-	-	-	-	-	
58		$	-	-	-	-	-	-	-	-	-	-	-	-	-
59															
60	Grade	Hours													-
61		Rate		-	-	-	-	-	-	-	-	-	-	-	
62		$	-	-	-	-	-	-	-	-	-	-	-	-	-
63															
64	Total Contractor	Hours	-	-	-	-	60	57	45	-	-	-	-	-	162
65		$	-	-	-	-	3,361	3,193	2,521	-	-	-	-	-	9,076
66															
67	Equipment														
68	Hardware	$													-
69	Software	$													-
70															
71	Material														
72	Tran/Factory Costs	$					28,538.01								28,538
73	Travel	$													-
74		$													-
75															
76	Total 1998	$	1,444	1,577	1,672	1,691	35,291	8,779	4,953	-	-	-	-	-	55,407

	Jan	Feb	Mar	Apr	May	Jun	Jul	Aug	Sep	Oct	Nov	Dec
BCWS	1,444	3,021	4,693	5,814	51,206	69,589	103,912	107,673	111,882	115,643	119,404	122,206
BCWP	1,300	3,877	5,348	6,405	32,656	61,233						
ACWP	1,444	3,021	4,693	6,384	41,675	50,454						

Cumulative Costs for Gauchito Rocket Assembly)

140,000
120,000
100,000
80,000
60,000
40,000
20,000
-

	Jan	Feb	Mar	Apr	May	Jun	Jul	Aug	Sep	Oct	Nov	Dec
BCWS	1,444	3,021	4,693	5,814	51,206	69,589	103,912	107,673	111,882	115,643	119,404	122,206
BCWP	1,300	3,877	5,348	6,405	32,656	61,233						
ACWP	1,444	3,021	4,693	6,384	41,675	50,454						

Summary / Roll-Up / Canadian Arrow / Cosmos Mariner / Lucky Seven / Vanguard Eagle / Falc

Ready

Tab Rubicon.

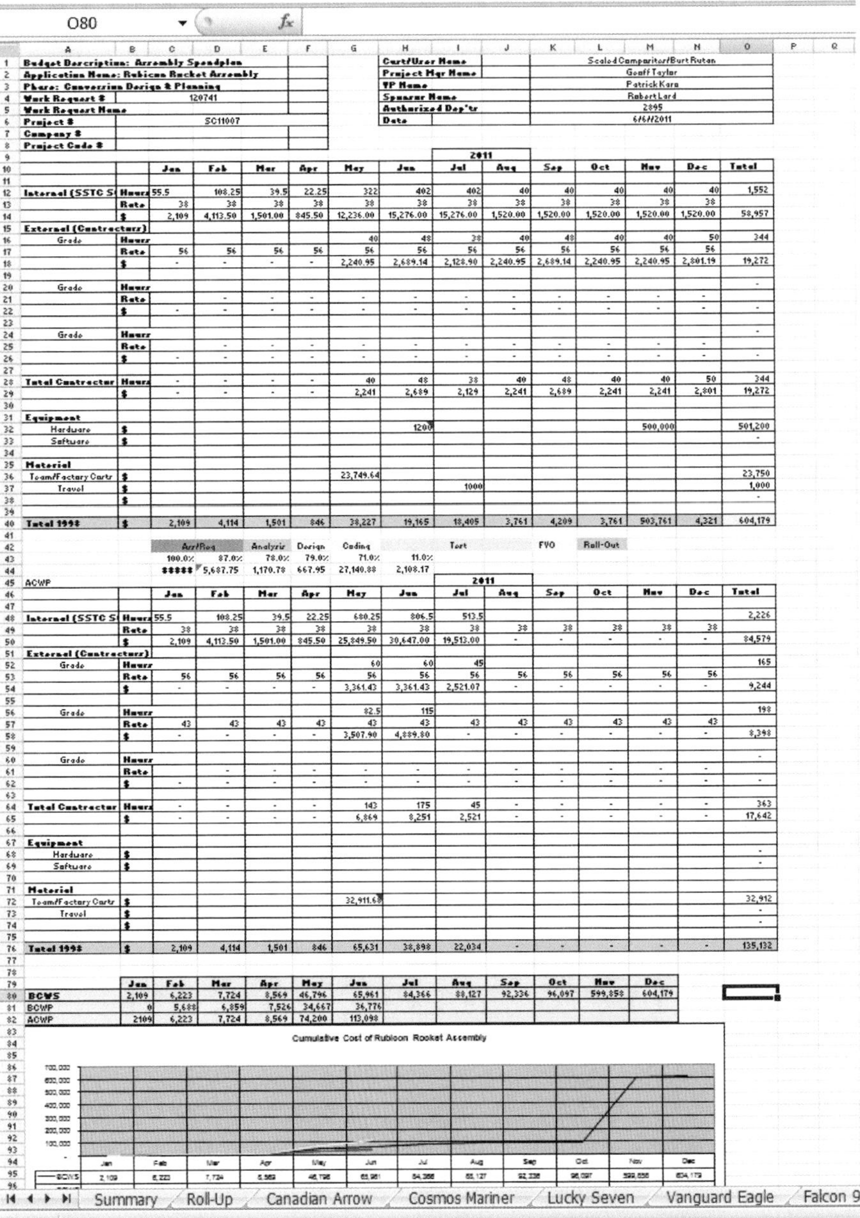

O80

Budget Description: Assembly Spendplan				**Cost/User Name**		Scaled Composites/Burt Rutan
Application Name: Rubicon Rocket Assembly				**Project Mgr Name**		Geoff Taylor
Phase: Conversion Design & Planning				**VP Name**		Patrick Kara
Work Request #	120741			**Sponsor Name**		Robert Lord
Work Request Name				**Authorized Dep'ts**		2895
Project #	SC11007			**Date**		6/6//2011
Company #						
Project Code #						

		Jan	Feb	Mar	Apr	May	Jun	Jul (2011)	Aug	Sep	Oct	Nov	Dec	Total
Internal (SSTC S	**Hours**	55.5	108.25	39.5	22.25	322	402	402	40	40	40	40	40	1,552
	Rate	38	38	38	38	38	38	38	38	38	38	38	38	
	$	2,109	4,113.50	1,501.00	845.50	12,236.00	15,276.00	15,276.00	1,520.00	1,520.00	1,520.00	1,520.00	1,520.00	58,957
External (Contractors)														
Grade	**Hours**					40	48	38	40	48	40	40	50	344
	Rate	56	56	56	56	56	56	56	56	56	56	56	56	
	$	-	-	-	-	2,240.95	2,689.14	2,128.90	2,240.95	2,689.14	2,240.95	2,240.95	2,801.19	19,272
Grade	**Hours**													-
	Rate		-	-	-	-	-	-	-	-	-	-	-	
	$	-	-	-	-	-	-	-	-	-	-	-	-	-
Grade	**Hours**													-
	Rate		-	-	-	-	-	-	-	-	-	-	-	
	$	-	-	-	-	-	-	-	-	-	-	-	-	-
Total Contractor	**Hours**	-	-	-	-	40	48	38	40	48	40	40	50	344
	$	-	-	-	-	2,241	2,689	2,129	2,241	2,689	2,241	2,241	2,801	19,272
Equipment														
Hardware	**$**						1200					500,000		501,200
Software	**$**													-
Material														
Team/Factory Costs	**$**					23,749.64								23,750
Travel	**$**							1000						1,000
	$													-
Total 1998	**$**	2,109	4,114	1,501	846	38,227	19,165	18,405	3,761	4,209	3,761	503,761	4,321	604,179

Ass/Req		Analysis	Design	Coding	Test			FVO	Roll-Out
100.0%	87.0%	78.0%	79.0%	71.0%	11.0%				
#####	5,687.75	1,170.78	667.95	27,140.88	2,108.17				

ACWP

		Jan	Feb	Mar	Apr	May	Jun	Jul (2011)	Aug	Sep	Oct	Nov	Dec	Total
Internal (SSTC S	**Hours**	55.5	108.25	39.5	22.25	680.25	806.5	513.5						2,226
	Rate	38	38	38	38	38	38	38	38	38	38	38	38	
	$	2,109	4,113.50	1,501.00	845.50	25,849.50	30,647.00	19,513.00	-	-	-	-	-	84,579
External (Contractors)														
Grade	**Hours**					60	60	45						165
	Rate	56	56	56	56	56	56	56	56	56	56	56	56	
	$	-	-	-	-	3,361.43	3,361.43	2,521.07	-	-	-	-	-	9,244
Grade	**Hours**					82.5	115							198
	Rate	43	43	43	43	43	43	43	43	43	43	43	43	
	$	-	-	-	-	3,507.90	4,889.80	-	-	-	-	-	-	8,398
Grade	**Hours**													-
	Rate		-	-	-	-	-	-	-	-	-	-	-	
	$	-	-	-	-	-	-	-	-	-	-	-	-	-
Total Contractor	**Hours**	-	-	-	-	143	175	45	-	-	-	-	-	363
	$	-	-	-	-	6,869	8,251	2,521	-	-	-	-	-	17,642
Equipment														
Hardware	**$**													-
Software	**$**													-
Material														
Team/Factory Costs	**$**					32,911.68								32,912
Travel	**$**													-
	$													-
Total 1998	**$**	2,109	4,114	1,501	846	65,631	38,898	22,034	-	-	-	-	-	135,132

	Jan	Feb	Mar	Apr	May	Jun	Jul	Aug	Sep	Oct	Nov	Dec
BCWS	2,109	6,223	7,724	8,569	46,796	65,961	84,366	88,127	92,336	96,097	599,858	604,179
BCWP	0	5,688	6,859	7,526	34,667	36,776						
ACWP	2109	6,223	7,724	8,569	74,200	113,098						

Appendix-F: EVM Project Example

A1 | Budget Description: Assembly Spendplan

Budget Description: Assembly Spendplan	
Project Name: Gauchito Rocket Assembly	
Phase: Conversion Analysis	
Work Request #	120742
Work Request Name	Scaled Composites 1106
Project #	GM593-100X
Company #	
Project Code #	MSM/MBA/MSIT

Cust/User Name	Scaled Composites/Burt Rutan
Project Mgr Name	Your Name
VP Name	Betty Vandenbosch
Sponsor Name	Professor's Name
Authorized Dep'ts	591/592/593/594
Date	6/6/2011

		Week 1	Week 2	Week 3	Week 4	Week 5	Week 6	Week 7 (2011)	Week 8	Week 9	Week 10			Total
Internal SSTC Staff)	**Hours**	38	41.5	44	29.5	413	413	413	40	40	40	40	0	1,552
	Rate	38	38	38	38	38	38	38	38	38	38	38	38	
	$	1,444	1,577.00	1,672.00	1,121.00	15,694.00	15,694.00	15,694.00	1,520.00	1,520.00	1,520.00	1,520.00	-	58,976
External (Contractors)														
Grade	**Hours**					40	48	38	40	48	40	40	50	344
	Rate	56	56	56	56	56	56	56	56	56	56	56	56	
	$	-	-	-	-	2,240.95	2,689.14	2,128.90	2,240.95	2,689.14	2,240.95	2,240.95	2,801.19	19,272
Grade	**Hours**													
	Rate													
	$													
Grade	**Hours**													
	Rate													
	$													
Total Contractor	**Hours**	-	-	-	-	40	48	38	40	48	40	40	50	344
	$	-	-	-	-	2,241	2,689	2,129	2,241	2,689	2,241	2,241	2,801	19,272
Capital (Detail Items)														
Hardware	**$**							15000						15,000
Software	**$**													
Other Costs (Detail Items)														
Team/Factory Costs	**$**					27,457.32								27,457
Travel	**$**							1500						1,500
	$													
Total 1998	**$**	1,444	1,577	1,672	1,121	45,392	18,383	34,323	3,761	4,209	3,761	3,761	2,801	122,206

Ass/Req	Analysis	Coding			Test	FVO	Roll-Out
90.00%	81.00%	88.00%	77.00%	56.00%	17.00%		
1,299.60	2,576.97	2,770.96	3,634.13	29,053.80	32,178.94		

ACWP

Gauchito

Ready

A1 | Budget Description: Assembly Spendplan

ACWP

		Jan	Feb	Mar	Apr	May	Jun	Jul (2011)	Aug	Sep	Oct	Nov	Dec	Total
Internal (MCI Staff)	**Hours**	38	41.5	44	44.5	89.25	147	64						468
	Rate	38	38	38	38	38	38	38	38	38	38	38	38	
	$	1,444	1,577.00	1,672.00	1,691.00	3,391.50	5,586.00	2,432.00	-	-	-	-	-	17,794
External (Contractors)														
Grade	**Hours**					60	57	45						162
	Rate	56	56	56	56	56	56	56	56	56	56	56	56	
	$	-	-	-	-	3,361.43	3,193.36	2,521.07	-	-	-	-	-	9,076
Grade	**Hours**													
	Rate													
	$													
Grade	**Hours**													
	Rate													
	$													
Total Contractor	**Hours**	-	-	-	-	60	57	45	-	-	-	-	-	162
	$	-	-	-	-	3,361	3,193	2,521	-	-	-	-	-	9,076
Capital (Detail Items)														
Hardware	**$**													
Software	**$**													
Other Costs (Detail Items)														
Team/Factory Costs	**$**					28,538.09								28,538
Travel	**$**													
	$													
Total 1998	**$**	1,444	1,577	1,672	1,691	35,291	8,779	4,953	-	-	-	-	-	55,407

	Jan	Feb	Mar	Apr	May	Jun	Jul	Aug	Sep	Oct	Nov	Dec
BCWS	1,444	3,021	4,693	5,814	51,206	69,589	103,912	107,673	111,682	115,643	119,404	122,206
BCWP	1,300	3,877	5,348	6,405	32,688	61,233						
ACWP	1,444	3,021	4,693	6,384	41,675	50,454						

Cumulative Costs for Gauchito Rocket Assembly)

140,000
120,000

Gauchito

Ready

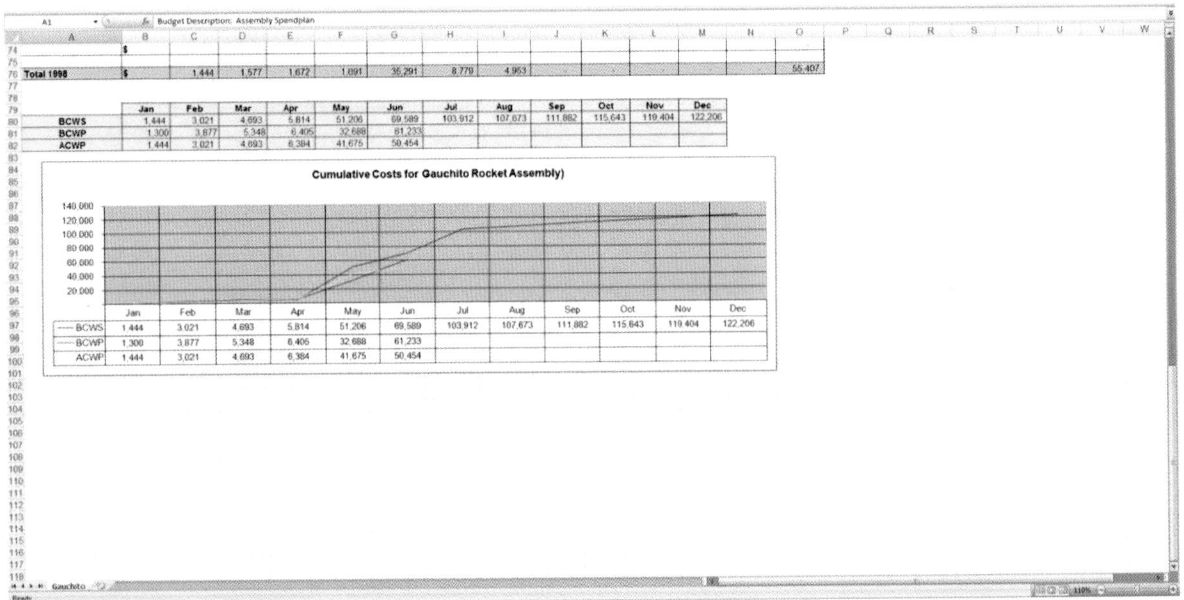

A1 Budget Description: Assembly Spendplan

	$													
Total 1998	$	1,444	1,577	1,672	1,691	35,291	8,779	4,953	-	-	-	-	-	55,407

	Jan	Feb	Mar	Apr	May	Jun	Jul	Aug	Sep	Oct	Nov	Dec
BCWS	1,444	3,021	4,693	5,814	51,206	69,589	103,912	107,673	111,882	115,643	119,404	122,206
BCWP	1,300	3,877	5,348	6,405	32,688	61,233						
ACWP	1,444	3,021	4,693	6,384	41,675	50,454						

	Jan	Feb	Mar	Apr	May	Jun	Jul	Aug	Sep	Oct	Nov	Dec
BCWS	1,444	3,021	4,693	5,814	51,206	69,589	103,912	107,673	111,882	115,643	119,404	122,206
BCWP	1,300	3,877	5,348	6,405	32,688	61,233						
ACWP	1,444	3,021	4,693	6,384	41,675	50,454						

Gauchito

Ready

Appendix-G: Gauchito Blank Template

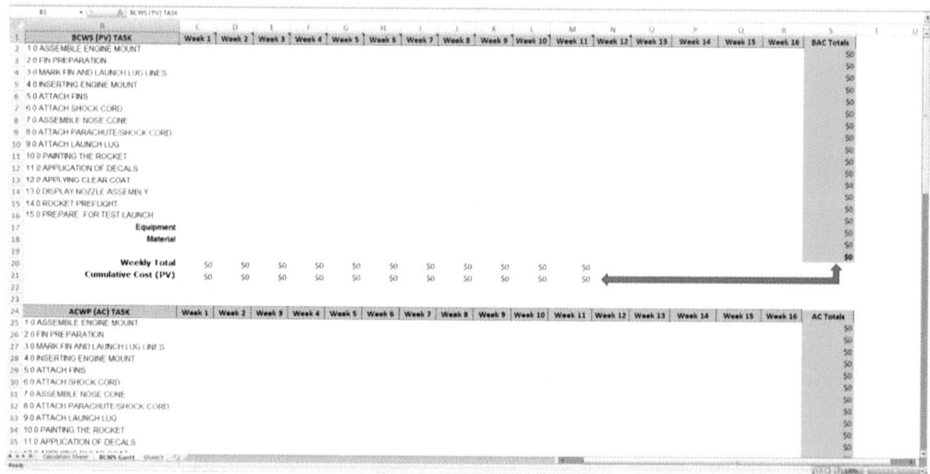

BCWS (PV) TASK	Week 1	Week 2	Week 3	Week 4	Week 5	Week 6	Week 7	Week 8	Week 9	Week 10	Week 11	Week 12	Week 13	Week 14	Week 15	Week 16	BAC Totals
1.0 ASSEMBLE ENGINE MOUNT																	$0
2.0 FIN PREPARATION																	$0
3.0 MARK FIN AND LAUNCH LUG LINES																	$0
4.0 INSERTING ENGINE MOUNT																	$0
5.0 ATTACH FINS																	$0
6.0 ATTACH SHOCK CORD																	$0
7.0 ASSEMBLE NOSE CONE																	$0
8.0 ATTACH PARACHUTE/SHOCK CORD																	$0
9.0 ATTACH LAUNCH LUG																	$0
10.0 PAINTING THE ROCKET																	$0
11.0 APPLICATION OF DECALS																	$0
12.0 APPLYING CLEAR COAT																	$0
13.0 DISPLAY NOZZLE ASSEMBLY																	$0
14.0 ROCKET PREFLIGHT																	$0
15.0 PREPARE FOR TEST LAUNCH																	$0
Equipment																	$0
Material																	$0
																	$0
Weekly Total	$0	$0	$0	$0	$0	$0	$0	$0	$0	$0	$0						
Cumulative Cost (PV)	$0	$0	$0	$0	$0	$0	$0	$0	$0	$0	$0						

ACWP (AC) TASK	Week 1	Week 2	Week 3	Week 4	Week 5	Week 6	Week 7	Week 8	Week 9	Week 10	Week 11	Week 12	Week 13	Week 14	Week 15	Week 16	AC Totals
1.0 ASSEMBLE ENGINE MOUNT																	$0
2.0 FIN PREPARATION																	$0
3.0 MARK FIN AND LAUNCH LUG LINES																	$0
4.0 INSERTING ENGINE MOUNT																	$0
5.0 ATTACH FINS																	$0
6.0 ATTACH SHOCK CORD																	$0
7.0 ASSEMBLE NOSE CONE																	$0
8.0 ATTACH PARACHUTE/SHOCK CORD																	$0
9.0 ATTACH LAUNCH LUG																	$0
10.0 PAINTING THE ROCKET																	$0
11.0 APPLICATION OF DECALS																	$0

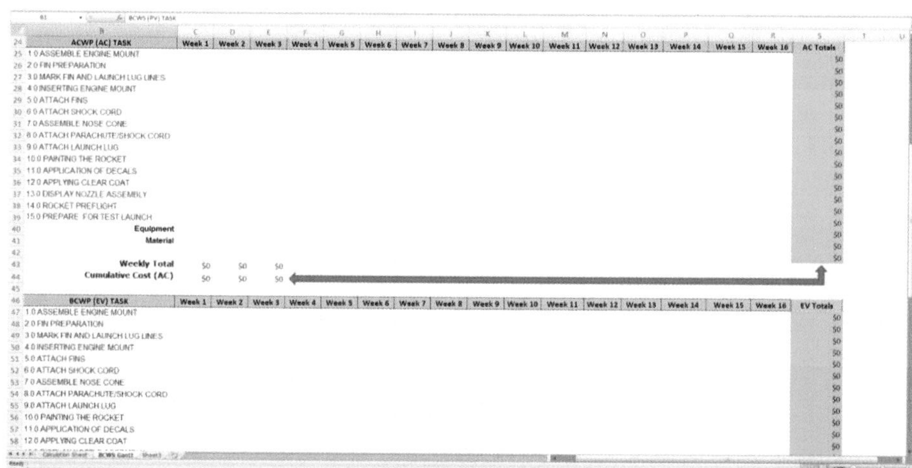

ACWP (AC) TASK	Week 1	Week 2	Week 3	Week 4	Week 5	Week 6	Week 7	Week 8	Week 9	Week 10	Week 11	Week 12	Week 13	Week 14	Week 15	Week 16	AC Totals
1.0 ASSEMBLE ENGINE MOUNT																	$0
2.0 FIN PREPARATION																	$0
3.0 MARK FIN AND LAUNCH LUG LINES																	$0
4.0 INSERTING ENGINE MOUNT																	$0
5.0 ATTACH FINS																	$0
6.0 ATTACH SHOCK CORD																	$0
7.0 ASSEMBLE NOSE CONE																	$0
8.0 ATTACH PARACHUTE/SHOCK CORD																	$0
9.0 ATTACH LAUNCH LUG																	$0
10.0 PAINTING THE ROCKET																	$0
11.0 APPLICATION OF DECALS																	$0
12.0 APPLYING CLEAR COAT																	$0
13.0 DISPLAY NOZZLE ASSEMBLY																	$0
14.0 ROCKET PREFLIGHT																	$0
15.0 PREPARE FOR TEST LAUNCH																	$0
Equipment																	$0
Material																	$0
																	$0
Weekly Total	$0	$0	$0														
Cumulative Cost (AC)	$0	$0	$0														

BCWP (EV) TASK	Week 1	Week 2	Week 3	Week 4	Week 5	Week 6	Week 7	Week 8	Week 9	Week 10	Week 11	Week 12	Week 13	Week 14	Week 15	Week 16	EV Totals
1.0 ASSEMBLE ENGINE MOUNT																	$0
2.0 FIN PREPARATION																	$0
3.0 MARK FIN AND LAUNCH LUG LINES																	$0
4.0 INSERTING ENGINE MOUNT																	$0
5.0 ATTACH FINS																	$0
6.0 ATTACH SHOCK CORD																	$0
7.0 ASSEMBLE NOSE CONE																	$0
8.0 ATTACH PARACHUTE/SHOCK CORD																	$0
9.0 ATTACH LAUNCH LUG																	$0
10.0 PAINTING THE ROCKET																	$0
11.0 APPLICATION OF DECALS																	$0
12.0 APPLYING CLEAR COAT																	$0

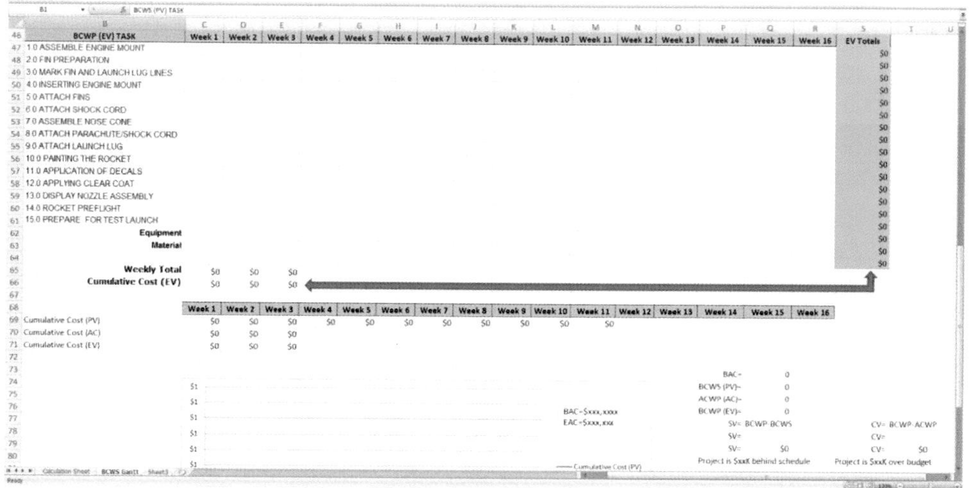

BCWP (EV) TASK	Week 1	Week 2	Week 3	Week 4	Week 5	Week 6	Week 7	Week 8	Week 9	Week 10	Week 11	Week 12	Week 13	Week 14	Week 15	Week 16	EV Totals
1.0 ASSEMBLE ENGINE MOUNT																	$0
2.0 FIN PREPARATION																	$0
3.0 MARK FIN AND LAUNCH LUG LINES																	$0
4.0 INSERTING ENGINE MOUNT																	$0
5.0 ATTACH FINS																	$0
6.0 ATTACH SHOCK CORD																	$0
7.0 ASSEMBLE NOSE CONE																	$0
8.0 ATTACH PARACHUTE/SHOCK CORD																	$0
9.0 ATTACH LAUNCH LUG																	$0
10.0 PAINTING THE ROCKET																	$0
11.0 APPLICATION OF DECALS																	$0
12.0 APPLYING CLEAR COAT																	$0
13.0 DISPLAY NOZZLE ASSEMBLY																	$0
14.0 ROCKET PREFLIGHT																	$0
15.0 PREPARE FOR TEST LAUNCH																	$0
Equipment																	$0
Material																	$0
																	$0
Weekly Total	$0	$0	$0														
Cumulative Cost (EV)	$0	$0	$0														

	Week 1	Week 2	Week 3	Week 4	Week 5	Week 6	Week 7	Week 8	Week 9	Week 10	Week 11	Week 12	Week 13	Week 14	Week 15	Week 16
Cumulative Cost (PV)	$0	$0	$0	$0	$0	$0	$0	$0	$0	$0	$0					
Cumulative Cost (AC)	$0	$0	$0													
Cumulative Cost (EV)	$0	$0	$0													

BAC= 0
BCWS (PV)= 0
ACWP (AC)= 0
BCWP (EV)= 0
SV= BCWP-BCWS
SV=
SV= $0
Project is $xxK behind schedule

CV= BCWP-ACWP
CV=
CV= $0
Project is $xxK over budget

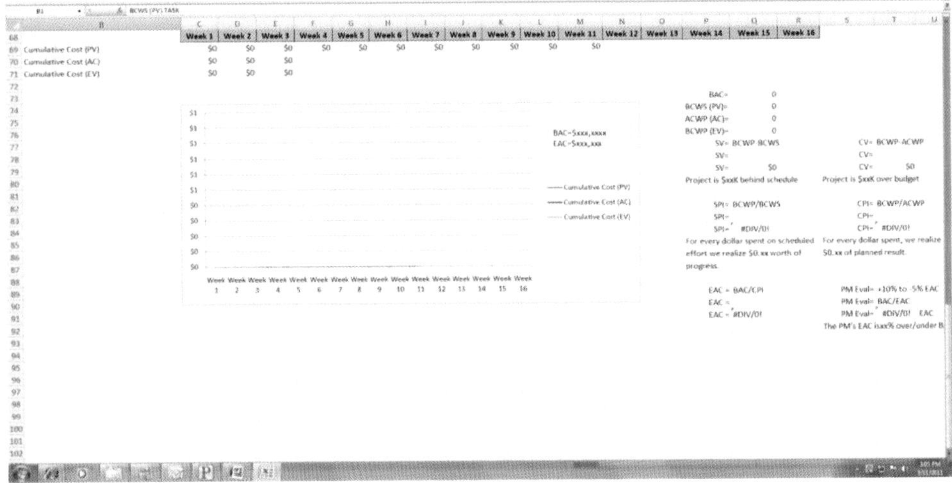

Complete view of spreadsheet.

B1 BCWS (PV) TASK

Calculation Sheet | BCWS Gantt | Sheet3

Ready

Appendix-H: Building the BCWS-PV-Project Baseline

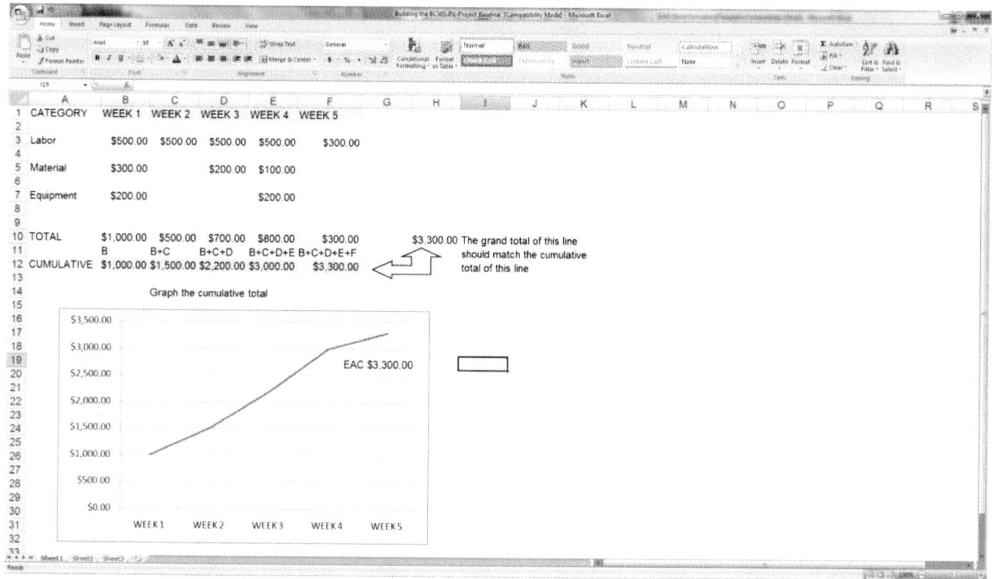

CATEGORY	WEEK 1	WEEK 2	WEEK 3	WEEK 4	WEEK 5		
Labor	$500.00	$500.00	$500.00	$500.00	$300.00		
Material	$300.00		$200.00	$100.00			
Equipment	$200.00			$200.00			
TOTAL	$1,000.00	$500.00	$700.00	$800.00	$300.00	$3,300.00	The grand total of this line should match the cumulative total of this line
	B	B+C	B+C+D	B+C+D+E	B+C+D+E+F		
CUMULATIVE	$1,000.00	$1,500.00	$2,200.00	$3,000.00	$3,300.00		

Graph the cumulative total

Appendix-I: Answers to the Assessment Quizzes

Chapter 1: Test Your Knowledge

Take the following practice quiz. Identify those where you are weak and then reinforce yourself.

1. Scope Management
   a) Is concerned with naming all activities performed, the end products which result, and the resources of the project manager
   b) Entails managing the project's work content
   c) Is a subset of configuration management and as such is performed by CM specialists
   d) Is not a concern of the project manager
   e) None

2. The scope statement provides
   a) A basis for future decisions about the project
   b) A baseline to accomplish verification measures
   c) A baseline to evaluate potential scope changes
   d) All
   e) b and c only

3. The project life-cycle can be describes as:
   a) Project concept, project planning, project execution, and project close-out
   b) Project planning, work authorization, and project reporting
   c) Project planning, project control, project definition, WBS development and project termination
   d) Project concept, project execution, and project reporting
   e) All

4. Customer influence in the project process is:
   a) Essential in accurately documenting the goals and objectives of the project
   b) Meddlesome and will slow down the process
   c) A minor consideration because the customer has difficulty in stating what he wants
   d) Best handled by the sales department
   e) None

5. A project is defined as:
   a) A coordinated undertaking of interrelated activities directed toward a specific goal that has a finite period of performance
   b) A large, complex undertaking with many objectives, multiple sources of funding and no discernible end point
   c) An undertaking of interrelated activities directed toward a specific goal that can be accomplished in less than one year
   d) A group of activities headed by a project manager who has cradle-to-grave life cycle responsibility for the end product
   e) All

6. Creation of project objectives
   a) Allows for data collection and analysis and progress reporting against which standards of performance can be measured
   b) Is accomplished by selection of measurable variables against which performance can be judged
   c) Is required before funding of the project by the project sponsor
   d) All
   e) a and b only

7. The Project Charter

a) Expresses upper management commitment to the project
b) Provides the authority by which the project may proceed
c) Establishes the organizational structure within which the project will operate
d) Specifies the overall objectives and timeframes of this project
e) All

8. A program is characterized as
   a) A grouping of similar projects having no definite end that supports the product(s) from cradle to grave
   b) A grouping of related tasks lasting one year or less
   c) A unique undertaking having a definite time period
   d) A project with a cost over $1 million
   e) None

9. The Project Charter is developed by
   a) Senior management
   b) The customer
   c) The project manager
   d) Both a and c
   e) None

10. A clear definition of the users' needs serves as the direct basis for the . . .
    a) Functional requirement
    b) Work Breakdown Structure
    c) Project cost estimate
    d) Selection of personnel
    e) Termination decision

11. A technical requirement has which of these characteristics?

a) Typically describe physical dimensions and performance requirements
b) Easy to understand
c) A communication tool between the user and the design team
d) Written in non-technical language
e) Developed in cooperation with the user

12. Selection criteria for project selection include . . ..
    a) Cost vs. benefits
    b) Risk
    c) Contribution towards organizational goals
    d) Rate of return
    e) All

13. Scope management is:
    a) a project control function
    b) employs change control
    c) a work authorization process
    d) considers Cost, Quality and Schedule
    e) all

14. The sequential steps that define the process for successfully completing a project is:
    a) Implementation Plan
    b) Development Plan
    c) critical path
    d) Management Plan
    e) a life cycle

Chapter 2: Test Your Knowledge

Take the following practice quiz. Identify those areas of Organizational Planning where you are weak and then reinforce yourself.

1. Using the time reference problem, which task is completed?

TASK	BCWS	ACWP	BCWP
Survey	500	2000	400
Remove Debris	2000	3500	2000
Dig hole	3000	2000	2800
Emplace forms	1200	1000	1100
Pour Concrete	5000	3000	2500

a. Pour concrete

b. Survey

c. Dig hole

d. Remove debris

2. On November 1, $1,000 worth of work on a task was supposed to have been done (BCWS); however, the BCWP was $850. Calculate the schedule variance.

a.-$100

b.$100

c.$150

d.-$150

3. If the project committed $1,000 worth of work resources but only completed $850 worth of work, what is the Cost Variance?

a. Cannot calculate from the information provided

b.$1,500

c.-$150

d.$150

4. The Cost Performance Index (CPI) measures:

a. cost of work performed vs. planned costs.

b. work performed vs. planned work.

c. work performed vs. cost of work performed.

d. direct costs vs. indirect costs.

5. The computation for Cost Performance Index is:

a. BCWP-BCWS

b. BCWP-ACWP

c. BCWP/ACWP

d. ACWP/BCWP

6. The Cost Performance Index is computed as:

a. budget cost of work performed divided by actual cost of work performed

b. budget cost of work performed minus actual cost of work performed

c. budget cost of work performed minus budget cost of work scheduled

d. budget cost of work scheduled divided by budget cost of work performed

Chapter 3: Test Your Knowledge

Take the following practice quiz. Identify those areas of Organizational Planning where you are weak and then reinforce yourself.

1. Free float is the amount of time that an activity may be delayed without affecting the:
   a) Early start of the succeeding activities.
   b) Late start of the succeeding activities.
   c) Project finish.
   d) Cost of the project.
   e) Late finish of any parallel activities.

2. The critical path is calculated by
   a) determining which tasks have the least amount of total slack.

b) subtracting the end date of task one from the start date of task two.

c) totaling the time for all activities.

d) determining the shortest path through the network.

e) determining the determining which tasks have the most slack

3. Which of the following is indicative of negative float?

   a) The late start date is earlier than the early start date.

   b) The critical path supports the imposed end date.

   c) The early finish date is equal to the late finish date.

   d) When leads are employed in the schedule.

   e) The project is sinking.

4. The critical path in a schedule network is the path that:

   a) Takes the longest time to complete

   b) Must be done before any other tasks

   c) Allows some flexibility in scheduling a start time

   d) Is not affected by schedule slippage

   e) All of the above

5. The first step in building a PERT/CPM network is to:

   a) Create a work-breakdown structure

   b) Create a flow chart

   c) Determine the critical path

   d) Show task relationships

   e) *None

6. The purpose of a dummy activity in an activity-on-arrow diagram is to

   a) Show a dependency

   b) Identify a task that could be replaced by another

c) Take the slack time into account

d) Show a task that is not necessarily needed

e) Denote a milestone

7. As a project is carried out and slack time is consumed on individual tasks, the slack left over for the remaining tasks is:

   a) Reduced

   b) Insignificant

   c) Unchanged

   d) Increased

   e) Doubled

8. As a control tool, the bar chart (Gantt) method is most beneficial for:

   a) Rearranging conflicting tasks

   b) Depicting actual versus planned tasks

   c) Showing the outer dependencies of tasks

   d) a and c

   e) a and b

9. Fast tracking means to:

   a) Speed up a project through parallel tasks

   b) Swap one task for another

   c) Reduce the number of tasks if possible

   d) b and c

   e) *None

10. The key purpose of project control is to:

    a) Keep the project on track

    b) Plan ahead for uncertainties

    c) Generate status reports

d) Develop the project road map

e) *All

11. The actual configuration of a PERT/CPM network ______________________ the amount of resources that can be devoted to the project.

a) Is heavily dependent upon

b) Increases

c) Is not affected by

d) Does not require

e) Is the only means for determining

12. In crashing a task, you would focus on:

a) As many tasks as possible

b) Non-critical tasks

c) Accelerating performance of tasks on critical path

d) Accelerate performance by minimizing cost

e) a and d

Chapter 4: Test Your Knowledge

Take the following practice quiz. Identify those areas of Organizational Planning where you are weak and then reinforce yourself.

1. The Cost Performance Index (CPI) measures:

a) floating costs vs. sunk costs

b) work performed vs. cost of work performed.

c) cost of work performed vs. planned costs.

d) work performed vs. planned work.

e) direct costs vs. indirect costs.

2. When comparing the cost of competing projects, which of the following is typically NOT considered?

a) Opportunity costs.

b) Direct costs.

c) Sunk costs.

d) Indirect costs.

e) Burden rates.

3. The computation for Cost Performance Index is:

   a) BCWP/ACWP

   b) BCWP-ACWP

   c) BCWP-BCWS

   d) ACWP/BCWP

   e) ACWP-BCWS

4. The following types of cost are relevant to making a financial decision except:

   a) unavoidable costs

   b) opportunity costs

   c) direct costs

   d) sunk costs

   e) none

5. The Cost Performance Index is computed as:

   a) budget cost of work performed divided by actual cost of work performed

   b) budget cost of work performed minus actual cost of work performed

   c) budget cost of work performed minus budget cost of work scheduled

   d) budget cost of work scheduled divided by budget cost of work performed

   e) actual cost of work scheduled divided by budget cost of work performed

6. Life Cycle Costing:

   a) is the concept of all costs within the total life of a project

b) is an activity devoted to optimizing cost/performance

c) is an activity of appraising the cost and technical performance of a completed project

d) is a process of predicting the life of a project

e) all

7. Managerial Reserves are:

a) allowances to account for price changes that can occur over the life of the project due to inflation

b) accounts to allocate and maintain funds for contingency purposes

c) Incentive fees paid to managers for good performance

d) funds used to offset poor cost or schedule estimates

e) all

8. Sunk costs are

a) Future costs held in reserve

b) Costs invested in commodities

c) Overhead costs

d) Tax credits

e) Expended costs over which we have no more control

9. Cost variance (CV) is which of the following equations?

a) CV = BCWP = BCWS

b) CV = BCWP - ACWP

c) CV = SV / BCWS

d) 1 and 3

10. Which of the following can best describe cost budgeting?

a) The process of establishing budgets, standards, and a monitoring system by which the investment cost of the project can be measured and managed.

b) The process of developing the future trends along with the assessment of probabilities, uncertainties, and inflation that could occur during the project.
c) The process of assembling and predicting costs of a project over its life cycle.
d) The process of gathering, accumulating, analyzing, monitoring, reporting, and managing the costs on an on-going basis.

11. Which of the following is a direct project cost?
    a) Lighting and heating for the corporate office
    b) Employee health care
    c) Piping for an irrigation project
    d) a and b

12. Which of the following can best describe cost controls?
    a) The process of gathering, accumulating, analyzing, monitoring, reporting, and managing the costs on an on-going basis.
    b) The process of developing the future trends along with the assessment of probabilities, uncertainties, and inflation that could occur during the project.
    c) The process of assembling and predicting costs of a project over its life cycle.
    d) The process of establishing budgets, standards, and a monitoring system by which the investment cost of the project can be measured and managed.

13. If the project was supposed to have $1,000 worth of work accomplished but only completed $850 worth of work, what is the Scheduled Variance?
    a) -$150
    b) $150
    c) $1,500
    d) Cannot calculate from the information provided
    e) None

14. If $850 worth of work is completed, but it actually cost $900 to perform the work, what is the Cost Variance?

a) Cannot calculate from the provided information

b) $50

c) -$50

d) None

15. Sunk costs are:

a) dollars that have not been invested but are in the management reserve.

b) cost that vary in total depending upon the activity of the project as compared to fixed costs.

c) another name for labor cost since these costs are already budgeted.

d) dollars already invested in the project and regardless of what is done will not affect the project's outcome.

e) a and c

16. Reserve funds are set aside to be used when:

a) anticipated problems have been identified but not completely expected

b) an up-scope of the project requires additional funds to compensate the initial budget

c) they are needed for the sporadic fluctuation in potential labor rates when a union contract is under negotiation.

d) none

17. Cost control is concerned with:

a) influencing the factors which create a change to the cost baseline

b) managing the actual changes when and as they occur

c) insuring that the customer knows that the project budget is under or over budget

d) a and b

e) b and c

18. Which is the most conservative of the work completion rules:

a) 0/100 Rule

b) 50/50 Rule

c) 20/80 Rule

d) 100/100 Rule

e) None

19. Which is considered the earned value?

a) Budgeted Cost of Work Scheduled

b) Budgeted Cost of Work Performed

c) Actual Cost of Work Performed

d) Budgeted at Completion

e) b and d

20. What does a positive Cost Variance indicate?

a) A cost under run

b) The project is over budget

c) There were not enough dollars allocated in the budget for the budget item

d) The project is behind

e) None

21. What does a negative Schedule Variance indicate?

a) The project is behind in the schedule

b) Up-scope is causing cost overruns

c) The project is ahead of schedule

d) The project is on schedule

e) None

22. The BCWS is $10,000 and the BCWP was determined to have a $7,000 worth, and the ACWP is $5,000. What is the Cost Variance?

a) $2,000

b) -$2,000

c) $3,000

d) -$3,000

e) Cannot calculate the answer since not enough data is available

23. The BCWS is $10,000 and the BCWP was determined to have a $7,000 worth, and the ACWP is $5,000. What is the Cost Variance percent?

a) 29%

b) -48%

c) 50%

d) 60%

e) Cannot calculate the answer since not enough data is available

24. If a CV was positive and the SV was positive, what does this indicate?

a) The project is under budget and ahead of schedule

b) The project is over budget but on schedule

c) The project is under budget but behind schedule

d) Cannot tell from the information given

e) The project is on budget and on schedule

25. If the variable cost of producing a unit is $100 per unit and all fixed costs equals $2,500, what will be the cost of producing ten extra units?

a) $1,000

b) $3,500

c) $25,000

d) $1,500

e) None

26. What is the purpose of the contingency money in a cost estimate?

a) Provides money to cover uncertainties in the estimate within the defined scope and schedule

b) Money to cover changes in scope

c) Money to cover unforeseen natural disasters

d) a and b

e) a and c

Chapter 5: Test Your Knowledge

Take the following practice quiz. Identify those where you are weak and then reinforce yourself.

1. The Cost Performance Index (CPI) measures:

a) floating costs vs. sunk costs

b) work performed vs. cost of work performed.

c) cost of work performed vs. planned costs.

d) work performed vs. planned work.

e) direct costs vs. indirect costs.

2. The computation for Cost Performance Index is:

a) BCWP/ACWP

b) BCWP-ACWP

c) BCWP-BCWS

d) ACWP/BCWP

e) ACWP-BCWS

3. The Cost Performance Index is computed as:

a) budget cost of work performed divided by actual cost of work performed

b) budget cost of work performed minus actual cost of work performed

c) budget cost of work performed minus budget cost of work scheduled

d) budget cost of work scheduled divided by budget cost of work performed

e) actual cost of work scheduled divided by budget cost of work performed

4. Cost variance (CV) is which of the following equations?

   a) CV = BCWP - BCWS

   b) CV = BCWP - ACWP

   c) CV = SV / BCWS

   d) 1 and 3

5. Cost controls can be best described by which of the following?

   a) The process of gathering, accumulating, analyzing, monitoring, reporting, and managing the costs on an on-going basis.

   b) The process of developing the future trends along with the assessment of probabilities, uncertainties, and inflation that could occur during the project.

   c) The process of assembling and predicting costs of a project over its life cycle.

   d) The process of establishing budgets, standards, and a monitoring system by which the investment cost of the project can be measured and managed.

6. If the project was supposed to have $1,000 worth of work accomplished but only completed $850 worth of work, what is the Scheduled Variance?

   a) -$150

   b) $150

   c) $1,500

   d) Cannot calculate from the information provided

   e) None

Appendix-J: Bibliography

B. Davis, P. (2008, December 10). PMI Quick Quiz. *Community Post* .

B. Davis, P. (2008, July 25). PMI Quick Quiz. *Community Post* .

B. Davis, P. (2008, August 8). Quick Quiz. *PMI Community Post* .

B. Davis, P. (2010, December 17). Quick Quiz. *PMI Community Post* .

Charland, J. F. (2010, October 1). *JF Charland*. Retrieved December 29, 2010, from JF Charland: http://jfcharland.com/post/1224279757/chuckfrey-love-this-visionaries-have-ideas

Duggal, J. (2008, November 14). Cultivating a portfolio mindset. *Community Post* .

Haughey, D. (2010, June 3). *Project Smart-Articles.* Retrieved June 3, 2010, from Project Smart: http://www.projectsmart.co.uk/how-to-implement-earned-value.html

Kerzner, H. (2003). *Project Management: A Systems Approach to Planning, Scheduling, and Controlling, 8th Edition.* New York: John Wiley & Sons, Inc.

n.a. (2010, December 7). *Spending Plan*. Retrieved December 7, 2010, from Business Dictionary.com: http://www.businessdictionary.com/definition/spending-plan.html

Project Managment Institute. (1998). *A Guide to the Project Management Body of Knowledge (Interactive Version).* Newton Square, PA.

Stackpole, Cynthia et al. (2008). *A Guide to the Project Management Body of Knowledge (PMBOK Guide) Fourth Edition.* Newtown Square: Project Management Institute.

Tyler, M. J. (1993-2010). Lecture Notes.

Tyler, M. J. (1998, June 30). NIS Y2K EVM Workbook. Colorado Springs, CO, United States.

Tyler, M. J. (1998). *True Sayings about Project Management.* St. Louis, MO: Webster

University.

Tyler, M. J., (2009). *Project Intiation, Planning, and Execution.* Boston: Pearson.

Waldrop, M. M. (1992). Complexity: the emerging science at the edge of order and chaos. In M. M. Waldrop, *Complexity: the emerging science at the edge of order and chaos* (p. 384). New York: Simon & Schuster.

Wideman, M. (2005, February 26). *Wideman Comparative Glossary of Project Management Terms v3.1.* Retrieved November 8, 2010, from Max's Project Management Wisdom: http://www.maxwideman.com/pmglossary/index.htm

Wilkens, T. T. (1999, April 1). *Project Smart-Articles.* Retrieved June 3, 2010, from Project Smart: http://www.projectsmart.co.uk/docs/earned-value.pdf

Appendix-K Index

Made in the USA
Charleston, SC
02 April 2015